T0294782

DECOLONIZING MORMONISM

DECOLONIZING MORMONISM

Approaching a Postcolonial Zion

edited by
Gina Colvin and Joanna Brooks

The University of Utah Press | Salt Lake City

Copyright © 2018 by The University of Utah Press. All rights reserved.

 The Defiance House Man colophon is a registered trademark of The University of Utah Press. It is based on a four-foot-tall Ancient Puebloan pictograph (late PIII) near Glen Canyon, Utah.

Library of Congress Cataloging-in-Publication Data

Names: Colvin, Gina, editor. | Brooks, Joanna, 1971– editor.
Title: Decolonizing Mormonism : approaching a postcolonial Zion/edited by Gina Colvin and Joanna Brooks.
Description: Salt Lake City : The University of Utah Press, [2018] | Includes bibliographical references and index. | Identifiers: LCCN 2017053344 (print) | LCCN 2017054556 (ebook) | ISBN 9781607816096 () | ISBN 9781607816089 (pbk.)
Subjects: LCSH: Globalization—Religious aspects—Church of Jesus Christ of Latter-day Saints. | Globalization—Religious aspects—Mormon Church. | Church of Jesus Christ of Latter-day Saints—Doctrines. | Mormon Church—Doctrines. | Church and minorities.
Classification: LCC BX8611 (ebook) | LCC BX8611 .D43 2018 (print) | DDC 289.309—dc23
LC record available at https://lccn.loc.gov/2017053344

Printed and bound in the United States of America.

CONTENTS

ACKNOWLEDGMENTS

The editors would like to acknowledge that a faith crisis is nowhere near as tragic as a smallpox epidemic, or a settler-on-settler massacre which is blamed on the local indigenous population, or the legal violations that appropriated millions of acres of Native land for the building of Deseret. The editors would not like to acknowledge those deep pockets of white, upper-middle-class Mormon men who have a penchant for commissioning books from other white, upper-middle-class Mormon men, whom they fly around the world. We have received not a red cent for this project. Our reward is in solidarity and in heaven.

We love each other, our husbands, the LDS Church, and our contributors. We love and tolerate our children. Thank you as well to Jane Hafen for her exemplary inspiration and unyielding endurance and to John Alley for his support of this project. We thank Lynn Matthews Anderson for Mormon feminist solidarity as expressed in the editorial work she did to help bring this project to completion. We also thank the generations who came before and did the work that made ours possible, especially our ancestors and the teachers and mentors at Brigham Young University; Brigham Young University-Hawaii; the University of California, Los Angeles; and the University of Canterbury. *Aroha nui.*

INTRODUCTION

Approaching a Postcolonial Zion

GINA COLVIN AND JOANNA BROOKS

When we were little Mormon girls attending church on Sundays in the 1970s, sitting on metal folding chairs and singing the same hymns in virtually identical LDS chapels in Southern California and New Zealand, we never could have imagined writing a book like this—for so many reasons and historical dynamics vast and deep as the Pacific Ocean on whose shores we lived. But this book is the product of a relationship made possible through the circuits of empire and their rewiring through the power of a shared faith. That an Anglo-American feminist and a Maori womanist should find each other in intellectual conversation and then collaboration is remarkable enough; that this shared conversation is fueled and infused by a shared appreciation of the beauties and challenges of Mormon theology, faith practice, and culture makes it all the more meaningful to us. Were it not for Mormonism, each of us would occupy distinctly narrower worlds, with fewer opportunities to travel outside our own domains of experience and to learn from the experiences of others. But these opportunities do not come without costs, and recognizing that inasmuch as Mormonism reproduces American colonial dynamics, those costs will fall unevenly on communities of color and non–North American communities is an essential step in the cultivation of a more responsible practice of Mormonism and more responsible work in the field of Mormon Studies.

This book features essays by Mormon scholars and writers—Indigenous Mormons, Mormons of color, white Mormons in the United States, white Mormons in Europe—who offer their own experiences, research, and learned perspectives on the inegalitarian power dynamics that structure and have often damaged or hobbled their faith.

The candidacy of United States President Donald Trump was initially rejected but then almost wholly supported by white American Mormons, despite his flagrant disregard for human rights of the world's most vulnerable populations from refugees to the disabled, his assaults on the dignity of immigrants and women, and his disdain for religious freedom—all values articulated in recent years by LDS Church leadership. His initial days in office were characterized by a series of executive orders that clash with Constitutional values in content and in form. We remember when the United States Constitution was held up by LDS Church prophets as a sacred document, and we note the silence of white American Mormons as their nation's chief executive compromised its protections for life and liberty. We cannot fail to point out the enormous economic and environmental repercussions that a Trump administration will have on the well-being of Mormon peoples around the world, especially in the global South. We wonder if in the months to come the hearts of Anglo-American Mormons at the faith's historic and geographical center will turn to their fellow Saints at the periphery, and whether they will feel called by a responsibility greater than unexamined American partisanship and nationalism.

We take heart in that we are not the first Mormon scholars to consider through the language of scholarship, reflection, and critique the promise of Zion attested by the LDS church. We remember how Hugh Nibley elucidated the Mormon Zion in his classic book of essays *Approaching Zion*, which first appeared in 1989:

> The Bible contains a fairly complete description of Zion, but there is one aspect of it that only the Latter-day Saints have taken to heart (or did formerly), and it is that doctrine that sets them off most sharply from all of the other religions, namely, the belief that Zion is possible on the earth, that men possess the capacity to receive it right here and are therefore under obligation to

waste no time moving in the direction of Zion. The instant one realizes that Zion is a possibility, one has no choice but to identify himself with the program that will bring about the quickest possible realization of its perfection. The call is to awake and arise, to "push many people to Zion with songs of everlasting joy upon their heads" (D&C 66:11). If undue haste is not desirable, delay is inexcusable; a sense of urgent gravity has ever marked the latter-day work: "I am Jesus Christ, who cometh quickly, in an hour you think not" (D&C 51:20). "Wherefore, stand ye in holy places, and be not moved, until the day of the Lord come; for behold, it cometh quickly" (D&C 87:8).

"When we conclude to make a Zion," said Brigham Young, "we will make it, and this work commences in the heart of each person." Zion can come only to a place that is completely ready for it, which is to say Zion must already be there. When Zion descends to earth, it must be met by a Zion that is already here: "And they shall see us; and we will fall upon their necks, and they shall fall upon our necks; . . . and there shall be mine abode, and it shall be Zion" (Moses 7:63–64). Hence, President Young must correct a misunderstanding among many of the Saints who "gather here with the spirit of Zion resting upon them, and expecting to find Zion in its glory, whereas their own doctrine should teach them that they are coming here to make Zion," that is, to make it possible. "The elements are here to produce as good a Zion as was ever made in all the eternities of the Gods." Note that Zion is an eternal and a universal type and that the local Zion, while made of the substances of this earth, "shall come forth out of all the creations which I have made" (Moses 7:64). "I have Zion in my view constantly," said Brother Brigham, making it clear that Zion for this earth is still an unrealized ideal of perfection. "We are not going to wait for angels, or for Enoch and his company to come and build up Zion, but we are going to build it," so that we will be ready. If we did not have a responsibility for bringing Zion, and if we did not work constantly with that aim in view, its coming could not profit us much—for all its awesome perfection and beauty, Zion is still our business and should be our constant concern.[1]

Nibley's critique of the state of the church in the late twentieth century is a powerful and disturbing indictment of the easy seduction of money and power. We find his searing appraisal of the sorry state of Mormonism's claim to Zion (a once urgent yearning among the early Saints) to be a fitting framework through which to refract this collection of essays. Each of these essays addresses a loss perpetrated by an institutional order that has made it difficult for those not living in the church's metropole to have their cultural needs accepted or their local wisdom heard. Instead, the church's institutional preference for homogeneity and standardization has served to excuse the church's global operations from adapting to larger scales of concern than those derived from its base in Utah.

Nibley's injunction for a renewed commitment to Zion reminds us that some of the organizational habits of Mormonism are not necessarily born out of a desire to expand the spiritual relevance of the church but out of an unchecked desire to grow the numbers of consumers of a ready-made corporate message to be sold on the religious marketplace. The fact that the LDS Church is run like a corporation, with an expanding financial base through ever-growing numbers of shell corporations and property portfolios, distrust of management systems that embrace complexity and adaptation, disinterest in financial transparency, legal protections that it invests in to protect its financial base, and a lack of sensitivity toward the diverse cultural systems that it overwhelms across the world, leads us to wonder if the yearning for Zion hasn't been abandoned in the face of a praxis that urges the institutional church toward the pursuit and safeguarding of capital as an end in and of itself.

Should the delights of Zion govern our spiritual instincts instead of the rigid financial, institutional, and legal mechanisms that protect the capital of the Corporation of the President, we might very well see a much-needed alteration to Mormon culture and a re-visioning of religious and spiritual intent. Indeed, Nibley was emphatic about Zion being undone, among other things, by the greedy appropriation of the earth's resources freely given by God for our nurture and sustenance, the conversion of the Earth into land title for sale, and the extraction of its bounties for cash.

As a condition of the heart, Nibley describes Zion as an end product, unalloyed with anything that would turn our human endeavors into capital. His strongest invective was against a cultural condition "that is quintessentially Babylon [and] now masquerades as Zion." Nibley strongly condemned the tendency of Mormons to avoid mental work. He derided the Mormon tendency toward zeal at the expense of knowledge. He argued that the current of sentimentality and preference for easy answers that thrives among Mormons needs to be checked. Thus, our intent for this volume is to highlight the voices of those most likely to be forgotten by both the institutional church and Mormon Studies scholars, who have each persistently sought to use the same materials, usually produced by a white, American, Utahn, colonial patriarchy to manage or challenge Mormonism's messaging.

The tension between two groups of white male insiders—some more orthodox, some less—seeking some kind of discursive power in the small world of Mormonism is not lost on us. Thus, our intention is to draw the reader away from attention to the circular and seemingly irresolvable tensions that erupt in the thick of the LDS Church and its elite white transgenerational cohorts, and turn to places of thinner presence, where Mormonism nevertheless lands with characteristic heaviness, managing its adherents into cultural contexts that seem wholly insensitive to local sensibilities and concerns.

The Mormon idea of Zion, we are arguing, seeks the unification of the best parts of the body of Christ, wherever they may be abroad on the Earth. Zion, with its vision of economic prosperity for all, its call for the wise and careful stewardship of the Earth, and its emphasis on informed and clear thought, would make space for the wisdom, critiques, and knowledge of those at the margins because we would see that we are not complete as a people without them.

Thus, in our moment, we are struck by the urgent necessity of informed, critical, heartfelt reflection on power and resource distribution in a global church. Mormon Studies has lagged significantly behind other religious studies fields in taking these questions seriously. But this must come to an end. Today, more than half of the world's Mormons live outside the United States, but Mormon wealth and authority is profoundly and exclusively concentrated in a narrow geographical band in the United States. In the US, the church does not disclose its financial records, and almost all of its business decisions are made by a very small cohort of homogeneously white, aged, multi-generational Mormon men who hail from elite Mormon families. Today, more Mormons speak Spanish than English, but English remains the Church's governing language. Today robust multi-generational Mormon communities exist across Latin America and the Pacific, especially in places like Samoa, where one in four Samoans is Mormon, and Tonga, which has the highest per capita rate of LDS Church membership of any nation in the world.[2]

Even within the Mormon culture region, indigenous, Polynesian, Latino/a, and African American Mormons have established their own distinctive communities and ways of being Mormon. Still, LDS religious practices from the most sacred temple rituals to quotidian Sunday School lessons and weekday church activities for youth are structured around North American Mormon cultural norms, expectations, and priorities. Today, the church is experiencing tremendous growth in Africa, but church leaders have stumbled in limited efforts to move white North American Mormons to recognize and reject the racism of Mormon doctrine that excluded men and women of African descent from priesthood ordination and temple worship. Virtually nothing has been done to make the suffused, suffocating racism of everyday American life a matter of Mormon moral priority.

For all of these reasons, non–Euro-American Mormons find themselves at times living in tension with Euro-American Mormons who have not reflected on inequality within Mormon life or beyond. It is time that the tensions and the pressures borne by Mormonism's global and Indigenous majority are better understood, for the well-being of the movement as a whole. Approaching a postcolonial Zion means undertaking a thoughtful, critical examination of how the Mormon faith as an American-born religion has interacted with and sometimes benefitted from the larger historical forces that have established the United States as a global power, often at the expense of the world's Indigenous peoples, especially in the Global South.

Because these questions of inequality within global faith communities are not new or unique to Mormonism, we have access to a vocabulary that others have developed over many decades for understanding global distributions of power and resources. *Colonization* is the physical conquest of Indigenous peoples and their homelands, including the expropriation of Indigenous land and its resources, dispossession and displacement of indigenous peoples, and exploitation of Indigenous labor; *neo-colonization* is a term used to describe the twentieth- and twenty-first century economic and political subjugation or exploitation of Indigenous peoples by modern nation-states and multinational corporations and industries that rely on nation-states for support and protection. Colonization and neo-colonization have incurred atrocious losses of population, land, natural resources, wealth, human rights, and self-government. *Colonialism* and *neo-colonialism* are systems of ideas, beliefs, and practices that justify the domination and subjugation of Indigenous peoples, often by disparaging Indigenous peoples or treating them as a separate and lesser class of human beings: the "other."[3]

Just as colonization has resulted in atrocious physical losses, colonialism has implanted in non-Indigenous and Indigenous peoples alike devastating ideas about the inferiority of Indigenous individuals and communities, ideas that have contributed to the destruction of Indigenous families, languages, and cultures as well as personal health and well-being. These ideas have been imposed through colonial institutions that have required Indigenous people to assimilate, adjust, or surrender to outsider-imposed political, economic, social, and cultural systems in order to survive. It was through the violent and exploitative mechanisms of European colonization in the sixteenth through nineteenth centuries that Christianity came to the Americas, the Pacific, Africa, and Asia. Mormonism's rise in the nineteenth century and its global growth in the twentieth century also took place within the context of colonization and neo-colonization and drew from colonialist and neocolonialist ideas and attitudes. Thus, the use of "post-colonial" in the title draws attention to the institutional practices and discourses that instantiate certain forms of cultural behaviors, ideologies, and narratives that reflect more closely the interests of the Utah church than they do local cultures, thus putting Mormons at the church's periphery at odds with their surrounding community.

Because these forms of cultural alienation exact a psycho-social price, this volume is an explicit attempt to create something of an inventory of these cultural costs. But because of its post-colonial orientation, it also seeks to highlight the points of resistance, adaptation, and innovation that work to make Mormonism work as a viable faith tradition at the margins.

Decolonization is the movement among Indigenous peoples to dismantle the visible and invisible structures of power that have contributed to their subjugation and dispossession. Decolonization movements were active in the formal unsettling of European occupying governments in Africa and Asia from the 1940s through the 1970s and in the return of governmental power to the hands of local and Indigenous peoples. Even today in countries such as New Zealand, Australia, Canada, and the United States, where Indigenous people continue to be outnumbered and governed by

Euro-American settler populations, decolonization movements are active as Indigenous communities uproot harmful ideas about the inferiority of Indigenous peoples sown in them by colonialism and work to heal and transform their communities to become self-governing, self-determining, and healthy. Decolonization projects and organizes spaces within or parallel to post-colonialism where it can be possible for Indigenous peoples and peoples of color to think, act, and live in a fully realized, safe, healthful, self-determining way. Our project of approaching a post-colonial Zion holds forth the hope that our faith can sustain these spaces.

As we have reflected on the histories and experiences captured in this volume, we have asked ourselves not just to look at but also to look beyond the political and economic mechanics of colonialism that scaffolded Mormonism's global expansion to matters irreducible to materialism: matters of faith and doctrine. What is it in Mormon theology and practice that won the hearts and lives of so many converts, first in North America, then in Europe, and then far beyond? Surely a belief in or hope for a literal gathering and establishment of Zion—a place for the pure in heart—attracted many early adherents. Some may also have been attracted to the metaphysical dimensions of Joseph Smith's early teachings, which in their attestation to the identity of spirit, matter, and light may have appealed to peoples with animist spiritualities. But perhaps even more powerful was the pull of Mormonism's audacious theology on the salvation of the dead and its expansive concept of redemption as eternal continuity of the generations.

Joseph Smith had a vision of his dead brother Alvin that led to his rejection of the orthodox Christian view that those who died without baptism or without a profession of faith were doomed to hell and to his subsequent innovation of salvific temple rites, including baptism for deceased ancestors. This important and distinctive theology held tremendous power for early Mormon converts in North America, as Samuel Brown has compellingly argued.[4] How much power it also held for those whose traditional belief systems incorporated connections to ancestors or who had seen their traditional connections across the generations catastrophically disrupted by imperial violence and dislocation!

For many hurting and dislocated peoples—white, Black, and brown—the growth of institutional bureaucratic twentieth-century Mormonism provided not only a theological and ritual salve for profound personal losses but also a resource that promised middle-class stability, security, social mobility, and access to education and broadened perspectives.

The LDS Church's establishment of schools, colleges, universities, cultural centers, and educational programs from Brigham Young University to the Church College of New Zealand and its aggressive worldwide program of building meetinghouses and temples created educational, employment, and travel opportunities for members from the working-class United States to the Pacific. The demands of its highly structured and time-intensive congregational life answered human needs for belonging and shared purpose, especially where traditional community life had been forcibly disrupted by colonialism. Even the Word of Wisdom—Mormonism's dietary code—offered a measure of protection against the pull of drug and alcohol use.

Mormon congregations and institutions could even serve, in a limited way, the continuity of traditional Indigenous kinship networks and some cultural practices (especially funeral practices and performance traditions), even across dislocated national contexts. Economic migrants to the United States for example, could join LDS congregations populated entirely with members from their home countries and continue to speak, sing, and pray in their home languages. However, these modest affordances came at a cost. LDS institutional spaces were deeply structured by mid- and late-twentieth century American Mormon conservatism, which was itself driven in part by the LDS Church's hunger to transform itself from an outlier sect to a mainstream American Protestant church. These spaces, from wardhouses to Church-sponsored university classrooms, did not support nor equip Mormons to participate in the critical conversations about power and resources colonized peoples around the world were engaging in from the 1940s and 1950s onward. Education in LDS Church colleges and universities and the culture of LDS congregations focused on preparing a globalizing membership to assume local responsibility for the administration of LDS Church units according to American bureaucratic norms. Limited cultural accommodation came at the cost of surrendering critique and sustaining a false sense of political innocence. Stability interlocked with the status quo.

To what extent were the spiritual promises American-based Mormonism offered the world in the middle and late twentieth centuries coded in the economic and political promises and aspirations of the American middle-class? To what extent were its comforts phrased in the idioms of the white suburban American nuclear family, with its patriarchalism, its nationalism, and its bourgeois consumerism? Several of the writers in this book and other researchers (such as David Knowlton) suggest that those who converted to Mormonism in non-American contexts were at least partly attracted precisely to this middle-class American ideal. We see a powerful physical legacy of this promise and its attraction in the LDS Church meetinghouses and temples built around the world from the 1950s through the 1990s with familiar American materials, on standard Salt Lake City designs, with green lawns and gated peripheries.[5]

Even the most sacred spaces of LDS temples construct heaven as an elegantly appointed but comfortable upper-middle class American living room furnished entirely in white. Similarly, Sunday dress norms for LDS men around the world and standard attire for LDS Church leaders acting in their public capacities align with the dress codes of aspirational white American middle-class manhood: the white shirt and tie. Without denigrating the sense of comfort wardhouse and temple environs actually afford their patrons, and while still honoring the pragmatism of Mormon faith practice and its radically accessible anthropocentric conception of God and the divine these material faith practices instantiate, we believe it is time to critique the notion that Zion can be understood or experienced as a middle-class American suburb. For the longer story of American history shows that the rise of the American middle-class and its security and comfort have been made possible in large part by the unjust expropriation of Indigenous land and resources, the appropriation of Black lives, nationalist domination of global relations, economic exploitation of global markets and global South resources and labor, racial segregation within the United States, and throughout it all, a seeping sexism and heterosexism that rationed life opportunities even within the suburbs according to gender and sexuality. None of these—economic exploitation, nationalism, racism, colonialism, consumerism, sexism, nor heterosexism—have a place in Zion. Zion is not and can never be an American middle-class suburb.

We claim this moment to look back reflectively on the compact twentieth-century Mormonism brokered with its global adherents. This compact allowed limited accommodations for traditional cultural practices and identities and promised access to worldly opportunities and moments of spiritual transcendence, to stable supportive institutions, and to theological and social comfort in the face of loss and pain. But the cost of this accommodation and access was obedience to LDS Church hierarchy and a bracketing of critique of the status quo, including the forms of systematic and structural violence and inequality that contributed to or created loss and pain. Both white North American members and members at the peripheries bought into this compact, which delivered something approaching a kind of Zion. But it could not deliver Zion itself.

Angels have a special role in Mormon faith and history. We have always imagined that our angels look forward, move forward in time, trumpets in hand, to bring new knowledge to prophets on earth. But perhaps moving forward requires looking backwards as well. We remember Jewish philosopher Walter Benjamin's compelling characterization of the angel of history:

> This is how one pictures the angel of history. His face is turned toward the past. Where we perceive a chain of events, he sees one single catastrophe which keeps piling wreckage upon wreckage and hurls it in front of his feet. The angel would like to stay, awaken the dead, and make whole what has been smashed. But a storm is blowing in from Paradise; it has got caught in his wings with such violence that the angel can no longer close them. This storm irresistibly propels him into the future to which his back is turned, while the pile of debris before him grows skyward. This storm is what we call progress.[6]

As does this angel, can the angels of Mormon history look back on the past? Mustn't they? Mustn't Mormons turn and face our own history and what has passed for Zion thus far and receive from its storms the energy that will propel us forward in understanding? In what has passed for Zion thus far, Mormons have been acculturated to bracket and seal off the catastrophes and mistakes of the past, so that they cannot be appropriated by those who would seek to harm. But we are in a new moment when the static, heavy, opaque, unreflective institutions of LDS Church life threaten the Mormon movement as much as any enemy without. We believe that twenty-first century Mormonism is in a moment of danger: we witness declining rates of LDS Church institutional participation, which, given the twentieth-century LDS Church's hostility to alternate channels of Mormon affiliation, participation, and learning, constitute a direct threat to Mormon continuity. Benjamin writes:

To articulate the past historically . . . means to seize hold of a memory as it flashes up at a moment of danger. . . . The danger affects both the content of the tradition and its receivers. . . . In every era the attempt must be made anew to wrest tradition away from a conformism that is about to overpower it. The Messiah comes not only as the redeemer, he comes as the subduer of Antichrist. Only that historian will have the gift of fanning the spark of hope in the past who is firmly convinced that even the dead will not be safe from the enemy if he wins. And this enemy has not ceased to be victorious.[7]

The enemies of Zion are not Missouri mobs nor evangelical Christian anti-Mormons nor even devoted ex-Mormons who expend tremendous energy seeking to publish incriminating episodes from LDS Church life, past and present. The enemies of Zion are the forms of violence and inequality that segregate and distribute chances for well-being in this life and the next according to nation, race, color, sexuality, and gender. Colonialism and imperialism are among the enemies of Zion. It is time to turn and face the catastrophes of Mormonism's colonialist and racist history with open eyes.

We believe that the Mormon people are more than capable of doing this work, and the integrity of that work will be augmented by our willingness to be awakened into new forms of consciousness upon hearing the stories of the marginalized. Opening ourselves up to the story of the oppressed among us and waking up to the reality of a Zion project that hasn't delivered on its promise of safe harbor, equality, and beloved community for all is an important first step. Inasmuch as Mormons do this, we develop the capacity to question the ways in which we have privileged and massaged our myths of social mobility and middle-class comfort into our theology of human becoming. Opening ourselves up to the stories of our own from around the world and at the margins serves to complicate and disrupt Mormon heartland certainties; it causes us to think more, feel more, to do more and to ultimately become more in our faith.

Mormons have shown how immensely powerful they can be when motivated by a potent vision, and that vision is energized and mobilized by the unique intimacy and bond they have with each other as a people. But the shared Mormon vision of Zion has become complicated by the

Ameri-centric political ideologies that have become pressed into and con-
flated with Mormon theology because so many of the church leadership's
concerns are overly concerned with the faith's continued viability and relevance in United States.

As a New Zealander, Gina Colvin has noticed how ideologies, mythologies,
and cultural practices that serve a unique suite of American political interests get massaged with impunity into worldwide expressions of faith even
when they don't belong, or worse still, when these practices make strangers
of church members in their homelands. In addition, Mormons not from the
United States of America are left unseen at best, or treated as the petted and
patronized prizes of Mormon evangelism at worst. This serves to do little
other than to undermine all that has been done, and all that could be done
in the service of Zion.

Faith communities, Mormonism included, can no longer survive with
great moral authority on tired and outworn truth claims at a time when
there is growing political literacy and increased familiarity with the competition of ideas that defines religion and spirituality in postmodernity. Certi-
tude is no longer a currency that can be sold on the marketplace of religious
ideas with any hope of great spiritual returns. Faith traditions need to be
anchored, rooted, and provide an offering that is centered on a hope for the
beloved community. James Cone's challenge gives us pause:

> The Church has not only failed to render service to the poor, but
> also failed miserably at being a visible manifestation of God's inten-
> tion for humanity and at proclaiming the message of the gospel to
> the world. It seems that the church is not God's redemptive agent
> but rather an agent of the old society. It not only fails to create an
> atmosphere for radical obedience to Christ, but also precludes the
> possibility of becoming a loyal, devoted servant of God. How else
> can we explain that some church fellowships are more concerned
> with nonsmoking principles or temperances than with children
> who die of rat bites or men who are shot while looting a TV set.
> Men are dying of hunger, children are maimed from rat bites,
> women are dying of despair, and churches pass resolutions. While
> we may have difficulty in locating the source of evil, we know what
> must be done against evil in order to relieve the suffering of the

poor. We know why men riot. Perhaps we cannot prevent riots, but we can fight against conditions that cause them. The church is placed in question because of its contribution to a structure that produces riots.[8]

Perhaps the great trial of Mormon faith in our time is going to be the need to purge ourselves of all narratives that shut us into narrow corridors of belief and yet refuse to entertain any disruption to our knowing. Jesus' promise, "the truth will set you free" (John 8:32) was not offered as a medicating balm to ease us out of discomfort. Jesus modeled his own truth seeking in his decision to conclude his ministry in Jerusalem, the seat of religious and state authority. He didn't stay in the wilderness, he went right to the beating heart of his polity to experience for himself the systems that held in place a brutal Roman occupation on the one hand and religious teachings that were leaden and heavy with their godless piety on the other, and in doing so he was released from any moral obligation to serve either master. Jesus asked us to reach out to God so that He alone could order our souls and our consciences. He spoke up against outsourcing our ethics and morality to the logic of capital and against systems that rely for their maintenance on structures of inequality. Doing so ourselves is perhaps one of the greatest expressions of faith in Jesus and discipleship to him. The very idea that we ought to stand up against principalities and powers sadly throws up a challenge for Mormons. If the Church of Jesus Christ of Latter-day Saints is to evolve in this world with a message of spiritual and transformative relevance, it must return to, and refresh its idea of Zion, and in doing so it must face up to its unholy alliances with Babylon. We might see individual expressions of Zion in the lives of a few of its adherents, but it hasn't become Zion, the Kingdom of God on the Earth, and it is taking huge spiritual liberties in posturing itself as such. Hugh Nibley was scathing of the confidence that the Mormons had that they had indeed established Zion:

> From the very first there were Latter-day Saints who thought to promote the cause of Zion by using the methods of Babylon. . . . [But we] have the word of the Prophet Joseph that Zion is not to be built up using the methods of Babylon. He says, "Here are those who begin to spread out, buying up all the land they are able to, to the exclusion of the poorer ones who are not so much blessed

with this world's goods, thinking to lay foundations for themselves only, looking to their own individual families and those who are to follow them. . . . Now I want to tell you that Zion cannot be built up in any such way." What do we find today? Zion's Investment, Zion Used Cars, Zion Construction, Zion Development, Zion Bank, Zion Leasing, Zion Insurance, Zion Securities, Zion Trust, and so on. The institutions of Mammon are made respectable by the beautiful name of Zion. Zion and Babylon both have their appeal, but the voice of the latter-day revelation makes one thing perfectly clear as it tells us over and over again that we cannot have them both.[9]

So, the question remains, has Zion fled or do we yet have it in our midst? And what relevance does the idea of Zion have for communities at the margins of Mormonism? As editors of this collection we have confidence that Zion can be called back into Mormon theology, but the light that we need to call it out of its shadow is not to be found at the church's metropole, it's to be found at the church's margins. It's at the margins that discoveries can be made as to what is spiritually relevant and what isn't. Where we find resistance, possibility, conflict, and questions is where our tradition's wisdom is best tested and burnished. At the margins of the church lies a body of experience that can tell us what matters, what complicates and what enlivens. But in order to draw that wisdom from the margins we need to provide the right conditions, and among those is an environment of honest storytelling.

For instance, Gina was recently teaching a Relief Society lesson in her ward during which a discussion ensued regarding Zion. As each woman talked about Zion they did so with reverence and wonder. They described "Beautiful Zion" with immense affection. This amazing and articulate group of mostly women of color—Māori, Tongan, Samoan, Chinese, Indian—spoke hopefully of a society that was tender, accepting, without exclusions and filled with the kind of social order that is founded upon principles of divine love. These women talked with fluency about a community that boldly refused war, division, and competition. Each of these women shared their reflections with eloquence because they had been schooled in the centrality of the doctrine and hope of Zion. Their eyes lit up with moving enthusiasm and they created a sacred space of shared aspiration for something more than the world offers. Because the lesson included a reflection on the arrival of the Saints into Utah, Gina spoke with great admiration about Utah, with its beauty, its productivity, and its industry. She talked with respect about the spread of temples across the valley and the great spirit of generosity among the people; the monuments and remembrances that are so familiar to Mormons across the world. She talked of the first time she went to Utah and found herself in the thick of something that felt like home because everything was so strangely familiar. Then she asked the class, "Was Zion established? Does Utah deserve to be called Zion?" These questions were greeted with a confused response. "They call it Zion, but does it meet the conditions of Zion?" This seemed to be the unifying question.

Gina continued describing the colonial incursion that happened during the settlement of Utah, the violence that erupted over resources between the settlers and the Native Americans, the murder and the policies and laws that legalized the confiscation of land. They discussed the Mountain Meadows Massacre and the blame that was so mendaciously misdirected at Paiutes. She apologized to the class as she observed the look of horror and shock on each of the faces. But they batted away her concern and asked her to proceed, they wanted to know, to be informed—these were mostly brown women raised in New Zealand where understanding the nation's colonial history is important cultural knowledge. "We know how this works," they said. And so the discussion returned to the question, "Was Zion established? How could it have been? How can you claim something to be Zion when its formation wasn't based upon the principles of Zion? The means surely do not justify the end!"

Thus satisfied that the beautiful name Zion could not be applied to the geographical area of Utah claimed by the Mormon pioneers, the conclusion was that "Zion, is yet to come." The idea that they were each responsible to exercise some integrity with respect to their commitment to Zion, that they all had something more to do, was more inspiring than the loss of innocence in learning about the atrocities committed by a community some in the class had been taught their whole lives to revere.

What if the approach assumed by this group of Mormon women at the peripheries defined a collective approach to Mormon history? What if we regard the entire history of the Mormon people as a series of errors from which we have over time learned what Zion is not and what it must become? Not an infallibly and teleologically God-ordained walk in certainty but a persistent dialectical engagement with our own failures and misunderstandings? What if one of the obstacles we have encountered in approaching Zion is that both white and non-white Mormons bought into the deception that white settler colonialism, or American nationalism, or late bourgeois consumerist capitalism, were actually Zion? The advantages of late capitalist mobility and access may have been a fueling stop providing access to resources, but these are not Zion itself. Returning to Hugh Nibley: "Zion is the pure in heart—the pure in heart, not merely the pure in appearance. It is not a society or religion of forms and observances, of pious gestures and precious mannerisms: it is strictly a condition of the heart" (*Approaching Zion*, 26).

Zion is not a status quo; it is a dialectical process of humble critique and reflection. It welcomes and takes pleasure in difference, in keeping with Mormonism's radically universalist theology. If we are not willing to do this work, what we will see is a Mormon movement torn ever more deeply by the conflict between those who insist on static perpetual innocence and those who cannot abide the arrogance of innocence or the disposability of Mormons whose lives do not sustain the master narrative. What we see in many areas of the global South are grand gated temples with great grassy lawns subsidized by North American tithing dollars while members baptized in the 1970s and 1980s become disengaged and walk away, leaving congregations and stakes to collapse.

If the work of the Mormon people is to move forward towards Zion, and a role of Mormon Studies is to produce understanding of and knowledge about Mormonism as it is actually practiced and lived, we believe our work as Mormon scholars is to be in service of this essential conversation. In inviting Mormons from around the globe to contribute to this volume, we have been committed to providing a broad reflection on how American Mormon religious cultural imperialism is experienced. With this in mind, we draw readers' attention to the following questions: What is the legacy of Mormon religious colonization in minority and non-American communities? What are the consequences of Mormonism's heavy administrative and cultural hand in these communities? What forms of cultural and material exploitation can we discern in the narratives herein? And most importantly, to what forms of consciousness, resistance and adaptation to American Mormon religious and cultural imperialism do the authors point and how can our acknowledgement of these adaptations better inform a shared vision of Zion?

Section one includes essays written by Indigenous authors. Gina Colvin (*Ngāti Porou, Ngapuhi*) begins with a reflection that positions her Mormonism in the crossfire of her Māori, class, and national identity. She concludes that the activities of the Church of Jesus Christ of Latter-day Saints upon Māori in New Zealand have the twin effect of healing and wounding: while the church has historically been a cultural prosthetic, standing in for the losses faced because of colonization, it hasn't been supportive of the politicization of Māori as they have over time sought to reclaim language, land and culture rights so that they could stand on their own feet, in their own land, using their own resources. In a personal reflection, Colvin concludes that innovation and creativity have been necessary to navigate the intersections of religion, colonization, race and identity.

Thomas Murphy (*Iroquois*) provides a compelling argument for the decolonization of the Book of Mormon. His argument is that if the Book of Mormon is indeed an artifact once belonging to an ancient American Indian people, then it ought to be returned to American Indians. Murphy provides point-by-point directives on how, in material ways, the Church of Jesus Christ of Latter-day Saints needs to deconstruct Lamanite identity, reconsider its truth claims, and move Indigenous voices to the center.

Angelo Baca (*Navajo/Hopi*) provides a compelling insight into the journey of a young native boy growing up in the confluence of Mormon dogma and Navajo custom. Baca charts a personal journey that led him to make a film, *In Laman's Terms: Looking at Lamanite Identity,* in which he speaks back to the LDS Church from a critical Indigenous perspective, stridently arguing against the appropriation of his identity in order to tell a story that simultaneously erases and co-opts, re-stories, and violently repositions his people's history and narratives to suit non-Native sensibilities. This, he argues,

> contributes to the invisibility, voicelessness, and neglect of American Indian thought, perspective, culture, and history. It is a clear demonstration of the continued subtle violence of colonization and one that needs to be addressed today in a real and cooperative way including Indigenous voices in this sorely lacking dialogue.

Elise Boxer (*Dakota*) leads us through a deeply personal experience wherein as a teen her peers required her, by virtue of her LDS Church membership, to privilege the Book of Mormon "Lamanite" re-telling of American

Indian history at the expense of her Dakota identity even though the Book of Mormon story had no cultural or social resonance with her. She again keenly felt the pressure to behave as a Mormon in ways that agree with white United States American sensibilities when as a young woman, she was asked to "play pioneer" during the sesquicentennial celebrations of the Mormon arrival and settlement of Utah. She refused. Some years later, Boxer reflects on her decision to return to the Assiniboine reservation in 2013 during the Days of '47 Pioneer celebrations in Salt Lake City. "I simply could not handle another 'Pioneer' celebration in which Indigenous peoples are marginalized or placed on the periphery of the historical narrative and geographically removed or placed on the periphery of 'Pioneer' celebrations."

Boxer captures poignantly how deep the psycho-social costs are in the ongoing pressure to assume a Mormon identity that agrees with the dominant religious discourse, constructed and reproduced in colonizing contexts. In the United States of America, one simply must believe the racial narrative of the Book of Mormon, and one must celebrate the incursion of white Mormon settlers into American Indian tribal homelands in order to "be" Mormon.

Alicia Harris (*Nakota*) beautifully describes the complexity and the difficulty associated with being mixed-race. For Harris, her spiritual experiences as a white/Nakota Mormon straddle two powerful traditions, both of which have claim on her. How she negotiates both in this "Middle" compels her to ask "about the ways that these two views of self-seeing in relation to the world and to Creation inform and enhance one another. I love to try to see the ways that each view can create space and time for the other. Is this what I am called upon, as a Middle, to do?"

Thus, section one describes how the dominant cultural discourses of the LDS Church continue to work their way into Indigenous ways of understanding the self, identity, settler colonialism and assertions of sovereignty. The authors in this section acknowledge race as a construct through which colonists see Indigenous folk, but they are more focused on how the appropriation of Indigenous identities have served to tell a colonist's story. Their claim is for ownership of Indigenous story-telling, something that the LDS Church has misappropriated for too long as its institutional domain.

We began this book with Indigenous voices to make the point that this anthology is not simply about working out harmful racialized narratives.

Questions of cultural appropriation, alienation, and colonization need to be answered as vital first questions. This is not to say that race isn't a powder-keg issue in Mormonism, and we acknowledge it as an ongoing problem that continues to have significance, particularly in the United States. The Church of Jesus Christ of Latter-day Saints has played its part in reproducing the discourse of white supremacy through its historical declarations of the cursed state of Black and Indigenous folk, for which it has yet to make a formal apology or retraction. Though the ban on the ordination of Black men was lifted in 1978, the ideologies that held the practice of exclusion in place for so long have not been repudiated and a thick strain of deep racist sentiment continues to run through US-Mormon feelings, as the authors will demonstrate. Thus, in the second section, the authors discuss how race continues to matter in the church. Rolf Straubhaar's personal and analytical essay raises powerful questions around his privilege as a white "heritage" Mormon. Using the critical pedagogy framework proposed by Paulo Freire, Straubhaar poignantly argues that being "born in the covenant" is too often understood as being born into competency by heritage Mormons who live or serve among the most economically disadvantaged Mormons around the globe. It became a matter of significant concern for him that regardless of the local expertise, his birth circumstances meant that during his mission in Brazil and while working in Mozambique, he was seen as more religiously authoritative than even those who had spent years in successful church service. As an antidote to this cultural habit of preferring the expertise of the metropole to the wisdom of the margins, he proposes that "the pursuit of critical consciousness is a pursuit of a reality in which the unique heritages, characteristics, and contributions of all are seen as worthy of recognition and emulation."

Mica McGriggs maps her personal journey through racial identity development as a Mormon woman. She charts this journey of identity through several affecting events growing up as the only Black child in her ward community and concludes that true liberation only came when confronting the mess. She describes, "Coming into contact with my truth set me on a path of development that has been both painful and beautiful. Finding through my identity development and research words with descriptions that perfectly embodied my experiences was liberation for me. Admitting that my spiritual home was and still is deeply flawed (in ways I believe are monumentally disappointing to the Savior) was painful, but necessary."

Ignacio Garcia retells his story of serving as a Mormon bishop in a Latino ward. The greatest roadblock he found to success was the gnawing pressure placed upon him to produce a congregation that was recognizable to the white hierarchy. Like Straubhaar, he noted the habit of deference both expected and given to white Heritage Mormon culture, where even middle-class Latino members exercised degrees of parallel racism, undermining Garcia's work because it didn't entirely comport or mirror a white middle-class Mormon congregation. As he honored the wisdom and creativity of his congregants and scaffolded a praxis that might not be recognizable to mainstream Mormons, his ward members responded with high levels of engagement and joy. Garcia reflects that, "Latino members and leaders need to discard the mythology of white member exceptionalism and of the colored Saints' 'expected' dependency, and see themselves as spiritual equals in the work of saving souls."

Straubhaar, McGriggs, and Garcia together address the importance of critical consciousness as a form of liberation from discourses and practices that have the harmful effect of dehumanization. They celebrate the freedom that comes from squaring up to social, cultural, and economic dynamics that construct regimes of privilege. They each argue in their own way that unnecessary racial, cultural, social, and economic divides as constituted in Mormonism hobble a faith tradition from realizing its potential vibrancy, relevancy, and humanity.

The final section includes chapters from scholars in Europe, North America, and Hong Kong who pay close attention to the community dynamics sustained within the global LDS Church. They note how uncomfortably many of the assumptions made in Salt Lake City cannot be realized without significant innovation because the conditions upon which these objectives are crafted do not exist in the international church. They also highlight spaces where global church members have innovated to adapt LDS practice to their own contexts and conditions.

Joanna Brooks provides a history—actually, two histories—of Mormonism, one as a project benefitting from American neocolonial networks, and one as a resource for those who seek to negotiate and survive those networks as Indigenous people or people of color. Ethnographers Melissa Inouye and Staci Ford both use their experiences serving in non-American Primary and Relief Society auxiliaries to reflect on the way in which Mormonism is practiced in the interstices of fragmented identities. These chapters turn to the academic in acknowledgement of the robust theoretical frameworks needed to make persuasive and decolonized assessments of complex contexts from which neither hail. Their authors' rigor is to be applauded.

Neither Inouye nor Ford avoids providing vigorous social context as a necessary precursor for any credible ethnography authored by an observer. In doing so they find beautiful complexity in the way in which the programs are negotiated and managed by the local congregations. Inouye's observations about LDS children's programming across three different contexts tell us that there is tremendous variability and innovation. She argues that the informal curriculum and leadership, while circumscribed by male patriarchy, is nonetheless a site of huge innovation and creativity and should not be overlooked as part of contemporary Mormonism's progressive call for the deinstitutionalization of the Church of Jesus Christ of Latter-day Saints. Ford's analysis of the church in Hong Kong demonstrates once again how flexible and creative the church can be if the conditions call for adaptation. The provision for weekday Sacrament services and Sunday temple worship for domestic workers highlights the structural advances that are possible. But within this community, there are other more touching grass-roots innovations that deepen the religious experience of women in the Sister branches. Says Inouye,

> To be a Latter-day Saint is to believe in collectivity, in gathering, in organization. In many cases Mormons choose institution-building over the cultivation of charisma, for feasibility over worthiness. In many instances this proves to be a dull and conservative choice. But I would argue that the tradition of institution-building, especially informal institutions created by local Mormons for local Mormons, is among the most valuable and distinctive things that Mormonism has to offer as a religious tradition.

The collection ends with an essay by Ingrid Sherlock who, having observed the church in Flanders (Belgium), notes the general complicity with the system as an American import if there is flexibility for adaptation. She notes that the Flemish approach to authority and control is present also in dealing with an American church and all that is prescribed from Salt Lake City: "In Flanders there is a tendency to listen and obey combined

with the national sport of bending or adapting the rules quietly and prefer-
ably without being caught."

We hope that this collection of diverse perspectives provided by a small
community of thinkers who have generously contributed their memoirs
and research is not taken as the final word. There is still much to be done.
But we do hope that in thinking broadly about the Mormon experience
across different nations and cultural contexts, and about how they have
played out in the face of an overt colonizing intent by the American church,
we can harvest the wisdom and the hope that exists at the margins. This
conversation, we believe, will provide a much-needed stimulus to re-center
and refresh the hope of Zion. For too long Mormonism has excluded the
very narratives and identities that will push it to become more than the
exclusive Great Basin Kingdom that has in recent generations bowed and
nodded too willingly to the narrow economic and cultural interests of the
United States of America.

> When the Saints of Zion
> Keep God's law in truth,
> Hate and war and strife will cease;
> Men and women will live in love and peace.
> Heav'nly Zion, come once more
> And cover all the earth. (Hymn #47)[10]

I

FIRST, WE NAME OUR EXPERIENCE

Indigenous Mormonisms

The Mormon practice of bearing testimony allows us to develop an under-standing of and a feeling for spiritual truths by listening to the experiences of others. But unspoken rules that govern the practice of testimony-bearing in LDS Church settings often stigmatize the telling of stories that diverge from familiar norms and contours or speak to complicated truths that do not map neatly onto orthodox Mormonism. These four essays by Gina Colvin, Thomas Murphy, Angelo Baca, and Elise Boxer open a space for the telling and hearing of Indigenous experiences in Mormonism. By naming their experiences, these authors offer a healing space of acknowledgment and recognition to Mormons who do not find themselves or their stories reflected in mainstream and official LDS Church media. They also offer an equally necessary and salutary space where Mormons who are accustomed to occupying a place of privilege at the cultural center can learn to surren-der their privilege and come to understand the limits of their own experi-ence and their own understandings of truth. Ensuring that the stories of Indigenous Mormons are fully heard, and learning to hear the stories of others, is fundamental to the work of approaching Zion.

One

A MAORI MORMON TESTIMONY

GINA COLVIN

If you tip a picture of the North Island of New Zealand upside down, it looks like a stingray. The North Island is known colloquially as *Te Ika a Maui* or "Maui's fish". Maui was a demigod, a trickster, who famously fished up the North Island from his boat, *Nukutaimemeha*. Out on the tip of the eastern wing is a small settlement called Horoera. Horoera today consists of a marae and a few scattered farm houses that look out upon a dramatic, rocky and unspoiled coast line. Kanuka grow on a lean bent over by the prevailing easterly winds that blow across the lowland steep lands and sweep up the hills into the Raukumara ranges. If you face east at dawn, you'll see the sun emerge from its ocean cave, lifting its tired head in a chaos of bright liquid yellows and oranges that skip and scatter across the watery expanse, coloring both cloud cover and sky in a riot of pink fire. From the shore, you'll hear the steady rumbling rhythm of the ocean as it throws itself into the rocky stands that stretch out from the coast into the sea in rows like sentinels. You'll hear the shriek and bluster of sea birds, and on hot days you'll hear the unmistakable rub and click of a noisy chorus of scrub cicadas.

Towering over this eastern corner of New Zealand lies Mount Hikurangi, which according to lore was the first part of Maui's fish to emerge from the ocean. Hikurangi is a sacred place for the Ngāti Porou people whose identity is weaved into their own. Nothing captures the spirit of the descendants of Porourangi more than Te Kani-a-Takirau's response to an invitation to be a part of the Māori Kingship established by the Waikato people to raise a parallel monarchy to Queen Victoria: *"Ehara a Hikurangi i te maunga haere"* (Hikurangi is not a travelling mountain)—meaning that Ngāti Porou already have their kingship, earned from their ancestors, and will bow down to no other regime.

The Waiapu River meanders down from the Raukumara ranges, and for a stretch of 130 kilometers it waters, feeds, and shelters the various Ngāti Porou clan who have made its banks their home. Thus, the people of Ngāti Porou always introduce themselves in formal contexts by saying:

> *"Ko Hikurangi te maunga."* (Hikurangi is the mountain.)
> *"Ko Waipau te awa."* (Waiapu is the river.)
> *"Ko Ngāti Porou te iwi."* (Ngati Porou are the people.)

I feel that it's important for readers to know that, like many Indigenous folks, I belong someplace. My land, my river, the ocean and my mountain give me a place to put my feet. I am made someone by these associations. I am part of something ancient that is behind me and beyond me, and knowing this in my bones gives me steadiness. I didn't grow up in Horoera, but I am sure, deep down that in this one place on earth I belong.

My grandfather's father, Ngawati Ruwhiu, was not Ngāti Porou—he was Ngā Puhi, a significant tribe who occupy the tail of the fish. He and his wife, Huhana Wharepapa, along with their children (including my grandfather Hau), migrated from the Bay of Islands to the East Cape at the turn of the century. As the chair of the Northland Māori Council, it seems that he ran from his tribal lands to escape the smallpox epidemic (brought to New Zealand by a Mormon missionary) that he was charged with trying to contain. In the end, the outbreak killed fifty-five people in Northland and displaced my ancestors.

Hau grew to manhood in the homelands of Ngāti Porou in sight of the Pacific Ocean that stretches east toward Chile and Argentina, while mountains, rivers and lush valleys form a dramatic backdrop in the west. Hau joined the Church of Jesus Christ of Latter-day Saints in July 1934 at the age of thirty-five, two months before the death of his first wife. Hau's first wife's death left him with the care of nine children, so it was arranged that he marry my grandmother, Te Here Taiapa, fifteen years his junior from Toko-maru Bay. Te Here was a daughter of Ngāti Porou, but unlike the majority of her tribe who joined the Anglicans, she had been baptized a Mormon two years earlier.

Hau and Te Here would be married for twenty-three years and together would have another eleven children, and though they had land and food enough to eat they were unable to turn their work into economic prosper-ity. While white farmers received low-interest loans to purchase stock and seed, and were able to turn a profit enough to reinvest in farming, Māori had no such advantage. This was intentional. The colonial government had very little interest in Native prosperity. They wanted Māori for their labor, and their land for white settler farmers, and used the fullest extent of the law to divest as many Māori of their property as they could since a colonial government was formalized in New Zealand in 1852.

The conditions for many Māori during the early twentieth century were a carryover and a continuation of a nineteenth-century assault on Native rights. So even though Māori had survived a violent and appropriative colo-nial incursion, and though there might have been moments of familial hap-piness, life for the Ruwhiu family was by all accounts hard and brutal.

I share this story to arrest the tendency to romanticize rural life among Māori. There is a penchant for some to get glassy eyed and dreamy about Indigenous wisdom, mythology, history, and lore, particularly when it comes out of beautiful landscapes and rushing tides. But that reflex to want the dreams more than the reality creates existential gaps in our understand-ing and does little more than silence the context, rendering a people only half seen. When we are only half seen, or only half see ourselves, it makes it difficult to be whole, and easy to repeat history.

When my grandmother Te Here died on 23 December 1958, she was work-ing at Hinerupe *marae*[1] catering for a funeral or a *tangihanga*.[2] She and her fellow workers were eating ice cream at the end of a hot, busy few days. From all accounts, her death was quite sudden, and indications from those present are that she suffered from a pulmonary embolism.

Back at the farm in Horoera, a few of her *tamariki* were sitting on the weathered tin roof of the family home watching out for their moth-er's return along the dusty road south from Te Araroa. Horoera is a tiny rural community near the eastern most point of New Zealand, and their modest house was nestled beneath the Raukumara Range overlooking a shimmering Pacific coast. As the day wore on, my aunt Huhana, who was ten years old at the time, became fretful wondering what was taking her mother so long. She ran down to *Matahi o Te Tau*, a local marae close to the farm house to use the community party line telephone but was unable to rouse anyone. It was then that Huhana saw the *koroua*[3] Hemi Paringaitai leave his home with his crude horse drawn funeral cart, a sure sign that someone had died, and her heart lurched. She told me, fifty-five years later, "I knew he was going for mum. I just knew it." When confirmation finally came through that Te Here had indeed passed, my young aunts and uncles were gathered in by neighbours and taken home for the evening. They were expected at Hinerupe for their Te Here's tangihanga the following day.

The next day, Christmas Eve, the weather was inclement, and with the Awatere River in flood, it was difficult to get the Ruwhiu children across to Te Araroa. Taking two distraught children at a time, the crossing was precarious, causing an already grieving young family even more anxiety. Upon their arrival at Hinerupe, sodden, frightened, and grief-stricken, the Ruwhiu children were brought onto the marae with a *karanga*, a chanting summons for visitors to ascend onto the marae. As is customary, Te Here was lying in an open coffin on the veranda, and as the children made their way up the path, their feet keeping up a soundless shuffle in time with the wailing of the old women's calls, they silently wept. Unused to being the center of attention, the children were also unsure of the formal protocols surrounding tangihanga, where in this instance the *tikanga*[4] was not a comfort.

The younger Ruwhiu children grew up in an era where the explicit practice of *Māoritanga* existed on the periphery of their awareness. Their parents spoke the language to each other, but never to their children. Hau and Te Here were fully involved at the marae but didn't admit their younger children into the cultural life that surrounded both marae at Te Araroa and Horoera fearing that they wouldn't progress in the *Pākehā* or English world if they had too much exposure to the Māori world. Huhana's grief turned to horror as Te Here's now silent and motionless form was presented to her as her beloved mother. Huhana recalls the terrifying experience of being made to kiss her mother's face—now discolored, bloated and disfig-ured. My young aunts and uncles listened as the people rose to speak about her mother, and to her mother, one at a time in the Ngāti Porou dialect.

Notwithstanding her daily proximity to this language, this was a cultural and a linguistic world in which she had not been prepared nor socialized to find comfort. And all the while as the grieving kept vigil over their mother, the wail and call of the *kuia*[5] lifted and soared down to the gate, bringing the next group of mourners up to the *whare whakairo*.[6]

I asked my aunt why it was that she didn't understand the funereal protocols that I had romanticized as fundamental to life "back home." She lived in proximity to two busy marae in a predominantly Māori community. Why was this all new to her? "Because we used to go to the marae and dance the Gay Gordon with the missionaries," came her reply. "I just loved the missionaries," she effused with a happy smile. "I used to stand on their toes, and they would swirl me around in time to the music."

For a moment in time, my Aunt's forlorn memory of her mother's death and her lack of cultural preparation was punctuated by a recollection of joy. But the irony was that the knowledge she needed to make sense of her mother's death was pushed out of her grasp by the Gay Gordon and the missionaries, and their encroachment into this sacred space. I felt bitter about that, notwithstanding her smiles.

When I heard my Aunt tell this story we were sitting on her porch in Campbelltown, near Sydney, Australia. She had enthusiastically and generously offered up these memories, warmly scolding her brothers (in absentia) for their hopelessness in keeping these family stories alive. "Too quiet," she said of my uncles. I saw the sadness in her eyes when she talked about her mother's passing. When she described their house, she laughed at how the newspaper that was used as wall coverings throughout the farm house interiors gave her good reading skills. When she talked about my grandparents' insistence on cleanliness, she became fiercely proud. But when she talked about the missionaries, her eyes danced with pleasure. My family loved the missionaries. My youngest uncle was even named after the missionary who baptized my grandfather. There is no doubt that the missionaries brought a sweetness with them that was compelling. The other churches were filled with stuffy, staid, and priggish missionaries or clergy from England or from New Zealand. The Mormon Māori got the Americans, with their youth, their audacious dreams, their optimism, and their remarkable openness and generosity of heart. How could a young girl on the verge of womanhood not fall in love with the handsome young men who were sent into the hinterland to dance with her?

The juxtaposition of two traditions, the ancient Indigenous and the modern American, is worth thinking about. For my aunt, colonization and language loss meant an illiteracy with the former, and pleasure in the latter. The question arises as to whether or not the easy joy of an American faith tradition that swept up my aunt lubricated her cultural alienation, or if the Mormon church has been a prosthetic, offering Māori a way of composing themselves in a world that has been aggressive and unkind to Indigenous folk? Maybe it's done both, because I can't deny that Mormonism has been an important vehicle that encouraged my and my cousin's intellectual training, thereby affording us the capital to work among our own. But I'm not sure that that has ever been the express intention of the Utah oligarchy, who then as now seem more intent on making Native people recognizable, but not necessarily equal, to themselves. That Māori have found other meanings in Mormonism wherein they have been able to leverage Mormon institutional resources to help their own should be a reason for celebration. That they do it against the tide of the metropole's feeling, sadly means that any wisdom that Māori have to offer will likely not be communicated to the center, so that white America can be enriched by the diversity in their midst.

The Mormon missionaries were different from the Anglican, Methodist, or Catholic missionaries. They were young; they were transitory; they didn't look to purchase Māori land; they didn't have a problem with polygamy; they learned the Māori language instead of insisting that Māori learn English; and they stayed in Māori homes. But even those spaces innocently and even enthusiastically inhabited by the American Mormons—such as they did in Horoera, a tiny settlement on the tip of a mythical sting ray— were not rendered neutral simply because there was no ill intent. There have been enormous consequences as a result of even the most well-meaning activities of the Church of Jesus Christ of Latter-day Saints' mission among the Māori.

For my grandfather, the church bought coherence, and provided him with a story that made sense of his *whakapapa*—his origins—and it gave him hope in a future radiant with eternal glory, upon the condition of his loyal Mormon adherence. With sights fixed upon the horizons of eternity, the present needed but to be endured. Whatever vicissitudes had to be suffered, would be suffered. Mormonism offered a story beyond the need to struggle over questions of Māori sovereignty, beyond the pressing necessity to preserve the language, beyond the Māori land court, and beyond the Treaty of Waitangi. It fixated beyond the legislative violence that left him bereft of the resources to develop his farm while those same state resources ensured prosperity to his Pākehā (white) neighbours.[7] In the dazzling reflection of a discourse that spoke compellingly of the wonders of celestial glory, the sharp contours of the political and social were now obscured.

Having said this, I'm not sure how many fingers of critique I can point at Mormonism for creating a politically impotent narrative for my grandfather to live into. Simple critique doesn't do the complexity of a Māori Mormon faith justice. Mormonism offered up a theology that pointed to universal concepts of equality and grace for all, and unlike other Christian faith traditions, allowed for and recognized the ancestors as a sprawling unit of salvific concern. Regarding the Book of Mormon, over the years I have personally witnessed the resonance in these stories that cover the arc of human prospering and decline. I grew up with Sunday school discussions that pointed to the fate of a people who became more enamored by the prizes of men, rather than the holiness of God. Furthermore, there is no guarantee that had my grandfather not been Mormon, he would have been more politically or culturally literate or active. There's no guarantee that Hau would have insisted on his children speaking the language, or having his children schooled in the arts, wisdom, politics, and culture of their forebears. What it does suggest is that in this respect Mormonism, even with its departure from mainline Christianity, even as it offered a replacement system for a people pushed to the margins, made no formal investment in turning its theology into political action, liberation, or social justice. While the Saints in Utah were actively pursuing a political course that would ensure their future protection, freedom, and prosperity, that kind of consciousness was not expected beyond the Great Basin kingdom.

Zion, it has become apparent, is a geographic location, a conquest of territory, not a state of mind. Though Joseph had imagined a society of equality and consecration, Māori were never allowed to participate in this Zion project of gathering on account of US skin color–based immigration laws. The very heart of Mormonism that imagines an earthly kingdom fit for God and Māori was not translated into something that could come alive in New Zealand in anything other than the buildings erected by the mostly Māori membership. Property acquisition and development from the 1940s onward is reminiscent of Zion-building in that it leaves the physical traces of a faith in view. But Māori have learned, precisely because of colonization, that property acquisition can leave as many scars as it leaves monuments. They have learned that the spirit of a people cannot be measured by building size or investment portfolio. Colonization has taught Māori that in the end:

> *He aha te mea nui i te ao?* (If you should ask me what is the greatest
> thing in the world,)
> *He tāngata, he tāngata, he tāngata* (I would answer, it is people, it is
> people, it is people).

Only traces of Hau's orthodoxy lingered in his and Te Here's twelve children. Mormonism added another complex layer of dogma to many of my aunts and uncles and their children who were already troubled by the social and cultural complexities as Indigenous subjects amidst a hostile colonial incursion. In the wake of postwar urbanization, rural Māori children were leaving their tribal homes in search of prosperity that they would never achieve at home as the government continued their onslaught of legislation to acquire native land. Some of my aunts and uncles were sent, in times of great financial hardship, to Church College of New Zealand. But for some Māori children, the cultural terrain of Mormonism during the 1950s and 1960s was too heavy with dogma and religious expectation to manage alongside the day-to-day struggle of being Indigenous in yet another white colonial patriarchal hegemony. In my family's case, an orthodox father who could be severe in his management of his motherless children was another compelling reason to leave. Thus, away from the parental control of their religious life, the youthful Ruwhiu offspring gradually made their way into towns and cities and away from the surveillance of their father, and for some, away from the church.

If you look at a map of the South Island of New Zealand and squint your eyes a bit, you could almost convince yourself that it's a boat—the same that Maui hid himself in when his brothers went fishing, thinking that they had left their annoying sibling on shore. Once out at sea, he stood up on this island canoe, threw in the magic jawbone fishhook of his ancestress Muri-ranga-whenua, and hauled up a thrashing stingray that he beat to death with his *patu*. My maternal ancestors made their way to Maui's boat from

Wales, Ireland, Scotland, England, and Germany, bringing with them the hope of a new life, knowing that they would likely never return to Snowden Beck in Yorkshire, or to Wadhurst in East Essex, or to County Antrim in Ireland, or to Stirling in Scotland.

I returned to Wadhurst a few years ago, navigating its narrow leafy lanes swathed in the deepest of green. I found the cemetery where the bones of my Colvin ancestors lay beneath unreadable and weather worn headstones, and I recalled their stories handed down to me, glad to put a place and an aesthetic to their names. There are still Colvins living in Wadhurst. The kind folk at the Wadhurst Parish office directed me down the main street to Daphne Colvin who worked at the local pharmacy. But she was having a day off when I opened the shop door with its welcoming chime. I didn't mind missing her. What does one say to family who have been separated by 19,000 kilometers for the last 160 years?

The Colvins, the Bairds, the Crofts, and the Grindlays brought little in the way of religious conviction with them to New Zealand. They were not Catholic—that is all that seemed to matter. While they were avowedly Christian, religion and godly conversation weren't my mother's progenitors' primary concerns, making a living was. One side of my mother's family were well-to-do farmers who worked the Ashley bank on the Canterbury Plains into productivity. The other side were hard-working tradespeople who had few aspirations beyond living in unpretentious comfort.

My mother Marie's decision to become a Mormon passed the faith of a rural Māori family from the back of beyond onto a working-class white city girl and onto me, the half-caste child with the blood and spirit of both sides of two very different families coursing through her. Though I was never raised in my father's family, I have always identified as Māori. Always. One of the reasons why is that I look Māori enough that I would simply never be allowed to say I was Pākehā. Not that I have ever wanted to say I was Pākehā. Some people have asked me, "Are you part-Māori?" And in simple jest my stock reply is, "No, I'm part Pākehā." This retort is often met with some confusion and uncertainty, as if whiteness is a base color that you mix into your gene pool, but you never discuss, because—well, it's just a base color. Once you add a tint, you can never claim that base color as your own. So I've never been able to hide from my Māori ancestry, I have been treated consistently as such, which has led me to identify as Māori, and that in turn determines who I understand myself to be.

But I've always felt mostly Māori—on the inside. It's difficult to explain, but it feels as though my Māori ancestors have always spoken with more insistence to my soul. It's not simply about the way I present in the world: there is a soul attachment to my *tupuna* Māori punctuated by too many dreams, too many encounters with something beyond myself or my imagination to dismiss. It's as if my ancestors left traces of themselves everywhere for me to find, and in finding them, I find a complete story of myself and my place in the world.

For all of that sense of connection, colonization meant that I was born unraveled from the rites and blessings to which every Māori infant is entitled. My passage into mortality was without the rhythmic cadence of the elders' incantations, it was without the calls and cries of the women folk who should have welcomed me into a mortal space brimming with the sounds and symbols that spoke to my potential. I was born into a shrill place, hollowed out by generations of colonization. I was born into a time saturated with British conceit, where Māori families were corralled into narrow city islands with oceans of whiteness between them and their own. All the while, Pākehā continued to grow fat and rich on land stolen from Māori, and were clever at schools shot through with white stories, histories, and ways of being in mind, spirit, and body.

I was born into a time of muteness, where the words, the language that might have connected the ancestors with their posterity, were silenced under the teacher's cane. I was born into a time where children like me paid a burdensome social tax for the offence of their skin color. I was born into a time of silence about my ancestral past—a silence so weighty and intentional I could feel it undulating across my heart in a constant throb of unsaidness. Even as a child the burden of this silence sat upon me like a nightmare. Silence like this isn't peaceful. Those words that should slip around a child's soul, helping them to gently make sense of a fractured world, were eaten up in wave upon wave of unrelenting colonial meanness and racism. Where taking from Māori and not giving back was lawful, where the child is made to feel that the burden and responsibility for the prejudice in the world are theirs alone.

But I was also born at the edge of the Māori renaissance, at a time pregnant with growing unrest. Treaty, language, and cultural rights were being argued in the public sphere as Māori moved into cities to gain an education and employment. I remember protests, marches, flags unfurled, and images of elderly Māori walking the length and breadth of New Zealand with their people, desperate for attention from the government for their plight. And perhaps my infant spirit vibrated with the energy of that time as my country and my people began looking over their shoulders at the past that needed attention.

At the same time, rivulets of ancestral blood burned through me like fire, so much so that there has never been a time when I have not felt wildly awake to the transcendent potential of the soul and its connection to a cosmic beyond. I have always been alive to the idea that being fully human is inseparably connected with the soul's mission to see the world's aching need for redemption and to bring it love, justice and healing. Māori resistance taught me that.

While Māori were taking to the streets, unfurling ensigns that declared sovereignty and demanded rights, the LDS Church chugged along a mirror image of the colonizing government of New Zealand with its imported curriculum and its white foreign leadership, its pioneer stories of invasion into Indigenous land. The church ignored Māori concerns. Instead, Māori were told to listen to Salt Lake City for guidance as to the conditions that should be met for our eternal salvation. We were told that our exaltation depended on the machinations of an institution beyond our borders or cultural control, that we would always be subject to the authority of Americans because our nationality, our culture, our skin color, our pedigree, or our residency is not enough to be taken seriously by those in religious power. Jesus apparently prefers the passports of the United States of America.

From the 1970s on, some Mormon church leaders set about problematizing the Māori rights movement. The Utah church has a past littered with incidents of racial exclusions. It had historically participated in the group murder and appropriation of Indigenous land in Utah; it had developed an increasingly rigid theology of gender and sex; as a growing corporate entity, it was increasingly embracing the politics of financial protectionism rather than social progress. As the civil rights disputes placed pressure on the United States government to change, the Church of Jesus Christ of Latter-day Saints opted to position itself behind more politically conservative sensibilities. At the same time, as Māori made their way into the cities for jobs and increased educational opportunities, a developing political literacy meant that even Mormon Māori were joining the movement to reclaim language, culture, and political and treaty rights. This challenge to the existing system of colonial authority in New Zealand must have resonated unfavorably with Utah who didn't want "their church" associated with protest.

The political climate in the United States and in Utah in particular during this time saw a swelling white supremacist conservativism, and American LDS church leaders thus infected brought these ideologies to the left-wing social democracy of New Zealand with impunity. Eventually this desire to regulate political feeling to agree with what was taking place in Utah was deployed as a religious injunction known as the "gospel culture." This term was frequently deployed to remind us that certain cultural practices don't comport with one's membership in the Church of Jesus Christ of Latter-day Saints. The gospel culture has become a ubiquitous term that reminds us non-Americans that we are obligated to "pursue a distinctive way of life, common to all members of the church." That culture, according to Elder Dallin Oaks, comes from the plan of salvation, the commandments of God and the teachings of the living prophets. Except that's not where culture comes from.

Culture is a complete way of life. Culture arises over time and includes a whole suite of human behaviors—from what we consider important to know to what we choose to believe, to how we respond through artistic expression, what we consider to be right and wrong; our community agreements, our daily habits, how we socialize our young, the customs we preserve and the languages we speak, and the practices that grow out of being in relationship with a certain geography or landscape. As a colonized people, Māori have had significant disruptions and assaults on their cultural systems such that it has been a temptation to grab on to Mormonism as a cultural prosthetic, something that offers a way of being that replaces that which has been lost—except that one religious tradition, particularly one from the Great Basin mountain home of the Mormon pioneers, is an inadequate substitute for Indigenous people in the South Pacific.

The gospel culture won't revitalize a language that holds all of the secrets and wisdom of an ancestral past. The gospel culture, as it is currently described by LDS authorities, won't arouse the resistance needed to claim and demand the material and political return of resources that were taken from a people in a slew of historical legal violations. The gospel culture won't make room for Māori to find the missing parts of the self that have been torn from them and their families by colonization. The gospel culture won't make Māori white, nor will it teach them to be proud of the color of their skin, the movement of their body, the shimmer of their thick wave of ebony hair, the arc of their generous lips, the spread of their nose, the twinkle in their chocolate almond eyes, or the thickness of their legs. Nor will it arouse pride in the mythologies that make those beautiful bodies make sense. And the gospel culture has little capacity to be the bridge of enlightenment needed by a bereft group of Māori children to cross into a sacred space of shared grieving and be held there by the tribe, attended to with words that attest to the continuity of life and meaning, simultaneously nourished by hope and laughter and stirred into a flow of tears until they are ready to let their mother go. And the gospel culture won't ease these children back into the world of light having been renewed by the old ones in an ancient practice that makes holy affirming and comforting connections between the living and the dead.

Thus, while Mormonism flexes and bends with elasticity to reinforce and add value to white American conservative national identities, the negotiations are more complex at the periphery of the church. At the center, political, social, cultural, and religious spaces coalesce and cohere. At the periphery, Mormonism has no language to apply with relevance and purpose to help the indigene recover those parts of their diasporic self. Rather, a new language is offered up that invites the Indigene to reconstitute the self in a new center of churched belonging. The church replaces the tribe. The temple is the context in which we talk about *whakapapa* (genealogy). *Tikanga* is set by the General Handbook of Instructions. The Treaty, the legal and political basis for colonial resistance, is constructed within the unwelcome rhetoric of protest—something good Mormons don't do because, as is indicated in the twelfth Article of Faith, "we believe in being subject to kings, presidents, rulers, and magistrates, in obeying, honoring, and sustaining the law." But to trust the law so implicitly is a privilege realized only by those who are benefited by the law. The reality for Indigenous folk is that the law has actively worked against them, and rather than protect the human rights and property of a people it has been leveraged to justify the systemic erasure of everything that makes Māori who they are and gives them a sense of coherence in the world.

How can Māori, or anyone for that matter, be expected to sustain laws that might bring about the extinction of their own people physically, spiritually, economically or culturally? In this respect, the Church of Jesus Christ of Latter-day Saints is doing a mischief by arrogantly and ignorantly raising a question over the place of resistance. The fact is New Zealand society has become more tolerant because of Māori resistance to the law. Māori defiance, protest, and their willingness to stand up for each other and future generations against a violent discursive colonial incursion has been a blessing for all New Zealanders brown and white.

This leads me to wonder if the white Utah church will ever soften enough to admit the stories and narratives from beyond their borders? And I wonder how its dogmas would endure an assault upon the certainties that are born out of a context that has relentlessly pursued a kind of authoritarian homogeneity that has a tendency to still any reflex to question and critique. But at the same time, the LDS Church is deeply implicated in the way that I have storied my world. When I was pregnant with my eldest son Isaac, my dreams were filled with *ngarara*, mythical reptiles in Māori mythology who have magical powers to either protect or to curse. My ngarara appeared in a brilliant array of colors. They weren't menacing, they were *kaitiaki,* or guardians, who stood in great numbers around me and with me. When Isaac was two years old I told my cousin about the dreams, and he replied matter-of-factly, "Our women often have dreams of ngarara when they are *hapu* (pregnant)." At which point he regaled me with stories of his own mother and her extra-spiritual encounters while hapu. "It's a thing," he repeated.

I share this story because I find myself having to take a syncretic approach to Christianity. At its traditional heart, Māori cosmology is animist, acknowledging that everything, whether seen or unseen, is part of a great cosmic ecosystem where there is no hard line between the physical and the spiritual and that in all things there is a need for balance. For some time in the church's early history in New Zealand, this cosmology co-existed unquestioningly with Mormonism where the mutual infusion of each other's wisdom traditions created a complementary partnership. This has left me with a unique spiritual legacy. So, as both Mormon and Māori, I came into maturity understanding the power of dreams and symbols or encounters with a spiritual realm and an attachment to guardian ancestors who continue to stand beside me. That I dream of mythical lizards, that I make ritual calls to the deceased beyond the veil sending them on their way, that I have pounamu blessed before I wear it, that I claim my mountain and my river as an extension of myself, that I sprinkle myself with water after leaving a cemetery or touching the dead, and that I fold this into my

Mormon practice means that I get to be more than one thing. In being more than one thing I extinguish the need for certainty, and in living out my life without rigid dualities, I become.

Being Māori has taught me to respect mythologies, to see their usefulness as well as their impossibility, and to hold both reflexes to embrace and to reject together. For instance, before my father passed away in 2006, he returned to church after several decades of inactivity, and like his father and some of his siblings he found in Mormonism a story of belonging and comfort that was shot through with flashes of orthodoxy. When I was sixteen, he handed me several pages of *whakapapa*. With hands like mine he stabbed at it with determination and asked me to remember my genealogy and to observe how this family tree, straight and tall and as confident as a *totara*, linked me back, all the way back, through Porourangi, and Hagoth, and Lehi, and Joseph, to Adam and Eve. He implored me to remember that I was of the blood of Israel, as he had been told he was.

Some years ago my cousins filmed my father's elder brother's testimony. I watched as tears filled his eyes and he recited:

> "*Kia hora te marino.*" (May peace be over all things.)
> "*Kia whakapapa pounamu te moana.*" (May the sea be like greenstone.)
> "*Hei huarahi mā tātou i te rangi nei.*" (A pathway for us all this day.)
> "*Aroha atu, aroha mai.*" (Giving love and receiving love.)
> "*Tātou, i a tātou katoa.*" (One toward another.)

And then with deep feeling he talked about how he imagined God guiding the hand of Hagoth and his Pacific Ocean migrants as they sailed across *Te Moana Nui a Kiwa* toward *Aotearoa*, the Land of the Long White Cloud, New Zealand. I watched my uncle's deep reverence for a story and was filled with feeling. This was not the first time I had heard this testimony; it was a narrative that I was encouraged to live into as I grew up. Even my patriarchal blessings affirm that the "Blood of Israel" flows richly within my veins, that I am a literal descendent of Joseph of Egypt. The fact that Mormonism saw my ancestry and weaved it into its theology offered me a sense of place and even confidence that no one else could.

I'm grateful that for a time I believed I was of Lamanite origin. Except now I have to face that it is likely that I'm not. Even as the rise of DNA research tells an entirely different story, I wonder how useful it will be to tap my aged uncle on the shoulder and inform him that for all of these years, through church building, church service and raising Mormon children he was under a delusion—that there is no evidence that these pronouncements are factual. Spencer W. Kimball proclaimed:

> And so it seems to me rather clear that your ancestors moved northward and crossed a part of the South Pacific. You did not bring your records with you, but you brought much food and provisions. . . . I would like to say to you brethren and sisters of New Zealand, you are some of Hagoth's people, and there is No Perhaps about it!

But the silence from the church in the face of growing evidence that Māori have Southeast Asian genetic origins suggests there to be more of a commitment to the authority and pride of an institution than there is to provide the ideal conditions for human flourishing and connection. Yet I still couldn't burst my uncle's bubble and tell him otherwise, that this story is not a truth, but rather a myth that stood in for the cosmological erasure that rendered Māori culturally bereft of their own origin stories. I couldn't do that because the story is part of his recovery and identity as a Māori man—and that makes this tale true for him. I can only hope that we don't feel the need now to reproduce or pass on tales and narratives that are misleading to our *tamariki/mokopuna* to imagine they are something they are not. In the face of mounting evidence as to the errant nature of this Mormon myth, it isn't emotionally or intellectually healthy to live with the dissonance that these kinds of "suppositions" supply, particularly the kind of dissonance that will only be sustained because we have more feeling for our American leaders than we do for our people. Besides which, in recent years the New Zealand government has embraced a policy of biculturalism, and the country and its people have been the better for it. This has been as a result of the protest that some US LDS church leaders found abhorrent. A bicultural political landscape means that Māori are more literate about their origins, more comfortable in their identity, and more assertive in their politics. The young simply don't need myths and fables about who they are from white men in the United States. Stories of Hagoth are occasionally recited in Sunday school classes or sacrament talks but they don't get much traction from young Pasifika people. They simply don't sit well in our cultural lexicon that has exploded out further than Mormonism has dared venture.

My identity as Māori and Mormon has required consciousness, resistance, adaptation, and integration as I stay on alert and cautious, just as my Indigenous forebears had to do, to structures of exploitation and power. In this tight spot between the single story of a religious tradition that is infected with the heavy weight of its historical evolution and my national culture still plagued somewhat by the sins of its past, I have to entertain hard questions to survive. I have to find the courage to resist anything that doesn't allow for human dignity and becoming. I have to innovate spiritually so that all parts of myself, wherever they are scattered across God's ecosystem can coalesce, and I have to push these disparate parts of myself into relationship with each other and make them talk. Because in the final analysis, this is where wisdom lies.

There is little doubt that my Mormon life has been a blessing. Where my Māori father was absent, my Māori church filled the emptiness. I have been rehomed by good people, loved by many, offered community and belonging, and I've become socially mobile because of the church's emphasis on higher education. But my Mormon life hasn't been an unproblematic one. Where the self sometimes requires spiritual reconciliation and redemption from sin, the attention that Mormonism encourages us to pay to ourselves can be transformative. At the periphery of the church, in our religiously colonized spaces, it flounders with few tools sharp enough reach into the blind spot and surface a language that will help the Indigene as a people deeply and profoundly heal from the vestiges of colonization. Some feel that it is enough to be Mormon, that the spiritual attention we and others give us is sufficient, that anything outside Mormonism is simply a distraction from all that is necessary and important for our salvation. For instance, in 1995 I trained as a secondary school English teacher. On my teaching practice, I chose to spend two months at Church College of New Zealand, a Mormon College in Hamilton. This was a teaching placement that I found as interesting as I found bewildering. In a school that boasted a significant majority of Māori learners, I was confused as to why their cultural expressions were limited to performance. This at a period in New Zealand's cultural history where we were grappling with questions of Indigenous self-governance and sovereignty, language and cultural rights, land claims and calls for a bicultural nation state. At lunch one afternoon I asked my teaching associate, herself Māori:

"Why doesn't this school place more emphasis on te reo Māori, or teach its Māori majority student body about the Treaty of Waitangi?"

She replied, "Our students need to understand that they are children of God."

To which I returned, "Don't you think that 'our students' need to understand why that child of God lives in poverty, while that one lives high on the hog without a care in the world?"

Yet for her and a few other Māori teachers at CCNZ, there was a palpable contentment in allowing the question of identity, reclamation, revitalization, and sovereignty to go unanswered. Social, political, economic, and cultural contexts were simply nuisances that the teachings of the church could neutralize as superfluous to the business of spiritual progression. In my younger years, I was often warned that I was straining at matters that were not necessary for my deliverance, yet my deepest spiritual yearnings were satisfied in the language of critique. In using a language that interrogated and demythologized colonial, racist, gender, and class regimes, in seeking for a higher critical consciousness, I was finding God, and me, and me with God.

Colonial incursions with their sometimes progressive policies of assimilation and integration have been woeful not only in their absolute lack of success but also in the immense damage they have caused hundreds of millions of Indigenous folk throughout the world. In the New Zealand context, it cannot be argued that the LDS Church hasn't played an important role in the social mobility of its Māori adherents. In 2014 more and more LDS Māori are present in the realm of Indigenous politics and activism. Yet we live a double life, where on the one hand we advocate for language revitalization and are working hard to raise a generation of Māori children who are fluent in a dying language, but we don't ask for this space at the pulpit. Nor do we give our children the language of God in the language of their forebears. While on the one hand we read the gospels, and like Te Ua Haumene, Te Kooti, Te Whiti-o-Rongomai, Rua Kenana and Paora Te Potagangaroa, we see a story of oppression and suffering, and a glorious redemption from the earth's injustices made possible through the political dissident, Jesus Christ, our LDS teachings waver tremulously toward a version of the savior as first and foremost a personal redeemer from personal weakness. And though we shake a fist at the legislative violations that alienated Māori land by the millions of acres, we are inclined to quietly turn a blind eye to the Māori land given up freely to the church for chapels, with little recompense, because we have been taught to see this as a holy sacrifice rather than a prudent and cunning commercial transaction between friends. And while we rage at the economic exploitation that caused Māori to sink into low-paid unskilled work, we glory in the years and years spent by our tupuna who worked as unpaid labour missionaries to build church-owned facilities.

While my spiritual journey has been made more meaningful the more I have sought to unlatch from and challenge colonial systems, my churched journey, once so simple, joyous and transformative, has become more and more complex. Yet my survival as an Indigenous woman is absolutely dependent upon the language I have acquired over the years as I have sought to reclaim parts of my diasporic self split apart in the wake of colonization, and the irony is that some of those sensibilities and that motivation to heal and to build a world of compassion has come from being a Mormon—as do some of my wounds. As a result, I have had to learn a language that when applied to Mormonism raises hard, hard questions for a church that faces the massive challenge of the diversity and differences of its membership. I'm hopeful that it can be done, but I don't think the answer to the church's greatest challenges will come from Utah or from white folk who have been privileged by an intergenerational system that has rendered many sightless.

The Utah-centric cultural hubris and rigidity that has turned Mormonism into more of a fortress than a faith needs to be questioned so that it becomes softer and open to a new spirit of generosity characterized by a will to let go of everything that causes existential harm to Indigenous folk who are already tenuously and painfully connected to their roots. The Utah centric cultural hubris that makes the desperate lives of those at the church's non-white, non-middle-class, non-Utah, non-patriarchal, non-heteronormative, colonized, oppressed margins needs to be challenged by an appeal to the wisdom, the faith, the resilience, and the resistance contained in those stories. Mormonism was never meant to be centered around a single unchangeable story. Mormonism has made a claim over and over again that it presents a truth offering to the world. As Antonio Gramsci argues: "Truth is revolutionary," meaning, I believe, that truth must catalyze change and motivate hope that things can indeed by different. Arousing the will to reach into that third space, that space that holds complexity, loss, and as Homi Bhabha suggests, "incommensurability," is surely Mormonism's most difficult but most redemptive future act. For it is in this space that wisdom and compassion dwell. It is in this space, in the cross-current of ideas and sensibilities, resistance, innovation, new meaning-making, symbols, and new and ancient forms of sacredness that wisdom and the beloved community is to be ultimately found.

Two

DECOLONIZATION ON THE SALISH SEA

A Tribal Journey back to Mormon Studies

THOMAS MURPHY

As a child growing up in southern Idaho in the 1970s, the Book of Mormon taught me that my "Lamanite" ancestors, celebrated in stories by my grandmother, had been cursed with a dark skin for their wickedness. The same Mormon scripture had promised we could become "white and delightsome" (2 Nephi 30:6) by abandoning the traditions of our forefathers and mothers and adopting the religion of the colonizers. As if in fulfillment of this prophecy, my skin was white, like that of my English, Irish, and Scandinavian ancestors, early converts to Mormonism who gave rise to a lengthy pioneer pedigree. My Dad's Irish ancestors, despite a sojourn in Mexico, also contributed to our light skin.

My maternal grandmother, Eunice Wayment Harmon, told us stories that she had learned from her Grandfather Gransbury about his Indian grandmother who was excluded by his parents from the family home. Charles W. Gransbury enjoyed his childhood experiences playing outside with his grandmother and passed that memory on to his descendants. It was to the Book of Mormon, though, that my mother, now Cheryl Harmon Bills, instructed me to turn if I wanted to know more about our Indigenous ancestors. Yet in this American scripture, "Lamanite" culture was suspect and supposedly the primary cause of wickedness and the purportedly fallen state of my ancestors. I was not satisfied with the answers it offered.

An anthropology course on North American Indians at the University of Iowa led me as a young adult to ask more questions about our heritage. When asked, my grandmother, an avid genealogist, said she thought our ancestors were Iroquois. Iroquois, though, was a confederation of six nations including the Mohawk, Seneca, Oneida, Onondaga, Cayuga, and Tuscarora. After my grandmother's passing, my mother's genealogical endeavors turned up more details about Susannah Ferguson, born about 1786 at the village of Tiononderoge in Mohawk Valley, a site renamed "Florida" by American colonists. My mother, who calls Susannah an "Indian princess," sent me an extract from a genealogical resource that described Susannah's Mohawk community as follows:

> [C]ommonly regarded by historians as among the most powerful and intelligent of our savage aborigines; of good stature, and athletic frames, naturally warlike and brave, they possessed in large measure all the qualities making up the savage's highest type of man.[1]

Such language characterized our Indigenous cultural inheritance, mediated as it was by a history of colonization.

The family of my wife, Kerrie Sumner, passed along similar stories but with more detail. She was a direct descendant of Peninah Shropshire Cotton, a Cherokee woman and a servant in the household of prominent Mormon patriarch Daniel Wood during the Mormon sojourn in Nauvoo during the 1840s. Family stories say Peninah was the first Native woman to go through the Nauvoo temple, where she wed Daniel Wood in a secret polygynous marriage in 1846. Her traditional knowledge on the Mormon trek west to the Great Basin during the following year would become legendary.

In the 1990s the Church News rediscovered this relic of early Mormon diversity and printed her husband's purported recollection:

> Peninah was a God-send to these people, as Sacagawea, the Indian maid, had been to Lewis and Clark's expedition. She knew the berries and plants that were good for food and medicine. And she made moccasins, gloves and clothing from skins; and from cloth she wove herself. She also had to drive one of the wagons.[2]

Kerrie now winces at the reference to Peninah as a Mormon Sacagawea, another colonial reframing of Indigeneity that was anachronistically added to family accounts in later generations.[3] Nonetheless, Kerrie is grateful that her grandfather passed along an immense pride in Cherokee heritage along with some of that traditional knowledge that had earned Peninah her fame.

As a couple, Kerrie and I have traveled a path of decolonization together, one that led us away from Mormonism and into careers in Indian country. As light-skinned professionals engaged in decolonization work, we are not comfortable putting our ethnicity into a box, especially one generated by colonial efforts intended to make Indians disappear. I am comfortable stating, though, that as the seventh-generation descendant of Susannah Ferguson from the Mohawk village of Tiononderoge, it is an honor to share my reflections on our journey through Indian country as part of a much-needed anthology focused on decolonizing Mormonism.

Mormonism presents a complex case for decolonization work. Book of Mormon images of Lamanites have framed Indigenous identities in a manner that privileges the authority of white men, a pattern that extends to the present in Mormon discourse.[4] White Mormons celebrated the genocidal removals of the 1830s that were so traumatic for the Iroquois, Cherokee, and other Eastern tribes. A high council meeting in Kirtland, Ohio in 1836, for example, praised President Andrew Jackson's removal policy, calling it a "wise measure" that "reflects the highest honor upon our government."[5] Mormons are deeply implicated in the colonization of Indigenous peoples in the Great Basin. For example, in Utah Territory in 1850, Brigham Young advocated for extinguishing Indian title to land, removal of Utes and other tribes "from our territory . . . because they are doing no good here to themselves or anyone else."[6] While actively participating in the colonization of Natives, early Mormons had also imagined a shared empire with American Indians, perhaps even with a red prophet. White Mormons, too, experienced a series of removals, wars, and colonization alongside Indigenous neighbors.[7] Decolonizing Mormonism promises to raise some fundamental questions both about faith and about decolonizing methodologies.

Three questions guide this auto-ethnography: (1) How do we decolonize ourselves when we are a physical and cultural product of the colonial effort to turn Indians "white and delightsome?" (2) How might decolonization reshape Mormon truth claims? (3) What are some models for the decolonization of Mormon Studies? I follow these questions using a narrative of my early forays into Mormon Studies, my departure from the discipline for work in Coast Salish communities, and my recent decision to bring the work of decolonization back to the religious community of my birth. Throughout this narrative I seek to unsettle Lamanite identity, in particular the way that this colonial ethnonym has buttressed white authority and privilege.

HOW DO WE DECOLONIZE OUR OWN WHITENESS?

Struggles with understanding my own identity and religious path inspired my journey into American Indian and Mormon Studies. As a college student, reflecting on my Mormon upbringing, I was appalled at the racism that permeated the Book of Mormon. I found it perplexing that any Native person, let alone some of my own ancestors, would join a religion that taught that a dark skin was a curse from God for wickedness. I could not go back and ask Lura Elmina Cole, Susannah Ferguson's granddaughter, why she joined the LDS Church or what she thought about Lamanite portrayals in the Book of Mormon. Instead, I applied for and was accepted for graduate studies in anthropology at the University of Washington with the intent of examining Native American understandings of Mormonism through ethnography among contemporary Indigenous Mormons in Latin America.

Ethnographic research took me to Mayan and Ladino communities in Antigua, Guatemala, and to Nahua communities in central Mexico. The conventional wisdom of the day, as articulated by David Martin, Mark Leone, and LaMond Tullis, was that Mormon institutions were simply turning Latinos into Anglos, that Indians were Mormon on white rather, than on their own terms, and that Indigenous Mormon movements in Mexico, while robust in the 1930s, had since floundered.[8] That was not what I found. Ladino Latter-day Saints in Antigua insisted in priesthood meetings upon a primordial birthright to the Covenant of Abraham vis-à-vis *los anglos* who were adopted into the covenant. Mayan and Ladino Mormons were using the Book of Mormon to validate a local Indigenous scripture, the Popol Vuh or Mayan Book of the Dead.[9]

In central Mexico, while searching for surviving relatives of the excommunicated Nahua leader Margarito Bautista, I stumbled upon the thriving utopian community of Colonia Industrial in Ozumba, Mexico, that Bautista had founded fifty years previously. These self-identified Lamanites similarly insisted upon a primordial connection to Abraham. They had restored communal living under the United Order and plural marriage, practices that the LDS Church had abandoned in capitulation to its own colonization by the United States. Ironically, while they continue to resist the colonial impositions of the United States, they have named their predominantly Nahua community Colonia Industrial.[10]

Ethnohistorical research, initially for my doctoral dissertation and currently for a forthcoming book about decolonizing the Book of Mormon, has helped me to understand the physical means by which Mormons in the United States sought to turn Indians white. These processes were myriad but implicated nineteenth-century Mormons in ecological practices dispossessing Native peoples; in perpetuating an Indian slave trade in Utah; in promoting strategic intermarriages between white men and Indian women while refusing requests for reciprocal alliances, in placing Indian children orphaned by war or purchased through the slave trade into Mormon homes; in establishing extralegal treaties, in targeted evangelizing of Indigenous peoples, participating in displacements, and in cultivating church-owned Indian farms.

In the twentieth century, the fostering efforts were formalized through the Mormon Indian Student Placement Program, and Mormon legislators played key roles in formulating a federal Indian policy of termination of tribal sovereignty at mid-century. While the LDS Church suspended the Placement Program by the 1990s, twenty-first century Utah has developed a reputation as a favorable destination to go to subvert the paternal rights of men of color.[11]

Intriguingly, though, Native converts did not simply capitulate to white Mormon demands. In each of Utah's nineteenth-century Indian wars, baptized Mormons led the combatants on both sides. In the twentieth century, the American Indian Movement and former participants in the Placement Program were its most vocal critics. While white Mormons had penned the legislation that targeted Utah tribes for termination, Native American Mormons would subsequently lead efforts to restore recognition to those same terminated tribes. In the twenty-first century, Indigenous parents continue to publicly protest Utah's subversion of parental rights as illustrated by Lorraine Martinez Cook, an Apache Indian from Reno, Nevada, who in 2003 fought the efforts of an LDS bishop and LDS Family Services to pressure her newborn grandchild's birth mother to subvert the paternal rights of Lorraine's son.[12]

To decolonize my own whiteness, I needed to understand the social processes that created the conditions leading to the decisions of my ancestors. I looked to Indigenous Mormons as models for how one might imagine Mormonism differently. I found thoughtful, articulate, and passionate people in the present and past that did not simply submit to white views of themselves but actively resisted their own colonization. Many Indigenous people found from within and outside Mormonism tools for empowering themselves and struggling against powerful social and ecological forces of change. Some, though, did internalize oppressive views of themselves and their ancestors but much less so than conventional wisdom had led me to expect.

HOW MIGHT DECOLONIZATION RESHAPE MORMON TRUTH CLAIMS?

Decolonization methodologies advocate identification of power imbalances and deconstruction of historical processes.[13] Much to my dismay, the critical analysis of images of Lamanites upon which I had embarked in my doctoral dissertation got overlooked and waylaid in the controversy that would erupt over an article about DNA research I had written at the request of a Mormon philanthropist and published in the anthology, *American Apocrypha*.[14] Mathew Latimer, my LDS stake president, invited me to a meeting in November of 2002 to discuss the article, "Lamanite Genesis, Genealogy and Genetics." In that interview, Latimer expressed particular dissatisfaction with one of my final paragraphs and requested that I reconsider the following conclusion:

> From a scientific perspective, the Book of Mormon's origin is best situated in early nineteenth-century America, and Lamanite genesis can only be traced historically to ca. 1828. The term Lamanite is a modern social and political designation that lacks a verifiable biological or historical underpinning linking it to ancient American Indians. The Book of Mormon emerged from an antebellum perspective, out of a frontier American people's struggle with their god,

and not from an authentic American Indian perspective. As Mormons, we have a moral and ethical obligation to discontinue this view of Native American origins and publicly disavow the offensive teaching that a dark skin is a physical trait of God's malediction.[15]

My refusal to reconsider that conclusion without contradictory evidence resulted in a highly publicized effort to excommunicate me for apostasy.

Throughout the subsequent ordeal, I told nearly every reporter I talked with that they were missing the deeper story by focusing on a science versus religion conflict. The story I encouraged the reporters to tell was the impact of shifting Mormon beliefs about Indigenous peoples, especially those of us who had come to think of ourselves as descendants of Lamanites. I encouraged them to speak directly with other Indigenous people for broader perspectives.

Only two reporters, Suzan Mazur for the *Financial Times* and William Lobdell at the *Los Angeles Times*, followed through on the recommendation.[16] Mazur's article, appearing in London, was the first to report on the issue. However, the only paper in the United States to carry her story was *Indian Country Today*. Lobdell, who followed my leads belatedly, was ironically the same reporter who saddled me with the unwelcome moniker of "a Galileo for Mormons."[17] Dozens of other reporters ignored the way the Book of Mormon's failure to withstand scientific scrutiny was a deeply traumatic betrayal for those of us who were raised to think we had Lamanite heritage.

There are four important lessons for decolonizing Mormonism that come from that difficult experience. The first is the dangerous obsession that Latter-day Saints have with our own truth claims. Decolonization necessarily de-centers and unravels universal truth claims. This methodology asks all researchers to recognize and acknowledge the cultural biases that we bring to our work. It seeks to undo the power imbalances inherent in hierarchical and patriarchal institutions and insists upon the sovereignty of Indigenous nations, especially in regards to intellectual property. Decolonization requires that we move Indigenous knowledge to the center of our analysis.[18] Science is not always an ally in that process, but in this case it was. Nearly all of the voluminous scholarly and journalistic responses to my article in *American Apocrypha* skirted the deeper questions of colonial power and focused instead upon whether or not the Book of Mormon was an ancient historical document. Few responses, outside of Indian country, considered the ethical implication of colonial scriptures or the recasting of Mormon views of Indians and Lamanites for Indigenous peoples.

I appeared in three full-length documentary films addressing the Book of Mormon in the following years, but only one came from a perspective of decolonization.[19] Living Hope Ministries produced "DNA vs. the Book of Mormon" and "The Bible vs. the Book of Mormon" with the express intent of converting Mormons to their own particular brand of Christianity.[20] This approach, in which I must acknowledge my own participation as an interviewee, is fundamentally a perpetuation of the colonization of Mormons, an effort led in the nineteenth century by Christian evangelists and the Republican Party. The current efforts to convert Mormons to evangelical Christianity perpetuate this colonial desire to remake others into replicas of self. These two films sought to change Mormons because the Christian producers, too, were obsessed with truth claims. Yet the critical analysis they directed towards Mormons was never pointed at their own perspectives. Intriguingly, Latter-day Saint response to criticism from evangelical Christianity has primarily been a refashioning that seems to have moved the faith away from its distinctive claims that connect it more with Indigenous peoples.

The second important lesson for decolonization is the importance of place and the centrality of Indigenous peoples in the work. This lesson is illustrated in the third full-length documentary film in which I participated, one that has been largely overlooked by Mormons but has been getting significant play in Native communities. Angelo Baca (Diné/Hopi) directed *In Laman's Terms: Looking at Lamanite Identity* as part of the Native Voices program at the University of Washington, a graduate program in communications committed to decolonizing methodologies.[21] Hopefully, Baca's essay in this volume will bring wider attention to his scholarship and media productions.

As penance for my participation in the previous two films, I negotiated with Living Hope Ministries to include Angelo in our travels to New York. For his film, Angelo suggested that we interview a representative of the Seneca Nation to hear an Indigenous perspective on the scripture that purportedly emerged from the dust of this Iroquois homeland. Our interview of Peter Jemison was, to my knowledge, the first academic effort to seek a Seneca perspective on the claims of the Book of Mormon. The important lesson here is that Seneca specifically, and other Iroquois nations more generally, need to be significant partners in the decolonization of Mormonism. It was, after all, from the land of the Haudenosaunee that Mormon scripture "sprang from the dust."

The third important lesson is the centrality of repatriation to the decolonization movement.[22] We must consider that if the Book of Mormon is the ancient American document that the Latter-day Saints claim it to be, then it is, first and foremost, the intellectual property of the Seneca Nation and the Iroquois Confederacy. It never belonged to colonizing Mormons from the beginning. The copyright, the gold plates (if they can be found), the seer stones and other Indigenous artifacts associated with production of this text should ethically belong to the nations from which they were removed. If we insist upon the truth claim that the Book of Mormon is an ancient Indigenous scripture, then an ethical decolonization effort requires that it be returned to the people from whom it was stolen. Either way, it is deeply troubling that disturbing Native burial sites, taking grave goods without permission or compensation, and destroying mummified corpses were central to the Mormon prophet's methods for producing scripture.[23]

The fourth important lesson is that there is an alter-Native to treating the Book of Mormon as a literal history. This approach can be found in Indigenous approaches to stories and diplomacy. In his thought-provoking classic, God is Red, Vine Deloria Jr., explains, "No Indian tribal religion was dependent on the belief that a certain thing happened in the past that required the uncritical belief in the occurrence of the event." The sharing of stories between "different peoples was regarded as a social event embodying civility. Differing tribal accounts were given credence because it was not a matter of trying to establish power over others to claim absolute truth."[24] Deloria invites us to reconsider the value of questions over answers. "Tribal religions do not claim to have answers to the larger questions of human life. But they do know various ways of asking the questions."[25]

To claim that the Book of Mormon is the history of the Americas is a breach of civility and an act of cultural violence that seeks to displace Indigenous histories with a colonial one. In a decolonized Mormonism, there would be no more efforts to displace Indigenous narratives with colonial stories that privilege whiteness. Instead, the value of Mormonism, like that of tribal religions, would come from the questions we ask, the ways that we ask them, and the relationships we build. The sharing of stories would replace evangelization and conversion.

A decolonized Mormonism would recognize that Joseph Smith was part of a particular culture that shaped his understanding of people, divinity, and ecology. The stories he produced were his stories, emanating from his cultural experience, reflecting the biases and prejudices of his time and place. They might lead him to seek understanding across cultures, time, and place, but his interpretations should not be expected to displace those emanating from other peoples, times, and places. The challenge for decolonization efforts is that his cultural setting was that of a settler colonial society engaged in a social and ecological displacement of Indigenous peoples, justifying those actions with racist and ethnocentric views of Indigenous peoples, along with a religious imperative to convert others to that same point of view. While Joseph Smith uncritically accepted many of the assumptions of his culture, he also struggled with them. It is from the questions that Joseph Smith asked and from his own doubts that decolonization can draw value. His doubts, for example, may have led him to revise the Book of Mormon's original prediction that the descendants of the Lamanites would become "white and delightsome" and to replace it with "pure and delightsome," a change that would be lost for over a century and then eventually restored to LDS scripture in 1981.[26]

A decolonized perspective might see Joseph Smith as something more like a complex trickster and thereby accommodate his flaws within a more holistic view of a prophet and seer. In fact, Iroquois oral tradition has robust and sophisticated understandings of dreams, visions, seers, prophets, and messiahs that might be employed to reevaluate the Joseph Smith story.[27]

Media attention led my stake president to suspend and then permanently halt disciplinary actions against me for my article in *American Apocrypha*. Nonetheless, I came away from that experience disheartened by the response. People who supported my work wanted to make me into some sort of "science vs. religion" martyr or to use my conclusions to advocate for the validity of their own religious views over those of Mormons. Apologists engaged in vicious attacks on my integrity, sought to disrupt my tenure evaluation, and fundamentally missed the significance of the decolonization work in which I was engaged.[28] Or perhaps they understood it and were afraid to address the real questions of power and authority. Meanwhile, my efforts to decolonize the academy were bearing considerable fruit in Coast Salish country, and as a result I shifted my attention elsewhere.

WHAT ARE SOME MODELS OF DECOLONIZATION
FOR MORMON STUDIES?

The advantage of having walked away from Mormon Studies a decade ago to continue work in a more promising arena is that I can now bring back some concrete examples of what decolonization projects can do to restore power balances. Decolonizing the LDS Church may be nigh to impossible, but if it is to be done, it will likely be led from the margins where both Indigenous communities and academia find themselves today. An alliance between academia and Indigenous communities could lead processes of change and would be a necessary precondition for unsettling the power imbalance that is the LDS Church. Remember, though, that Mormonism is much bigger than the LDS Church and decolonization gains its strength from the margins, not from the center. A decolonized Mormonism may never be centered in Salt Lake City. It might instead find a home in places such as Ozumba, Mexico, or among the Maori, or in Coast Salish country.

Early in my teaching career I began a series of innovations in pedagogy that would culminate in the creation of the Learn and Serve Environmental Anthropology Field (LEAF) School at Edmonds Community College in Lynnwood, Washington, in 2006. The LEAF School, as a partnership with Coast Salish tribal communities, aims to use Indigenous methodology and pedagogy to change power relations in higher education and in our surrounding communities.[29]

As I made a series of changes in the way I taught, I drew inspiration from field experience I previously had as a research assistant for Eugene Hunn on the Zapotec Ethnobiology Project in the state of Oaxaca in southern Mexico in 1996. Our task had been to document the traditional environmental knowledge of a Zapotec community while studying the cognitive ways that humans organized and transmitted that knowledge over generations.

What we found astounding was the breadth and depth of familiarity with plants, animals, and their ecological niches that even young children in this community possessed. Our assessments found that children as young as seven could name hundreds of species of plants and animals (often in two languages), explain where and under what conditions you might find them, and identify a variety of uses to which they might be put.

This was information that they did not learn in school. Instead, they learned it outside, in a multigenerational context with elders, parents, mentors, and peers. Learning came through meaningful hands-on tasks of gathering plants and animals for food, medicine, or other practical purposes. It also came through play and was reinforced with stories told by elders.[30]

The LEAF School seeks to incorporate these Indigenous ways of learning into higher education. In doing so, we partner with local tribes to use traditional environmental knowledge to help solve modern problems.[31] We offer a series of courses in human ecology and archaeology that are community-based with a service-learning pedagogy and designed using a mentoring model. This approach breaks down some of the power relationships involved with Indigenous knowledge. Instead of me, the anthropologist, being the authority on traditional knowledge, my students work in the field alongside Coast Salish elders and professionals working for the tribes. Their meaningful tasks are selected by our partners to advance the aims and goals of the community and often include activities such as archaeological and ecological support of salmon habitat restoration, fishery rehabilitation, fish and wildlife monitoring, traditional food preparation, surveys of culturally modified trees, and the production of cultural events. The products of our work are not publications that enhance my career but which instead provide tangible benefits for the community. Examples are data that informed new government policies to protect vital crab and prawn habitats, and streams to which salmon have now returned after a fifty-year absence; improvements to the design of wildlife crossings on local highways; ethnobotanical gardens and traditional knowledge trails used as teaching and gathering places; a cultural kitchen on our campus used to prepare traditional foods; presentations about ecotourism opportunities at tribal community meetings; and cultural events that have included powwows, coastal gatherings, canoe journeys, and first-food ceremonies.

My role as a teacher became more that of a facilitator and a networker. In addition to creating bibliographies, I build relationships with the people, plants, and animals of the Salish Sea. Students, interestingly, learn better in this hands-on, relationship-building, community-based setting. The anthropology department at Edmonds Community College, where we implement elements of this approach in all of our courses, has had the highest success and completion rates in our Social Sciences division. The more intensive and community-based our fieldwork, the better our students do. We do this while targeting Native American and low-income students along with those who failed high school. A majority of our students are low income; up to 50 percent in our field courses are Native (contrasted with 1–2 percent of our college population); and many did not earn a traditional high school diploma. These results show that decolonization can have significant impacts on student success and completion, especially but not only for Indigenous students.

My wife Kerrie has been a key partner in these efforts to decolonize the academy. Earlier in our careers, Kerrie and I both worked for the Native American Science Outreach Network at the University of Washington and helped middle and high school teachers develop more culturally relevant science curricula. Kerrie's involvement at Edmonds Community College began as a volunteer helping our Native American Student Association put on an annual powwow. Eventually, Edmonds Community College hired her to direct our Occupational Safety and Health program, and in that capacity she collaborated with Tulalip Tribes to offer culturally relevant safety training. She now works for the Indigenous Wellness Research Institute (IWRI) at the University of Washington, an international leader in the decolonizing approach of community-based participatory research.[32] Our daughter, Jessyca Murphy, has also worked for IWRI; her graduate studies at the New School in New York have facilitated her scholarly application of critical theory to cultural appropriation in the fashion industry.[33] Our social and professional worlds are now deeply embedded in the decolonization movement.

Important practices drive this work and have some promise for decolonizing Mormon Studies. Perhaps most important to all of this work is that the voices of Indigenous communities need to be included in all steps of the research and educational processes. The community, not the institution of higher education, identifies the questions we pursue and the projects we undertake. Our classes, our events, and our projects are, as much as possible, opened and closed by tribal leaders. The products of our work belong to the tribes or other partners, not to the college nor to us as teachers and researchers. Some of the traditional knowledge is used only in specific applications and is not to be shared beyond our projects and those involved. Our tribal partners play key roles in academic events that we host. We reciprocally participate in academic events that they host.

Our partnerships involve reciprocal relations that stretch well beyond our obligations of employment. For example, Donald Bond, a former

Mormon and member of the Snohomish Tribal Council, asked to adopt Kerrie and me in 2009 at one of our public events in stəl̕jx̌ʷáli, an ethnobotanical garden we had built together in a city park. We now have the same sorts of reciprocal responsibilities with the Bond family and Snohomish tribe that we have with the families and communities of our births.

Kerrie and I risked our careers at Edmonds Community College while removing barriers to Indigenous practices on campus. We faced significant objections to cultural protocols such as offering cash prizes to pow-wow dancers and singers, smudging students and campus facilities, giving gifts (including tobacco) to our guests, harvesting Native plant material on campus, offering prayers at events, holding zero-balance cultural events at which we give away all the money we raise, hosting traditional salmon bakes, and parking RVs on campus. Thanks in large part to our white privilege and a growing Indigenous presence on our campus, we have successfully overcome each of these challenges, but the struggles do not end. New administrators often mean that we have to repeat the same old struggles all over again. These are big investments with rich rewards, but they have great potential for destabilizing our relationships at work and have certainly disrupted our relationship with the LDS Church. We have been fortunate that our decolonization work has been more supported than opposed, but the path has not consistently been smooth. Scholars engaging in this endeavor need to be aware of the challenges as well as the rewards.

Mormon Studies has barely gained my attention over most of the past decade. A few events, though, propelled me to reconsider my decision to withdraw from active scholarship in the field. Most notably, the Mitt Romney campaign for president of the United States in 2012 gave me considerable pause. Romney's disparaging remarks about poor people, his presumptions of his own cultural superiority, his intolerance of immigrants despite his family's history in Mexico, and his unwavering support for the interests of the wealthy over those in need struck me as disappointing examples of Mormon ideologies to display to the world. His ethnocentrism is not surprising or uncommon among Mormons. Racism runs deep in Mormonism but is masked today by presumptions of cultural superiority and victim-blaming discourse about poverty. Romney's embrace of neoliberal capitalism; the LDS Church's political endeavors to prevent same-sex persons from marrying; its overwhelmingly Republican membership in the United States; and its continued resistance to equal rights for women illustrate the depth to which Mormonism itself has been colonized by the very same political party that led the nineteenth century assault on this faith tradition. With Romney's campaign in the news every day, I began to question my decision to step away.

My questioning this decision solidified after I accepted an invitation to review *The Book of Mormon: A Biography* for *Nova Religio*.[34] Paul Gutjahr, just like Terryl Givens (author of a similar text I had reviewed a dozen years previously), completely overlooked Indigenous perspectives on the Book of Mormon.[35] It appears that my white privilege that helped so much in making changes at Edmonds Community College is still needed in this effort to decolonize Mormonism. I am now turning my attention back to Mormon Studies. If the scholarship represented in this anthology of working towards a postcolonial Mormonism is well-received, then presses at universities such as Princeton and Oxford will never again publish books on Mormon scripture that so glaringly ignore Indigenous perspectives.

A TRIBAL JOURNEY THROUGH THE SALISH SEA

I began this essay shortly after Kerrie and I returned from participating in one of the most powerful examples of decolonization work led by the nations of the Salish Sea: a tribal journey that consisted of paddling approximately five hundred miles in canoes from the Lummi Nation in western Washington to the Heiltsuk Nation in Bella Bella, British Columbia, Canada. We traveled an ancestral route, guided by traditional knowledge of elders along the way who hosted us in a different village each evening. In Canada, unlike in much of the United States, many of the First Nations we visited retained possession of their ancient village sites, now home to reserves created through colonization. In these ancient homes we spoke Native languages. We sang ancient songs. We shared dances that connected us with the dolphins, porpoises, black fish, eagles, and cormorants that traveled with our canoes.

Along with my students, representing Haida, Tlingit, Cheyenne, Arapaho, Lakota, and Cherokee nations, I traveled in the Snohomish Tribe's Blue Heron Canoe, and we accompanied the Lummi Youth and the Oliver Canoe Families. We were joined en route by dozens of other canoes representing nations from as far south as Warm Springs, Oregon and across the sea from

Hawaii and Aotearoa. Even more canoes joined us as we paddled together beyond the Salish Sea, through Queen Charlotte Sound, and up the Inside Passage to Bella Bella.

This 2014 tribal canoe journey was an iteration of the 1993 Paddle to Bella Bella, a journey that had helped bring the cedar canoe back to many of the shores we traveled after an absence of nearly a century. At the "Paddle to Seattle" in 1989, the first event of its kind in generations, Frank Brown from the Heiltsuk Nation had issued a challenge to Coast Salish nations to paddle to Bella Bella. The trip was arduous, but those who had been on the first journey testified to the way that the Heiltsuk Nation had changed the world with that invitation, initiating an annual journey that has transformed lives. Examples of decolonization were evident all along our route. The canoes brought back the languages, songs, and dances that we shared in Big Houses that once again dot the inside shores of Vancouver Island. The protocol we practiced respected the diplomacy and sovereignty of our hosts.[36]

Kerrie and I could not help but contrast the experience of this tribal journey with our visit to the LDS-owned Polynesian Cultural Center (PCC) in Hawaii only a few months previously. In both situations, Indigenous languages, songs, and dances were central. Yet the economics and the setting were fundamentally different. At PCC we paid a rather high price for admission and every time we turned around someone was asking for more. The whole experience seemed to be designed to extract as much money as possible from the tourists. The performers at PCC, while talented, let their body language remind visitors that they were employees doing a job. The cultures at PCC, while vibrant, were not free. They were contained by colonial economic relationships and subservient to LDS Church leadership.

Tribal Journey, in contrast, was a series of potlatches hosted by sovereign nations. A potlatch, or giveaway, operates on an economy of reciprocity. It so reverses the logic of capitalism that colonial powers in the United States and Canada had banned potlatches for decades. In a gift economy, one gains prestige through the wealth you give away rather than by what you accumulate. The generosity of our hosts was abundant. We never paid for food, lodging, showers, or laundry. Our hosts fed us generously with salmon, halibut, crab, herring eggs, and other prized foods. Communities opened their parks and people shared their front lawns so we could camp. Community members came by and invited us to their homes so we could shower and wash our clothes. In return we shared our stories, songs, and dances, and gave gifts of our own.[37]

On Tribal Journey our First Nation hosts were sovereign. We asked permission to land upon our arrival and for permission to leave upon our departure. Our hosts welcomed us as diplomats from other sovereign peoples. Our hosts were living on their own land, not on property owned by the LDS Church. They were not employees, but were citizens with the right to govern themselves. These First Nations spoke freely and clearly about the dangers of capitalism and the threat of the oil industry to the health of the Salish Sea, the Pacific Ocean, and neighboring waters. They spoke of the betrayals of colonialism and the hope of decolonization so eloquently represented by the life of the cedar canoes and the cultures they carried. The elders spoke proudly of their traditional knowledge and gifted it generously to ensure our safe travels. Our hosts shared their own stories and listened intently to ours. At times the stories were different, but that did not matter because no one story had to take priority. Customs we practiced in one nation might vary at the next, but both sets were treated as equally valid. Mormons, it is clear, have a lot to learn from the diplomacy of Indigenous communities.

A decolonized Mormonism might be one in which Indigenous peoples are welcomed to its headquarters as ambassadors from sovereign nations and are treated with the same respect that dignitaries from settler states receive. Mormons might work hand in hand with local tribes and the nations of the Pacific to return as much land as possible to the people from whom it was stolen. Protecting cultural resources and restoring harvesting rights on public- and church-owned properties would be a valuable first step towards the ultimate repatriation of land.

In a decolonized Mormonism, we might very well see the Red Prophets dreamed about by early Mormons, but long since forgotten. Certainly, the leadership would support marriage equality and would include women and people of color, proportionate to their representation in our community.

In a decolonized Mormonism, our Indigenous ancestors would not be framed through such colonial images as a Lamanite, an Indian princess, and/or a Sacagawea. These images are damaging because they project European ethnocentrism, social categories, and systems of aristocracy onto Indigenous cultures. These images value Native women primarily for the services they provide to white men and not for their own dignity and authority.

A decolonized Mormonism would honor the original intent of the Indian Child Welfare Act and ensure that Indigenous communities, as sovereign nations, choose who raises their children. In such a setting, no baptism of the Indigenous dead would take place without consent from the sovereign nations of their descendants. A decolonized Mormonism would welcome all Indigenous peoples and their descendants into the effort. It would recognize that racial categories themselves are a product of colonial institutions and destructive to our communities. It would seek to undo the ecological devastation of capitalism and restore balance to ecosystems.

A decolonized Mormonism might take seriously the Book of Mormon's message that the canon is not closed and welcome such Indigenous narratives as the Popol Vuh and *Black Elk Speaks* into our body of scripture. A decolonized Mormonism might consult with the Seneca and Iroquois Confederacy and return the artifacts stolen from Iroquoia in previous centuries. Meetings might open and close with the inspiration of Indigenous elders who shape the agenda, curriculum, and objectives of those meetings. In a decolonized Mormonism, missionaries might partner with actual "elders" to lead service projects that meet community rather than church needs.

A decolonized Mormonism would gain prestige from the wealth and knowledge it gave away, not from the tithes it collected nor from the businesses accumulated. In a decolonized Mormonism, education would not be a tool for changing people's culture but would instead be a tool for reinforcing and strengthening diverse cultures. Diplomacy and relationship building would take priority over baptism.

The field of Mormon Studies can lead this effort, beginning with some changes of our own. We can read the growing literature of decolonization coming from our peers.[38] We can assign this literature and that of Indigenous Mormons in our college courses. We can deconstruct our own history and bring to the forefront counter-narratives of resistance to colonization, especially those coming from Indigenous voices. We can implement community-based research methods in which our Indigenous partners are involved in every step of the research process, from forming the questions to disseminating the results. We can ensure that we are following the institutional review policies of our Indigenous partners who may be the subjects of our research. We can partner with Indigenous communities to host academic conferences that address issues related to Mormonism, but of preeminent concern to Indigenous health and well-being. We can preference tribally owned facilities to host our conferences. We can invite elders, council members, and employees from our host nations to play leadership roles in the design and implementation of the program. We can serve traditional foods at our events. We can attend conferences hosted by Indigenous communities and seek guidance on the challenges we face in decolonizing Mormonism. Throughout these actions, we would need to be prepared to feel pain and heal together from the historical trauma that we have all collectively inherited, but often in differing measures.

Those of us working in Mormon Studies can employ Indigenous methodologies in our research and teaching. This would include situating ourselves culturally at the beginning of a narrative rather than burying our biographies in a preface, in an acknowledgement, or at the end of a book. We can use proper cultural protocols and ceremonies in our research, even when that might entail sharing tobacco, kava, peyote, or other items that may be taboo in Mormon circles. We might reconsider our fetish of writing and open our methods up to more diverse options that include storytelling and multimedia. We might use whatever privileges we may have at our institutions to expand tenure and other reward systems to value the unwritten products of Indigenous methodologies such as storytelling, the restoration of a salmon stream, the production of a cultural event, or the building of relationships. We can take our students out of the boxes we call classrooms and into talking circles and outdoor settings in our communities. Finally, we can give priority to mentoring and empowering young Indigenous scholars to carry on this work.

CONCLUSION

The elders on the Paddle to Bella Bella told us that decolonization, just like colonization, is a seven-generation project. One elder in particular spoke of a prophecy from her ancestors that the seventh generation would return to Indigenous ways. She acknowledged the paddlers in our canoes as the promised return of that seventh generation. As I sat in one of those canoes, I could not help but be inspired by seeing myself, even with my light skin, in that prophecy as well. While the revitalization of culture on Tribal Journey was profound, the elders also cautioned us that the changes we were initiating might take another seven generations to reach fruition. As we unsettle Lamanite identities and embark on a robust decolonization of Mormonism, we should take heed from the wisdom of the elders.

Three

PORTER ROCKWELL AND SAMUEL THE LAMANITE FISTFIGHT IN HEAVEN

A Mormon Navajo Filmmaker's Perspective

ANGELO BACA (NAVAJO/HOPI)

I was born on the Navajo Reservation and I have family all over the Four Corners area in the desert Southwest. Growing up in southeastern Utah, as well as in numerous places on and off the Navajo reservation, I had many contrasting experiences in my culture and in the LDS culture. My grandmother taught me many traditions, and she taught me the importance of language. She saw the influx of non-Native people into our lands her whole life and remembers a time when there were no roads and no white people in the territory. My mother was a member of the LDS Church and a graduate of BYU, and I have vague memories of being on the campus when she was in classes. We participated in both cultures and had valuable insight into both, but we knew where home was, who our Navajo people were, and how important the Navajo culture and way of life was to us.

My family was Mormon because the community was Mormon; we were also traditional Navajos. Religion, as much as anything else, is a culture, too. We went to church because that's where people went, it was where the opportunities were, and where the educational, business, and social worlds intersected. It was almost impossible to live in Utah and not have the LDS influence touch some aspect of your life. Mormon influence is so strong that I felt it to my very core ever since I was a young boy. As a Navajo Mormon, I struggled, but the single biggest sentiment I shared with George P. Lee was that the Church showed me "[n]ew experiences and a vast new world existed beyond anything I had dreamed. My Navajo roots were strong and would provide stability in the years to come."[1] At one time, he was the highest-ranking Native American general authority of the LDS Church, demonstrating that you could be Indian and Mormon. At the same time, my grandparents told me the harsh truth about Mormon settlers who took land, water, animals, and language away. My traditional Navajo grandmother, who is still here with us today, can give life to those stories with her own words from personal experience as a marginalized minority of Navajos who suffered at the hands of Mormon encroachment, colonization, and missionary efforts. Reading about such stories is different from listening to the testimony of those who were there and experienced real and tangible oppression, no doubt stemming from an Anglo-Mormon view of Navajos who were Lamanites and "filthy."

Perhaps for this reason, from a young age I always questioned the Mormon faith, knowing deep down the effects of its colonialism. I always had questions about the gospel as an Indian, but it was pointed out to me in Sunday school that it was disobedient to question God and His wisdom. Going back and forth to the city in Utah from our rural home made Mormon culture normalized and cultural expectations LDS-centric. I knew that my grandparents loved me and taught me traditional ways, but outside the home, the dominant settler-colonial structure reared its ugly head and taught me to hate my culture, language, ceremonies, and myself.

I didn't start really questioning the Church until I was a teenager, when I saw many asymmetrical power dynamics beginning to emerge. I saw connections between the fact that my Navajo relatives who had been incarcerated were put in jail by a largely white Mormon police force, the fact that willful ignorance of Native Americans and their ways dominated my Utah community, and the fact that an overwhelmingly non-Native majority ran the local businesses, schools, and land ownership systems. Needless to say, I wanted to believe that it could be better.

When I was about fourteen or fifteen years old, I went on a trip to the Seattle Temple. I was "blessed" enough to get to go to on the trip with the rest of my youth group from my ward. I was already skeptical because I knew that I wasn't ready or worthy, and I felt a sense of discord because I wanted confirmation from my bishop, but he didn't care or notice. We were there to do baptisms for the dead, which I see now with the benefit of hindsight, is a major affront on many levels—morally, ethically, and legally—to Indigenous peoples and, as famously amplified in the media, Jewish ancestors whose names were being co-opted in some of these ceremonies. Told to take with me twenty dollars for food, I did as I was told, like a good Mormon boy, but thought it was because we would eat together later. I discovered that after the ceremony in the temple, we all were to eat in the cafeteria in our little white jumpsuits in a prison-like, sterile setting of homogenized LDS members eating in silence, with not one person talking. How odd this was to me—strangely uncomfortable to the point that I could not articulate it until I was older. Now I see that it was the complete opposite of my experience as an Indigenous person. The Mormons made me pay money when our Navajo ceremonies would prepare, cook, and serve food for you because you are a guest, maybe even a patient, and part of the community, so they take care of you. In a Navajo ceremonial context, everyone was supposed to talk, joke, catch up, use our own kinship terms with each other, and re-establish our close community and cultural relationships with each other. You put care into the food you cook for people: it is a sacred act. Something as simple as eating and making food has always been sacred to Navajos and other Native peoples.

As I reflected over the years, I thought about many colonial aspects of my temple experience: the power to name and claim from a dominant societal position; the colonization of obtaining names of dead Indigenous ancestors; obvious displays of disproportionate wealth clearly demarking class, status, and social hierarchy; a singular and universalizing mechanism designed to make diversity non-existent by rejecting one's own culture and accepting the LDS rituals of wearing all white and questioning nothing; and finally, no acknowledgement of the people who cooked the food or the plants and animals that generously gave of themselves to nourish us and give us life. Here I was, wondering why everyone was so alone and separated while we ate our generic and impersonally served meals of overpriced chicken fried steak in a hospital setting in a multimillion-dollar facility—multimillions that could have easily gone to help my Navajo people get clean water, warm homes, electricity, and access to their traditional lands by helping them manage their lands instead of taking them over. It appeared to me that in their effort to progress spiritually, LDS people had forgotten many of the simplest and basic elements in the process.

I clearly recall another the time when I was in the young adult Sunday school class in my ward and learned about the Book of Mormon figure

Kohihor who questioned the validity of God and the truthfulness of the gospel in Alma 30, demonstrating the wrath of God if one disobeyed. Even now as I read it again, I still can't believe how harshly God strikes Kohihor "deaf and dumb." He was trying to question logically and reasonably, and to systemically think of how God could exist. No different than scholars or academics, philosophers or artists—they are trying to think and feel their way to something divine, truthful, and real. Yet this man was punished for questioning and asking something that all of us do, privately or publicly. To top it off, Kohihor ends up trodden upon and dies. I was the only young brown kid in a class filled with well-to-do Mormon teenagers who never thought about gentrification, assimilation, colonization, or cultural difference. They only thought about obeying the teacher, while I was the one questioning everything. The story was horrifying to me because in my own Navajo culture, all of Creation helped each other, in harmony, in "hozho" (the Navajo worldview philosophy of all things beautiful and good in balance with each other). What kind of deity that cares about its creation treats them like that and calls it just?

When I became an adult, I decidedly went back to my traditional Navajo spiritual and ceremonial ways. Yes, I could live in two worlds and manage it the best I could honoring both ways of belief. Yes, I do respect each as its own way and can see how the two of them can be compatible together. But I can't let go the fact that so many Indigenous people don't know who they are, where they come from, which family or clan they belong to, how to speak their ancestral language. Nor can I let go of how they are taught to abandon what they might still know even after the pressures of Christianity, capitalism, boarding schools, assimilation, disease, warfare, and racism have ravaged our Indigenous peoples while Mormons have ignored their checkered history with Indians. If Mormons believe that Indigenous people are the "chosen people," then why are we continually subjugated and diminished as the literal "other," and made to be background characters in a colonial story?

I made the film "In Laman's Terms: Looking at Lamanite Identity"[2] in order to change this dynamic. The film was a way to enter the world of the LDS Church through a very simple question: "What is a Lamanite?" I think definitions are a part of the colonial structure but also help people to understand what something is. The irony is that there is no term for Lamanite in any Indigenous language, as we have always had names for ourselves in our own languages.

The Native Voices Program at the University of Washington backed my project and took a huge risk in doing so. We realized that there are many spheres of influence in LDS circles and they include many powerful scholarly and academically administrative people who could make this project difficult. However, it was to the great credit of my committee members and co-directors Dan Hart and Luana Ross that they pushed for me to complete my project in its entirety. In fact, Terry Macy and Dan Hart had created a documentary short called "White Shamans and Plastic Medicine Men" in 1996, produced by Native Voices, about the cultural appropriation of New Age groups and hippies claiming to be Native American "healers"; it was well-received at the Sundance Film Festival. This project was monumental for me because I could literally see a film that said what many Native people have always wanted to say to these New Age people but didn't know how to say it—just like Oneida comedian Charlie Hill in the film remarks, "You say you were an Indian in a past life, well . . . you're White now!"[3] The bravery of this Native filmmaker, among many inspiring and influential others who broke a path for upcoming directors like myself, left its mark on my mind that something similar in film could be done with Mormons and Indians as well.

Film for me is closely aligned with storytelling, an Indigenous tradition. American culture doesn't understand the high value Indigenous people place on our oral traditions, storytellers, and songkeepers. I would come to understand that my own grandfather, though I was never there to witness it, was a highly regarded storyteller in the Navajo community before my time. I see film as a new shape for an oral tradition that will continue long after the cameras, monitors, projectors, and smartphones turn off. An even newer twist may be that Indigenous peoples will be behind the camera telling their own stories the way they think they should be told, giving rise to agency, creativity, independence, and sovereignty on a whole new level. It is possible to bring the obscure to the big screen, literally into the light. This is the primary mode of decolonizing our own stories, the opposite of the colonizing nature of Mormon cooptation and appropriation of our histories in the Book of Mormon.

Documentary film gives an opportunity to privilege the Native American voice whereas previously we had little to no voice in the knowledge, production, accumulation, study, preservation, and management of information concerning Indigenous peoples. In essence, we can provide audiences with Indigenous views that are important to us but that also simultaneously erase the lies of years of inaccurate, racist, and misinformed books and research about Native peoples.

For me, filmmaking is an act of sovereignty. Sovereignty is about being able to determine for and by yourself what you want to do and how you want to do it. Making a film is no different. You choose what you want to make a film about and then go about planning how to bring it all together and successfully complete the project with a team of people. Being able to communicate the issues and the matters that are most important to Indigenous groups using mass media is a turning point in our history. Authoring, or directing (as it were) a cinematic work is a huge task and organizing such an effort requires more than one person and one kind of ability. It is a relatively difficult and rather new process to get our Indigenous peoples trained in film production and technique. With its own access to computers, internet, and smartphones, the middle class of America often takes for granted the resources, access, and technology that are not as available to Indigenous peoples.

Running a nation and running a film production can be seem like two very different things, but I say that when a film production is successful, you have something to show for it, just as keeping a nation together is a daily exercise in management, optimism, and faith. Yet at the end of the day, a film is a story that you can see, and stories are powerful actors in the world. Therefore, every act of filmmaking by an Indigenous person is an act of sovereignty.

My film begins with an introduction of myself, my background and my investment in the church's history, and my motive for making the film, focused primarily on the question, "What is a Lamanite?" Second, the film addresses the graphic nature of the Book of Mormon's stories and how these stories influence ideas about what a Lamanite might be. Third, it offers a brief overview of the Book of Mormon's origin story about how Lamanites came into existence, along with the settler-colonial narrative of Middle Easterners colonizing the North American continent, culminating in a racist battle for ultimate supremacy in favor of the light-skinned peoples, represented by Nephites in the Book of Mormon. The great moment here is when this storyline is confirmed by the University of Washington's LDS Institute of Religion by their public recruitment leader, using missionary talking points.

Fourth, I travel to Palmyra, New York, to the original Book of Mormon printing press and meet a Nahua woman LDS tour guide from Mexico who directly rejects her Indigenous traditions calling them "bad"; visit the Hill Cumorah Pageant and talk to the actor portraying "Laman," and ask his opinion about playing this role while being threatened with removal from the grounds; and then visit Ganondagan, a Seneca tribal village site maintained by Seneca scholar and artist Peter Jemison, who comments on the Indigenous perspective of the Indian people of the area versus the official LDS standpoints.

Fifth, I conduct interviews with Dr. Tom Murphy and Dr. Simon Southerton, who both wrote scathing indictments of the LDS claim of historicity, demonstrating that scientific studies of DNA and genetic testing clearly disproved the Lamanite idea in the Book of Mormon. Sixth, I interview Forrest Cuch, the former Executive Director of Indian Affairs for the state of Utah, talking about obvious cultural and societal biases towards Indian students and their cultural worldview in a state full of Mormons. Seventh, my own mother, Ida Yellowman, volunteers to talk about her experiences of being converted and going to BYU as someone who identified as "Lamanite" and how complex the identity dynamics were in her day and still are for believers who are Native.

I then travel to Hawaii, where I interview Dr. Haunani-Kay Trask, a native Hawaiian academic who criticizes the results of the Christian missionary efforts on her Indigenous islands and the lasting impact of colonization's negative backlash upon her people, including the LDS influence and the Polynesian Cultural Center's Mormon hold on her proud culture.

In the final installment, I conclude with calling for the redefinition and a re-appropriation of the word "Lamanite" on Indigenous terms.

Although I tried mightily to get other LDS members to become involved and even went personally to invite and ask members to come to the premiere on the University of Washington's campus, no one wanted to initiate a conversation about what my film was about nor why it would be important. The only response was a tripled number of missionaries on the University of Washington campus. I couldn't demand any genuine interaction, even though that was one outcome I had hoped for, but I felt it was vitally important to start a dialogue. However, members were reluctant to participate even in this: none of those whom I invited came to the opening screening. In my mind, I thought to myself, "American Indians are cited on the first page of the introduction to the Book of Mormon and no one thinks this is important enough to talk about?" I was incredulous about the film not being taken seriously, as the Book of Mormon is a cornerstone of the faith in so many ways, and for so long the Book of Mormon has been presented as a history of Indigenous peoples. That this is literally taken for granted by members and leadership contributes to the invisibility, voicelessness, and neglect of American Indian thought, perspective, culture, and history. It is a clear demonstration of the continued subtle violence of colonization and one that needs to be addressed today in a real and cooperative way by including Indigenous voices in a dialogue that is sorely lacking.

To move a dialogue forward about Mormonism and colonization, certainly we need address the repatriation claims about the artifacts of the Book of Mormon. If the church does have them in their vaulted archives, and they are indeed of American Indian origin, they need to be properly examined by outside anthropologists and archaeologists as well as through consultation with Native American tribes as per regulations of NAGPRA (Native American Graves Protection and Repatriation Act of 1990).

We also need to think critically about by what measuring stick Indigenous peoples must be evaluated, and what representative figures we should model ourselves after. Is it the same as the continuum from "savage" to "civilized" that sprang forth from the early days of anthropology? I think about two dichotomous Mormon figures—Samuel the Lamanite and Porter Rockwell, the former the quintessential "good" Lamanite who can work towards salvation and whiteness by serving his white master, and the latter a classically westernized legendary figure who used violence to benefit his Mormon people in the untamed American West. Just like the Lone Ranger and Tonto (and just as ridiculous) we have two very different figures who are thrown into the same time and place but interpreted through the lens of the colonizer, the one with the power and resources to overwhelm the minority voices of the Indigenous.

Porter Rockwell, a murderous thug for the early Mormons, was a right-hand man of both Joseph Smith and Brigham Young. He was the muscle behind Young's threats, the enforcer, a soldier of the new Zion mafia of the West in Utah. He did the dirty work of early Mormon settlers, fighting Indians and the enemies of his Mormon brethren. He was tough customer and a warrior in his own right, not hesitating to defend his religion and his LDS group with any violence he thought was justified. Let's not forget that he was also a real figure in history, as opposed to Samuel the Lamanite, who was more of a metaphorical figure designed to elicit defense of the gospel by the act of preaching "unto all the corners of the Earth." Rockwell actually killed people and was good at doing it, a fact that the LDS Church has ignored and continues to actively ignore. Legends estimate the number of people he killed in his lifetime from 150 to 400—making him sound more like a plague than a human being. Many empires were built on the blood shed by their soldiers' acts, and the Mormon Zion was no different. Rockwell thought and believed he had the God-given right to commit such crimes.

Indeed, Rockwell had faith he was another permutation of Samson from the Bible, never cutting his hair nor his beard since Joseph Smith had legendarily told him, "Cut not thy hair and no bullet or blade can harm thee!" This is rather ironic counsel considering what Mormon leaders required of Native American men who served the LDS Church as priesthood holders and missionaries, and who of late have tried to attend Brigham Young University. Hair is sacred in many of our Native cultures and cutting it can be a form and expression of mourning. When it was cut in boarding school times in an attempt to assimilate Native American children into American society, many youth would wonder in silence who had died in their family because they didn't know enough English to ask and they weren't allowed to speak their Native tongue.

BYU has recently decided not to continue to allow American Indians to have long hair. This suggests that colonial relationships are still very much alive. When you hear and learn of these stories from various Native communities from across the country, it's easier to understand why Indigenous peoples associate both school and church as negative, oppressive, and controlling assimilative institutions.

Samuel the Lamanite, now as in the Book of Mormon past, represents a kind of voicelessness and the silent violence enacted upon Indigenous peoples. He preached to people and no one would listen to him standing on that wall. Even while arrows were shot at him, he continued to warn them about their wickedness. He reminds me of William Apess of the Pequots of New England, an educated Indian, preacher, and writer, much the Martin Luther King Jr. of his day, and a contemporary of Joseph Smith. Apess tried to bring awareness to non-Indigenous peoples of colonial abuses of Indigenous peoples. He was an Indigenous intellectual and Christian who tried desperately to use religious rhetoric and impeccable logic to reach the European masses who lived in east coast Indigenous lands. Just like Samuel, he pleaded with non-Indigenous peoples and tried to shine light on the ignorance and destructiveness of their settler-colonial ways to no avail.

In the Book of Mormon, Joseph Smith disarms Samuel: he speaks but does not fight. The "good" Lamanite, in Mormon eyes, is the one who is a pacifist. I like to think of Samuel as the warrior going to his death. He was trying to tell those people at the bottom of the wall that what they were doing was wrong, and he was trying to help them. Whether it was a moral or ethical wrong he was talking about in the Book of Mormon, or if it is about today's self-proclaimed "Lamanites" bringing attention to the historical trauma, lies, and inequality of the religion upon their people and lands, the charge remains the same: decolonization is the first step to addressing the historical wrongs of Mormonism. Taiaiake Alfred, an Indigenous scholar, stresses "Without a substantial change in the circumstances of colonization, there is no basis for considering the injustice historical. The crime of colonialism is present today, as are its perpetrators."[4]

The ultimate sin of the people at the bottom of the wall was not listening to Samuel, even as he was moved to help his white-skinned brothers. Even as they shot their slings and arrows at him, he continued on, knowing the danger. He knew his ancestors were with him and he would be protected. I think of him today whenever Indigenous people do decolonizing work. I think: spit your fire, sing that truth, Brother Samuel. As far as I can tell, the light-skinned populace of Mormons and Gentiles still isn't listening to you. They can shoot their slings and arrows at you or at me, but now we have our cameras to shoot back.

Four

"THIS IS THE PLACE!"

Disrupting Mormon Settler Colonialism

ELISE BOXER

Mormon settlement of the Great Salt Lake Valley has often been depicted as a story of pioneers seeking refuge from religious persecution. Their migration west illustrated their willingness to sacrifice all that they had, including their lives, to freely practice their religion, Mormonism. The Mormon historical and religious narrative ignores the presence and ultimately, the removal of Indigenous peoples from their homelands. I seek to complicate this narrative by utilizing settler colonialism as a framework of analysis to better understand the process of Indigenous removal, and how this colonial society destroyed Indigenous ways of living and being and replaced it with Mormon worldviews. I will specifically focus on this historical and religious narrative of Mormon settlers as "pioneers" and "This is Place" Heritage Park, located in Salt Lake City, Utah, that reifies this narrative of Mormon exceptionalism.

(In my work here as in other works, I disrupt the use of the term "pioneers": putting it into quotes undermines attempts to normalize Mormon settler colonialism. I similarly denormalize the Mormon term "Lamanite" by putting it into quotes.)

Adria L. Imada explores the production of colonial settler nostalgia as a "dominant mode of organizing temporality and space" in Hawaii, an ongoing colonial site. I argue that the state of Utah is an ongoing colonial site in which the institution, the Church of Jesus Christ of Latter-day Saints, and its members continue to dominate, shape, and demarcate the landscape as "Mormon," one that can only exist because Indigenous peoples and communities are erased from the historical and contemporary narrative of Mormon settlement in Utah. Imada argues that the production of colonial nostalgia is just one aspect of settler colonialism: "the displacement of Indigenous peoples through the expropriation of land and institutions by foreign settlers [that] relies on and produces an investment in uncomplicated, ahistorical fantasies."[1]

Imada's work is useful in understanding how the Mormon historical and religious narrative is a production "in uncomplicated, ahistorical fantasies." Mormon settlers are depicted as "pioneers," and this term implies that the first wave of Mormon settlers were in fact the first into this region. This is simply not true. Jared Farmer's *On Zion's Mount: Mormons, Indians, and the American Landscape*, explores how Mormons created their own homeland at the expense of Indigenous peoples by using Indian place names to mythologize and nostalgically infuse Indigeneity into the land and the historical narrative.[2] Indigenous peoples exist only when it can give meaning to Mormon identity.

While Imada's work is useful in understanding how the production of colonial nostalgia is tied to the creation of a religious historical narrative that naturalizes the presence of Mormon settlers, it does not adequately explain the process of Indigenous removal, or what Patrick Wolfe has termed the "logic of elimination." Wolfe's work on settler colonialism helps us understand the presence of Mormon settlers in present-day Utah as a process, rather than as an event. The process of settler colonialism "may or may not be ethical, but it is always exculpatory."[3] He further states, "[a]s the settler takes over the territory, so does the territory take over the settler . . . [i]ts seizure is not merely a change of ownership, but a genesis, the onset of a whole new way of being—for both parties."[4]

Put another way, "settler colonizers come to stay: invasion is a structure, not an event."[5] In other words, one can use Wolfe's definition of settler colonialism to better understand the invasion of Mormon settlers into the Great Salt Lake Valley, not merely as a historical event, but as the "erection of a new colonial society on the expropriated land base."[6] This new colonial society existed on stolen land, but it has never been fully acknowledged by the LDS Church, nor by members who now live on this land. Instead, religious rhetoric is employed to justify the arrival of Mormon settlers to extinguish Indigenous title to land and access to valuable resources.

Terminology also plays a significant role in how Indigenous peoples are removed from the religious historical narrative. It must also be highlighted and deconstructed to better understand how Indigenous peoples became the "absent presence." Myla Vicenti Carpio defines the "absent presence . . . or deliberate exclusion, of the 'other's' history works to construct and reify the master narrative, as does the utilization of a historical 'presence,' or inclusion, that only benefits the dominant narrative."[7] Indigenous history is

> the "absent presence" in American history, deliberately erased or radically transformed to maintain the master narrative . . . a retelling or distortion of Indigenous history is designed to justify the colonizers; violence and exploitation of Indigenous peoples, lands, and resources.[8]

This description is not just applicable to American history, but to Mormon history and by extension, to Utah history as well. The retelling of Mormon history is not just about the erasure of Indigenous peoples, but also about the justification of Mormon settlement. Mormons justified their presence through the production of colonial nostalgia disguised as Mormon history.

Rather than use the term "pioneer," I employ the term "settler" to acknowledge the process of Indigenous dispossession. Mormon settler colonialism was not just only about the land they claimed as their own, but about how Mormon settlers claimed the historical narrative as their own, too. The religious historical narrative regarding their arrival and subsequent colonization of the Great Salt Lake Valley can exist only through the exclusion of Indigenous peoples or by placing Indigenous peoples at the periphery of the narrative as advocates of Mormon settler colonialism. Finally, I seek to disrupt the Mormon religious historical narrative not just by dismantling the narrative, but by centering my experiences as a Mormon Dakota member. In doing so, my presence and voice challenge the assumption and portrayal of Indigenous peoples as willing participants in Mormon colonization.

One of the primary reasons that Mormons became the target of increasing harassment was largely due to their religious beliefs. A fundamental belief of Mormonism was the Book of Mormon. Mormons believe this to be a significant religious text, like the Bible. The Book of Mormon documents Jesus Christ's visit to the Americas and his subsequent teachings to the "ancient inhabitants." Many non-Mormons believed the Book of Mormon to be a work of fiction or "blasphemous nonsense, silly story, pretend prophecies [and] history."[9] Mormons were viewed as "fanatics, or knaves, (for one or the other they undoubtedly are) who pretended as they did . . . to hold personal communication and converse face to face with the Most High God."[10] The Mormon "golden bible" alarmed non-believers, who ridiculed the Mormons for their beliefs.[11]

In addition to believing that the Book of Mormon contained additional teachings by Jesus Christ, other specific religious doctrines alarmed non-Mormons.[12] Various references in the Book of Mormon and the Doctrine and Covenants assert that Jackson County, Missouri, would become the "New Jerusalem," a second gathering site for Mormons in the search for the "land of promise" where they would create a Mormon "Zion."[13] Jackson County became a place where the sacred and profane met to create a refuge for Mormon Euro-Americans; however, non-Mormons began to fear that their own properties would be violently expropriated by Mormons for the establishment of a Mormon empire.

The increasing Mormon settler presence in Kirtland, Ohio, and Jackson County, Missouri, further agitated non-Mormons. Mormon settlers purchased lands, building homes and businesses to serve the needs of the community. Many non-Mormons viewed Mormons uneasily because they tended to create Mormon enclaves in which they patronized Mormon-owned business. They also tended to trade and buy exclusively from one another, angering non-Mormons who lived in Kirtland and Jackson County, because it threatened their economic and political livelihood.

Ever-increasing Mormon migration also constituted a potential political threat, the tenuous balance that existed between these two communities constantly was threatened by increasing Mormon migration. Mormons had formed their own voting bloc, much like other religious groups. Ultimately, ongoing conflict between Mormons and non-Mormons reached its apex on October 27, 1838, in Independence, Missouri, when local non-Mormon citizens gathered at the courthouse. Governor Boggs placated non-Mormon citizens' demands for removing the Mormons by calling for the Mormons' extermination: "The Mormons must be treated as enemies and must be exterminated or driven from the state, if necessary for the public good. Their outrages are beyond all description."[14] Church leaders, including the "prophet" Joseph Smith, were jailed, but later escaped to Nauvoo, Illinois. Eventually, Joseph and Hyrum Smith would be arrested again under initial "charges of riot" and additional charges of treason.[15] Ultimately, Joseph and Hyrum Smith were killed by a mob on June 27, 1844 at the jail in Carthage, Illinois, and Brigham Young effectively gained leadership of the LDS church by August 8, 1844.

Growing up Dakota, I knew that Mormons were not the only people or community to experience persecution due to their belief system. As Indigenous peoples, our ways of living and being have been under constant attack since contact. Indigenous peoples have also been under attack by the federal government and its policies designed to assimilate and exterminate Indigenous peoples and communities. Despite the Mormon historical narrative that argues that they have been the only people who have had extermination orders issued against them, this is simply not true.[16] Mormons were not the only group of individuals to be expelled from a state. My own people, the Dakota, were expelled from the state of Minnesota by Governor Alexander Ramsey on September 9, 1862, when he declared, "The Sioux Indians of Minnesota must be exterminated or driven forever beyond the borders of the state."[17] Our people had fought bravely during the US-Dakota War of 1862 to protect our right to live as Dakota people. Settlers had continued to encroach upon our lands in violation of the 1851 Treaty of Traverse de Sioux. Bounties of two hundred dollars were placed upon the heads of my people. On December 26, 1862, President Abraham Lincoln ordered that thirty-eight Dakota men be hanged in what remains the largest mass execution in United States history.[18] But there is little acknowledgement by Mormon historians of state-sponsored Indigenous genocide; instead, the call for Dakota extermination is ignored, thereby resulting in their "absent presence" in the historical narrative.

Mormon historians and members have been so focused on their own religious persecution and expulsion from Missouri that they cannot see how other peoples, including Indigenous peoples, have also been marginalized and pushed to the periphery of society. This comparison is not about determining who has suffered more greatly, but rather it is symptomatic of how Indigenous peoples are continually relegated to the margins of history. It further illustrates how Mormons become so focused on their own history that they effectively silence Indigenous history, despite the fact that our histories are inextricably linked to one another.

Increasing religious persecution served as a catalyst for the Mormon migration west. The West became a symbol of refuge. A Mormon expedition was sent out to explore potential options for future Mormon settlement. Eventually, they determined that settlement of the Great Basin region would be an ideal location. It was isolated, surrounded by mountains that offered protection, and had sizeable tracts of fertile land for farming. Mormons saw a potential site to build to a Mormon empire, a space they could claim and transform as their own. Planning for the move west had begun before the death of Joseph Smith Jr. Once Brigham Young became leader of the LDS Church after Smith's death, he continued to organize members to begin to move west.

The first wave of Mormon settlers left Nauvoo, Illinois, in April 1846 due to increasing pressures by non-Mormons. Mormon settlers were not prepared for their migration west but quickly set up a camp at Winter Quarters, Nebraska, where they organized and outfitted themselves in preparation for their long trek west. The Mormon historical narrative highlights this period as one of great sacrifice by its membership. Mormon settlers became "pioneers" as they moved west. According to the Mormon historical record, these "pioneers" were guided by their faith in the hope they could practice Mormonism freely in the West, just outside of the political boundaries of the United States. The initial migration west paved the way for the influx of other Mormon settlers who continued to claim land and resources as their own.

The first Mormon settler company, composed of 142 men, three women, and two children, entered the Salt Lake Valley on July 24, 1847. Brigham Young did not know the exact location of their final destination but stated, "I will show you when we come to it. . . . I have seen it in a vision, and when my natural eyes behold it, I shall know it."[19] Wilford Woodruff, then an LDS apostle, recalled, "I drove my carriage with President Young lying on a bed in it, into the open valley, the rest of the company following. . . . President Young arose from the bed and took a survey on the country; . . . [On] this occasion he saw the future glory of Zion and Israel as it would be planted in the valleys of the mountains."[20] Upon seeing the Salt Lake Valley, Young declared, "It is enough. This is the right place."[21] Mormon settlers immediately began to plant crops and prepare for the influx of other Mormon settlers. Their first migration, a historical and pivotal moment in the Mormon experience, became the foundation for their "ahistorical fantasies." They envisioned and reimagined their history that did little to acknowledge their role in the dispossession and removal of Indigenous peoples in the American West.

"THIS IS THE PLACE" MONUMENT AND HERITAGE PARK

A critical component of Mormon settler colonialism was not the elimination of Indigenous peoples, but "access to territory."[22] Integral to gaining access to land was the process of renaming or demarcating space and place as Mormon. This section will focus primarily on the "This is the Place" Heritage Park located in Salt Lake City, Utah, because it demonstrates how a space is claimed and demarcated as Mormon. "This is the Place" Heritage Park also illustrates how the history of a space can also be written through the erection of monuments that venerate Mormon "pioneers" while simultaneously erasing Indigenous peoples as integral to the Mormon religious historical narrative. The very presence of "This is the Place" Heritage Park reinforces this space as Mormon. Indigenous peoples are scarcely included in and around "This is the Place" Heritage Park, because according to the Mormon settlers, Indigenous peoples were not present or integral to Mormon settlement of the valley.

The sixty-foot-tall "This is the Place," monument with a twelve-foot, four-inch statue of Brigham Young, Wilford Woodruff, and Heber C. Kimball was unveiled during the centennial celebration on July 24, 1947 to mark and "record the unequaled achievements of these men and women" who were the first Mormon settlers to arrive on Ute and Goshute lands.[23] Located in a park at the mouth of Emigration Canyon, where the first Mormon company led by Brigham Young entered the valley and where he declared, "this is the place," this imposing monument cannot be missed. The statue of Brigham Young takes on mythical proportions at "This is the Place." Young's monument dominates the entrance to the park and the landscape. As one drives up to the park, this monument looms on the horizon, growing larger as one nears the park. The monument faces "slightly north of west and . . . toward Temple Square" four miles in the distance and offers a panoramic view of the valley.[24]

The reliefs and plaques located at the base of the monument also retells a story of mythical proportions or "ahistorical fantasies." At the base of the "This is the Place" monument, the principal plaque reads:

"This is the Place" monument, dedicated July 24, 1947, commemorates the arrival of the Mormon Pioneers into the valley of the Great Salt Lake, one hundred years, and also the role of others— Spanish Catholic Fathers, trappers and fur traders, official government explorers and California immigrants, who contributed to the successful founding of an empire in "The Top of the Mountains." Driven from their homes in Missouri and Illinois because of political and religious prejudice, the Mormons began their historical fifteen-hundred-mile trek from Nauvoo to the Rocky Mountains. . . .

This plaque highlights not only the presence of Mormon settlers but the process of Mormon settler colonialism that "destroys to replace" and contributes to the absent presence of Indigenous peoples in the historical narrative. The first step requires the displacement and removal of Indigenous peoples from their homelands. Mormons and the Mormon religious-historical narrative rarely acknowledge the presence of Indigenous peoples. Instead, the religious-historical narrative portrays this land as open, set aside by God exclusively for Mormon settlers. Similar to American manifest destiny, Mormons became even more exceptional, their claims to land superseded other claims, including the claims of Indigenous peoples, because land and natural resources were claimed in the name of Mormon religious refuge. The plaque implies that Mormons, along with "Spanish Catholic Fathers, Trappers, official government explorers and California immigrants" built an empire on lands that Indigenous people did not use or inhabit. Indigenous peoples simply cannot be mentioned because the mere acknowledgement of Indigenous peoples forces Mormon settlers to also acknowledge their role in the theft of Indigenous lands and resources. This illegal land theft not only contributes to Indigenous displacement but to the genocide, in all aspects, of Indigenous peoples. Second, Mormon settler colonialism was about the expropriation of this land. The primary goal of Mormon settler colonialism was access to territory. Mormon settlers immediately began to make Indigenous lands their own. Indigenous title to land was terminated and instead, Mormon settlers claimed land in the name of religion. Mormon settlers hold title to this private land and continue to assert their dominance over all non-Mormons, especially Indigenous peoples. The majority of downtown Salt Lake City was demarcated as Mormon space and built upon private land, allowing for complete control of the physical space and narrative that naturalizes Mormon settler colonialism.

One hundred years after their arrival, Mormon settlers continued to demarcate Utah as a Mormon space. The examination of "This is the Place" Heritage Park highlights how the space continues to remain Mormon. The physical space is dominated by Mormon structures that create a historical narrative that "produces an investment in uncomplicated, ahistorical fantasies." The plaque focuses on Mormon religious persecution and on the fifteen hundred mile trek to create what Benedict Anderson defines as an "imagined community" of what I term a "pioneer" identity. Ultimately, this Mormon "pioneer" identity belies the Mormons' role as settlers and the process of Mormon settler colonialism.

"This is the Place" monument becomes a settler colonial site in which Indian peoples become the "absent presence" evident in the monument inscription. Indigenous peoples' presence in the Salt Lake Valley was not acknowledged nor included in the main plaque but was rather included in the much smaller plaque on the east side, which is representative of their inclusion in the Mormon religious, historical narrative. Mormon perspectives regarding Indigenous peoples are one-sided at best. On the east side of the monument, Indigenous peoples are finally acknowledged and included this imposing monument. A bronze relief of Chief Washakie, Shoshone chief, was included as a representative of all Indigenous peoples and nations in the Great Basin region. Mormon settlers considered Chief Washakie to be a "[g]reat Warrior, wise leader of this people, known all over western country as one of the most intelligent and able Indian chiefs . . . [a c]lose friend of Brigham Young and the Mormon people." Chief Washakie becomes the only chief and the only Indigenous person included in the narrative and on the plaque.

The image of Chief Washakie becomes appropriated and part of the Mormon settler narrative because he was "friendly" to Mormon settlers, meaning that he welcomed Mormon settlers. His friendliness to Mormon settlers implied that he and his people accepted and sanctioned their presence and settlement of the region. Chief Washakie's religious conversion to the Mormon faith is also another important feature of Mormon settler colonialism.[25] Chief Washakie has been used to sanction and support the claim that land was open, ready for Mormon settlement. Mormon settlers were welcomed by Chief Washakie and his people. Mormon settlers become exculpatory in this narrative perpetuated at "This is the Place" Heritage Park.

As the park's website highlights, "[w]ith several notable exceptions, relations between the Native Americans and the settlers were relatively cordial during the settlement era." These "notable exceptions" range from the Bear River massacre to the Blackhawk war.[26] None of these "notable exceptions" are mentioned at the park, including the Bear River massacre, especially the fact that unarmed Shoshone men, women, children, and elders were killed after settlers slowly claimed more land and resources. The Bear River massacre site is located near present-day Preston, Idaho, just over 114 miles north from "This is the Place" Heritage Park. Mormon settlers constantly encroached upon Indigenous lands, claiming resources as their own, causing conflict between the two groups. As a result, Indigenous ways of living were dramatically impacted and ultimately, many fought back against the increasing presence of Mormon settlers. The cause of these "notable exceptions" has never been included on the monuments or plaques in the "This is the Place" Heritage Park despite being integral to the region's history.

The presence of Indigenous peoples at "This is the Place" park can also be found at the "Native American village nestled against the mountains." The Native American village located within the 450-acre park, along the eastern bench of the Wasatch mountains. The park was designed to be an educational experience where visitors can "step back in time" into a historic village filled with actors who provide an "authentic" experience of Mormon settler life on the frontier. There are over fifty buildings in the park, complete with livestock, a blacksmith, a tinsmith, craftsman, and a saddle maker who use their skills to demonstrate "how the West was built." These buildings were original, but relocated to the park so that visitors could not only reimagine the past, but play Mormon "pioneer."

As visitors wander the park, they can also visit a "Native American village," located far away from the recreated nineteenth century Mormon settlement. On the website, the Native American village describes Indigenous peoples and lands as a "world long since gone." This statement reinforces the notion that Indigenous peoples are a people of the past. They become the "absent presence" at the park because they are pushed to the edge of the park. Visitors must actively seek out the Native American village to learn more about the Indigenous peoples and nations whose homelands were claimed by Mormon settlers.

Further, the rich histories of five Indigenous nations—Shoshone, Paiute, Ute, Goshute, and Navajo—are erased from the historical narrative and park. Only two tribal nations, Shoshone and Navajo, along with their typical primary dwellings (tipi and hogan, respectively), are included. The park has attempted to use authentic materials in the construction of the tipi and includes both female and male Navajo hogans. However, while both tribes lived within the boundaries of present-day Utah, they primarily lived in northern and southern regions. The park also selected dwellings that are decidedly "Native American." The tipi is arguably one of the most recognizable American Indian dwellings and further romanticizes Indigenous peoples. It also reinforces the notion that Indigenous peoples were nomadic, that they did not have ties to homelands.

"This is the Place" Heritage Park is an educational site that fails to meaningfully include Indigenous peoples, and fails

to shift the paradigm from Indigenous peoples as exhibition subjects, to educate the different publics visiting the museum about the Indigenous people of the Americas, and, more importantly, to make Indigenous history "present."[27]

Indigenous peoples' cultures were appropriated to further the purposes of this park: they were put on display to attract tourist curiosity and further Mormon settler-colonial nostalgia. Similar to settler-colonialism in Hawai'i, Mormons continue to reimagine and reconstruct their past through the "This is the Place" Heritage Park. Visitors can step back into the historical past and "play Indian." The inclusion of Indigenous peoples at the park was done on Mormon terms. Visitors can enter into the dwellings, grind corn, make arrowhead necklaces, and sand drawings. Park visitors get to "play Indian" and consume Indianness without any meaningful conversation about the genocide and/or dispossession of Indigenous peoples of their lands and resources.

Finally, if there are no Indigenous people present today, then Mormon settler colonialism remains unchallenged. However, the presence of

Indigenous peoples within the boundaries of what is now the state of Utah also contradicts the eliminatory nature of settler colonialism. Despite Mormon settler and federal government attempts to remove Indigenous peoples from their homelands, seven tribal nations reside within the boundaries of Utah state. These present-day reservations are a far cry from vast traditional homelands they once inhabited and from their traditional ways of living, but the Indigenous peoples living within the boundaries of the Utah have fought to retain their identities and maintain their intimate connection to the land.

CHALLENGING MORMON SETTLER COLONIALISM: A PERSONAL REFLECTION

I was born and raised in The Church of Jesus Christ of Latter-day Saints. My parents were both converts at a time when Indigenous peoples were revered as "Lamanites." When they met one another at Brigham Young University, it was at the height of the "Day of the Lamanite." My father is Dakota, Sisseton-Wahpeton bands, and my mother is Chicana. My mother was conscious of her Indigenous roots: her family was from Mexico and my great-grandmother spoke Nahuatl, an Indigenous language. My four siblings and I were raised as Dakota, but we also knew that our indigenous roots ran deep on both sides of our family. We were raised on the reservation, and our identity is rooted in our Dakota identity. I grew up primarily on two reservations: the Fort Peck Assiniboine and Sioux reservation in Poplar, Montana, and the Yakama Nation reservation in Toppenish, Washington. My heart will always be connected to my family and community on the Fort Peck reservation.

The LDS branch in Poplar, Montana, grounded my experiences as a member of the LDS Church. Our branch was very small, but we knew one another. Our membership fluctuated, but I felt a sense of home and belonging. It was a safe place where we could be Dakota. While there were wasicu members, Dakota/Assiniboine members made up the majority of the branch membership. It was our reservation, our homeland, our church. When we gathered as LDS members, we greeted one another warmly: we were not just members who held the same religious beliefs, we were relatives.

Our family was one of very few Dakota/Assiniboine families who were steadfast in participation, largely due to my parents' commitment to raise their family in the Mormon faith. Our branch also had potlucks and it reminded me of our community feasts. Everyone was welcomed, and we shared our food with one another. Food brought us together as relatives. Looking back on these formative years, I recall feeling this was a safe space for me to be Dakota and Mormon. Our small Poplar Branch has always felt safe and welcoming. I never had to choose between being Mormon and Dakota. I belonged.

However, my experiences living in another tribal community were very different from one another. As in many reservation communities, tribal politics played a role when my father decided to leave our community. He had earned a master of social work degree from Eastern Washington University. We had returned home immediately after he had graduated. He had worked as a social worker, but other tribal social workers resented my father. They were angry that he had been promoted, and eventually my father could no longer tolerate his work environment. After living in Poplar, we left and he relocated us to the Yakama Nation reservation in Toppenish, Washington. This move was not welcome. My siblings and I did not want to leave our home. My father and mother had waited a year to relocate us.

Toppenish, Washington, is a very unique place. While it is located on the Yakama Nation reservation, it does not fall under tribal jurisdiction. Toppenish is an incorporated town and falls under state jurisdiction. The Yakima Valley encompasses the Yakama Nation reservation and is known for the variety of crops they grow annually. As a result, there are a high number of migrant workers who either temporarily reside in and around Toppenish during harvest or live there throughout the year. There are three major racial groups who live on the Yakama Nation reservation: Latinos, whites, and Indigenous peoples. According to the 2010 census, 8,949 citizens reside in Toppenish, Washington. Of its 8,949 residents, 33.8 percent are white, 8 percent are American Indian/Alaska natives, and 82.6 percent are Hispanic or Latino (per census guidelines, "Hispanics may be of any race, so also are included in applicable race categories," thereby accounting for the total greater than 100 percent).[28] American Indians, including Yakama Nation citizens, are the minority on their traditional lands.

The Toppenish Ward of the Church of Jesus Christ of Latter-day Saints reflects the diversity of its citizenry. There is an English-speaking ward that the majority of white and Indigenous members attend. Latino/a members attend the Spanish-speaking branch. I attended the English-speaking ward. This ward is where I first felt marginalized as a Mormon Dakota and became cognizant that I was somehow different. At this young age, I did not have the knowledge to articulate why I felt like an "outsider," but I now have the language to articulate my experiences. I had experiences both as an "insider" and "outsider." I consider myself to be an "insider" since I was born and raised in the LDS Church. I understand the culture and doctrine of the church. My critiques are aimed at the culture of the LDS Church and its membership, not at doctrine. However, I believe that many lay members of the faith use their own worldview to interpret doctrine resulting in prejudicial and/or racist attitudes towards Indigenous peoples. For example, I have been told at various times that I am a "good Indian" or even that I am not a "traditional Indian" because of my education. Both of these phrases are loaded and imply that the only "good Indian" is an educated Indian. Even more dangerous is the implication that being traditional is bad, or as I have been told, is reminiscent of our "Lamanite ancestors." I have never accepted these "compliments." Instead, I use them as opportunities to educate these individuals. As Dakota people, we value our elders. They are the keepers and protectors of our language, culture, and people. Even though I have a PhD, I will always value the education of my elders over my own.

I simultaneously consider myself to be an "outsider" because I never felt as though I fully belonged or that my perspective was reflected in church history, classes, or activities. My perspective has always been different from the mainstream, primarily very American Mormon identity, even at a young age. I recall asking doctrinal questions, such as why the Book of Mormon changed "white" to "pure" when discussing Lamanite peoples? My teachers usually avoided directly answering or instead would tell me it was not our place to question doctrinal changes. Other teachers answered that the change in terminology was to clarify the real meaning, i.e., it was discussing the faith or spiritual countenance of a people, not their pigmentation or race. If it was not about race, then why was my Indigeneity or skin color equated with being a descendent of the "Lamanites"? Many of my Sunday school classmates continued to buy into and perpetuate the idea that I came from a line of "cursed" ancestors. One young man had stated that the reason why Indigenous peoples were brown, was due to the fact that our ancestors were unrighteous. This contradicts LDS beliefs that we have individual agency and that we do not pay for the transgressions of others, including our ancestors. However, this young man indicated that I was paying for our ancestor's unrighteous behavior and beliefs because I was Dakota. I knew this to not be true.

One of the fundamental beliefs of the Church of Jesus Christ of Latter-day Saints is that Indigenous peoples were descendants of "Lamanites." From the very beginning of the LDS Church, white Mormon members defined what it meant to be indigenous. In my article in the *Journal of Mormon History,* I explore the origins of this "Lamanite" identity and its application to Indigenous peoples.[29] "Lamanites" emerge from a family division and where they were once

> white, and exceedingly fair and delightsome . . . the Lord God did cause a **skin of blackness** to come upon them . . . [and] cause that they **shall be loathsome** unto thy people, save they shall repent of their iniquities. And cursed shall be the seed of him that mixeth with their seed; for they shall be cursed even with the same cursing.[30]

This passage reveals how "Lamanites" were once a promised people, "white, and exceedingly fair and delightsome," but because they were disobedient and challenged the patriarchal power of their father and younger brother Nephi, they became a fallen people cursed by God. "Lamanites" became a people marked not only by their darkened skin, but also by their savagery. The descendants of "Lamanites" and their "skin of blackness" made them easily identifiable, they became the racialized "other."

Even though this text changed in 1981 from "white and delightsome" to "pure and delightsome" people, Mormon culture continues to cling to the idea that Indigenous peoples will one day become "white." This became a topic of discussion in various religious classes. I had classmates who really thought that we Indigenous peoples would become "white and delightsome" as long as we accepted Mormonism. My parents had taught me well regarding this issue. For example, when my mom first converted and became a member, this phrasing, "white and delightsome" did not make sense to her. She did not believe that she would become "white and delightsome," but more importantly, she did not want to literally become white. My mother was and continues to be, a proud Chicana woman. Despite this phrase, she felt that it would be changed later. My mom relied on her faith and converted in the early 1970s despite this appearance of textual racialization.

When the text changed in 1981, from "white and delightsome" to "pure and delightsome," her faith was reaffirmed. She knew she would always remain Chicana and that her phenotype was not tied to her eternal salvation.

Despite the textual change in 1981, the idea has been woven into Mormon culture. Individuals continue to insist that my complexion, or the complexion of my ancestors and relatives reflect our lack of faithfulness and righteousness or that our Dakota beliefs are inherently wrong. Others have even remarked that because I have a lighter complexion than my siblings I must be more righteous than they. What they are telling me is that my "righteousness" is being reflected in my physical countenance, i.e., my race. Whiteness becomes valued, prized above Indigeneity. Comments such as these continue to remain problematic as they demarcate Indigenous peoples as a religious and spiritual "other." My Dakota identity was being denied. The focus on my race and connection to my perceived "righteousness" erases the rich history of my people and my lived reality as a Dakota woman. I will always be Dakota.

Indigenous peoples occupy an interesting space in the LDS Church in which we are a fallen and promised people simultaneously. I remember one vivid instance in which I realized the problematic intersection of Indigeneity, Mormonism and righteousness. I was on vacation with a friend from graduate school and she had also invited two friends. All three women were white and former missionary companions. Two had completed bachelor degrees at Brigham Young University, and the third woman had taken classes at BYU. While I was apprehensive about going to a foreign country with two people I did not know, I ignored these feelings and embarked on what I anticipated would be a fun adventure. One evening, we were having a conversation about American Indian reservations. These women had neither been to a reservation nor had they had any meaningful relationship with Indigenous peoples. As they were asking me questions, the usual stereotypes of American Indian peoples emerged from their questions. Why are Indians alcoholics? Why are they so poor? As I attempted to ground their questions within a historical context, they were not happy with my responses. I talked about the current conditions found on reservations as a direct result of colonization, including Mormon colonization. I used the LDS Church's Indian Student Placement Program as an example of how colonization affects Indigenous peoples and communities. I had argued that while the intentions of the church were good, the reality was that American

Indian foster children were dramatically affected by their participation, often not always in positive ways. I described that the driving purpose, the idea that Indian people were deficient in their morals, and religious and educational beliefs, and that Mormonism was a solution to these issues, was problematic. American Indian foster children were marginalized as "Lamanites," were seen by Mormon religious leaders as a people in need of religious uplift. I should not have been surprised that this made them uncomfortable. One young woman in particular had a very difficult time accepting anything I said.

As our conversation moved to my own identity as a Mormon Dakota, our conversation became more heated. One woman asked if I viewed the Book of Mormon as my history or as the history of my people. I have pondered this many times, but the Book of Mormon does not align with traditional Dakota beliefs. I had responded that no, it was not my history. It was not Dakota history. While this may seem controversial, it is only Mormon Indigenous members who are informed that our history, our ancestors, can be found in the Book of Mormon. This young woman became very angry and then stated, "if you knew your history, you would know that the Book of Mormon is your history and that your people have always been a violent people. They have always been a bloodthirsty people." Needless to say, I was initially shocked but then responded to her question. I challenged her uniformed assumptions regarding Indigenous peoples and asked her to refrain from making unfounded, anti-Indian statements. I offered up Dakota history as a challenge to her spurious assumptions about Indigenous peoples.

While this exchange was heated, I learned an important lesson. Race and racism continued to be a problem in American society, including the LDS Church. Indigenous peoples continue to be not only a racialized people but also a religiously marginalized people within a predominately white LDS Church. Our histories, our identity as Indigenous peoples arc not only ignored, but dismissed and denied when it makes others uncomfortable or challenges the narrative of Mormon settler colonialism. Instead, we are expected to reaffirm a religious identity that too often does little to acknowledge our Indigeneity.

Challenges such as these, which eschew historical and political context and makes sense of race only within, have been relatively commonplace in my experience growing up in the LDS Church. As a young woman, the narrative I was taught about Mormon settlers and their arrival in the Salt Lake

Valley in 1847, was both celebratory and triumphant. Mormon settlers who made the trek west were revered for their faithfulness despite the hardships they endured along the trail. Many journeyed with very little, others lost their lives or loved ones and material resources in the hopes of finding religious refuge beyond the boundaries of the United States.[31] Their arrival into the Salt Lake Valley was in large part due to their faith and religious belief that this land was set aside especially for their use. It was as if this land were free, unsettled, and ready for Mormon settlement. This perspective was not unique, nor exclusive to Mormon settlers for that matter, but indicative of settler colonialism that seeks to eliminate and replace Indigenous peoples. It is also American history.

Indigenous peoples were rarely mentioned while I was growing up, and if they were mentioned, it was because they were "uncivilized" or made Mormon settlement difficult. This became clear during the Church of Jesus Christ of Latter-day Saints' 150th anniversary celebration on July 24, 1997 of the first Mormon settlers' arrival in the Salt Lake Valley in 1847. The sesquicentennial was one of the largest celebrations of Mormon "pioneers" within the LDS Church. Mormon "pioneers" are also celebrated annually by the LDS church, and in Utah, July 24 is a state holiday: everything shuts down so that members can remember and celebrate these "pioneers" who paved the way for Mormon settlers along the Wasatch mountains. There are parades in Salt Lake City and in various other towns along the Wasatch Front to venerate these first "pioneers" who moved west seeking religious refuge.

I remember very vividly the push for young men and women to participate in the sesquicentennial celebration when I was a seventeen-year-old girl. In the run-up to the celebration, my seminary teacher made a point of presenting various lessons in our class about the Mormon "pioneers," even going so far as to dress as a Mormon "pioneer" in period clothing that she sewed herself. I was fortunate that my older sister was with me in this class because we were able to resist in our own way. We feigned a lack of interest, but what we were really resisting was the assumption that Mormon settlement was inevitable or that the "pioneers" were worthy of celebration. While we were not vocally resistant, we were subversive in our resistance: we would not let our presence be used to sanction a celebration that removed other Indigenous peoples from their homelands. We would not play "pioneer." Instead, we used humor to address the pain, we joked that we would "play Indian" and attack the handcart re-enactors to give them an "authentic" experience.

The sesquicentennial celebration felt like a year-long event, and I remember feeling anxious and angry. I did not want to participate in any of the events planned by my local church leaders. Our church leaders had admonished all parents to encourage their children to participate in these sesquicentennial activities. I was fortunate that my parents were very critical of our local church leaders and refused to allow us to participate because it was a direct assault against our identity as Indigenous peoples. One specific activity that many LDS youth participate in is a recreation of the "pioneer" experience. For example, we had to dress in period clothing, long skirts and bonnets for girls, and push a handcart. This is an experience that many young men and women, ages 12–17, participate in annually. The purpose of this recreation is for young men and women to have an understanding and appreciation for the "pioneers" who made the long trek west due to religious persecution. It is also intended to be a religious experience for the individuals who participate. Young men and women who participate recall the spiritual aspects of this reenactment; it reaffirms their faith in the truthfulness of the LDS Church but also the affirmation of these Mormon "pioneers" whose trek west was sanctioned by God.

I did not participate in these reenactments because I knew they were part of the religious colonization process. I would not buy into this narrative because it conflicts with my Dakota identity. As a Dakota young woman, I made sense of this day on my own terms. I believed this event to be hypocritical at best. How could we celebrate the Mormon move west to escape religious persecution yet remove Indigenous peoples from their traditional lands because they were not Mormon? How could I celebrate a church holiday that did little to acknowledge Indigenous peoples as an integral role in the Mormon historical narrative? Indigenous peoples were not included in any historical narrative and I knew if we included Indigenous peoples, there would have to be an acknowledgement that Mormons settled on Indigenous lands. Furthermore, not only did they claim land as their own, but from the Mormon perspective, this land was open and free for colonization. However, this was never the case. Utes, Paiutes, Shoshones, Goshutes, and Navajos lived within these boundaries of what we now know as Utah. While they did not clearly demarcate their land as Ute, Paiute, Shoshone, or Goshute the way Mormon settlers did, they had made this land their own long before Mormon "pioneers" arrived. They were knowledgeable and intimately connected to the land. Instead, Indigenous peoples remain invisible not only in the historical narrative, but their lived experiences remain invisible to the larger LDS community.

The invisibility of Indigenous peoples remains even today. There is little meaningful discussion of Indigenous peoples and Mormon "pioneers." In my own work, I have tried to disrupt even the usage of "pioneers." Putting the term "pioneers" into quotes also undermines attempts to normalize Mormon settler colonialism. I employ the term settler rather than "pioneer" to disrupt the narrative and to name settler colonialism as a process that seeks to replace Indigenous peoples. Mormon settlers were foreign to Utah, their settlement and colonization of Indigenous lands was not accidental. They claimed and remade Indigenous land into their own. Annual Mormon settler celebrations continue to marginalize Indigenous peoples. Indigenous peoples who are included are those who do not challenge Mormon authority or perform "Indian." Both of these contexts are considered safe because neither challenges Mormon hegemony over the narrative of Mormon settlement. Again, there is no engagement in the histories that overlap and intersect. Individuals who chose to challenge the Mormon colonial discourse are considered threats that must be quickly dismantled or dismissed.

For example, I left Salt Lake City, Utah, for home on the Fort Peck Sioux and Assiniboine Reservation on July 24, 2013. Excited about my return to my home for a community celebration and to leave the state of Utah on "Pioneer Day," I posted an update on my personal Facebook page on which I stated that I simply could not handle another "pioneer" celebration in which Indigenous peoples are marginalized or placed on the periphery of the historical narrative and geographically removed or placed on the periphery of "pioneer" celebrations. In response to my post, a white member from my former ward in Toppenish, Washington, stated:

> Elise . . . don't start with more devisive [sic] rhetoric . . . we already have enough with the white-black issue. Please with all your influence spread more love and compassion to all people of the U.S. Yes, there have been many problems with all of the groups who have come to America seeking freedom . . . one of them dating back to the Nephites and Lamanites. I'm so sorry for all the hardships of each group and hope you can feel better towards the Mormon Pioneer Day celebrations.

This particular comment angered me. I embraced my anger. As Haunani-Kay Trask has articulated, righteous anger is the "emotional/psychological response of victims of racism/discrimination to the system of power that dominates/exploits/oppresses them. Righteous anger is *not* racism; rather, it is a defensible response to racism."[32]

My response reflects the ongoing anti-Indianism that exists institutionally in annual celebrations of Mormon settlers. I do not want to be silenced because my perspective may be deemed divisive. Instead, this comment reveals the ongoing racial tensions between white and Indigenous peoples. Whiteness becomes normalized within this religious institution. My perspective challenges the Mormon "pioneer" narrative, therefore, it must immediately be dismissed as an incorrect or inaccurate perspective. As this sister articulates, she hopes that I "can feel better towards the Mormon Pioneer Day." I will feel better when we can be honest about our past and have a honest conversation regarding our shared past, no matter how different our perspectives may be regarding Mormon settlers.

When I was younger, I was much more conciliatory. I would have caved or said something to assuage her hurt or indignation. However, as I have gotten older, I realize that it is not my job to make others feel better. I have a responsibility to my community and to Indigenous peoples to tell our histories that may be painful or uncomfortable to non-Indigenous peoples. While it has been a slow process, I will no longer allow myself or Indigenous peoples to be silenced. Her comment, "[p]lease use your influence to spread more love and compassion to all people of the US" is just another example of how my experiences as a Mormon Dakota are being dismissed. This sister is pushing me to "use my influence to spread more love"; as a Dakota historian with a PhD, I am using my influence to spread truth. This chapter is about truth-telling, even if it makes non-Dakota Mormons uncomfortable. I can no longer stay quiet about issues that continue to dismiss my experiences because it makes others uncomfortable when their white privilege is being checked and challenged. Truth-telling is integral to challenging and disrupting Mormon settler colonialism.

Some Mormons argue that race no longer exists as an issue in the LDS Church since the ban against Blacks holding the priesthood was reversed in 1978. However, as this sister has demonstrated, race continues to be an issue amongst the membership. Her reference of the "white-black" issue highlights her erroneous belief that racism or prejudice operates solely along the black/white binary. We need to move beyond this limiting binary of race and expand our analysis and perspective to include Indigenous peoples. In order to heal from racism and the wounds it has caused, we must have a candid conversation about race within the LDS Church, especially the notion of Indigenous peoples as "Lamanites." Truth-telling in the religious and historical narrative becomes vital to healing past wounds and moving forward.

Even though this sister attempts to acknowledge that various groups have experienced hardships, she still fails to understand that Indigenous peoples never migrated to what we now know as the United States. We have always existed as a people on this continent. We were not the first immigrants. We have always existed and will always exist as a people. It was only through the arrival of settlers that our ways of living and being were dramatically affected through colonialism—in this context, Mormon colonialism. Our hardships that we endure as a people are due to colonization. People have sought to change our ways of living and being because we were seen as "savage."

Despite all the federal and private policies that have sought to "kill the Indian, save the man,"[33] we have been a resilient people. We continue to define our identity on our terms. As a Dakota woman growing up in a predominately non-Indian institution, it has been difficult to maintain my identity. I am Dakota. This has not always been easy because attacks on my Dakota identity occurred growing up in the church and continue to happen, especially when I challenge the widely accepted narrative of Mormon "pioneers" within the LDS Church.

It has been these experiences that made me realize that race, especially in regards to Indigenous peoples, remains invisible within the LDS Church and amongst its members. It is difficult to exist as a Dakota woman within the LDS Church if our perspectives and lived experiences continue to be pushed to the periphery or outright challenged, ignored, or worst of all, dismissed. Instead of understanding my perspective regarding the celebration of Mormon settlers, church members framed my resistance in religious terms: I simply lack faith. My attacks have never been anti-Mormon. I seek to complicate the notions of Mormon identity and to include Indigenous perspectives and experiences as part of the Mormon experience and history. More importantly, my goal has been to raise awareness regarding the diversity of Indigenous peoples' experiences. Our experiences are vast and diverse, yet our voices, especially those that are critical, continue to be silenced by other members, including other Indigenous Mormon members who have internalized their own colonization.

As a Mormon Dakota, I have learned to challenge the institutional and individual racism displayed by members throughout my lifetime. It has not always been an easy process. Initially, when I experienced racism as a young child and adult, I did not have the tools to articulate and pinpoint why a statement or a comment was racist or anti-Indian. Eventually, I found my voice. I know I am not the only Indigenous person who has had questions about the gospel that have challenged our faith. I also know that I have been blessed with an intellect and a voice that demands I speak up and become an advocate for those who fear speaking out due to backlash or for those unable to speak out. My hope is that my voice and work will pave the way for others to articulate a space within the LDS Church that not only welcomes their Indigenous identity, but also acknowledges Indigenous identity as an integral part of the Mormon experience and history.

II

LIVING THE PERSISTENT LEGACIES OF COLONIZATION IN LDS CONTEXTS

While some think of colonization as a historical event, colonialism—the systems of thought and structures of power that privilege colonizers over colonized peoples—continues to dominate human life around the world today. Among the most persistent legacies of colonialism in the Americas are systems of racial privilege that distribute life chances according to skin color. These systems of racial classification derive from colonial economic, legal, and political systems that exploited African labor and appropriated indigenous and Mexican lands to create the modern United States of America. The descendents of colonized peoples from Africa and Indigenous and Spanish-speaking North America continue to be marked by their "race"—a non-scientific category of human classification invented in law and culture in the seventeenth through nineteenth centuries—as available for exploitation. The four essays collected in this section ask us to reckon with the extent to which these systems of racial privilege structure Mormon contexts and experience, and what resources the faith can offer as we seek ways to abandon the systems and approach a postcolonial Zion.

Five

UNPACKING WHITE-HERITAGE MORMON PRIVILEGE

A Latter-day Saint Pursuit of Critical Consciousness

ROLF STRAUBHAAR

When I was a junior in college, I participated in a study abroad program in Salvador, a historical colonial city in northeastern Brazil. I had lived in Brazil as a child and served a proselytizing mission there, and I jumped at the opportunity to return to a country I loved.

My first Sunday I found the local LDS meetinghouse and attended services. I met some amazingly talented, experienced and well-traveled people, among many others: a woman who had recently returned from serving as a missionary in another part of Brazil and was attending the flagship college in the area, a bishop who was bilingual in Spanish from his mission in Colombia and owned a successful local business, and a young man who had traveled throughout Brazil as an accomplished musician.

Yet despite this abundance of fascinating, talented people, most of whom had life and church leadership experience that far exceeded my own as a recently-returned missionary, my attendance as a white heritage Mormon in this relatively small congregation made me a bit of a celebrity. Five minutes before sacrament meeting started, the bishop pulled me aside and asked me if I could give an introductory talk. I asked if another speaker had been unable to make it, and he shook his head. "No, no, no, all our speakers are here. But we think the congregation would love to hear just a few minutes from you. The other speakers will get less time, but that is fine—after all, it is not every day that we get visitors from the US!"

This experience in college was one of many similar occurrences during my times participating in church among those who did not share my background: without any motive beyond my personal history as a white, born-in-the-covenant heritage Mormon with pioneer ancestry, I would see my experiences, opinions, and words privileged above those of other members. While such experiences always made me a bit uncomfortable, only with time and study did I begin to realize the extent of the negative repercussions of such social dynamics within the church—negative in that it dehumanizes and spiritually stunts both those who lack and those who possess the characteristics and heritage which are privileged.

From the perspective advanced by the Brazilian educator Paulo Freire, socially privileged individuals benefit from a cultural environment that dehumanizes those who do not share that privilege. In *Pedagogy of the Oppressed*, Freire draws a clear line between those who are benefitted by structural social inequalities and those who are the victims of it, calling them (respectively) the oppressor and the oppressed. To Freire, "the oppressor consciousness tends to transform everything surrounding it into an object of its domination. The earth, property, production, the creations of people, people themselves, time—everything is reduced to the status of objects at its disposal."[1]

To both the oppressors and the oppressed, "oppression is domesticating."[2] Both groups receive myriad messages justifying their unequal placement within social hierarchies, messages which can make our social positionalities seem natural, or even deserved. For those from oppressor classes, Freire astutely notes that "the oppressors do not perceive their monopoly on having more as a privilege which dehumanizes others and themselves."[3]

Within a Mormon context, this divide of privilege is notable between white North American church members who often have long family histories of church membership and the people of color within the US and the rest of the world who primarily represent growth in church membership over the last half-century. For those white North American Mormons who engage with Mormons of color, whether through missionary work or fellowship in local congregations, this privilege often exhibits itself as a sense that white North American church members have a unique degree of power to spiritually uplift, edify, and strengthen—an idea that results in privileging such individuals' voices, ideas, and actions in church settings.

The existence and effects of this privilege in society at large, experienced at various intersections of race, social class, nationality, and gender, has been explored at length in literature[4] and film.[5] The need for privileged individuals who work in marginalized communities to "unpack" their privilege has become a staple of many teacher education programs.[6] However, a similar discussion of privilege (in all its sexual, social, racial and national intersections) within Mormonism, and more especially the ways in which socially privileged Mormons may begin to recognize and address that privilege, has yet to be undertaken in Mormon Studies literature. I have purposefully crafted this essay as an initial entry into this needed conversation.

As a white, middle-class, married, straight Mormon man of Utah pioneer heritage, I arguably embody privilege at all possible intersections within Mormon religious culture. During many periods in my life—as a child of an American expatriate family living in Brazil and the Dominican Republic; as a missionary in northern Brazil; and as an educator and researcher working in Brazil, Mozambique, and in various communities of color in the US—I have spent much of my Mormon religious life in local congregations in which I held privilege that was not shared by the majority of my co-religionists. In this essay, I will share a number of personal experiences through which I came to recognize this privilege and the power relations it represents in Mormon religious settings. Building upon my own experience, I will then argue that the philosophy of Paulo Freire can effectively problematize this privileged mindset. More specifically, I argue that Freirean theory itself outlines a process of reflection and action (or praxis) that, by promoting continual self-evaluation in the pursuit of what Freire[7] would call critical consciousness, can be effectively used by privileged Mormons to try to counter and mitigate the effects of their privilege in their religious lives—privilege that dehumanizes oppressor and oppressed.

THE SACRAL WORK OF FEEDING NORTH AMERICAN MISSIONARIES

While serving as a missionary in northern Brazil, mostly in areas right on or next to the equator, noon was one of the most anticipated parts of my day. After three hours of morning tracting in the Amazonian sun, my companion and I would typically already be dripping with sweat when we would arrive at the doorstep of whichever member had volunteered to prepare us lunch that day. To have an hour to sit in front of a fan or air conditioning unit, a cup of fresh juice in hand, and enjoy a lovingly prepared meal was a much-appreciated reprieve.

In addition to the rest, the meals I was served as a missionary were, on the whole, decadently extensive: a large plate of rice and beans with a well-seasoned side of meat or fish, a fresh-cut salad, mashed potatoes, one of several potato- or yucca-based sides, and some form of dessert involving cream and tropical fruit, *cupuaçu* (an Amazonian fruit) being every missionary's favorite. Compared to the meals I ate in my middle-class North American home growing up, this felt like Thanksgiving every day.

After several months in the mission field, these huge midday meals began to feel more and more routine, even expected—so much so that when a family first served me a modest lunch of grilled river fish and rice in their very modest home, I remember feeling an initial sting of disappointment. Picking the small bones out of my fish while looking around from my seat at the cracked walls, bare dirt floor and mud-encrusted windows, I first began to consciously realize the enormous disparity between what I had become accustomed to eating every day and the daily gastronomic reality of the people I was visiting and serving. This home was no different from most of the members' homes where we ate more lavish meals, but the chasm of difference between those meals and the humble circumstances in which they were served became much starker when the meal seemed to more accurately fit the surroundings.

Though members always shrugged off our thanks and said they were happy to help missionaries who were doing so much for them and their communities, from that moment on I began to notice more and more the high priority placed on missionary meals in the everyday life of a north Brazilian Latter-day Saint. Bishops regularly held up the missionary meal calendar over the pulpit, guilting members for leaving blank spaces when it was their obligation as a ward family to feed us. Upon arriving in poorer areas with more sparse member meals, I had one companion who took it upon himself to visit members personally and challenge them to provide us with more frequent meals. The simple truth was that missionaries had come to expect large, lavish meals, and members were left to spend significant amounts of their monthly income to satisfy those missionaries' tastes.

Though I would not have described it in such language then, what was bothering me was the realization that missionary well-being was prioritized over member well-being. This is problematic everywhere, but at least in congregations like the suburban middle-class US wards in which I grew up, members had the income to be able to feed themselves and the local missionaries. Also, most member families in such settings could see missionaries as one of their own—they looked like them, were typically raised in family settings like their own, and might even remind members of their own children or of themselves at a younger age.

In Amazonian Brazil, on the other hand, the vast majority of members were converts themselves, lacking the same life-long connection to the LDS faith or to the US context in which it took root. Amazonian members' relationship to missionaries was one of imbalanced power, one in which missionaries (despite barely having reached adulthood) were seen as higher authorities than those whom they taught or with whom they served in local congregations. Members and local church leaders would come to us missionaries, particularly those of us who were from the US and raised in the church, for advice. The fact that an eighteen-year-old boy from Utah could be seen as a wiser, higher authority than (for example) a sixty-five-year-old man or woman with children and grandchildren and a lifetime of experience is evidence that this is not a relationship of peers or equals. It also helps explain why members were willing to sacrifice their own personal well-being for North American missionaries—because the missionaries' well-being, simply by virtue of the place and faith into which they were born, was given higher privilege and priority.

BORN INTO THE COVENANT IMPLYING BORN INTO COMPETENCY

Similarly, in several places in which I've lived and served in the church, I have noticed a tendency among Latter-day Saints of color, particularly those who are recent converts to the church, to defer in decision-making to those (like myself) who are white heritage Mormons with generations of LDS ancestry.

While working in the development sector in Mozambique, I served as the executive secretary of the local district, which included six branches. I was extended this calling within a week of arriving in Mozambique, despite being only twenty-four years old and not having anywhere near the life experience of the other members of the district presidency.

I remember clearly many meetings in which, while planning a particular activity or deciding upon a particular course of action, one of the other members of the presidency would turn to me to ask me what I think. When I would defer to their opinions, especially given the fact that the secretarial position is not intended to provide the same level of input or counsel as the president or his counselors, I would often be asked again, upon the premise that, "well, you're from the US, and you were raised in the church. You would know how these things should work better than we do." Effectively, the years I had spent goofing off in church as a youth were appraised as more valuable life experience than the decades these other men had spent as husbands, fathers, and working professionals. Being born in the covenant with pioneer ancestry trumped all these other credentials.

Several years later as a newlywed elementary school teacher working in Washington Heights in New York City, I remember a special sacrament meeting program in which several white members were invited to speak about how much they enjoyed the service they were able to provide in the Spanish ward that met in the same building. The program was designed to encourage other members to "help out" by switching to the Spanish-speaking ward and taking on leadership callings. One speaker made a point of noting that you didn't need to speak Spanish to take advantage of this opportunity: "Most of the children speak English, and you will be so blessed for using your experience to serve the less fortunate."

What struck me as particularly odd and troubling about such statements is that I knew many members of the Spanish-speaking ward. One of them was the assistant principal at my school, as well as the Relief Society president in the ward. She was extremely capable in both roles, as were a number of Latino/a men and women in that ward. Yet the bishop and most of the leadership of the Spanish-speaking ward were white men who had just finished up a sacrament meeting trying to recruit more white members to come "help" run the Spanish ward. What exactly were they lacking? What exactly made us better? I could think of no other explanation for such behavior than that the experience and spirituality of white heritage members was seen as inherently superior to that of largely convert Spanish-speaking members from the Caribbean and Latin America.

COUNTERING MORMON PRIVILEGE

As I grew older and spent more and more of my religious life in places where white heritage Mormons were the privileged minority, I became more and more interested in finding a way to push back against the social dynamics exacerbated by such privilege. Through my work with progressive educational nonprofits and my later graduate studies, I found an answer in the writings of Paulo Freire.

Freire calls for those in privileged positions, such as white heritage Mormons, to be willing to "commit class suicide,"[8] or to give up the privileges associated with their identity and upbringing. Only by doing so can white heritage Mormons become "completely committed to the deepest aspirations of the people to which they belong"[9]—that is, their co-religionists who do not share their privileges. In a later book of his, Freire (who was himself a committed Catholic involved in the development of liberation theology) makes a more religious argument that privileged individuals must "live the profound meaning of Easter,"[10] letting their previous privileged selves die and beginning new lives in which they commit to living equally with their brothers and sisters, rather than as their implicit superiors.

This type of repudiation of the privileges one enjoys within the status quo requires serious spiritual work: it means questioning the very social structures in the church in which we have been raised and learned to function socially. Any white heritage Mormon has lived their entire spiritual life and experienced the divine wholly within a system that prizes their feelings and experiences by virtue of who they are; to question that, and to try to see one's co-religionists of color as one's complete equals goes contrary to one's lived experience, and in the case of problematic passages in the Book of Mormon and Book of Abraham, against one's doctrinal instruction.

More specifically, various passages in the Book of Mormon (2 Nephi 5:21; Jacob 3:8–9; Alma 3:5–10; 3 Nephi 2:15) and the Book of Abraham (Moses 5:40), both canonical texts within the LDS faith, associate dark skin (or a "skin of blackness" [2 Nephi 5:21]) with divine curses intended to help make sure that those people who are in favor with God do not "mingle [their] seed" (Alma 3:9) with less-preferred dark-skinned peoples. While at various times in the Book of Mormon narrative these people gained God's favor and had their curse removed (in one case, according to the text, their skin literally "[becoming] white like unto the Nephites" [3 Nephi 2:15], the text's chosen people), and while many passages (1 Nephi 15:4, 2 Nephi 9:53, 3 Nephi 21:1–7) prophesy of the eventual salvation of these people (who were commonly viewed by LDS church leaders throughout the nineteenth and twentieth centuries as being the progenitors of contemporary Native Americans and Polynesians), this curse associated with a literal darkening of skin implies a clear separation between white and non-white peoples on the basis of past (or present) righteousness. In the case of many white Mormons like myself raised on these texts, it is easy to gain an implicit feeling of moral superiority simply on the basis of skin color.

While it may seem difficult to challenge assertions of one's inherent superiority when those claims are made in scripture itself and are reinforced by voices carrying prophetic authority, it is precisely this process of problematization that is necessary to reach critical consciousness. In Freirean thought, critical consciousness "refers to the process in which men [and women], not as recipients, but as knowing subjects, achieve a deepening awareness both of the socio-cultural reality which shapes their lives and of their capacity to transform that reality."[11]

Similarly to how Mormons view testimony-building, Freire sees critical consciousness as a process rather than a single transformative experience. This process is meant to be a difficult one, based in inner struggle:

> Those who authentically commit themselves to the people must re-examine themselves constantly. This conversion is so radical as not to allow of ambiguous behavior. To affirm this commitment but to consider oneself the proprietor of revolutionary wisdom—which must then be given to (or imposed on) the people—is to retain the old ways. The man or woman who proclaims devotion to the cause of liberation yet is unable to enter into communion with the people, whom he or she continues to regard as totally ignorant, is grievously self-deceived. The convert who approaches the people but feels alarm at each step they take, each doubt they express, and each suggestion they offer, and attempts to impose his 'status,' remains nostalgic towards his origins.[12]

Unfortunately for white heritage Mormons like me, the LDS focus on reverence for our pioneer ancestors makes it particularly easy to feel nostalgia towards the power and privilege inherent in our origins.

SEEKING CRITICAL CONSCIOUSNESS

In the process of seeking critical consciousness, Freire talks first about being able to "name the word and the world"—in this case, I see this as being able to give a name and a face to the structural inequalities that prevent the full humanization of all our brothers and sisters in LDS culture and society.

As I read and reflected on Freire's writings and applied them to my spiritual life, I came to see that I needed (and still need) to change—I needed to not only recognize my privilege, but be willing to find concrete ways to abandon it, granting my co-religionists the same trust they so often placed in me. In recognizing my privilege and the inequalities it created, I learned over time to "name the world," or notice the elements of my religious world that needed changing; all that was left was the hard work of trying to do it. I had begun to ask hard questions—questions without simple answers, and which led to critical thinking and reflection. As Freire and Faundez have written, "thinking about questions that may not always or immediately arrive to an answer are the roots of change."[13] In "naming the world," I had taken that first step towards critical consciousness and begun my process of personal change.

"ENDURING TO THE END" WITH CRITICAL CONSCIOUSNESS

One of the difficulties in seeking critical consciousness is recognizing that there is no concrete end point to which one can look and hope to have one day "made it." Though I have studied Freire's writings for over a decade now and consider myself a Freirean, I do not think I have come to a place yet where I fully understand Freire, and I doubt I ever will. That, however, is part of the point. As Freire has put it, we are unfinished beings, "unfinished yet conscious of our unfinished state,"[14] always growing and changing in our thoughts and feelings.

In my efforts to recognize and counter my privilege as a white heritage Mormon, this is part of what I find easiest to love and embrace about

Freirean thought—the notion that, just as Latter-day Saints believe it is our purpose in this life to continue to grow and progress and to try to become more like the Divine, it is part of our unfinished nature to continue to ask questions, to challenge our preconceived notions of truth and righteousness, and to continuously interrogate our understanding of what it means to live a moral, socially just life. As Freire has said, "I like being human because I am involved with others in making history out of possibility, not simply resigned to fatalistic stagnation."[15] Freire lived this ethos of humility and reflexivity beautifully, listening carefully when challenged by other theorists or thinkers, and at times completely re-thinking various aspects of his own work. (For a beautiful example, read about his interactions with bell hooks regarding the lack of discussion of race and gender in his early writings.[16]

In my ideal world, this is pure religion: a constant struggle to reconsider my own convictions and consider new information that could change the way I think, teach, and act. This is one of the central themes of Freire's work—a call for each of us to push ourselves, to work to reconsider the choices we make through our daily lived existence, and in so doing become more and more "fully human."[17]

While this essay and each of the anecdotes in it has an end point, this process of reflection and change does not: as we follow the Freirean injunction to re-examine ourselves and push ourselves towards critical consciousness, reinvention and recommitment become our daily lived experience. I cannot claim to have completely abandoned the privileges I enjoy as a white heritage Mormon; however, my hope is that in daily working to unpack my ingrained preconceptions and to live accordingly, I can mitigate the damaging effects of such privilege. After all, a power dynamic that privileges the experiences and feelings of the few over the many not only damages the many, it also dehumanizes the few.

As Freire characterized it, what makes a situation oppressive is when "it keeps people from being fully human."[18] While the dehumanization of those who are oppressed may seem obvious, Freire also clarified that oppressive circumstances dehumanize those whose power leads them to oppress, as "no one can be authentically human while he prevents others from being so."[19] Challenging oppressive structures in the church is not an exercise in trying to get to a point where all members are treated as white heritage Mormons are now treated, as that treatment is predicated on implications of inherent superiority; rather, the pursuit of critical consciousness is a pursuit of a reality in which the unique heritages, characteristics, and contributions of all are seen as worthy of recognition and emulation. In Paul's familiar phrasing, "For as the body is one, and hath many members, and all the members of that one body, being many, are one body: so also is Christ. . . . If the whole body were an eye, where were the hearing? If the whole were hearing, where were the smelling?" (1 Cor. 12:12, 17). Unfortunately, the status quo in LDS culture is one in which the white, born-in-the-covenant heritage parts of the body with pioneer ancestry are seen as the crux of the whole, while others are often left feeling lesser, broken, "more feeble" (1 Cor. 12:22), "less honorable" (1 Cor. 12:23). To challenge and systematically disregard such deficit mentalities, all members must personally consider them through the pursuit of critical consciousness, especially members who, like myself, benefit the most from their propagation.

Six

AN ABUNDANT GOD KNOWS
THE MIDDLE ALSO

ALICIA HARRIS

I wasn't raised on a reservation. I was born in prosperous Ogden, Utah in the 1980s. I was raised and viewed by my family and my community as a "normal" white Mormon girl. I wasn't raised speaking Nakota or knowing any traditions associated with my tribe. But since I was a little girl, I've wanted to know more about them, learn from them, and inhabit them. I knew for sure that I was Mormon, and I had a pretty good idea that I am also Native American, but any depth to that latter notion was simply absent. In many ways, my experience with the church complicated my Indigeneity: my identity as a mixed-race person in the LDS Church has been romanticized and simultaneously trivialized. As I've grown and tried to learn more about my heritage (a common element in almost every Latter-day Saint's life), this situation has become increasingly problematic and curious to me.

While I was in the third grade, my mom flirted with the idea of homeschooling my sister and me, and I remember being excited at the prospect of throwing myself deeply into a study of Native American history. My notebook from that period is probably still sitting in a box in one of my parents' garages, gathering dust. It's full of drawings of feathers and ideas for stories about a history that I have since recognized as an entirely romantic fiction. In my childhood drawings, my mom always had blonde hair. In my imaginative musings, I erased and denied her Indigeneity, her rich red-black hair.

This erasure has become symbolic for me of my discomfort with my own Indigeneity, and the lack of place and time where that Indigeneity was nurtured and allowed to grow. Though I was fascinated with all things "Indian," I couldn't ever really think of myself as Assiniboine, except when it was convenient for me. My drawings reflect the inability to fully embody the lived reality of what it actually meant to be a Native American person. This reality was secondary to my imagination. I look at those drawings with love for the child who I was: I have love for a girl who was so fully colonized that her own identity was irreconcilable to reality. My childhood was spent caught in a place where I couldn't fully embody my Native heritage, because I was always expected to enact and celebrate my European Mormon pioneer ancestry, and my Indigeneity remained a mystery, eternally ancillary.

I learned to call that mystery my "Lamanite" heritage. To be clear, I never wanted to be known as a Lamanite. It wasn't really a very attractive thing to be. Even after I went to Brigham Young University and encountered the BYU Indian Princesses, whose portraits line a back hallway in the Wilkinson Student Center. Within the context of Mormonism, it might never be fully okay to be "among the descendants" of the Lamanite people. I fear that I have always been perceived as secondary because of this heritage. I never saw living examples of how to live with the gospel, with the church, and also with a Native American family and past. Maybe others did; I hope that others did. I didn't. And while the BYU Indian Princesses were beautiful, and likely very accomplished young women, pioneers in their own right, they were not presented to me in a way that allowed for full personhood. Their identity was always shrouded in the mystery, romance, and near-secrecy of the European gaze upon Indigeneity. These women perpetuated the romance of my girlhood drawings and ramblings about what it meant to be "Indian." I was never encouraged to fully embrace this Indigeneity until I left the comforting bubble of Mormondom for graduate school. Instead, I subverted one half of myself and sought more ready acceptance through never really talking about the truth of my family and my heritage, and found refuge in a more common (in the LDS Church) European-American history.

I easily pass for an ambiguously ethnic or (just very capable of tanning) white person. So most often when I was with Mormon friends, I tapped into that ability. Many people confessed that they thought I was Mexican after I started to talk about my own heritage and my interest in it. *Passing* refers to the process by which a member of one racial, gender, nationality, or sexually oriented group adopts the guise of another.[1] This idea has been important to my development of identity, especially within LDS culture. Many scholars have focused on the idea of a person of color passing as a white person as a socially advantageous practice.[2] I have known from a young age the value of looking like the people who are around me. My mom told us stories of abuse because she simply did not look like the blonde-haired and blue-eyed half-siblings or friends with whom she associated in the racially charged 1960s and 70s.

Even further, I know what it means, and I know the value of belonging in Mormonism specifically. Belonging is a part of our ritual (and ceremonial) practice in the church. We dress the same and talk the same and read the same books; our Sunday school answers (and questions) are set like a script. Except in unusual circumstances, American Mormons vote the same in elections. As a culture, generally, early twenty-first century American Mormonism is cohesive. Aberration from normative culture comes at a high social and practical cost to practicing American Mormons. Deviation raises social questions about worthiness, reliability, trustworthiness, and ability to lead. These are important social markers in the practice of Mormondom. Especially as it pertains to darkness, to one's worth and worthiness exhibited on the skin—the outward signal of righteousness—LDS culture sets up a paradigm that encourages subordination of any ethnic heritage. These pieces of cultural identity-making are dramatically exacerbated through LDS scripture which seems to make the darkness of skin a reasonable, accepted, and doctrinally founded marker for righteousness and worth. I am not going to deal with these problematic scriptures here—I have not yet come to a place of reconciliation with those scriptures, and I still feel a weight about them. I will leave that discussion for someone firmer in his or her conviction.

Rather, I'll say this: generally, I forgive Mormonism for its near-monolithically normalizing culture. I understand that it is a common feature for many religions and cultural institutions, especially in the nineteenth and twentieth centuries. My concern, rather, lies in the supposed universality of the LDS version of the gospel, and the ways that this uniform stretch of culture effects non-white and mixed-race peoples. If the LDS Church really can work for all peoples, we need to more attentively listen, hear, and be represented by a much greater variety of voices. We must more actively prepare a place for dual identities to be touched and nurtured in the culture of the gospel. There are a great many of us who fit squarely in the midst of more than one world. The church of Jesus Christ surely can afford to carve out a place for us. For me.

The situation of between and both are hardly if ever acknowledged, accepted, or supported, either broadly in US culture, or even more acutely in American Mormonism. I have slowly learned that an abandonment of belonging in one world does not equate to perfect belonging in another. The requirement to and incentives for selecting an identity which is complementary and congruent to dominant white American society are incompatible with the universal message of the gospel and the global church. Any expectation that a child of God express and acknowledge themself as an unwhole person ought to be viewed widely within LDS culture with sorrow, empathy, and support. We ought to anticipate in our brothers and sisters a full and complete expression of all the racial variants which compose our genetic and cultural ancestry. A component of the project of decolonizing Mormonism, then, is the work of softening the lines that keep us apart: apart from one another, and apart from ourselves.

At times belonging in Mormonism has come at the peril of my dual identity. I am increasingly interested in what I give up through racial (white) passage. I was raised to confront a culture that subjects and imperils one part of me to another. Language about Lamanites throughout Mormonism is often negative and devaluing, showing a cursed people who, through a direct and literal reading of sacred text, are not permitted to enjoy the blessings of the gospel's promises. They are cut off from the arm of the Lord, made a darkened and cursed race. But what is the message that is given to people like me: people who are in-between? I am a person who literally embodies the white and delightsome-ness and cursed darkness: my father from Danish, English, and Swiss immigrants; my mother from English, French-Canadian, Ihanktonwan Dakota, and Assiniboine peoples. For a growing population of Mormons, this is a question that needs resolution. An increasingly large subset of Mormonism must confront what it means to exist as both colonized and colonizer in one blessed body-temple. My intent, then, is to delve into the complications of living in a complex world, and advocate for a church whose mission must become large enough to robustly support this population.

This is a story that is inherited over generations. It is an account that is intrinsically different for each new group that rises up to ask it, because

Indigenous relationships to dominant cultures are necessarily in constant flux. This fact continues to shape identity for Native and mixed-race peoples, as the subjugation of one group must submit to dominating cultural forces. This interaction and relationship forms, for some, the core of personal value and self-worth. Cultural politics of interaction and interrelating inform and re-inform each new generation, which must wrestle and re-wrestle with the implications of a history of difference and division. These are the issues with which I have wrestled and continue to wrestle as I seek to find a place within Mormonism, and also assert, understand, and advocate for my Indigenous culture. I am not removed from either culture, but also not wholly embraced by either. I seek to define an identity of wholeness. To do otherwise feels dishonest.

The perspective of history is relevant and crucial to any attempt to give critical meaning to the account and the questions that rise from it. This story, then, is not mine alone. Dr. Marianne Hirsch, a professor of English and comparative literature at Columbia University theorizes the idea of the "postmemory" in her writings. Postmemory describes the relationship that later generations bear to personal collective and cultural traumas and changes for ancestral generations. Beyond epigenetics, these relationships are created through stories, images, and social interactions with which one is raised. They are not the lived experience of the latter generation, but are transmitted so effectively as to almost constitute memories in their own right.[3] I believe that this is an effective model and theory for understanding my own relationship to my Mormon heritage as well as to my Assiniboine ancestry and culture. I see the activity of this theoretical framework when I think about the drawings that I created as a little girl, and how I would go out of my way between classes to view those Indian Princesses during my time at BYU. I am an inheritor of the trauma of the historical and pervasive romanticization of Native American culture. I echoed the lines of a romantic past in lockstep, rarely critical of my own work or my own position. This romanticization ignores and denies the actual lived history and erases the reality of Indigenous people who are living today. In the mode of decolonization, then, I have felt compelled to critically examine the larger paradigm of my identity at large.

I link back, then, to my grandparents who first bravely left their homes in Denmark, England, and the Swiss Alps because of the compulsion of faith. Their need to belong and join in with the westward march of

Mormonism runs deep in me, their faith and devotion a characteristic to which I aspire. In the same measure, I link to my grandmothers and fathers who followed the North American bison herds of northeastern Montana and Saskatchewan. The people who saw the face of God in the prairie that stretched out unendingly and knew the way that the earth moved in relationship to the stars, a macrocosm of their own bodies. Their connection to place and reverence for the sacred all around is rooted in my core, and I aim to better understand, honor, and revitalize those faith traditions. The blood of both of these lines pump through my veins. My sense of self is a negotiation between these. Identity politics, then, are not abstractions, but lived daily and personal realities which extend into the lived experience of functioning as a practicing LDS individual. Because I am not in a position to reject one heritage or the other, I am subject to the history and the post-memory of both. These are the underpinnings and the structure of my own identity. Subjugation of my Assiniboine heritage to my Mormon heritage is the privilege of the central polis. This is not a privilege I seek to enact in my own life, and the process of decolonizing and expanding Mormonism must recognize and reconcile this position.

In *A Colonial Lexicon*, Nancy Rose Hunt explores the idea of a race based social class made of "Middles." By this term, she is referring to the subaltern of any colonized society: the people who are in closer proximity to the central polis of culture, but still not wholly in that dominant culture.[4] Her specific attention is given to light-skinned, well-educated, or miscegenated generations of colonized Africans, who propel the economies of colonization throughout the African continent. I find value in the idea of a racial "Middle," and see myself in that position with Mormonism and my Native American heritage.

One advantage to this type of structure is that it critically reminds us of the colonizing project at large. It asks us to consciously define "low" and "high" culture, while positioning oneself in between: in the cultural, social, and visual borderlands. This position is made possible through the action of passage, and of a cultural and social literacy in both cultures. I accept that my particular position is removed from Assiniboine culture. I have spent much of my academic career, social life, and professional career seeking to correct this. I have worked to find a greater understanding and rooted comfort in this substantial part of my own blood. Because I live in a colonized society, the removal from my Indigenous family and past appears invisible.

People actively question my decision to study Indigenous American art history. Why did they not question me when I studied European art? When I move towards my Native heritage, and towards the outskirts of dominant Mormon and American society, my movements are excruciatingly and sometimes devastatingly visible. It is work.

I am in the position of "Middle." This station replaces the privilege of ignoring and overlooking the project of colonization with a new privilege that allows and demands an exploration of the seam which joins two sides together, rather than the bifurcated whole. In positioning myself as a Middle person, I am pushed to reinterpret doctrine and teachings as they are presented to me. I am in a psychological place that requires me to interpret one side of the story for the other, apologize to the one side of my ancestry for the actions of the other. I am in a position to be an agent of decolonization.

Bifurcation is a major theme in my lived experience of Mormon culture. I have seen the "us vs. them" and "with us or against us" dichotomies played out countless times, in countless juvenile micro-aggressions. This is because American Mormonism in the western United States is a settler colony. In settler colonies, the colonizer must create dramatic differentiation between itself and the colonized. Settler colonies ingratiate themselves with native communities, bestowing their perceived religious (and racial) authority upon the naïve and supposedly godless. This bestowal is often enacted as benevolence. The end result of this quagmire is extreme cultural passive aggression.

I don't think most Mormons (historically or presently) have done this wittingly. Rather, I suspect that this cultural tradition is bred of fear—fear rooted in uncertainty, in the possibility that we are maybe wrong, or that there is something beyond our orange or purple meeting hall carpet that is somehow threatening to our practice. Fear within Mormonism is fostered and raised with impending threats about our ultimate salvation, demanding that we reassess our lives on a constant basis. Historically, we have perceived ourselves and have been seen by others as a people set apart. We make sure to recite the aphorism and claim that we are in but definitely not of the world. We have been on the defensive since our inception.[5] From Joseph Smith's trials and ultimate martyrdom, to the so-called "Extermination Order" issued in Missouri in 1838, through the exodus to the Salt Lake Valley and the Utah War;[6] from legal and cultural attacks on Mormon polygamy all the way up to the 2014 release of new web and Facebook pages dedicated to "Religious Freedom" sponsored and run by the Mormon Newsroom.[7] Persecution has almost always been an essential aspect of culture in the church.[8]

This discourse creates a reading of doctrine in a forked and detached way, one in which the righteous are removed from "the world." It limits our ability to truly grasp the experiences of cultural "others," while simultaneously requiring submission of entire groups whenever they encounter Mormonism. The expectation is that all "others" will inherently submit because of the good truth of the Mormon version of the gospel, or else they are thoroughly and completely our enemies. One example of this (surely there are a great many) is the cultural ban on kava ceremonies in LDS Tongan communities. A *Deseret News* article from 1999 reports:

> Mormon Tongans say they haven't lost their culture; they have simply taken the best of both worlds.
>
> "It's not that we want to be white or that we want to be Tongan," said Elenoa's husband, Haloti Moala. "The scripture in the church—that has become our culture now."
>
> Adhering to Mormon scripture has meant making some cultural compromises.
>
> Tongans drink kava, an intoxicating beverage made from the roots of the Polynesian pepper tree. It is a staple at weddings and funerals. It is also part of the dating ritual. A suitor takes the kava root to the one he is courting. As she serves the kava, he serenades her.
>
> "Kava is tradition," said Haloti Moala.
>
> Because of its intoxicating potential, the Mormon doctrine bans kava.
>
> "That was a big cultural contradiction for us," Moala said. "The two cultures kind of clashed heads and it was left for us to decide between the two."[9]

It is the subjugation of the one to the other that is of interest to me in the role of Middle. Traditionally, Mormons have interpreted the Book of Mormon passage in Alma 17:9–11 as a justification for this subjection, that the foolish and "base" traditions of the Lamanite fathers might be done away with to bring them into subjugation to Mormonism. This is the root of Mormon colonial benevolence. How often does this attitude invade contemporary Mormonism? How many missionaries are sent to African and Oceanic countries with this attitude? How many well-intentioned white Utah families baptized and then adopted Native American children with this exact text in mind? How prevalent was this narrative present in the arc of Mormon settlement from Idaho through Utah, Nevada, and Arizona, to California? Why do we, as a culture, persist in denying Native and Indigenous ways of knowing and seeing the world? Though the specifics don't look the same, Indigenous peoples have been turning towards God for millennia.

I have had to ask these questions of my own experiences. I think of the many occasions when Lamanites were discussed with Mormon friends in an extremely negative light, until I point out that the Mormon belief system has taught that *I* am the descendant of Lamanites, and awkwardness ensues. In an LDS Institute class, I told the story of my pioneer grandfather who was in prison with President George Q. Cannon for the crime of polygamy.[10] My heritage was praised that week, and I felt like a celebrity. The post-memory of the experience in this instance was a remarkably positive one. The very next week, I told that same institute teacher and class that I was also Native American when we started studying and discussing Lamanites. The teacher looked at me grudgingly and muttered, "Oh, that's what's wrong with you."

The parallel and contrast of these two occasions couldn't have been starker, or more poignant in displaying the practical ways church culture squeezes and sublimates Indigeneity. Using a folk "doctrinal" background, we have problematized and othered members of our own. In my case, this experience problematized and othered a small part of my whole person. What was the message that I was to receive from these two congruent experiences? How am I to divide myself and also see that I am fully a daughter of God? Is only one part of me worthy of the heritage that is my whole?

For every pioneer success story, there is an Indigenous submission or oppression. The story about my own Mormon pioneer ancestors entering into the Salt Lake Valley doesn't ever include a story about how the Shoshone, Ute, Paiute, Goshute, or Bannock who had to move for, submit to, and give way for them. The stories of the railroad etching itself across the continent and finally uniting in northern Utah almost never comes with a story about the disappearance of bison herds or of the dividing up of prairie land into convenient 160-acre sections, forming a checkerboard across the entire continent as a means of control of "savage" populations.[11] The silent absence of these stories is the effective domination of culture, one over the top of another. The history of one culture prevails and rewrites, overwrites, and silences the other. This practice will become increasingly unacceptable as Indigenous populations regain sovereignty and power. It will do increasing damage to Indigenous peoples who learn about the gospel message. This is an ineffective model for bringing mixed-race souls towards God. The attitude is one of aggression towards Indigeneity in general, and an extension of the fear-based "us versus them" culture that defines western American Mormonism. As a person in the middle of two worlds, I have a claim staked in the reexamination of this cultural practice. I would like to see the goodness of the gospel message spread, but I fear that this is an ineffective and damaging means of so doing.

A deep reading of the verses in Alma 17 might elicit a different reading, one that is less hostile to Indigenous culture. Alma the Younger and the Sons of Mosiah are traveling about, preparing themselves to enter into Lamanite territory. They spend their time praying and asking God to bless them to be "an instrument in the hands of God to bring, if it were possible, their brethren, the Lamanites, to the knowledge of the truth" (Alma 17:9). The specific "truth" that they are seeking, it seems, is that the old ways, the Native culture is "not correct."

And then, remarkably, God answers them.

God responds to their preparatory cry by first comforting and calming them. Rather than engaging their specific complaints, God goes on to tell these young missionaries to go in and be exemplary of the life of a disciple. He doesn't lay out a plan to point out perceived Indigenous idiocy or stupidity. He doesn't even acknowledge that part of the prayer they offered. Rather he simply instructs these young eager missionaries to be patient, simply requiring them to be good and kind examples of discipleship.

From an Indigenous perspective, from a Middle interpretation, this passage proclaims the love of God for Indigenous peoples. It points out the ways that we might carry our preconceived prejudices before our face, in the work of attempting to spread the gospel. To me, this passage is filled with hope for a God who doesn't singularly value the "white and delightsome,"[12] but also loves the varying shades of brown. It is the work, then, of the Middle populations of the church to see the ways that cultural and religious practices from both of our worlds function together to turn us towards heaven. I use the word work intentionally here.

This interpretation of scripture is not what I learned in Sunday school. What I was always taught was the colonial narrative that seeps through this story. I have had to struggle to come to terms with what I was hearing from teachers and from the pulpit with what I felt from reading this passage. There are many instances where I have struggled to do so—this was not an isolated incident. Functioning as Middle requires the mental exercise of reinterpretation, a reassignment of value, and a deep search for truth.

That type of work is, at its best, grueling. At its worst, it is destructive and pushes people out of the church. It is a thing that I struggle to balance on a nearly daily basis. Every time I burn sage or put on my garments, I wonder if I am doing harm or dishonor to the Other that resides inside of myself. But truth has come to me from both of these worlds: I cannot excuse my Mormon testimony with any more speed than I can dismiss the spirit that speaks Nakota. There is value and truth to be found in seeking to see that God knows both of the languages, and I think that there is value in asking the church to think critically about how it encourages me to find that God. This value compels the interpretation, presses me onward (ever onward) to reassessment, reassignment of value, and a deeper and ever-larger dig for the truth of a practical Gospel.

My Mormonism is a substantial and profound component of my identity. I was "born into the covenant" of my parents' temple sealing, and I was baptized into the church when I was eight years old. Certainly, I was unable to deal with, let alone comprehend the complexities of that decision when I made it. It felt, more than anything, like the only option. I didn't know that I could wait. I also didn't know that I didn't actually know "with every fiber of my being" if the church was true or not. Even still, I remained faithful to the covenants I made as a child and tried so hard to live what I was taught at church. I tried very hard to be a good Mormon girl. I graduated from early morning seminary and attended Brigham Young University, where church attendance and religious courses were not only a requirement, but also often a delight. I stayed close to the church through some very dark personal days, constantly trying to see the light of the gospel, constantly trying to vest my faith in the Mormon edict of "put[ting] my shoulder to the wheel" and the grandiose promise of "eternal perspective." I have gone on dozens of temple trips and campouts and I even know how to suspend the fruits and vegetables perfectly in my Jell-O. I participated in marathon group readings of the Book of Mormon and cried during more than one testimony meeting about how much I loved my BYU roommates. I understand how hard it is to find a dress that appropriately covers my temple garments but is also fashionable.

And deeper still, I claim a cultural and ancestral legacy in Mormonism. My ancestors left Denmark and England and Switzerland because they felt constrained by the good news of the gospel to do so. Those people unequivocally believed that they could do the work to build Zion far far away, in the West. I am a great-granddaughter of someone I was told was "the Last Living Son of a Utah Pioneer." I rode through the streets of Salt Lake City with my entire family on a parade float celebrating this fact in 1997 during Utah's sesquicentennial celebration. My people long before me answered a call to faith and practice in the Mormon way. They settled and they thrived in Utah. Unabashedly.

My Native American heritage is also a major source of my identity, one to which my heart is increasingly turning. Growing up, my Indigeneity was the sort of family lore that nobody could really give much substance to or prove to be truth. In my own psyche, my earliest years created a fantasy about what it meant to be "Indian" and how I could make meaning from that. It wasn't ever as easy as making meaning about being a Mormon, because it was mostly based on false stereotpyes about Indigeneity.

My maternal grandfather was born on the Fort Peck reservation in northeastern Montana around 1932. He left the reservation to join the US Navy as a teenager and met my grandma in Los Angeles, where she had gone in hope of becoming a film or television star. It was the 1950s, and the promises of Hollywood shone brightly for an Anglo-American Mormon girl from Utah. When she met my grandpa, they quickly became intertwined with one another, abandoning the fantasy of Los Angeles. Ultimately their decisions resulted in three daughters, the second of whom is my mother. For a variety of reasons, some of which I will likely never know, and definitely don't feel good publicly exposing, my "real" grandpa left our family before that last daughter, my sweet aunt, was born.[13]

Because of his absence, a hole was created in the narrative of my family's life. The only evidence of the substance that might have filled up this hole was only hinted at with my mom's deep gingerbread-brown skin and her and her two sisters' black hair and almond-shaped eyes. My grandma would later marry a German man with whom she had six additional children. They are tall, blonde- or red-haired, and blue-eyed. At family gatherings, sunscreen flies around wildly. There is a marked divide between the groups of cousins from my grandma's first daughters and her later children. We did not know our "real" grandfather, and always referred to him as "real grandpa" or by his name, Ernie. When we spoke about the man my grandma is still married to as "grandpa," it was always with a tinge of secret subtext for us. Within the "Indian" cousin group, we grew up fantasizing about and adding to the mythical nature of our Native grandfather. We knew some basic facts:

He was in the military, most likely the Navy.

He was Assiniboine, or maybe Dakota.

He was gone.

Until I was in high school.

Sometime around 2001, my mom used a pay-to-find search engine where you could enter in the social security number of anyone and find out their address, if they were alive. She entered his number into the search bar and was given the address of a nursing home for veterans in a town in Southern Texas. The home was less than five miles from where my grandmother and my "adopted" grandpa was serving a mission for the LDS Church. My mom and her eldest sister travelled to Texas as soon as they could make arrangements, certainly seeking answers to questions of their own identity. I cannot fathom the impact of this event on their lives. Finally, healing might come to these women, and to the rest of our family through them.

For me, this is a pivotal point in my own identifying narrative. I imagine that my cousins and siblings share the sentiment to some degree or another. The realness of my Indigeneity is marked from the moment in time when my mother found her dad, and also when I met him. Upon meeting him, I gained permission to dig into the side of myself that was always passed over. He looked like us. He looked like me. The experience of finally realizing a childhood fantasy, the surprising verity of an urban legend proving to be truth rather than simply myth, is monumental. For all of the time that we spent looking different and "Other" within our own family, we now had a verifiable claim to an actual person who gave validity to our story. I was shocked at the walnut-brown skin and almond shaped eyes, the nose whose outline echoes my own, the soft hairlessness of his arm and his chest. These were not character traits of the white grandfathers I was raised knowing.

The experience was a legitimizing force in my life. The timing of our introduction raised questions for me that have guided my studies and my academic work. I have spent my intellectual time asking questions about why it felt so good to have someone who looked like me. I haven't fully found answers yet, but I believe that this was my first step towards a decolonization of my own self and my own identity. These questions have unfurled and stretched themselves into my spiritual and faith practice as well, as I have sought out a feminine divine, and as I have struggled and fought to find a place for myself in the LDS Church and in LDS culture.

In graduate school, I met a mentor who was from my tribe—he knew some of our relatives. He invited my mom and my sister and me up to Montana to participate in the Sundance. The Sundance is the central religious ceremony for Native tribes in the northern Great Plains of America and southern Canada. Prayers and sacrifices are offered for family, community, and world during the four-day-long event. There is a great deal of preparation that goes into the sacred event. Special plants, objects and people are gathered as the community turns towards divinity in a spirit of renewal, sacrifice, and gratitude. The Sundance was illegal in the United States as recently as 1978. The invitation felt unendingly big. It felt like reclamation of a part of me that I didn't really know was missing. There were things that I experienced there that I have felt too tenderly and respectful about to heretofore speak or write of publicly. Some ritual practices in the actual ceremony of the Sundance find correspondence in LDS temple practice. My mother would add that many Assiniboine ceremonies have correspondence with LDS ceremony. The Sundance is the only one that I can speak to personally, but this correspondence feels profound to me. It feels like the seeds of truth are sewn in the overlap. I in no way want to diminish the sacred practices that I witnessed on that big open prairie, nor do I intend to diminish my experiences in my worship in LDS temples. Both are major sources of strength, truth, and peace for me. Neither practice need submit to the other, nor either experience be secondary.

I felt the same love as a child of divinity on that sweeping plain exposed directly to heaven that I have felt in any celestial room of any LDS temple. That experience taught me that God is abundant. I've drawn closer to an understanding of what is meant when Peter opens his mouth to testify that God is "no respecter of persons," because God and godliness are everywhere, and that the "us versus them" is actually enmity (Acts 10:34). More often than not, I felt like I was in a sacred place, witnessing a temple covenant. A few moments were more proximate to divinity for me there than I have ever felt when accidentally wearing the exact same white poly-ester dress as my neighbor in Mormon temples.

I am not done digging yet. I have tried to bring my family with me on the journey, which is a process that is making me more of a person, requiring me to more fully magnify my role as Middle. I'm still awkward; my edges are unrefined. I am still, and might always be learning to function in this role; my translation between these two sides might always be a bit jagged.

The process of functioning in such a position is heavy and hard. It requires me to ask questions and interpret received knowledge, especially received knowledge from the LDS Church. It is a position that is inherited from the history of settler colonialism. I have had to question stories and attitudes about what it means "to be a Lamanite," whether I even believed a book that would position my people in such a negative light, or a God who would command that it be written. I have had to reinterpret the way that God interacts with my people in sacred text and the way that they have been treated by dominant culture generally, and by Mormon culture specifically. As a means of survival, I have had to question what family is, and why it is so crucial to the doctrines of the church. I still have questions about how one side of my family seems to be portrayed as more important and worthy than the other. I am deeply wrestling with these questions. I foresee this wrestle as the struggle of my lifetime. Perhaps beyond.

Some have argued that settler colonies in America had to colonize American Indians as a means to reimagine their future on their own terms.[14] As a colonizing power, religion extends this reach into the mind and the spirit. In my own life, the colonizing power of Mormonism has required me to submit more wholly into the strictures of Mormon "righteousness" than it allows me to ask questions about what it means to me to exist as both Native and Mormon. My Indigeneity, and the spiritual life that sustained my grandmothers on the open Montana prairies for centuries, has always been problematically subject to the faith and truth claims of the Mormon Church. I often worry that the submission of the one is unsustainable, and is avoiding larger truths.

I have to consistently pretend that people don't mean to denigrate me when they talk negatively about "Lamanites," or when they unintentionally other my experiences. I have found myself often feeling compelled to prove that I deserve a place in Mormonism, often relying on my pioneer heritage, pushing my Indigenous roots to the back of people's attention so that I could stake a claim in the legacy of Mormon grandeur. One portion of my history is feted; the other is a secret. As I have come to reconcile my identity, settling with and reclaiming my Indigeneity, I have had to establish more firm boundaries with Mormonism at large—boundaries that challenge orthodoxy, but protect my sovereignty and the truth of who I am.

In functioning and performing as Middle, I have had to be selective about the things I believe in. I have had to do away with some teachings found in Mormonism; I am yet unwilling to wholly commit to Assiniboine spiritual practice either. I am put into a position of duality about which I feel a great responsibility to be very careful. Even when I feel my most hopeless about Mormonism and my doubts and questions seem insurmountable, even when I am almost certain that I no longer believe in the ideas that the LDS Church presents in a friendly smiley package, my Mormonism is ingrained. Some of my cells are made out of little pieces of blessed sacramental Wonder Bread and funeral potatoes. And even when I still feel like a complete outsider looking at and studying Assiniboine traditions and culture from the position of "white girl posing," even when I burn every last piece of frybread and stumble tremendously over glottal and nasal sounds in Nakota, I still have roots in the soil of northeastern Montana. A friend recently asked me where, if anywhere, I would call home. The only answer I could really firmly commit to was Montana. Even though I didn't grow up there, and have only been an infrequent visitor; even though I still feel like I have to prove that I have legitimacy when I go there, have to prove that I'm "Indian" enough, I feel as though my body or my spirit is settled there. The place keeps drawing me back.

In his masterful comparison of Western and Native American religions, *God is Red*, Vine Deloria Jr. posits the argument that Indigenous religion is place-based, and that Western religion is time-oriented.[15] In the West, we have a "Plan of Happiness," a first-we-do-this-and-then-we-do-that linear progression. In Indigenous culture and religion, we see all things as a container and reflector of God, and we are not disconnected from those things, nor even from our Creator. I am not completely convinced that I know which one of these is correct or even that Deloria's dichotomous argument is sound. I am compelled, however, to ask about the ways that these two views of self-seeing in relation to the world and to Creation inform and enhance one another. I love to try to see the ways that each view can create space and time for the other. Is this what I am called upon as a Middle to do? I cannot say that I know how to relate to God wholly, but at this moment, my faith is in a God who is much larger than the LDS Conference Center or Temple Square or even the "worldwide" LDS Church. Rather, the God that I want to rush towards speaks Nakota very slowly and carefully, and can stretch all the way across the open face of the Montana prairie. And that finally is starting to hint at what home feels like.

Seven

WHAT I LEARNED AT GIRLS CAMP

or Developing a Racial Identity Leads to Liberation

MICA MCGRIGGS

By the end of the first day of my first LDS Church girls camp, I realized that I was indeed a stereotype: Black folks don't camp. Pretending that you are homeless on the weekend is a white folk activity. It may not be true for all of us, but it proved to be true for me. Why in the name of all that is holy would one forgo sleeping in a perfectly good home or hotel to rough it with the wild things? No showers, no beds, hiking in the heat, nearly falling off a cliff, eating terrible food, crafting shrinky-dinks, and singing silly camp songs all while donning the bright floral print trousers my grandma had sewn me (because shorts were not allowed and I refused to wear jeans in the heat) was not my idea of a good time. Even as my pleasing personality was long gone (probably on its way back to the comfort of suburban Salt Lake City), jokes and "sassy attitude" alongside a unique ability to connect with adults (likely one of the benefits of being an only child) branded me a "keeper." Every single one of my incredibly thin (especially for having multiple children) blonde leaders loved me. Despite my abhorrent attitude about Smokey the Bear and all other things "outdoorsy," they wanted to keep me. My counterparts were either chastised or on the rare occasion sent home for such behavior, but not me: I had solidified my place in the community.

My intellect and quick wit paired with my brown skin and kinky curls served me well. My mom is white, and my dad is Black. In the suburban neighborhoods where I grew up, surrounded by white family members, friends, neighbors, classmates, and fellow church members, I was unique, and my milky-white community enjoyed unique. I was a deviation from the norm, a muse of sorts, preserved during my time of what scholars call low-level racial identity development.[1]

Development of racial or ethnic identity is described as a process of constructing the identity over time through experience and interaction. It includes gaining knowledge of in-groups as well as a sense of belonging to a racial or ethnic group.[2] A key feature of racial identity development is gaining knowledge. For me, I gained knowledge about my identity as Google searches led to combing through academic literature, to reading popular and scholarly books, and to attending events and trainings that addressed race. Looking into the term racism also led me to scholarly articles on critical race theory, privilege, white supremacy, multicultural competence, liberation theology, and racial identity development itself. I was blessed to have the time and resources to access the information. By the time I had arrived at graduate school, I knew that multicultural issues in psychology were what I wanted to study.

Through my racial identity development I have gained insight about my experiences and the language to articulate my feelings about those experiences. In the lower levels of racial identity development, the individual identifies more with the majority group. They do not see themselves as "the other" until some sort of contact either with their racial group or with the majority racial group occurs. This contact could be positive or negative. Sometimes the contact is a result of feelings of fictive kinship. Fictive kinship,[3] entails feelings of being connected or related to people who are not related through blood or marriage ties. For example, a young Black man being raised by a white family may not feel connected to the African-American community or to the Black experience until he recognizes a part of himself in Trayvon Martin or Michael Brown (both unarmed Black teenagers who were tragically killed). This young man sees their faces on the news and reads about their lives on the internet, and through fictive kinship he feels connected. Contact with their stories and his recognition of himself in them propels him into the process of developing a racial identity. This contact could be one event or experience or it could be a series of occurrences that move a person forward.

Another feature of psychosocial racial identity development is that it is very difficult for an individual to recognize where they currently reside in their development.[4] It is easier to look backwards or forwards. I am not one hundred percent sure where all my points of contact in my racial identity were. I can identify one of them. I had the opportunity in college to do a study abroad program in London, England. The university I attended in London was one of the most culturally diverse in all of the United Kingdom. I was a psychology major and a social work minor, so I signed up for classes in my designated fields of study. When I arrived at my community work class on the first day of the semester, I was shocked to see so many Black students. The class was composed mostly of brown and black faces. I would estimate that two-thirds of my classmates were Black and the rest were Middle Eastern. The professor was Pakistani, and the teaching assistant was a Black woman. Never in my life had I had a Black instructor. It took me traveling over five thousand miles to see myself reflected in my people. It was an incredible experience to be taught by and learn with others who looked like me. While I doubt this was the sole point of contact that propelled me into the process of racial identity development, it most certainly was one of the most impactful.

There are four major features of my experience as a biracial Mormon woman that I now (through my racial identity development) have the language to identify and critique: paradox, tokenizing, code-switching, and racial micro-aggression. All are expressions of white supremacy in Mormonism. My purpose in this essay is to detail how recognizing white supremacy at an individual level (through the themes highlighted) has led me to my liberation as a biracial Mormon woman. I see liberation as a higher level of racial identity development. Liberation is an actualization of sorts; again, because it is difficult to identify where one currently stands in his or her development, calling it liberation is the best descriptor I currently have. I see liberation as awareness, stability, and confidence as it relates to the self in a racial context.

PARADOX

Being biracial is a paradox in and of itself. Being born half-white and half-Black sets a strong foundation for seeing unique paradoxes in nearly every area of life. The ability to balance two worlds is imperative for survival when you are a person of mixed race. Not losing yourself in the process is the key to thriving. The welfare of the individual must be placed ahead of a philosophy or ideal.

From the age of around twelve or thirteen I had internalized a belief that I not only represented myself and family but my entire race. I can recall being a Beehive and having a conversation with one of my youth leaders about my desire to be the best I could so that every person I met would have a positive experience with a Black person. Today, tears well at the thought of my barely pubescent self carrying that much weight, confusion, and pain. To be twelve and feel the need to fix so much wrong that has been projected unknowingly upon the self, and to have internalized such violence at such a tender age, is heartbreaking to me now. I really believed it was up to me to change the hearts and minds of anyone with whom I came into contact.

My daily agenda went something like this: 8:00 a.m. school, 3:00 p.m. basketball practice, 5:00 p.m. homework, 7:00 p.m. church youth activity . . . and twenty-four hours a day, every day: heal the wounds of an entire nation, enable others to see past the "inadequacy" of my melanin, encourage their colorblindness, and reassure their Christian kindness. In my state of underdeveloped racial identity, I unequivocally believed that these tasks were my responsibility. Not only was I attempting to balance my racial identities, I was also attempting to balance the Mormon teaching referred to as "living in the world but not of the world." I loved my non-member friends, but I kept a cautious distance as to not get involved in some of the activities that were normal for them (swearing, R-rated films etc.) I also had to balance being an adolescent with being the spokesperson for an entire race. How does a child exist to be a child but also exist to be global representative? My existence was a paradox of epic proportions. It was depressing, anxiety-provoking, and hard.

TOKENIZATION

Why did I get away with winning the "ward's worst camper award?" Because I was a token. I was the token cute mixed girl, the token Black person in my ward, the token Black student, friend, and babysitter. As a token I was both scrutinized more closely than other youth and at the same time given leeway in some areas.

The reason I could push the limits was due to tokenization.[5] My anti-camping campaign delivered with "attitude" was met with amusement because it fit the acceptable narrative. A mini-Black woman being dramatic in reference to a reductive stereotype was amusing to my white youth leaders, whose exposure to Black people and culture was likely limited to me and media portrayal. In order to become a token, one must simultaneously entertain and amuse, through reifying myopic cultural clichés, while conforming enough not to threaten. I was a straight-A student who completed the LDS Church's Personal Progress goal-setting program for young women by the age of fourteen; at the same time, I had enough "sass" to keep everyone around me in stitches. I was the perfect token. Because I didn't have the maturity or language to express why this felt good and bad at the same time, I engaged in cognitive dissonance to ignore my feeling of unease. Enjoyment and resentment were being bred in my green mind.

CODE-SWITCHING

The paradox of being biracial impacts nearly every aspect of existential and daily life. My speech patterns are no exception. Linguists and sociologists describe this phenomenon as code-switching: alternating between two or more languages or language varieties during a single conversation.[6] Code-switching serves several purposes and occurs in a variety of situations; however, the type of code-switching that occurs in my life is called SAE to AAVE (Standard American English to African American Vernacular English).[7]

Because of my experience of growing up in a whitewashed world, I speak with a SAE or "white" dialect, but on occasion—depending on the crowd or content of conversation (usually when speaking with passion)—my dialect switches to a AAVE or "Black" sound. This is an unintentional switch: it is completely subconscious. Of course, I know once it is happening—I, too, can hear the sound of my voice change)—however, I don't plan or choose to engage in this switch or dialect consciously.

Here is an example of how code-switching worked in my LDS world: when I returned from that first year of girls camp, I had won my leaders and the other girls over. They laughed until they cried when I told stories over those four days at camp. That first Sunday home from camp, several people told my mom how funny I was. She of course took the compliment and agreed with their sentiment. I think I am funny; however, I'm not hysterical by any means. To my leaders, all of whom were white and mostly raised in homogenous areas, I was funny because of my code-switching. It was the sound of my voice that was cute and amusing. I was a novelty and the "act" of being myself was entertaining. Again, I fulfilled the cultural cliché.

Today, I still encounter people who are very entertained by my "humor," and while I take it as a compliment and am glad to know the sound of my voice made someone smile, I also see the problems. It was reductive, and when I first realized what about my stories were actually making people laugh, it made me angry. I was angry at my white leaders and counterparts for their ignorance and denial of privilege. Anger is feature of a mid-level stage of racial identity development. Today, I am not angry: I am disappointed, and even sad. But I am not the only person who code-switches and becomes a free source of entertainment. Many people of color code-switch, including Oprah, Will Smith, and Tyra Banks. While the process of deconstructing the fact that my natural speech pattern was being mocked, I took comfort in the prolific company I was keeping.

RACIAL MICRO-AGGRESSION

Racial micro-aggressions are "brief, everyday exchanges that send denigrating messages to certain individuals because of their group membership."[8] Micro-aggressions are covert assaults rather than overt; many are completely lacking malicious intent, and some are benevolent racism. One that I often heard growing up in LDS contexts was that I wasn't "really Black" because of how I often spoke or carried myself in public. This is a micro-aggression because the underlying message that is being conveyed is that if I am not fulfilling a negative stereotype then I couldn't possibly be Black. If I am "being good" or being seen as good, then I'm "being white." This was a troubling and confusing message to receive time and time again during my youth.

One Sunday each month, I reserved my evening for the local youth fireside. One fireside stands out in my mind as powerful example of micro-aggression. The theme of this fireside was modesty. The standard opening hymn and prayer were offered, as to adequately set up an environment where the Spirit could be invited. The first talk was given by a newly returned missionary who spoke about why he appreciated and preferred to date young women who dressed modestly. The second and final speaker of the night was the first counselor to the stake president. About halfway through his talk he said we should avoid extremes in hair style "like bright colors and braids." I was shocked he would give such counsel. I touched my head and felt my long strands sweeping across my back and shoulders: my hair had been styled in box braids for the past month. His insinuation that my braids were immodest annoyed me. When I looked around the chapel and saw several young women taking down their braided pigtails and French braids I was mortified. How could I win? It seemed impossible because my natural self was not, and seemingly would never, be enough.

Undoubtedly, the most difficult racial micro-aggression I have faced, and still face today, is the unspoken damage left in the wake of the priesthood and temple ban. The ban is a tangible product of white supremacy in the church. While it is no longer in practice, the impact is lasting. The language surrounding the ongoing speculation among members of why the ban was implemented in the first place boils down to a belief in the inferiority of Black people. Because this message is inextricably tied to the diminished worth of Black people, it becomes a part of our interactions at the most fundamental levels without us even realizing it.

From my earliest recollections I have felt an expectation for me to prove my worth. I must exemplify to white people that I can overcome the "lack of valiance" of my forebears and rise to a condition acceptable to white folk. Black people seek to rise, and white people watch and evaluate our performance. The expectation of accomplishing this lofty and counterintuitive goal is very low, but if accomplished, will be met with surprise and praise. I believe this is primarily a subconscious process for both groups of people; however, a shared experience is being co-created. The experience that is being created is one that reifies the current structure: a structure that lacks mutuality. While white members of the church have direct and rather seamless access to spiritual edification, people of color (particularly those of African descent) are left out on the margins faithfully just trying to get a crumb much like the Canaanite woman of old (Matt. 15:21–28; Mark 7:24–30).

It wasn't until college that I found the language to pair with the emotions and experiences I was having. Coming into contact with my truth set me on a path of development that has been both painful and beautiful. Finding through my identity development and research words with descriptions that perfectly embodied my experiences was liberation for me. Admitting that my spiritual home was and still is deeply flawed—in ways I believe are monumentally disappointing to the Savior—was painful, but necessary. Sweeping the mess under rug does not get rid of the mess, it only creates a tripping hazard. As I study more and more I continually liberate myself, and as I become increasingly liberated, I am able to help others liberate themselves. Once we as a church can face our truth, even our mess, we can move toward liberation at both the individual and systemic level.

Eight

EMPOWERING LATINO SAINTS TO TRANSCEND HISTORICAL RACIALISM

A Bishop's Tale

IGNACIO GARCIA

A friend of mine tells a story about a friend of his who cannot wait for the resurrection. At that moment, his friend expects to shed his Peruvian features—short, dark, and Indigenous—and rise up a tall, white, golden-haired, blue-eyed Saint. My friend, a patriarch, follows up the story with a chuckle and then tells of how many others of his short, dark fellow country-men conjure up similar but more private thoughts about being "white and delightsome."

While I never spend time worrying about my or my family's skin color, I know that it often plays a role in how some Latinos see themselves and more importantly, in how they relate to the larger white world. This is par-ticularly true among some Latino Latter-day Saints who, after all, were promised that one day they would be "white and delightsome," though we have replaced the term "white" with "pure" in my lifetime.[1]

The term "delightsome" is difficult to define and is usually translated as "delightful," meaning to please or to be charming. So Latino Mormons will one day be more pleasing and charming, characteristics that conjure up images of one doing things to please others, which in itself can imply either some form of superiority as in "being nice" to someone of a lower status or subservience in trying to please those whom you see as above you in one form or another. It is the latter that often creeps unconsciously into the thinking of some Latinos and other Saints of color. This happens particularly to those who focus on simply being loyal and obedient members of the institution, and even more so to those who are called as representatives of the church to their people.

In seeking to be true to their role in the kingdom, Latinos often adopt the attitudes, characteristics, and prescribed parameters of a conceptually white institution whose leaders have often (though not always consciously) rationalized racial, ethnic, and class differences among its members by buying into racial interpretations of scripture in its early years, and more recently by unquestioningly embracing capitalism. While promising the full blessings of heaven to all of God's children, LDS theology for most of its early years promoted—and in some instances still promotes today—a pecking order in which whites are the immediate recipients of the blessings of membership, while the rest of God's children were to wait either for a "blossoming," or in the case of people of African descent, until the next life at worse (or in the best of situations, after all others had received their blessings). By its nature, this theology which I call a "soft racialism" also asserts the premise that the advantages that white members have in this life will be maintained throughout eternity.[2] In terms of leadership, this "racial theology" saw God as choosing leaders based on their abilities to handle the work of the kingdom without regard to how differences in abilities are often created by racial and class prejudices both within and without the institution. To apologists at least, the redeeming value of this theology allowed for the eventuality that all of God's "other" children would someday become "delightsome" (and possibly white) if they obeyed the commandments and followed their white brothers who were supposed to be their "nursing fathers" (Isa. 49:23, 1 Nephi 21:23), but who ended up being their taskmasters instead. This theology provided and still provides white members with an advantage over Saints of color when it comes to church governance, to interpretation of doctrine, and to the perception of what awaits in the eternities.

This "theology of difference" creates gaps in the fellowship of Saints by treating some as more inherently blessed than others, and makes any attempt at equality in the church one based on "merit" and "worthiness." Such notions of worthiness often reflect a mixture of strict institutional loyalty and worldly success—as can be seen in the composition of some of the church's most influential bodies, whose members who are for the most part white, male, conservative, and tend to come from business, law, and educational administration. While Mormonism is fluid, and economic and worldly success has never been a prerequisite for service nor for "worthy" status, an institutional comfort with or tolerance of economic and racial differences does influence how poor Mormons and Saints of color are integrated into the fold and how they are perceived when it comes to leadership callings and theological interpretations of what makes a "good" member.

In my own leadership experience in the church I've rarely confronted strong racial prejudices, but I have encountered the effects of this legacy of racialism that keeps one group (whites) privileged over another (Latinos), causing the latter to assume an inherent unfitness—or a mindset of waiting for the appropriate time—to lead beyond prescribed religious bounds and to contribute to a theology of discipleship. This racialism has been the cause, in my view, of why Latino wards, and other wards of color, often struggle in their organizational function, and why Latino concerns over poverty, unemployment, social inequality, and inferior status in the church seem to draw such little theological interest from the higher echelons of the church, in spite of the numbers of Latino members and the promises of the Book of Mormon and early church founders about their eventual blossoming.[3]

Thus for me, changing that sense of unfitness or "not ready for primetime" mentality among Latino members is more urgent and in the long run more necessary than reminding my white brothers of their white privilege and their unrecognized perceptions of their superiority. This in no way means that we shouldn't sound the clarion call when we encounter prejudices or racism within the church, only that this is my way of confronting a form of religious subordination based on race and ethnicity from the bottom up. It is a way to stop waiting for our white brothers and sisters and our leaders to reject this racialism. The biggest challenge in engaging in this effort, however, has often been Latino members' own sense of inferiority in the church given that they've not known any other way of being a Mormon of color. The building of a white theology in the church occurred from the earliest days of the missionary effort. In this essay, however, I will not deal with the history of this secondary status, but rather will focus on a personal effort to change this legacy of racial theology within a Latino ward family.[4]

While not completely oblivious to it, it was not until I was called as a bishop in Tucson, Arizona, that I more fully understood the effects of this soft racialism among Latinos. I learned how ingrained this way of thinking was even among members who saw themselves as socially and intellectually equal to whites, and who often pushed back against prejudices on the outside. Yet they remained silent about prejudices within. For them the church was different from the world. It had the gospel of salvation, was led by a prophet, and offered many "promises to come" for them. While they often experienced bias and wondered why their wards struggled so much in being like "regular" wards, they rarely saw their second-class citizenship in the kingdom as responsible. When they even dared to articulate it, they mostly blamed individual white members or leaders rather than institutional structures. Their view was if only the local leaders did what the church asked them to do, things would be different.

When called, I replaced an incredible individual who had served as the bishop for nine years. He was tall, handsome, of fair complexion, and his persona spoke of success and worthiness in ways that I have rarely seen in my life. Vice-president of a large defense industry in town, he once confided to his two counselors (I was one) that sometimes in a day he had breakfast in Tucson, lunch in San Francisco, and dinner back home courtesy of a company plane. The working-class people in the ward loved him because he was deceptively funny and loved most of them, even though they were not the kind of people he usually hung out with having been picked from a distant stake to come preside over the Mexican ward. The middle-class members loved him because he was successful, he stood up for us with the white brothers, and he was a Latino Mormon that few whites could look down on.

Releasing him and putting me—a fellow still in graduate school, with too small a car for his family and cheap suits—proved shocking to some. I remember one sister confiding to my wife that her young daughter had asked her, "Why is someone with an old car and a horrible suit our bishop?" While I was well-liked and initially welcomed with open arms by most of the ward membership, my efforts to treat all ward members as equal citizens of the kingdom, and my willingness to lead from within rather than from the top was soon seen as very "un-Mormon" by several of the middle class families in the ward and a challenge to how they had been reared in the church.

I was a veteran of the Chicano civil rights movement, a PhD student in Chicano history, but most importantly a product of a barrio church in the west side of San Antonio that had mostly evolved on its own, while most of the members in this Tucson ward had either grown up in wards in Mexico or in white wards in the US.[5] Most had never experienced a "successful" barrio church in the United States, and while my predecessor had initially been part of a Latino ward in his youth, he attended English-language wards most of his adult life, and had fully integrated into traditional Mormonism and become politically conservative. His one great attribute, and the one that endeared him to the members with whom he shared little in terms of education, economic status, or outlook in life, was a strong strain of humility within a noticeably self-confident demeanor.

The Mexican ward I grew up in was poor and faced many challenges but it reflected a sense of certainty in who we were and was largely devoid of class divisions—we were all quite poor. We did not shy away from speaking of ourselves as Mexican, nor of the promises of the church to us that we all believed would be fulfilled in our lifetime. It was there that I learned that we were all children of God, and though the world made exceptions, He did not. We were in the United States because the hand of God had brought us here; it had nothing to do with immigration laws or nation-to-nation treaties. All of us could be worthy of serving the Lord regardless of our lineage, or whether we were of pioneer stock, and economic security was not a prerequisite to being called to serve God. He searched our hearts and not our pocketbooks. I also learned to serve young, as a Primary teacher at sixteen and young men's president at eighteen.

While much of my Mormon character was forged there, my understanding of my own people, including those in the church, began when I went off to college and learned about a scholar named Octavio Romano.[6] At the time (around 1974) Romano was an anthropologist at the University of Southern California. Like me he was an immigrant, his family having left Mexico when he was five; mine left when I was six. Orphaned one month after his arrival in the states, he grew up in an extended family of aunts, uncles, and grandparents, amid the harsh work of the agricultural fields and fish canneries of California. That experience forged both his character and his philosophy of life. To many of my generation of young Chicanos facing some deep questions about their identity and future, Octavio Romano was a godsend.

In a series of articles that became the foundation for Chicano or Mexican-American intellectual thought, Romano gave context and substance to the life of the Mexicano in this country. He did so by providing an interpretation of our life experiences that differed greatly from that which we got at school and which freed us from the guilt that came from being seen as poor, unassimilated, and voiceless. First, he posited that Mexicans had a history of their own—not an appendage to that of whites, but one forged by their own experiences, their sufferings, their triumphs, and their ability to survive the harsh domain of American society. This history, he argued, deserved more than the occasional paragraph in the huge history books that we read both in high school and college. It did not appear out of thin air when white America noticed, either because it needed laborers, or was deporting us, or was sending us to war, and it did not disappear when the need for us (or our bodies) did.

As a Mormon growing up in San Antonio, I sensed we Latino Saints "had history" because I read the Book of Mormon, and church leaders told us that was "our" history. As a devout Mormon, I, too, obsessed over the past, but Church history ignored my people, and the Book of Mormon seemed to condemn them except when prophesying of a future "blossoming" that even fifteen hundred years later seemed to be way off in the distant future. Thus, in reality, "our" Mormon history was imaging how we would have acted as pioneers and early founders, and given the self-deprecating humor among us, the images were not always uplifting.[7]

From Romano, my generation learned that Mexicans had resisted exploitation, racism, and political and economic marginalization, that Mexicans had not stood passively as things happened to them. Resistance to oppression and discrimination was an affirmation that there was courage in the barrio, and that it was not "troublemaking" to engage in protest and to fight for rights. Mexicans, he said, had been pushing back against misconceptions and outright racism for more than a century, but had rarely understood the foundation of the discrimination they faced. He taught that Mexicanos had an intellectual thought that came out of their experiences in Mexico and in the struggles of the fields, factories, canneries, and restaurants, and from the creation of internal communities in which they learned to live as people and not just as exploited minorities. Mexicans and Mexican-Americans had been writing, debating, and reforming for as long as they had been in this country. It was also not our fault that the stereotype of the Mexican as a lazy, mañana-oriented beast of burden had been created. Instead, white educators and politicians had doubly victimized

Mexican-Americans by blaming them for their condition and by making it solely their responsibility to overcome it.

He called social scientists "intellectual mercenaries of our age" who had institutionalized Mexican inferiority through "reports," "monographs," scholarly presentations, and classroom lectures, all of which offered the same fundamental message:

> Mexican-Americans [a]re simple-minded but lovable and colorful children, [with an] inferior . . . culture [who choose] poverty and isolation instead of assimilation into . . . a superior culture.[8]

There were times when the praise of visiting stake leaders to the wards I attended also sounded like a description of "lovable and colorful children" whose major attribute was the "spirit felt" and not the duties or functions performed in the church. Initially, I chose to interpret the praise in a positive manner, but its repetition everywhere I go has made it a bit hollow and stereotypic, a reflection of our "humble" status in the kingdom. (Admittedly, my interpretation often has much to do with the person who says it and with the spirit in which it is said.)

Romano accused social scientists of using a rhetoric that was not really science but a "crafted soliloquy" to explain away America's part in the oppression of the Mexican-American. He labeled the scholarship that sought to interpret history by blaming the victim for his/her victimization as "insidious rubbish." To interpret the historical process in this manner, he argued, "is to believe utterly that God, nature, society and rationality are all solidly on the side of success."[9]

Romano's writings put context to thoughts whirling in my head about the things I saw around me, including in church. I came to understand my people's circumstances better and to be less judgmental of them. While I rarely spent time blaming them for the conditions in which they lived, I had not been able to articulate an explanation that did not, at times, include a criticism of "not trying hard enough" and in the church of "lacking faith and succumbing to sin." For a time in the ward of my youth, I had even resented new converts because they threatened the stability of the church with their "worldly" ideas and "unrefined" ways, and because few seemed ever ready to pay the price of discipleship. But I have since learned that most of us long-time members are usually not ready either, at least not until we are converted to a gospel that transcends traditional institutional practices of focusing on obeying leaders, paying one's financial obligations to the church, accepting callings, and avoiding controversy.[10]

Through Romano I came to understand that most people in difficult straits—including those inactive in the church—usually confront structural challenges in their lives that they do not understand nor have control over. People in these circumstances can't simply be inspired out of their dilemmas: they have to be empowered to overcome those limiting structures, taught to validate their personal and collective history, and assisted in developing strategies to live lives that make a difference to them and to others. Some called it cultural or ethnic pride, but to me as a Mormon, it was more about recognizing self-worth and our eternal genealogy. It was also about affirming our place in society, or in the case of Latino Mormons, about affirming our place in the church. Whether we were ready or not, we had to assume an equal role in the kingdom and affirm it by contributing to the religious and spiritual lives of the whole.

I remember telling the stake president shortly after I was called that I did not see the Sonora Ward as a minor league team that prepared the members to move into "regular" wards—which is the way most stake leaders differentiated our ward from the others. If we accepted our role as minor spiritual players in the church, we could only expect to be treated as such, always being nurtured and protected and unbothered by the difficult demands of the gospel. My desire, instead, was to strengthen and develop a strong Spanish-language ward that met its obligations, understood its role in the church, and could serve as a beacon of faith to the barrios of Tucson. I naively thought that that was what most people in the ward wanted, but I soon realized that what some of the middle-class members wanted instead was a "regular" ward that happened to be comprised of mostly Mexican and Mexican-American members. They had been weaned in a Latino church culture constructed to fit into a traditional white Mormon umbrella that made allowances for God's other children if they conformed, assimilated, and acquiesced to white leadership and culture.

Whether they admitted it or even whether they liked it or not, these members had accepted the notion that we were to be led by our white brothers until some later day—which seemed never to come—when we would become whiter over time (or at least become the more palatable "delightsome"), and we would know that the promises of the Lamanite were fulfilled when our white brothers and sisters told us so. We really had little control over our organizational vision. Inspiration about the particular circumstances of our members was to be maintained within the parameters of the manuals and the *Handbook of Instruction* that were written for "regular" (white) wards.

I understood that deviating from this approach to church life presented a dilemma for some of the members. For poor immigrant members, the stability of the white-run church was welcomed after having come from countries where order, organization, and stability were often lacking. Most had never governed themselves in life or in church, and while white leadership was at times distant and cold, it was reassuring, because to them that was the way things would be in heaven.[11] To middle-class members who had learned to accommodate and find a niche in American society, there was no other way of worshiping, despite their misgivings on how they were seen or treated. In the church they had learned to become "as one" with the white members, even if they saw that not all things were equal. Having their own wards in which to prove that they could be good members gave them a chance to live the fulness of the institutional gospel in their own space while retaining a sense that they were part of the whole.

I did not fully understand these qualms initially, so I set out with optimism and passion to convince the ward members that we had to make changes in the way they perceived themselves and in the way the ward functioned. I knew, however, that to gain the space to implement those changes, the ward members had to learn to do the math, engage the bureaucracy, and get the numbers up. I had seen this over and over: the Latino bishops who took care of business operated at arm's length from the stake, and those who didn't found stake leaders on them like a tight noose. When I sat down with the stake president, I had to show him high numbers, reports done, positions filled, and significant attendance at stake training meetings so that I could keep him—and his counselors and high councilmen—in his office and not in my sacrament meetings every other Sunday.

The ward my predecessor left me was not a bad place to worship. The members were friendly, people could feel a good spirit during the services, and we had a few good teachers and dedicated leaders. The ward was less than ten years old and members were grateful to be worshiping in their own space, and particularly grateful for a bishop who, through strength of character, had kept the stake leaders at bay. Yet after nine years of existence we had hit a wall in our institutional progress and we were losing members, could not keep our auxiliaries staffed, our scouting program functioning, get members to attend stake activities or training meetings, and we were not baptizing people—a rarity for a Latino ward to which members come in droves, even though they often leave at the same rate. We had become complacent in our mediocrity, and some rationalized it with the all-too-typical Mormon reaction of "well, I'm doing my part," or with the terrible and self-deprecating rationale of "what do you expect from Mexicans?"

At the time of my calling I was writing my dissertation on "Chicanismo," the underlying philosophical tenets of the Chicano Movement.[12] Influenced greatly by Romano's writings, I argued in it that Mexican-American leaders and activists, as well as their supporters, had gone through a four-stage process in their fight against second-class citizenship. Since I saw most Latino Latter-day Saints as having a somewhat similar status within the kingdom, I thought it would be useful if our ward leaders, and then eventually our members, rid themselves of their own conception of being children of a God that favored his Ephraimite white children more.

The four-stage process pointed out that Chicano activists had "rejected the liberal agenda," or what was then in the early 1960s a status quo, that argued that "hard work and civic duty"—not demands, protests, or marches—earned Latino people the fruits of American democracy. The activists had engaged in a reinterpretation of history rather than just finding a place for themselves in the American narrative, had affirmed their race and class by accepting their differences and embracing those social and cultural elements that had allowed them to survive in American society, and had finally developed their own political (social/cultural) agenda.

In my mind this was a process that Latino Saints had to experience—with some slight variations—in order to better locate themselves within Mormonism. It was the way to de-institutionalize (or decolonize) ourselves from practices that had yielded low numbers, few leaders, and a complete lack of influence in the larger church.[13] I did not want to politicize the process, having already learned that politics in church rarely leads to unity or to the desired effect, but I did want the members of the ward to see themselves in a new light and to be empowered to act on their own behalf.[14]

The first step was to have them see themselves as their own agents and not just as followers who had little to say about their spiritual lives. I wanted them to reject the much repeated "wisdom" among both some whites and Latino Saints that we were incapable of governing ourselves, that many of the problems we confronted were self-inflicted, and I wanted to strip away the notion that some of us were more active because we were more faithful than others.

To this end, we began emphasizing to the members of the ward that though poor, they sought to meet their financial obligations to the church as best they could, travelled long distances to be there on Sundays, and sacrificed the little time they had because of multiple jobs and extended familial obligations to perform their duties. Years later, it became clear to me that poor and working-class members pay a heavier price for their membership because their offerings are often the "widow's mite," and their willingness to teach, serve, or administer in the church requires greater effort than from those who have greater resources and more ample education and experience. Callings and service often also bring a cost in the perception of their self-worth. While many gladly serve and revel in the success of their wards, rarely do they expect, except in generic ways, to receive recognition for their efforts. It cannot escape them that they are not seen as exceptional, as likely to lead, and their struggles are usually chalked up to character or spiritual flaws, rather than to any systemic problem. Poor people and people of color are not exceptional unless their story is one of having little, giving it all up for the church, and then resigning themselves to waiting for the second coming. Their lives become mere anecdotes for some speaker to prove a point about "sacrifice." As a former Chicano activist and the by-product of a poor but beloved Mexican ward, I see things differently, and I wanted them to know that they, and not necessarily leaders, were most responsible for the success of the ward.

We extolled their faith but explained to them that those who were not with us were just as capable of being good Saints and we needed to bring them back into the fold. They weren't as much unfaithful as they were people who had not fully tasted the fruits of the gospel. We also emphasized that our particular challenges as Mexican Saints sometimes required a different approach to fulfilling the mission of the church to bring all unto Christ. We did not criticize the approach of our white leaders, but simply interpreted our actions within our understanding of the doctrine rather than through traditional experiences. And we stressed the members' abilities to be faithful followers as well as good leaders while interpreting (rejecting) the failures of the past as simply times in which training and resources had been lacking. We were not naïve to think that all the members were willing to make the difficult decisions to "come unto Christ"—though we hoped they would—but we allowed them and not us to make that choice.

The second step was to help the members see their development as Saints. It was okay to tie ourselves to the pioneers and to other Mormon historical players as most other church members did, but it was just as important to remember those in our past who had kept the faith and were responsible for some of the traditions we had. Having no written Latino Mormon history at the time meant that we took the events in our lives and put them in the realm of history. Because a large number of the members came from the same region of Mexico, and some of their former branch leaders had followed them here, we created a historical link of faith by inviting these former leaders to be part of the change—some via callings and others as advisors.[15]

I got our ward to participate with other Latino wards and branches around the state in several youth Lamanite conferences at which we had cultural and sporting events, religious training, and a workshop about our history as Mexicans in this country. We were still hampered by a lack of sources for Latino Mormon history, but did the best we could by teaching the youth secular Latino history and explaining how often those challenges and successes were also ours. Most of the youth were bright enough to remember the times when "the world" had entered their religious space, and when they, too, had been victims of discrimination and prejudices, but we taught them that these challenges were simply a process by which they were "refined" to fulfill the promises given them by prophets and in scripture. In essence, we were writing our history in much the same way that scripture did, which is to assume that things had happened, or were happening, rather than that they would happen in the future.[16]

Bringing hundreds of young people together to play, learn, and worship created an incredible energy among the participants. They saw what a well-led Latino Mormon world could be like, and learned that their culture and their talents, put forth in a positive way, could provide them with the tools they needed to succeed in both the world and the church. In our well-executed "Lamanite" religious world, the participants and the volunteers were seeing what the church as whole could be like when we were seen as equals, too. Our stake president, who presided over our Sunday devotional, was astounded when he heard more than three hundred voices sing the missionary preparation song "Called to Serve" (in Spanish) and nearly one hundred youth bear their testimonies. Even my predecessor, who had taken only a slight interest in the conference, was amazed by the powerful message these young brown Saints were sending about the role they wanted in the church.

The last part of the process was having the members design their approach to their callings and to develop goals for the ward. At the start of my bishopric we set up a retreat for all the ward leaders, including my predecessor, as well as those members who were natural leaders and those whom I saw as the next wave of leaders in the future. We talked about the needs of the ward, divided into working groups, and prayerfully came up with goals and the processes to accomplish them. Whether the leaders realized it or not, we were developing a "theology of action" meant to empower us to resolve those problems unique to us. While they were couched in the language of the traditional church, these goals were nonetheless challenging some of the premises of that tradition. Once we agreed on them, I presented them to the membership in a Sacrament meeting for their approval. In my view, it was necessary that the members have a say in the affairs of the ward. To this end I also submitted the ward budget to them at the start of each year for discussion and a vote. I wanted our members and leaders to think about the particular challenges of a Mexican ward. This was new to members who had been taught to see problems in the church as culturally neutral and ahistorical, thus making all the ward problems "matters of faith."

Since I saw many of the problems our members faced as systemic, it was not enough to simply teach them to have a good attitude and a little more faith. We had to change the way things were done, and the first change was to remove the top-down approach that seem always to be the norm in wards of color where the leadership is small and leaders are often picked because they have the strength of character to get their members to obey. Our ward councils were opened to wide-ranging discussions—though by using an agenda we kept the dialogue moving—and we made decisions by majority vote. We hoped but did not expect or demand consensus in all decisions because we understood that doing so might pressure some leaders not to express their feelings for fear of destroying unanimity or of being seen as outliers.

We engaged in lots of leadership training and then let the leaders run their meetings and organizations without looking over their shoulders, and unless it was something that violated church policy or completely undermined what we in the bishopric sought to do, we let them make the decision of whether to change course or not when we disagreed. We also never chastised or critiqued the collective membership from the pulpit. We reasoned, we instructed, and sometimes we pushed back on some things, but we never reproved them publicly.[17] We wanted the members to feel like spiritual adults, not as charges of the church, and we did not want to undermine our auxiliary and quorum leaders' own efforts to lead their organization's members.

Within the first year we turned the disasters we called "home and visiting teaching" into a success story—at least in terms of people being visited—by going from somewhere in the low 20s to 90-plus percent. Our reports came in on time and the auxiliary and quorum secretaries, instead of a white ward clerk, did them right; and our attendance at stake meetings was the highest of any of the wards.[18] Our youth church activity nights, campouts, combined activities, firesides, and sports programs ran so well that the stake president later shared with me that he refused a request by five families in the stake to have their children be part of our youth program.

The ward members had so much talent and enthusiasm that they jumped at getting involved, and so our biggest contribution as a bishopric was simply identifying the right person(s), providing some guidance, training, and resources, and then getting out of the way. The more leeway we gave them, the more they took it upon themselves to be self-sufficient in performing their work. I was rather shocked when we hosted the second youth Lamanite conference and found out that we had more than three hundred kids coming, and all had to be housed in members' homes and fed three meals a day for about four days. But when I arrived at the reception site, I found that our conference coordinator Sister Gonzalez and her staff had set up tables with names, information on housing, meal assignments, workshop schedules, and sporting event times and that everyone got situated as soon as they got off their buses. After being processed, they were sent out to the church baseball fields for numerous games and activities to introduce them to youth from other stakes. The conference committee also set up a wonderful fireside that got the youth involved in making and burying their "weapons" in a large hole to commit themselves to a more peaceful approach to life (Alma 24).

I expected all the members to appreciate what we were accomplishing with our resources and our ideas, and most did, but I also found that some of the middle-class members were, for the most part, unmoved by our accomplishments and bothered by the things we were involved in. They were conspicuous by their absence during the conferences because their youth might "miss out" on their scouting. They were willing to trade spiritual lessons, identity-building, recreational programs, lessons on higher education, and association with Latino youth from across the state and Mexico so their children could collect merit badges. To me at least, that reflected their inability to see themselves beyond caricatured members who could do nothing beyond what they saw their white brothers and sisters do. It also reflected a class bias because they were unwilling to open their homes and kitchens, provide transportation, or concern themselves with the spiritual lives of the mostly working-class youth—who by the way turned out to be some of the nicest and most disciplined youth I ever met in the church.

(The irony was that no previous leader was as committed to scouting as I was. As soon as I became bishop, we changed mutual nights from one in which the bishop had interviews to one when all of the bishopric put on their scout uniforms and assisted with the program. I had been a scoutmaster for several years and had always gone to scout camp, and as bishop I spent one week each summer in summer camp.)

The more I did, however, the more alienated the middle-class families became. The scoutmaster—a dear friend before I was called—became alienated from me even as my support for his troop grew. My "sin" was that I did not force all the youth to be in scouting. I had a number of immigrant families who had converted or moved to our ward with youth past the early scouting age. They did not like and did not want to be part of scouting. Some saw it as childish—given the behavior of most youthful scouts—while others disliked the hyper-patriotism reflected in the uniform and ceremonies, which to some meant that they were to strip themselves of their Mexican citizenship, something they were not ready to do just yet. My predecessor had struggled with what to do with them and one of his counselors had taken to chaining the gym doors to prevent them from playing ball or hanging around the church. After I became bishop, we stopped that practice—a huge mistake in some people's eyes.

We developed activities so those boys could participate in mutual even though they were not scouts. That was our second mistake. Then we developed a successful athletic and cultural arts program that added to their distrust because it took boys away from scouting. But what could I do? I had fine young men who were not scouts, including a couple of the boys from these families. Not having been able to get them into scouting frustrated some of the parents who thought that without scouting their boys would not go on missions, marry in the temple, or serve in leadership positions. I understood the significance of scouting to the church's youth program, but I did not see it as panacea for all the troubled the youth of our ward, nor did I think that participation in the program necessarily guaranteed the afore-mentioned desired outcomes. In fact, many boys from my non-scouting group went on missions and more of them came to serve as branch presidents and bishops than did those in scouting. It had nothing to do with participating in scouting or not, it was simply that they were good young men and we gave them a chance to develop spiritually, socially, and culturally.

The most harmful effect of these families who kept their children apart was that their children became alienated from their peers, and distant from me. When the other boys were playing ball, the dance group was practicing, or we were fine tuning our plays, those youth would watch from a distance with an expression of someone looking at some foreign or exotic people. They refused to speak Spanish—even those who knew how—and no matter how much we tried, we could not get them to participate. Even my spending a week with some of them in summer camp or other monthly campouts did little to bring them closer to me or to the other youth.

As much as I supported scouting I did not think of it as the only option especially for young men of immigrant background who had no familial history in it or who saw themselves as too old to be wearing uniforms and tying knots. I also understood that an obsession with scouting tended to marginalize young women in the ward because all the attention went to the young men. I tried to change that by providing equal funding for the young women's program, attending all their activities, and celebrating their achievements as much as we did the boys'. The women of the ward were important in the process of change because women have always been the key to success in most Mexican and Mexican-Americans wards through their service, loyalty, and often through their leadership, whether unrecognized or appreciated.

We thus gave the women's programs the largest budgets and the Relief Society president became the most important person in the ward council.

I met with her regularly and we talked on the phone often not only about the women's issues, but about the needs of the whole ward. And I turned to other women in the ward for advice and feedback. My wife, always much more beloved than I, went out into the peripheries of the congregation to find those who needed to be embraced by the ward family. She also served as the person that members could talk to when they felt unsure about talking to me. I have found it strange that in Mormonism the wives and husbands of leaders are expected to blend into the woodwork and simply "take care" of the family. In my case, Alex is fundamental to any success I have in church leadership because she is an excellent organizer and a natural leader.

I was not a great feminist and at the time some of my feminist credentials were suspect, but I had grown up among strong working-class women who were the strength in the churches I attended.[19] My own leadership style had been greatly influenced by the women of my youth and though I had once dreamed of being a "fire and brimstone" Mormon bishop. I turned out to be rather gentle, more willing to negotiate, motivate, and be "loving," which I later found was another thing that some of the middle-class members disliked about me. They complained to the stake president who then advised me to simply "seek respect" and stay away from that "love and one-in-purpose" stuff. I chalked that up to the priesthood correlation program, which has often prized efficiency and order more than siblinghood.

By the third year things began to change as our approach to the ward function became the norm and some of the resisting families either came over to our side or simply stopped fighting. A number of them began to see the positive changes when two of our youth were singled out for church-wide exposure. One of our young women was chosen for a cover story in the New Era in which she spoke of her Latino heritage and her "wonderful ward," while one of our young men gave the youth address in the last televised church-wide commemoration of the Aaronic Priesthood broadcast. He spoke of the need of Saints to learn the gospel in their own language. Ironically, he came from one of the families that was often critical of me. He never liked scouting, but he participated in all of our activities, and he currently serves as bishop of one of the Spanish-speaking units that split from that ward.

The middle-class members who eventually became supportive did so because throughout the process, we never condemned, criticized, or sought to marginalize their roles in the ward. Why would we, since they, too, were victims of the racial theology that they had come to embrace? One redeeming value I had as a church leader was that I never really felt "worthy" and thus could not get myself to look down on those who criticized or opposed me, so I kept trying to embrace them by making them part of our efforts. When their boys earned their Eagle Scout award or their girls earned their Young Womanhood medallion, I made sure that we had a wonderful ceremony. When they chose to play sports—I was usually the coach—I made sure that the experience was enjoyable and successful. I praised them publicly for their commitment and pointed out their long history of service. When we had our tenth anniversary commemoration of the founding of the ward, I made sure their efforts were recognized and that my predecessor—still a hero to many of them, and now a counselor in the stake presidency—was the principal speaker.[20]

Many of the ward members soon shed the sense of inferiority that had often been just beneath the surface. They were more willing to serve and offer up ideas and strategies than simply wait to receive instruction as in the past. They took to attending stake activities and participated with ideas and even assumed leadership within stake auxiliaries. The jokes about Mexican "deficiencies" and white exceptionalism ceased for the most part. The more secure they felt in their brown skins, in their history of faith, and in their ability to contribute, the more they felt "at one" with their white brothers and sisters. More importantly, they began to be treated as such by the other members in the stake, and in the process, the cultural notions that "unprivileged" them were challenged, which in the long run was also good for our white members.[21]

I remember that at the conclusion of the sacrament meeting during which I was released (I had received my first academic appointment in Texas) my old friend, the scoutmaster, came to me in tears, almost shaking, and wrapped his arms around me and repeated several times, "I'm sorry, I'm sorry." For a moment we cried together as we hugged again as brothers in the faith. Others of the distant group came to me—maybe they were relieved that I was leaving—and expressed through their embrace that they were now again my friends. Even a former counselor's wife who had been a critic and forced her husband to resign his calling and move to a white ward eventually came to embrace us and acknowledge the good that was done.

While fond memories of my time as bishop are the things I most remember, I occasionally still wonder why some of my friends were resistant to change. Had they been more receptive, we would have quickly moved toward the more important goal of bringing people unto Christ and not spent so much time trying to establish a different and more empowering paradigm for our Mexican ward. Today I see more Latino bishops engaging in a rejection of the status quo, in historical reinterpretation, and even in formulating a new approach to ministering to their congregations, yet they often lack the training and the philosophical—or better said, theological— foundation to fully detach them from the traditional racialism through which they interpret their Mormonism.

Their approach is often a Latino Mormonism that has ample space and a higher ceiling, but is still constrained by history—were we really cursed with dark skin?—and by discussions of the celestial pecking order—will whites still be our leaders? Is God white? Will we become white? Eventually those questions and the problems they create will be resolved, but for now, too many Saints of color will continue to see themselves lesser children of a loving God. Many Latino wards and branches as well as other wards of color will remain dependent on white leaders for direction, and their leaders will continue to see one of their major obligations as helping their members "fight the curse."

To many Latinos, the church remains *ajena*—not theirs—and their failures continue to be seen as mostly a lack of discipline and faith. Octavio Rivera, the first Latino bishop in Utah and possibly one of the first in the US church, pointed out the problem of the church's shift from converting and training American Latinos to mostly baptizing immigrant Latinos. This has created an undocumented immigrant church whose leadership must not only deal with the inherent institutional challenges in their units, but also with navigating the turbulent legal waters in which their members now swim.[22] For a time, and even somewhat today, this shift has induced non-immigrant Latinos and other Saints of color to move to white wards, causing deficiencies in trained leadership and often meaning the recycling of the same leaders. I believe this is changing and I've noticed a slow reverse migration in recent years, but for some Latinos, white wards remain an attractive alternative because they are "regular," the programs are "run better," and because within them they feel a part of the "whole" in the kingdom.

The current disinterest among church leaders in publicly challenging the institution's past racialist theology (beyond the essay on its website) does not allow many Saints of color to discard the self-doubts about their ability to fully integrate or to lead in the church. This affects not only rank and file Saints of color, but also those called to the church's hierarchy who feel the need to so steep themselves in the institutional culture that they leave no room for a ministry that stretches the institutional one. Though they might worry about what is happening to Saints of color, they have no paradigm to change the conversation nor to offer alternative approaches. They will continue to strive to be "regular" church authorities, concerned with the needs of the "whole" church, but still worried that their brothers and sisters are not up to the demands of the kingdom—while waiting for the time when all of God's children are seen as the same, and when they will be able to sit in council with more leaders of color and fewer white leaders to remind them of their people's perceived inabilities. Some believe that then (and only then) they will be able to speak to the needs of their fellow Saints of color.

Latino members and leaders need to discard the mythology of white member exceptionalism and of the colored Saints' "expected" dependency, and see themselves as spiritual equals in the work of saving souls. This will, however, not be accomplished by alienating people of color from the main-stream of the church, particularly from the ward family, but rather through grassroot efforts of empowerment using the resources, callings, and pro-grams within the ward structure, and adding those other things that are necessary to fulfill the mission of the church in their congregations.[23] Like Eugene England, I also believe the church can be as true as the gospel itself, but only if it provides us the space in which we can work out our fellow-ship, develop our discipleship, and assume leadership; and it can be so only if Saints of color discard the theological burdens of the past.[24] Empowered people rarely feel unequal or inferior.

As a church concerned with historical precedent and profoundly tied to a prophetic vision, it is important for both our Latino and white leaders to officially and energetically debunk our past racial theology and its vestiges today, and develop one that demonstrates not only that we are committed to a gospel for all, but that we have faith in all of God's children's ability to lead in the ministry. This is not likely to happen, however, until Latinos and other Saints of color engage in discussing, theorizing, and questioning the circumstances in which they find themselves, as well as the conditions, deci-sions, and theological foundations that led them there. They must develop their religious scholarship, intellectual work, life experience literature, and the sermons necessary to push back against the racial assumptions that undergird much of Mormon historicity.

At the moment none of this exists, as there are few Latino scholars or other scholar-Saints of color who are being read or even published, and the world of Latino Mormon bloggers, essayists, and religious writers is near-nonexistent. Interpretations of the Latino Latter-day Saint experience by white LDS intellectuals and critiques by Latino anti-Mormons are not enough, nor should they be for creating a Latino Mormon voice. Paraphrasing what one Mexican-American intellectual said in the 1960s, "only the mexicano (Latinos, Saints of color) can speak for the Mexicano (Saint)."[25] This does not mean that Latino scholarship and intellectual work cannot be part of a larger critique of Mormonism's racialism, but only that Latinos first have to construct and solidify their own space or they will be drowned out—as often happens to minority voices when they are part of a larger "cry."

Despite its potential for a historical and theological disruption of Mormonism as we know it, a paradigm shift away from the old racialist theology to one that truly sees all of God's children as equals in the kingdom is essential—not only for people of color, but for the whole of the church.[26] This change should not be left to a "natural evolution" in which theological equality is eventually assumed, which has often been the way that previous Mormon leaders have "resolved" the messy issues of our church past.[27] A new theology that embraces inherent and historical worthiness of all of God's children will make this not a white church, nor a Latin American church, nor anybody's church but that of Jesus Christ. Then all who come unto Christ will find that they can "fulfill the measure of their creation" in whatever ward of Zion they choose to attend.

III

POWER, DIFFERENCE, AND NATION IN THE GLOBALIZING LDS CHURCH

Mormonism has been defined by the ambition and reach of its global missionary efforts that have created sizable, multigenerational Mormon communities across the Americas and the Pacific. Committed LDS Church members persist in Asia, Europe, and Africa as well. But in each of these places, Mormonism has been adopted and adapted into national and local contexts shaped by ancient indigenous and modern national cultures, human migrations, economic crosscurrents, political exigencies, and wars. It has sometimes benefitted from the mainstream LDS Church's twentieth-century alignment with international flows of American capital, and it has sometimes been claimed by those whose historical fortunes have suffered under colonialism and neocolonial globalization. The four essays included in this section examine various interpretations of Mormonism in global contexts among colonizers and colonized, and the more and less oppressive ways Mormon communities have worked across differences to strive for something approaching Zion.

Nine

MORMONISM AS COLONIALISM, MORMONISM AS ANTI-COLONIALISM, MORMONISM AS MINOR TRANSNATIONALISM

Historical and Contemporary Perspectives

JOANNA BROOKS

I am a scholar of American religion, race, and colonialism and an Anglo-American-identified member of the LDS Church. My ancestry includes English, Scots-Irish, Irish, Basque, and Native American ancestors; I was raised in middle-class and upper-middle class Southern California suburbs with robust Mormon communities. I grew up identifying primarily with my maternal grandmother's multigenerational Mormon England-to-Utah-and-Idaho ancestral pioneer history and my Basque grandfather's deep roots in the city of Los Angeles; my life was also shaped by my father's deeply working-class Los Angeles "Okie" family history replete with hard-drinking Johnny Cash–like uncles, mixed-race grandmothers, and Cherokee connections I was never taught to claim but that have asserted themselves in my life in many quiet ways. In Mormonism, all of my parents and grandparents found a respite from the confusions of history's dislocations, displacements, and losses. I write now as an intersectional Mormon feminist who traces her essential political and spiritual values—justice, mercy, kindness, work; a hunger for belonging and shared enterprise—to her upbringing in the faith. For all of these reasons, it is important to me to understand how Mormonism has interacted with and been shaped by the larger historical forces of colonization and colonialism—a historical imbrication and site of responsibility that

Mormon Studies has done little so far to claim and understand. It is impossible to live my values as a Mormon and a scholar without turning a critical eye on my own religious heritage and on my own location in, responsibility for, privileges derived from and losses sustained due to colonialism.

From its beginning, the Mormon movement has claimed a distinctive relationship to Indigenous peoples in the Americas and the Pacific grounded in the faith's chartering book of scripture, the Book of Mormon. First published in 1830, the Book of Mormon is a narrative of ancient Israelites who migrated to the Americas and there divided into two rival civilizations—Nephites and Lamanites—each working out its own relationship to God. Native Americans, according to traditional Mormon teaching, are the descendants of rebellious Lamanites who were cursed with dark skin for their early disobedience to God's will, but who as members of the House of Israel are destined for restoration to glory. As early as the 1850s, Mormon leaders also connected the Indigenous peoples of the Pacific to the Book of Mormon narrative, citing four verses in the book of Alma (Alma 63:5–8) describing a Lamanite named Hagoth who departed the Americas by boat for points unknown to become ancestor of Polynesian peoples. In 1863, Brigham Young wrote to King Kamehameha V of Hawaii:

> [The Book of Mormon] teaches us that the aborigines of this continent are of Israel[,] descendants of that Joseph who was sold into Egypt and that their ancestors were a highly enlightened people, blessed of God, and enjoying His favor; but that, subsequently through transgressing His laws and sinning against the great light and knowledge which they possessed, His anger was kindled against them and He punished them with a heavy punishment. Nevertheless, He had promised their fathers, by a covenant that they should be held in remembrance by Him and that in His favor and blessings, when they should become a mighty people in the land of their fathers. We have not a doubt in our minds but that your Majesty and the people of your Majesty's Nation . . . are a branch of this same great family. You are of the House of Israel, and heirs of all the promises made to the chosen seed: the Book of Mormon . . . is your book; for the promises and covenants of the Almighty which it contains, are applicable to your Majesty's Nation as to the nations of this continent.[1]

The idea that American Indians and others of the world's peoples were descended from the house of Israel predates Mormonism by centuries and can be found in seventeenth-century writings by such Jewish rabbis as Manoel Dias Soeiro (Menasseh ben Israel, 1604–1657) and by Protestant clerics as well. But Mormonism is unique in that one of its canonized books of scripture centers around Indigenous peoples in the Americas. Consequently, Euro-American Mormons have regarded themselves as bearing a responsibility to "restore" through the Book of Mormon the connection between Indigenous peoples' ancient legacy and their sacred destiny. This is not the same salvific role assumed by European and Euro-American Christian missionaries who envisioned salvation as a conversion from Indigeneity to whiteness. American and Pacific Indigeneity have a potentially sacred place within Mormonism. Even in the more orthodox sectors of Mormon life there is a special place reserved for some expressions of Indigenous identity.

Mormonism's scriptural teachings about the Indigenous peoples of the Americas and the Pacific propelled Mormon missionary activity and substantial conversion rates in many Indigenous communities and contributed to the globalization of the faith. Discovery of DNA evidence that disproves any genetic connection between Middle Eastern peoples and Indigenous peoples has not dismantled the value of Indigeneity in Mormon culture. It did lead the church to modulate its claims about Lamanites being ancestors to contemporary Indigenous peoples in prefatory materials to newer editions of the Book of Mormon.[2] But many Mormons—Indigenous and not—still view Indigeneity as having religious significance. To what purposes has this discourse been put? Exploitation? Emancipation? The answer depends on how one tells the Mormon story, or, more precisely, on which Mormon story one tells.

Told one way, the story of Mormonism is the story of a white minority that despite its own ambivalent position in American society has pragmatically cooperated in the Euro-American colonization of Indigenous peoples, inflecting their participation in colonial projects with a distinctive Mormon sensibility and using them whenever possible to meet their own theocratic purposes. Mormons have by no means exonerated themselves from the larger history of religious racism in the United States. Verses in the Book of Mormon connect the dark skin of Indigenous peoples to a curse from God, drawing from the broader Christian tradition of ascribing the phenotypical difference of African-descended peoples to the curse of Cain or Ham. The scripture 2 Nephi 5:21 describes how the Lamanites, the faction of ancient peoples who chose not to obey God's instructions, became dark-skinned: "[God] had caused the cursing to come upon them, yea, even a sore cursing, because of their iniquity. For behold, they had hardened their hearts against him, and they had become like unto a flint; wherefore, as they were white, and exceedingly fair and delightsome, that they might not be enticing unto my people the Lord God did cause a skin of blackness to come upon them." 2 Nephi 30:6 promises that if Lamanites change their ways "they shall be a white and a delightsome people." Beginning as early as 1830, Mormon missionaries brought to the Sac and Fox, Delaware, Wyandot, Cattaraugus, and Shawnee nations a double message: first, that they were peoples of a sacred legacy and destiny that they could come to understand through the Book of Mormon; and second, that the disobedience of their ancestors was the source of their Indigeneity. Nineteenth-century LDS church presidents, including Brigham Young, John Taylor, and Wilford Woodruff used the language of the Book of Mormon to publicly characterize Indigenous peoples of North America and the Pacific as "dark and loathsome" people who could through conversion be made "white and delightsome."[3] Nineteenth-century Mormon missionary discourse was no less racist than mainline Protestantism, the distinctive storyline of the Book of Mormon notwithstanding.

Anglo-American Mormons were also unexceptional in their participation in United States-backed colonial and neo-colonial projects. They did so whenever it suited the pragmatic interests of the Mormon people, sometimes muting their own justly developed criticisms of the United States in order to gain resources and protection from mainstream society and the federal government. Throughout the 1830s and 1840s, Mormon settlements in the Midwest were the target of mob violence; their requests for assistance and protection from the federal government went largely unanswered. Still, when Army officers appeared at a Mormon refugee settlement at Council Bluffs, Iowa in 1846, to request that a detachment of Mormon men serve in the Mexican-American War, LDS church leaders obliged, dispatching the five hundred member "Mormon Battalion" on a two-thousand-mile march through Kansas, New Mexico, Arizona, and California to support US interests. They did so in order to secure additional resources for Mormon migration and to demonstrate their loyalty to the US government. Mormon mass migration to Utah territory in 1847 to 1855 blended in almost seamlessly with the larger US-backed "Manifest Destiny" settlement of western North America. Mormons' establishment of what historian Leonard Arrington called a "Great Basin Kingdom" in Utah was distinctive in its theocratic character and its emphases on collective economic development and its rejection of outright genocide against Indigenous peoples. Still, pragmatic decision-making ruled Mormon colonization of the west. As Hawaiian Mormon scholar Hokulani Aikau writes:

> Through the religious principle of gathering Saints to Zion and the religious mythology that Native Americans were a lost tribe of Israel, LDS leaders and their followers rationalized their inter-actions with Indians even as they dispossessed and exploited them . . . Although the intent of the gathering principle was not colonial, as it was rationalized by religious doctrine and a desire for the freedom to practice their beliefs without fear of reprisal, as more Latter-day Saints set out for Zion, the pressure to make more and more land available for white Mormon settlement neces-sitated the removal of Native peoples from their territories. In con-trast to the rapture-filled descriptions of Zion documented in [his-tories] of Mormon migration to Utah are the stories of violence and dispossession enacted by these same Mormon settlers and federal Indian agents against local tribes. Through dispossession and exploitation, Mormonism, like Zionism, became in practice a colonialist project.[4]

Ultimately, Mormon colonization of the west did not differ substantially from US-backed colonialism in its material impacts on Native people: namely, disease, population loss, displacement, and loss of territory.[5]

Even as it blended into larger patterns of "Manifest Destiny," the Mor-mon migration to Utah territory and establishment of the "Great Basin Kingdom" fostered an image of Mormons in the American national con-sciousness as a special class of colonial "others." Theocratic territorial gov-ernment and open resistance to federal oversight and occupation by federal troops marked Mormons as a dangerous, ungovernable population. Images in nineteenth-century American popular media focused especially on the practice of polygamy, which became the object of a national eradication crusade that portrayed Mormons as white savages in need of civilization. The practice of polygamy also drew orientalist anthropologists such as Sir Richard Burton from their explorations of Asia and the Middle East to visit Mormon Utah, where Burton wrote his ethnographic *City of the Saints* in 1862. The 1879 US Supreme Court *Reynolds vs. United States* decision which held that polygamy was not protected as an expression of religious freedom and could be criminalized was argued on the explicitly colonialist grounds that polygamy represented a "barbaric" and "odious" practice which the United States as an agent of civilization had a moral warrant to prohibit. Legal reasoning in the *Reynolds* case drew comparisons between the British Raj's prohibition of the Hindu practice of sati in colonized India and the United States' prosecution of polygamy in Utah territory. In fact, the *Reynolds* decision was later used as a precedent in cases defining the scope of American imperial power.[6] For their part, Mormons in Utah Territory maintained a distinctive quasi-nationalist identity and resistance to US-backed military, legal, and political efforts to recolonize them until the 1890s, when church resources were exhausted. Public Mormon disavowal of polygamy, admission to statehood, and early twentieth-century assimilation within national culture reflected pragmatic choices by Mormon leaders; at the grass roots, however, many Mormons continued (and continue) to maintain a distinctive sense of identity differentiated from if not oppositional to mainstream American culture.[7]

Their distinctive sense of identity again did not prevent Anglo-Mormons from utilizing US-backed colonial and neo-colonial networks to advance Mormon missionary efforts beyond the western US. Addison Pratt, who had worked the Pacific as a sailor before joining the Mormon movement, returned to French Polynesia as a missionary in 1843. Nine Mormon missionaries arrived in Hawaii in 1851 and New Zealand in 1854, seeking in both places first to convert white settler populations but eventually turning their attention to the islands' Indigenous peoples. Early Anglo-Mormon missionaries to the Pacific followed pathways and networks established first by merchant sailors and American Protestant missionary societies, carving out a distinctive Mormon groove within European and Euro-American circuits of economic and religious colonization.[8] Sometimes LDS church leaders pragmatically found opportunities to exploit conflicts between rival missionary societies and colonial governments to establish a niche position as an independent minority faith. They also sought to differentiate themselves from the US government or from competing Protestant sects by leveraging distinctive Mormon teachings about the scriptural history and sacred destiny of Indigenous peoples—including Pacific Islanders—to appeal to Indigenous leaders' desires to maintain their peoples' sovereignty and well-being. Writing to King Kamehameha V in 1863, Brigham Young voiced Book of Mormon–backed support for the survival and self-determination of the Hawaiian people and emphasized that Anglo-Mormons had no desire to conjoin religious missionary work with political subjugation:

> We believe there is nothing to prevent your Majesty's people working out a glorious destiny for themselves, if they will avail themselves of the opportunities which are presented to them. They are capable; and Heaven will help them if they will only exert the powers with which the Great Creator has endowed them and seek to help themselves. It will be a pleasure to my friends, in their comparatively limited sphere, to cooperate with your Majesty in advancing the well-being and development of your people. Their aim will be to gather the people at a suitable place or places, and inculcate in them good morals and how they can best be elevated from their present low condition to a state of enlightenment that will make them suitable associates for the most refined. They will take special pains to impress upon them the absolute necessity there exists for them to observe such laws as will stop their decrease and enable them to perpetuate their race. There is no reason why they should perish and their lands become the property of the stranger. The same God watches over and cares for all His children, and, if they will be fully obedient to His laws, His preserving care will be equally extended unto them all. My friends will endeavor to open schools for their benefit, teach them trades and the arts of industry by which they may learn to know and appreciate the value of the favored country which providence has assigned them as a habitation. . . . In planting this mission in your Majesty's Kingdom, we have no political purpose to subserve. My friends will seek for no power of this kind. In selecting representatives for Parliament from the District or Districts where they and the people who may gather with them will settle, they will endeavor to learn your Majesty's choice, and elect such person or persons as your Majesty may

designate, to represent them. It will be their constant effort, in their intercourse with the people, to sustain the power of the throne and to recognize and uphold your Majesty's Kingly authority to the fullest possible extent. I trust that my friends will be obedient to your Majesty's wishes in all these things.[9]

In exchange for access that would allow Mormonism to win converts to build their own Mormon "kingdom," Young promised Kamehameha that Mormons would not seek to govern his Hawaiian kingdom. This pragmatic political disposition contributed to Mormon missionary efforts in the Pacific, as did the Mormon teaching that Indigenous identity was vestigially sacred and not in need of eradication, as was taught by their Protestant rivals. Mormon doctrine emphasizing spiritual connectedness between the living and the dead, expressed through the practice of genealogy and vicarious temple baptisms for the dead, also attracted Hawaiian and other Pacific peoples. In 1913, Mormon missionaries estimated that 22 percent of Hawaiians were members of the LDS Church, as were 10 percent of Maoris and 5 percent of Samoans in the early twentieth century.[10] The growth and stability of Anglo and Indigenous Mormon settlements in the Pacific in turn secured for ranking Anglo-Mormons positions of influence at the local-global interface of plantation industries, including sugar. Pragmatic opportunism in the service of theocracy characterized Anglo-Mormon participation in the colonization of the Pacific.

As did other colonizing Christian religions, Anglo-Mormons also endeavored to establish Western-style educational enterprises among Indigenous converts. But whereas mainline Christian traditions viewed Western education as necessary to the eradication of non-Christian cultures and beliefs, LDS colonial schools were motivated by a distinctively pragmatic and theocratic agenda to develop the Church's global base of operations and prepare local Indigenous leadership to function within its American-style bureaucracy. Mormon-backed schools were established in many mission areas starting in the early twentieth century. Under the leadership of President David O. McKay, the LDS Church developed a system of private elementary and secondary schools and colleges in Tonga (1953), Hawaii (1955), New Zealand (1958), Mexico City (1964), Fiji, Samoa, and Kiribati. In the United States, at the decline of the American Indian boarding school era, the LDS Church launched its own "Indian Student Placement Program" in

1954, assigning Native American Mormon children ages eight to eighteen to live with Anglo-Mormon families in non-reservation towns to attend school and church and experience what one program brochure described as "educational, spiritual, social, and cultural advantages"—the same colonial rhetoric used by government-backed boarding schools in the US and Canada to remove children from their tribal and family contexts at deep costs to the well-being and continuity of Native peoples and communities.[11] Participation in the Indian Student Placement Program peaked at five thousand participants in 1972, coinciding with a moment in American history when an unprecedented and unjustifiable number of Native children were being taken from their families and communities by government agencies and placed with non-Native families. Though framed differently than mainstream US governmental and private fostering and education, placement for many participants caused the same damages to individual well-being, family cohesion, and the continuity of tribal culture and language. It is estimated that thirty to forty thousand Native American youth participated before the termination of the program in 2000.[12] Many former participants harbor deep hurt, anger, and sorrow over the costs of participation in placement.

In the mid-twentieth century, the rising economic and educational status of Anglo-Mormons in the United States positioned LDS people in positions of access and influence that they used to extend the church's global reach. Just as Mormon missionaries in the nineteenth century had utilized their positions within colonial networks of seafarers and merchants to establish initial proselytizing efforts in North America, Mexico, and the Pacific, Mormons in the twentieth century used positions in neo-colonial US-backed government and economic enterprises to establish LDS church infrastructure in Latin America, Asia, and Africa. As Mormon anthropologist David Knowlton writes, "The church's elective affinity with formal economic enterprises and the expansion of regimes of business and governmental management . . . is part of its location within the broader American postwar expansion into the world."[13] When church leaders staged their entrée into formerly colonized countries in Africa, they relied upon advice from former officers of the British empire: for example, church leaders consulted with Sir Alfred Savage, former governor general of Nigeria, when developing a strategy for establishing the church in that country in the 1960s, seemingly unaware of the negative impression such associations would harbor for the citizens of the newly decolonized state.[14]

Anglo-Mormons who received missionary training in foreign languages utilized their knowledge in the service of business and governmental careers, leading to what Knowlton calls Anglo-Mormon "overrepresen-
tation" in neo-colonial corporate and governmental endeavors; given the
Mormon tradition of lay leadership—there is no paid LDS clergy on the
local level—they often pivoted on their footings as global businessmen to
work after hours in the service of church affairs.[15] Church leaders also used
these connections to organize business entities that could bring more LDS
lay leaders into African countries, and Mormons who worked for US-based
multinationals played key roles as liaisons in international church affairs.[16]
For example, Merrill Bateman, a BYU business professor who later headed
the Mars Candy Company and then served as a high-ranking church official and president of Brigham Young University, used consulting trips to
West African cacao plantations for US-based multinational candy manufacturing companies to help establish LDS church operations in Ghana.[17]
Church leaders appear to have been totally innocent to the idea that their
reliance on and positioning within these neo-colonial economic networks
would define the church's trajectories of growth and tinge its global image
with associations unfriendly to working-class people in the Global South.

Historical Mormon racism and the close imbrication of international
Mormonism with economic neocolonialism and neoliberal globalization
led locals to see the church as an imperialist enterprise and engendered
strong anti-colonial pushback. During the 1960s, the nation of Nigeria
shut down the church's missionary program after Nigerian students in the
United States came into contact with the church's racist priesthood segregation policies and asked them to withhold visas.[18] Mormonism's reputation for political conservatism in the United States, church leaders' public
expressions of support for right-wing and fascist politicians in the Global
South, and Mormons' participation in US-based efforts to intervene in and
reform Latin American economies and governments contributed as well to
Bolivian leaders' threats in 1970 to ban the LDS Church from that country.[19]
Oversupplies of Anglo-LDS missionaries, large-scale LDS church building
campaigns, and double-digit LDS church growth rates in South America
in the 1970s and 1980s compounded perceptions of an association between
the LDS Church and US imperialism. Consequently, Mormon missionaries
and church buildings became the targets of radical leftist groups. In Chile,
between 1983 and 1992, radical leftist groups bombed 278 Mormon church

buildings, set fire to an additional eleven buildings, and committed eighty-nine acts of vandalism. In Bolivia, members of the Zarate Willka Armed Forces of Liberation—an Aymara-led Maoist group fighting the expropriation of Indian land—bombed five LDS chapels between 1980 and 1990; threatened Bolivian mayors if they did not close LDS chapels in their cities; and killed two Mormon missionaries, Jeffrey Bell and Todd Wilson, on May 24, 1989, after which they issued the following statement: "The violation of our national sovereignty cannot remain unpunished. The Yankee invaders who come to massacre our peasant brothers are warned the same as their internal lackeys. The poor have no other path than to rise up in arms."[20] In August 1990 and March 1991, Maoist rebels of the Sendero Luminoso movement in Peru staged nineteen attacks on LDS chapels and killed three Native Peruvian Mormon missionaries—Manuel Antonio Hidalgo, Andreani Ugarte, and Oscar Zapata.[21]

Told this way—as a story of a US-based religious movement that tactically carved its own strategic niche within neocolonial and neoliberal political and economic networks, established schools to groom local leadership capable of assimilating to American middle-class and bureaucratic norms—the story of Mormonism seems to be the story of another strand of Protestant colonialism, albeit one with a distinctive regard for Indigenous North and South American and Indigenous cultures. It appears, in Hokulani Aikau's words, as an "unconventional colonialism," but colonialism nonetheless.

But it is possible to tell the story another way—several other ways, in fact, reflective of the many varieties of Mormonism lived and cultivated by Indigenous and global South Mormons themselves. These are stories that find scriptural footings not in verses of the Book of Mormon that depict the ancestors of American and Pacific indigenes as the benighted descendants of a fallen civilization, but in Book of Mormon storylines that center around the destiny of Indigenous peoples. Using the Book of Mormon, Indigenous and Latin American converts have forged Mormon identities parallel to but differentiated from those of Anglo- and Euro-American Mormons, whose identities have been grounded in histories of persecution, migration, and western settlement. As for the racist elements of the Book of Mormon, for every verse that refers to Lamanites as "cursed," there is another that asserts that "all are alike unto God"—"black and white, bond and free, male and female," as says 2 Nephi 26:33, among several others that indict economic exploitation, inequality, and class and racial division, as does the entire book of 4 Nephi. These scriptural texts predicated another way of living the Mormon story, one articulated by people of color in colonial contexts who have claimed Mormonism as their own, despite the tradition's historic racism and implication in neocolonialism and neoliberalism. Just as Anglo-Mormons have used their advantageous position within business and government to advance the work of "building the kingdom," Indigenous peoples have used their position within the "kingdom" to advance their own communities' needs for resources, access, power, continuity, and well-being. As Hokulani Aikau writes of indigenous Hawaiian Mormons, "Devotees themselves have the power to transform religion."[22] Throughout the Americas and the Pacific, they did so by fully claiming an identity as Book of Mormon-descended "Lamanites" and moving themselves, as anthropologist Thomas Murphy notes, from being the proselytized objects of a Mormon story to a "central position as the subjects."[23]

Early Hawaiian/Kanaka Maoli converts to Mormonism utilized their position as "chosen people" to secure for themselves a renewed tenure on traditional lands at a time when colonial policies of allotment known as the Mahele were causing Indigenous dispossession. LDS church leaders took advantage of a government-backed land privatization scheme by purchasing six thousand acres on Oahu at La'ie. Anglo leaders envisioned the land as a gathering place for Book of Mormon peoples of the Pacific; Indigenous Hawaiians recognized La'ie as a historic pu'uhonua—a site of refuge. Mormon teachings about the importance of genealogy, the transgenerational quality of salvation, and the spiritual responsibility of the living for the dead aligned with Hawaiian traditions that connected land tenure to lineage. "The integration of Polynesians into the broader cosmology of the church allow[ed] Hawaiian members to trace their genealogical line back through the Book of Mormon, and in these tracings new connections to the land begin to emerge alongside older ones," writes Hokulani Aikau. These practices of genealogy aligned in the constitution of the Mormon Hawaiian community at La'ie.[24] Kanaka Maoli "were motivated to settle in La'ie," Aikau continues, "because of the opportunity it afforded them to maintain customary food practices within an ahupua'a [traditional land tenure] system at a time when access to land became increasingly difficult."[25] They established traditional Hawaiian water gardens along streams and cultivated taro and even awa [kava] on land legally owned by the Church of Jesus

Christ of Latter-day Saints but held by the church collectively for the benefit of its people. Gathering as a community of Hawaiian Mormons allowed Indigenous peoples to sustain traditional economic, cultural, and language practices as well as a sense of collectively held identity at a time when both Indigenous collectivity and identity were under devastating pressure from the colonial state.[26]

Early Mormon converts in Mexico also found in Book of Mormon teachings a resource for fostering anti-imperialist collectivity. Among the first converts in Mexico was Plotino Rhodakanaty, leader of a circle of socialist anarchists in Mexico City. Attracted by the Book of Mormon's utopian visions of an egalitarian, anti-racist society and by early Mormon practices of communal economic living known as the "United Order," beginning in 1875, Rhodakanaty led a group of twenty self-declared Mexico City Mormons, who wrote to Salt Lake City in 1878 requesting missionaries. He was baptized in 1879, but soon grew frustrated with the US-based bureaucracies' refusal to support the organization of Mormon "United Order" communities in Mexico.[27]

Another significant figure in the early Mexican Mormon church was Margarito Bautista, who converted to Mormonism in 1901 after being healed by missionaries and soon moved to Utah, where he helped found a Spanish-language congregation. Inspired by the Mexican Revolution, in 1935 he wrote and published, with financing from fellow Mormons, *La Evolución de México: Sus Verdaderos Progenitores y su Origen, El Destino de América y Europa*. Dedicated to the heroes of the revolution, Bautista's book used Book of Mormon-informed historical narratives to position Mexican people as the descendants of an elect ancient civilization that had fallen but was destined for world leadership. Bautista claimed pan-tribal, transnational solidarity between Indigenous Mexicans and other Indigenous peoples of the Americas and Pacific, again referencing Book of Mormon-informed views of Indigeneity. European colonization was only a consequence of the apostasy or falling away of Lamanite peoples from their heritage status, Bautista claimed. Citing Book of Mormon scripture, he criticized exploitation of Mexico's agricultural and laboring poor, voiced support for agrarian reform, denounced the mercantilization of Mexican agriculture and exploitation by foreign investors and speculators. He also compared Mexican revolutionary leader Benito Juárez to Book of Mormon hero King Mosiah. Inspired both by the anticolonialism of the Mexican Revolution and by the honoring of

Indigeneity in the Book of Mormon, on April 26, 1936, Bautista convened a gathering of Mexico City Mormons to petition for installation of local Indigenous Mexican church leadership—*de raza y sangre* (of race and blood)—rather than United States-based Anglos.[28] After a strong backlash from the Salt Lake City-based hierarchy, Bautista and seven other convention leaders were excommunicated. Some Mexican Mormons estranged from the North American church over the question of Indigenous leadership successfully organized their own parallel Mormon congregations and published a magazine titled *El Sendero Lamanito* (The Lamanite Path). Bautista led another group of Mexican Mormons to found a utopian community practicing Mormon economic communitarianism and polygamy in Ozumba, Mexico, the remnants of which still exist today.[29]

If some early Mexican Mormons found support in the Book of Mormon for socialist utopia, many twentieth-century Indigenous Mormons have found in the church pathways to education and forms of social mobility they believe are necessary to survival and well-being in the globalized world. These include the Native American parents who sent their children on the Indian Student Placement Program in the hopes that it might give them opportunities beyond underfunded and dilapidated reservation schools or abusive and impoverished conditions at home.[30] These also include labor missionaries from Tonga and Samoa who travelled to work on church construction projects in New Zealand and Hawaii hoping to acquire construction skills that could give them an advantage in negotiating the economic crosscurrents of the globalizing world. As economic forces pushed Indigenous peoples out beyond their homelands and into diaspora, LDS church institutions and activity offered both access to some forms of opportunity and nodes where traditional culture and language could be retained, transmitted, and even regenerated. Pasifika students who enrolled at the Church College of Hawaii (later Brigham Young University—Hawaii) could finance a college education by demonstrating Indigenous culture at the Polynesian Cultural Center. Although its use of Pasifika students and employees often prioritized the financial benefit of the Church over that of the workers themselves, the PCC became for some Pasifika people a space where they could make lateral contacts with other Polynesians, learn cultural practices from elders, and foster cultural continuity.[31] The church's establishment of so-called "ethnic wards," congregations designated for Tongan, Samoan, Native American, Latinx, or African-American members living in the United States, Australia, and other sites of diasporic settlement, offered a refuge from white racism in LDS congregations and another node where Indigenous language use and cultural practices (notably, funereal practices) could be sustained.[32]

Although "ethnic wards" have been the site of perpetual struggle between assimilationist and separatist impulses among church leadership and membership—leading, for example, to the church-wide disbanding of ethnic congregations in 1972 and their reinstatement in 1977, they have continued to function as potential spaces for the formation of distinctive non-Anglo ethnic Mormon identities. With supportive local Mormon leadership, ethnic wards have served as sites for the indigenization of Mormonism, or for developing programs that advance self-determination. Wards in Tuba City, Arizona, on the Navajo reservation, for example, have sponsored programs to support members in developing home vegetable gardens that integrate traditional Navajo farming techniques with a traditional Mormon emphasis on home gardening and preparedness. While community gardening has a tribal and political history in Tuba City that precedes the LDS Church, and while the program does hearken back to historic agricultural "development" programs motivated by colonialist interests, for local members, the ability to leverage the resources and authority of a major religious institution in support of grassroots community food production is a valuable help to self-determination and well-being.[33]

Around the world today, for some of its Indigenous members, Mormonism offers a way to access educational and economic opportunities while still affirming and valuing Indigeneity in a religious setting that offers distinctive scriptural and historical contexts for doing so. Demographic studies of Mormonism in Latin America suggest that the LDS Church has the strongest hold, not among the rural Indigenous poor, but in urban and suburban areas populated by economically displaced, middle-class-aspiring Indigenous people.[34] Retention across the global South has also been strongest among the emergent middle and professional classes.[35] For some Indigenous and Global South Mormons, the historic alignment of LDS church bureaucracy with multinational capital creates individual pathways into employment and church leadership.[36]

For other Indigenous Mormons, mobility and access to education fosters a consciousness and a vocabulary to critique power dynamics within the LDS Church that align the institution with neocolonialism and foster racial, class, and gender inequality among its members. As did early converts in Mexico, these contemporary Indigenous Mormons are drawing upon Book of Mormon scriptures and the faith's minor histories of movement building, millenarianism, and economic communitarianism to voice critiques of contemporary Mormonism. Moana Uluave grew up in a working-class Tongan Mormon community in Salt Lake City and is now a Gates Millennium Scholar at Harvard University. She writes about the cultural refuge the LDS Church in the United States has provided for Pasifika peoples, as well as the racism Pasifika peoples have encountered within the Church:

> The Tongan Church is not a church; it's a community center in the diaspora. And it saved me. In the shadow of the temple, I see all the dark faces that taught me faith. In many ways, my chapel walls were sites of cultural preservation away from the assimilating world. A place where my grandparents could be teachers, my father could be bishop, and my mother could be Relief Society president in their own tongue. Where they were revered for their faith and talent. Where we practiced consecration through home deliveries of frozen fish, community babysitting and tutoring, and sharing of information. Where we wouldn't have to deal with people telling us to dance for them on command or sing those songs or control our children. This is not to say that the Tongan Church has not been affected by cultural policies that have regarded cultural Tongan practices as uncivilized and targeted them for civilizing into the Mormon (US white) "gospel" culture. But for all the damage that could have been done, we've at least had our space demarcated for over twenty years in the Salt Lake Valley. We've been allowed our bounded autonomy. Our worship is complex. Our people are complex. My view, too, hasn't always reflected that complexity. I can hear myself speak it. Stories of how silly my people are for their blonde wigs, gold teeth, leopard prints pressed against woven mats tied tightly around rotund waists belting out hymns in bush tones. Stories of Cain's curse, tokenism, deficit-based thinking, oppression, and colonialism. Our lives are informed by the stories we've been given, created, and continue to tell. My story as a Tongan American working class Mormon woman is the place where I sleep, work, and worship.[37]

Gina Colvin, a Maori Mormon writer and scholar, has used her globally read internet column *KiwiMormon* as a venue for voicing criticism of colonialist church policies—past and present. In one recent column, she writes:

> Colonial politics are not inspired—they are oppressive. Revisioning colonial politics and recasting them as having a divine origin are not just oppressive—they are malicious, and the negative effects are incalculable. . . . From the casserole making door-to-door service orientation of the English, to the soaring Maori karanga which privileges a deep connection between the living and dead, to the generosity offered at the table of Samoans. . . . Church leaders might be better off understanding these processes and expressions, and allowing [members] to adhere to gospel principles rather than disciplining when they don't see recognizable behaviours that agree with their own cultural norms. Mormonism has constituted its own kind of cultural tyranny, and we would all be better off in our pursuit of the "holy highway" if that were to end.

Colvin also uses her situation as a member of the global church who lives in a progressive social democracy at what she calls the geographic "antipodes" of the church's Salt Lake City headquarters to criticize how the privileging of white United States perspectives distorts the theology and practice of Mormonism worldwide, including its political and bureaucratic priorities.[38]

These thinkers put Indigenous Mormons at the center of their Mormon stories. They reflect thoughtfully on what Mormonism has meant to Indigenous peoples and document the range of motivations that have led them to claim the faith as their own. For some, it has meant a powerful attraction to distinctive dimensions of Mormon theology and practice, among them its historical and now residual emphasis on communalism, its theological emphasis on the significance of ancestors, and its Book of Mormon-based acknowledgment of the "special" histories and destinies of Indigenous peoples. It has for some offered an opportunity to relieve heavy tribal or ethnic obligations to land and community subjected to extreme stress by colonization. It has meant access to resources, including social and economic mobility. It means a portal through church schools and colleges and missionary service to education, international contact, mobility, employment: in short, a distinctive and alternative port of access to the resources of the contemporary globalized world. It has also meant the opportunity to persist and preserve Indigenous language and cultural practices in global diasporic Mormon ethnic congregations even as economic forces press Indigenous peoples out from their homelands. What Mormonism has meant to Indigenous peoples is itself an evolving story, one that reflects how the attractions of Mormonism's early communitarianism and millennialism have given way to emphasis on middle-class values and bureaucratic regularization, and how that has renewed the tradition's attraction for some Indigenous adherents of some generations, while raising ethical questions for others.

Indigenous Mormon writers and thinkers also point to how the adoption of Mormonism has evacuated or deferred crucial conversations about political economy within Indigenous communities and discouraged critical engagement with the neo-colonial political, cultural, and economic dynamics at work within Mormonism itself. Indigenous Mormon writers seek to bring this work of unsettling colonialism home to their own faith tradition. They articulate tensions between the official story of bureaucratic Mormonism and the Mormonisms lived on the peripheries. In so doing, they create a space for critique of the racism, classism, and colonialism of bureaucratic Mormonism and the North American Mormon culture region. They hold the faith accountable for its internal structures of inequality and its complicity with and instrumentality within American colonialism; some claim that this complicity is a betrayal of principles taught in Mormon scripture. They challenge the assumption that the transportation into global contexts has taken place without struggle, tension, dislocation, or cost. They acknowledge complex relationships between Indigenous Mormons of the global diaspora and the local Indigenous peoples in whose homelands they reside. They also acknowledge complex and sometimes fraught relationships between white and Indigenous Mormons. Their stories reflect that Mormons of color and Indigenous Mormons have developed a range of ways for dealing with racially exclusive hierarchy and ground-level white racism in the LDS Church. Some have quietly developed for themselves and taught within their own families and circles of influence a mode of critical thinking that decenters the colonialist and racist presumptions of US-based bureaucratic Mormonism and quietly rejects or remodels racist and colonialist elements of Mormon theology and practice.

As progressive Mormons have always done, critical-thinking Indigenous Mormons and Mormons of color have quietly waited for the church to catch up, waiting for the process Mormons call "continuing revelation" to move policies, theologies, institutional emphases, and the gerontocratic Salt Lake leadership. They have waited for the church to change the language of its scripture to revise out the racism of its nineteenth-century origins, as it did in 1981 when it changed the language in the most current editions of the Book of Mormon to replace 2 Nephi 5:21 from a promise that Lamanites would someday become "white and delightsome" to "pure and delightsome." They have waited for the church to finally and publicly reject as racism its past efforts to legitimate the historic segregation of the priesthood and temple participation from members of African descent, as it recently did in a quietly released statement on the internet. Some have waited while continuing to practice their faith as Mormons within LDS congregations. Some have stepped away from day-to-day activity within the church or even from church membership, but theirs is also a vital part of the Mormon story: part of a long tradition of Mormon progressives who have rejected bureaucratic and institutional Mormonism but continued to maintain a deep if ambivalent personal, spiritual, and cultural connection to Mormonism as writers, scholars, and critics.

There are multiple ways of telling the Mormon story. At times, Mormon leaders working to globalize the movement have exploited colonial and neocolonial economic and political channels established by the nation-state or by multinational corporations. But as a minority religion with a sometimes cooperative, sometimes ambivalent relationship to its imperial and national host societies, Mormonism has also carved out its own distinctive globalized networks. It resembles what postcolonial theorists Françoise Lionnet and Shu-Mei Shih have called a minor transnationalism. Lionnet and Shih developed the idea of minor transnationalism to account for globally distributed peoples who have cultivated their own relationships parallel to but differently articulated from state-backed imperial modernity. Minor transnationalisms, Lionnet and Shih write, have "multiple, paradoxical, or even irreverent relations with the economic transnationalism of contemporary empires" and their own affective registers for working out the "traumas of colonial, imperial, and global hegemonies."[39] They also have their own axes of verticality and horizontality, their own internal power relations, their own hierarchies and inequalities, their own "above" and "below."

Decolonizing Mormonism means choosing to see the transnational Mormon story through the eyes of Indigenous members and with a willingness to identify, unsettle, and if possible redress whatever there is in our faith tradition that has compromised the well-being of Indigenous communities. It means unsettling our assumptions about who this faith belongs to and what it is supposed to mean for politics and ethics. It means that that peoples long positioned as the object of Book of Mormon-based narratives of sacred history and campaigns of proselytization now move to a subject position as narrators of the Mormon past, present, and future. And moreover, that they leverage this subject position as a resource to advance the well-being of Indigenous communities, not sparing criticism of historical and contemporary church practices that ignore or contravene the priorities and perspectives of Indigenous peoples.

This is not an easy endeavor for several reasons. First, institutional Mormonism's twentieth-century adoption of corporate bureaucratic management practices and its deep imbrication in neocolonial and neoliberal global economic networks has led to what David Knowlton calls a "sacralization of management" that makes criticism of the corporate church—or sometimes even corporations in general—seem tantamount to heresy.[40] Second, this sacralization of management is reinforced among grassroots Mormons as an ideology of faithfulness that commands assent to church bureaucratic decisions. Hawaiian Mormon scholar Hokulani Aikau draws the phrase "ideology of faithfulness" from the writings of feminist thinker Jacqui Alexander; among Mormons, the "ideology of faithfulness" is used to "leverage faith to solicit community consent to church projects," including those that have less to do with theology or religious outcomes and have more to do with the bureaucratic and business-oriented prerogatives and priorities of the church and its officers. In her study of Hawaiian Mormons, Aikau notes moments when ideologies of faithfulness were mobilized to achieve profitable outcomes for church business ventures and for the business interests of prominent haole church leaders in the sugar and rice industries, and in obtaining free labor for church enterprises such as the building of the Polynesian Cultural Center and other building projects. In these and other situations, Aikau writes, "explicit critique is missing" and that "faithfulness to church business and managerial practices" is often compelled.[41]

The ideology of faithfulness in turn contributes to a third obstacle to decolonization among the grassroots Anglo-Mormon membership:

resistance to collective self-criticism. Anglo-Mormons who strongly identify with the LDS church hierarchy and have absorbed the culture's repres-
sion of critique are often resistant to reflect critically on structures of
inequality within the church and on their own privilege as white Mormons.
Few formal structures within the bureaucratic LDS Church support institutional self-examination: there are no synods, no conventions, no official
forums where policies are debated. Consequently, unless they have learned
norms of critical thinking outside of church settings, most Mormons are
ill-equipped to undertake the critical thinking that leads to the disarticula-
tion of core principles of the faith from the colonialist and white-privileging
practices that have shaped its institutional character. Navajo Mormon
scholar Moroni Benally writes:

> The members of the Church of Jesus Christ of Latter-day Saints
> who interpret and actualize the mission of the church are largely
> informed by settler-colonialism. As a result, their interpretations
> and practice of doctrine are informed by a series of moves to inno-
> cence, designed to relieve or unburden them from their complicity
> to egregious acts of colonization, while retaining their privileged
> status.[42]

Finally, a fourth condition that makes the work of decolonization challenging is declension among Indigenous Mormons themselves. Demographic studies of global Mormonism suggest that the resilience of Mormon identity that has fostered comparatively high retention rates among
members in the United States' Mormon culture region may not have the
same hold in Latin America.[43] Adherence among rural and working-class
Polynesian members in the Pacific and the diaspora also appears to be
declining. Those who continue to identify as Mormons and voice critique of
colonialism and racism within the church often persist against opposition
from fellow Indigenous and Anglo-Mormons who view any form of criticism of Mormon institutions and mainstream Mormon culture as heretical.

But there are also forces that are making it easier for thoughtful, critical
Mormon voices to break through and find audience. First, as has been the
case throughout Indigenous history, colonial institutions that bring Indigenous peoples from different backgrounds together often serve as powerful incubators for change. When Tongans, Samoans, Latin Americans,

Native North Americans, Maori, Hawaiian, and African-descended Mormons meet in LDS church congregations, at a church-sponsored school or university, at church-sponsored businesses such as the Polynesian Cultural Center, or in the mission field, they have opportunity to compare and discuss their experiences within the global church on their own terms rather than in terms scripted by the official bureaucratic discourse of the LDS Church. Informal lateral associations among Mormons of color offer spaces to reflect, compare notes, observe patterns, and theorize across local histories of minority Mormon experience. Second, the internet has amplified these lateral Mormon-to-Mormon conversations by giving Indigenous Mormons and Mormons of color potential platforms for sharing their experience in the robust universe of independent Mormon blogs and Facebook groups. The twentieth-century LDS Church tried to manage global growth by centralizing, simplifying, and managing information about Mormonism, generating it vertically top-down through official church-sponsored publications and institutional channels. In the twenty-first century world of Mormonism, content flows horizontally as well, as it is published on independent blogs and then propelled via email, Facebook, and Twitter along kinship and congregational networks, from region to region and across the globe. Critical perspectives by Mormons of color that have no chance of being heard over the pulpit or appearing in a church-sponsored magazine can reach significant audiences via digital media.

Those networks have made possible many of the relationships that undergird this very book and made more available the perspectives and personal faith narratives of Indigenous and global South Mormons. From its very foundations, Mormonism has been a faith propelled by personal narratives that use immediate experience with the divine to sanction new ways of being in the world. As he himself tells it, Joseph Smith was fourteen years old when he entered a grove of trees in upstate New York seeking answers to his questions about conflicts between rival Protestant denominations, and his personal search was rewarded by immediate contact with the divine. Mormons continue to retell the Joseph Smith story and to feature parallel personal stories of questioning and finding in collective faith life. For Indigenous and global South Mormons especially, personal narratives that tie together immediate experience of the divine within the context of indigenized Mormonism create the foundation for complex and robustly diverse Mormon ways of being: the many Mormonisms of global twenty-first century Mormonism. In the words of Mormon scholar Hokulani Aikau, personal narratives enact a "knotting together" of ethnic and religious identities. Where there are tensions between facets of being Indigenous and Mormon—confrontations with institutional racism, economic and racial inequality, conflicts between bureaucratic policies and decolonizing priorities—they are often resolved, Aikau observes, through such narrative devices as dreams, visions, or appeals to tropes of gathering or Lamanite destiny that affirm God's priority for Indigenous and Global South peoples and God's care for the individual believer and his or her community of origin.[44] Personal stories told in the service of decolonizing Mormonism reposition the act of criticizing inequality within the contemporary bureaucratic LDS Church and its host culture as an expression of fidelity to God and the Mormon movement.

These stories also hold the potential to open up and contribute to a general refashioning of contemporary Mormon identity, bearing implications that radiate beyond the lives of Indigenous and Global South Mormons to Mormons at large. They ask us to consider whether we will be in the twenty-first century a people who prioritize the bureaucratic prerogatives of the modern LDS Church or the growth and well-being of all Mormon people. Are we as a people defined by a stiff defense of the scientifically untenable literal facticity of Mormon scripture—including stories of Mormon scripture's ancient origins, or the literal Middle Eastern ancestry of the Indigenous peoples of the Americas and Pacific—or by a seeking, questioning, deeply felt, open-ended, and sometimes contradictory relationship to these founding texts? Are we people of the LDS church corporation, or people of the historic Mormon movement? Mormonism has always been a potential resource for dreaming a different way of being in the world, a better world, a Zion. The work of decolonizing Mormonism is the work of critically reconstructing that legacy to mobilize our faith as a resource for redress, reconciliation, self-determination, and wellness.

Ten

THE LDS CHURCH IN FLANDERS

Their Way, Our Way, or Their Way in Our Own Way

INGRID SHERLOCK

In 1972, my parents converted to the Church of Jesus Christ of Latter-day Saints (hereafter LDS Church) some months after my father actively searched out the LDS Church by flying to Salt Lake City on a free weekend while on a business trip in the United States. In the same year we moved from a large city in The Netherlands, a country full of rules and regulations, to a tiny rural village in the Flemish east of Belgium. My childhood was idyllic amidst the farms and the forests, I enjoyed an excellent education in Catholic schools, and was a member of the local Catholic youth organization and an internationally acclaimed youth choir. Last but not least, I attended a very small branch of the LDS Church. The branch existed by virtue of an average of eight to, at one time, up to sixteen missionaries being assigned to it so that a handful of local members could attend church somewhat near their home (a forty-five-minute ride each way in our case). For most of my childhood and youth, there were no other children in the branch. My mother started Primary at home when I was eight and my brother was a four-year-old. We continued Primary at home until the consolidated program came in, by which time I had already graduated from Primary. My mother taught Seminary, too, at home. My friends and neighbors knew that I was a Mormon and that Mormons were neither Catholics nor Protestants. I felt perfectly part of the local community and the fact that I was a Mormon was neither an issue, nor was I mocked or ridiculed because of it. If I was teased, it was because I was Dutch and therefore a *kaaskop* (cheese head).

Even as a young child I knew that the church had its roots in the United States and that the headquarters were in Salt Lake City where that big grey temple stood (the one on all the promotional material). The United States, however, was far away, a place on a map. The people I met in church, aside from the missionaries with their funny accents, were local people. As I grew up, contact with the missionaries proved very useful for learning English, but the whole American background of the church was just that, ever-present in the background, yet personified only in the American missionaries and sometimes in the funny food they so eagerly brought to church parties, such as medicinal-tasting pumpkin pie or root beer (a drink that tasted like liquid toothpaste). Why had I not felt an overarching American influence in church as a child while at times eight or more mainly American missionaries were holding together our tiny branch? Why did I know so little about the costs associated with joining a foreign faith?

There can be no question but that the outside world continues to perceive Mormonism as American. The LDS church leadership structure also bears responsibility for this perception. Even though the LDS Church works with areas and area presidencies, stakes, missions, wards, and branches, most real executive power remains in the United States with the top tier of the leadership. There are indicators that the LDS Church is starting to become more aware of the needs and the experiences of the global church; however, as with any big institution, the process is excruciatingly slow.

Scholars have been attentive to how European Mormons negotiate the relationships between their American-centered religion and their home countries and cultures. Kim B. Östman discussed "otherness-promoting and otherness-removing discourses" relating to Latter-day Saints in Finland, writing that the "mainstream Finnish population finds the Mormons foreign in many ways, while Mormons themselves feel that they are simultaneously part of the regular mainstream population in many ways yet different from it."[1] Flemish scholar Wilfried Decoo has addressed the struggle of retaining European converts and the difference between Mormon culture and gospel culture within an American worldwide church.[2] Walter van Beek, an anthropologist, offered an analysis of the how the American church impacts the experience of European Mormons attending the "Dutch

Temple" in Zoetermeer (The Hague Temple, The Netherlands), where the American hierarchy (as it does in all temples worldwide) maintains absolute control over all temple issues, including whether or not a chair can be moved.[3] But it is significant to me that even as he writes about the balance of power between the American church and its Dutch members, van Beek makes no mention of the two Belgian stakes that are also part of the temple district, which would seem to validate what is in the minds of Flemish Mormons—that there is an unequal power dynamic between the Flemish and the Dutch.[4]

Flanders was never an autonomous entity, yet throughout history Flemings cherished and managed to maintain their identity and their language. At times this was extremely difficult, as is evinced even in modern times by the treatment of the Flemish majority when Belgian independence was declared in 1830. Flanders was not a willing participant in the process and became a reluctant part of Belgium only after the intervention of a French military force. Flanders was bigger geographically and more densely populated, but poor and agricultural, whereas the French-speaking Walloons were a minority but rich through industry, and influential because they spoke a world language—which incidentally was the only official language of Belgium until 1919. Being treated as a sort of second-class citizen and having to obey others while at the same time trying to hold on to one's own identity and language made the Flemings resourceful. As a result they became masters at obeying rules—but naturally, only after adapting them.

Marinel Gerritsen has found that the 1980 assertion of sociologist Geert Hofstede still stands today, namely that no two countries with a common border and a common language are so far apart culturally as Dutch Belgium (Flanders) and The Netherlands.[5] These differences are magnified in church settings when church officials (whether from Salt Lake City or area authorities, who are often Dutch) merge these two cultures into missions or stakes and expect members to work smoothly together because they speak the same language or because they believe that "the gospel knows no borders or nationalities."

As a Flemish Mormon with Dutch roots, I stand in a complicated position as a European member of a hierarchical Mormon church and an ethnic minority in the nation where I live. How do Mormons like me negotiate the multiple hierarchies that shape their religious experience? The answer may be captured in remarks I heard at a local church meeting at which some new ideas were presented. Someone reacted to the new instructions with "oh well, that is how Americans and probably the Dutch do it; this would not work here, but if we change it a bit here and there, it'll work." I have heard remarks like this frequently: regulations and instructions were frequently adapted to local needs, sometimes out of necessity, but most of the time because "that is how they do it in America (or elsewhere), but we do it differently." One brother who had been a member for almost forty years called this approach "obeying through adaptation," an approach essential to minimizing the social costs that LDS membership exacted from Flemish converts and to preserving one's identity as a Flemish Saint even as historical and secular tensions between The Netherlands and Flanders spilled over in church life. This essay explores through ethnographic interviews with Flemish Latter-day Saints the history of this lived approach to LDS faith. To understand this history, I have organized this essay by the decade in which Flemish Mormons converted.

1950s

After halting missionary activity for about half a century, the Dutch Mission sent missionaries to Flanders in 1947. (The lack of missionary activity was possibly due to the fact that people at church headquarters in America erroneously thought of Flemish as a different language from Dutch and consequently assumed that there were no missionaries who spoke it.) Missionary efforts met with successes and practical challenges, such as finding suitable buildings to meet in, accommodations for the missionaries, and filling local leadership positions. There was also opposition from the conservative Catholic Church, which was itself struggling to maintain its power against surging progressive secular liberalism, especially in urban areas. Consequently, Catholic priests in cities like Antwerp and Mechelen viewed Mormon missionaries as a threat to their hold on their membership and actively discouraged people from having contact with or accommodating the American missionaries who spread their message from door to door.[6]

The church was, without any doubt, perceived as an American church by members and non-members alike. In one anecdote, a lady upon opening the door for the missionaries remarked: "truly everything comes from America, now religion too."[7] Americans were very welcome, since they had assisted the Flemish who had been made destitute by the First and Second World Wars with The Commission for the Relief of Belgium, an international food relief program, and the Marshall Plan (1948–1952). Growing Cold War tensions between Eastern and Western Europe also opened Flemish hearts towards American missionaries. The American origins of Mormonism were seen merely as either an incidence of history or as logical because America and all things American stood, at least in people's minds, for freedom and unlimited opportunity. Those I interviewed did not view the American leadership of local Dutch and Flemish units as an inappropriate exercise of power. Most felt that because of a lack of local experience or know-how, it was right to have the church administered in the exact image of the church in Utah, although Flemish converts admitted having less understanding for the American church's obsession with numbers and statistics. My respondents also indicated that missionaries were more integrated not only in the church community but also in the community at large, due in part to the lack of formal rules for missionary life at the time and the participation of missionaries in social activities with members.[8]

One man I interviewed fondly described the missionaries as his ever-hungry adoptive brothers. A trip to the cinema was as normal as missionaries introducing children to popcorn at family home evenings. Missionaries were not time-restricted visitors who came for a lesson or dinner and a short message, but rather a temporary part of local families as they spent long hours at investigators and members' homes to teach, dine, and play with the children. Respondents noticed but tended to forgive missionary conduct that implied American bias or that reinforced a colonial dynamic, such as the habit of the missionaries to dress up in folkloristic clothing, have their pictures taken, and then send those photographs home. People remember feeling uncomfortable, not because the missionaries dressed up and sent the photographs home, but rather with the fact that more often than not the *Volendammer* costume and/or clogs, which are actually Dutch, were used for the photos. One could possibly argue that this was because Flanders does not have a "native costume" or because the missionaries were serving in a cross-border mission. Nevertheless, interchanging Dutch and Flemish cultures in any context never was and still is not a good idea. In addition to that, traditional clothing in Europe is worn only at folk festivals and their wearing it for dress-up was (rightly or not) seen as somewhat condescending.

A second example was missionaries' irrational fear of going to a local doctor because they thought that American doctors were more capable. Third, was the missionaries' limited understanding of local politics and their imposition of the binary thinking of American politics. Liberals were good, probably because their ideas were close to the concept of the American Dream; socialists were bad; communists were naturally the root of all evil. Missionaries simply could not, or would not, accept that members in good standing could also be socialist, and they did not hide their opinions. They held on to this opinion in spite of the fact that they had, according to one respondent, more success among people with a socialist background than among the (lapsed) Catholics. Furthermore, one could argue that this irrational dislike of socialism was curious, to say the least, because the very colonization of Utah, the United Order experiments, and the Cooperative Mercantile Institutions are perfect examples of a combination of religious and socialist principles.

Flemish Mormons noted but tended to overlook these dynamics. Why? Was it the gospel message, the proffered escape from the yoke of Catholicism, or was it simply the friendly innocence of the young missionaries?

1960s

The 1960s saw the climax of the linguistic disputes the Flemings had engaged in with the Walloons on and off since 1878. A federalization process started in 1970, which transformed Belgium into a federal state with communities, regions, and language areas; this transformation was finalized with the change to the Belgian Constitution on May 5, 1993. Flemish identity and consciousness, which had always thrived—albeit surreptitiously due to the political reality on the ground—surged up and permanently changed the Belgian establishment. In this context, why would a church with essentially Anglo-American origins attract converts in Flanders after such a prolonged process towards recognition?

There are probably as many answers as there are converts. A number of respondents felt that the affirmation they found in the LDS Church that each individual is a cherished child of God with a pre-mortal identity was in line with their Flemish aspirations. It was also suggested that when the iron grip of the Catholic Church was broken, this not only opened the door to secularization, but it also paved the way towards acceptance that a person could choose a third option: to change religions. Notwithstanding this new tolerance, changing religions was at times painful for the individual and/or for the extended family, and family and social pressure negatively impacted the retention of new converts.[9]

Quarrels between members also contributed to retention problems. These quarrels would happen because at times the eager missionaries baptized bizarre and/or volatile people, a problem that is perhaps inherent in door-to-door proselytizing, or they engaged young people through the infamous "basketball baptism program."[10] (Respondents who were young at the time looked back with great fondness at the basketball sessions with the missionaries.)

The 1960s also saw the LDS Church embark upon an ambitious building program in Europe as a perceived means of attracting converts. In Belgium two chapels were built in Wallonia, one in Liège and one in Charleroi. A third chapel was built in bilingual Brussels. Young American missionaries were no longer called on proselytizing missions only, but some were called as building missionaries.

Both the presence of building missionaries and the lavish funds from the US that facilitated chapel building underscored the American identity of the church, but Flemish converts seemed not to be too concerned. LDS doctrine captivated those who endured and kept the faith. For them, everything fell into place as they found answers to long-held questions, rather than having to hear that some things were just a mystery to be recognized and accepted as such without further probing. It was logical to most respondents that the restoration was necessary because of the great apostasy, and that this was possible only in America because Europe was under the yoke of "Church of the Devil." The fact that Bruce R. McConkie identified this "Church of the Devil" as the Catholic Church in his somewhat infamous book, *Mormon Doctrine*, completed the picture. The plan of salvation healed wounds opened by the Catholic doctrine that children who had died before they were baptized and had been consigned to hell, but were now inheritors of celestial glory per Mormon doctrine. God was a living, physical, and personal being who cared for His children on earth and who wanted all His children to become like Him. The New Jerusalem was in America, but that did not matter because it all fell into place as part of LDS doctrine, and local Saints were convinced that in the midst of Babylon they could be instrumental in saving the nation. Flemish Saints imagined that one day Flanders would have its own wards, stakes, leaders, and missionaries in far-flung areas.

1970s AND 1980s

The LDS Church made Flanders an independent mission from 1975 until 1984. All respondents unequivocally hailed this period as the best time in Flanders's church history.

After the conference at which the independent Flemish mission was announced, my mother overheard a few members saying rather enthusiastically, "*eindelijk zijn we van die rot Hollanders af*" (finally we are rid of those rotten Dutch). It was not that they necessarily harbored ill will against Dutch church members, quite the contrary, but an independent Flemish mission was in line with secular events in which Flanders was endeavouring to gain more independence. Still, the LDS Church was not consistent in recognizing the Flemish hunger for recognition and independence. A number of respondents shared some examples of this. One was the painful situation of the Frankfurt Temple dedication in 1987. Of course there was joy and gratitude at having a temple closer to home, but during the main talk, then apostle Thomas S. Monson kept repeating "nobody can beat the Dutch," even though it was a joint Dutch-Flemish dedicatory service. Moreover, I was told by a number of respondents that there was not a single Flemish member in the celestial room where all the Dutch leaders, their families, and other "important" families had situated themselves, and that even the Antwerp district president (a Fleming) was following the dedication by video link in another room.

It was also widely perceived that general authorities never visited Flanders. Some remembered that a few months after the dedication of the Frankfurt Temple there had been a special fireside with a general authority for Flemish members only. What most did not know was that a member living in Belgium but with Dutch roots wrote a letter to the First Presidency about the occurrences at the dedication. Since this person had friends living in Salt Lake City, they delivered the letter for him and it actually landed on the desk of the First Presidency, who organized the special fireside as an effort to address the problem.

Respondents also look back on this period as a time of great fellowship and great unity among the small flock. They look back with great fondness to temple trips to Switzerland and later to Germany twice a year for a full week when members travelled together and engaged in temple work together. They also regaled me with stories of dances and musical evenings or cultural events organized by the larger branches but attended by all. In short, members feasted on the word of the Lord and on the wholesome things the world had to offer and did so in group. This worshipping and socializing within the church group is something that definitely displays the American character of the LDS Church. Members are used to it, but some respondents mentioned that family, friends, and acquaintances found this very strange indeed. In Belgium, you go to church for worship services, and then you go home.

Converts of this era, like converts of earlier decades, noticed but forgave Mormon impositions of American hierarchy and priority. The American roots of the church were part of the doctrine and thus accepted as logical. American habits such as celebrating Pioneer Day, Halloween, or Thanksgiving were largely ignored. If the missionaries organized something, some members would attend, others did not. At Thanksgiving, there was quite often families who felt sorry for the missionaries missing home on their important holiday and they would invite them and cobble together a Thanksgiving-like dinner.

A few mentioned that they looked upon some counsel leaders gave as American and somewhat alien. One of them was the Church teaching that mothers should stay home to take care of the children. Flanders did not, and still does not, have a stay-at-home-mom culture, not least because people have to work to build up a pension. A lot of sisters, therefore, continued to work outside the home, which at times led to lively Relief Society lessons, but unfortunately also to recriminations and hurt feelings.

It was also interesting that many Flemish Saints desired to travel to Utah to see it all for themselves. Many, but not all, had actually undertaken the trip, and some had even travelled to Nauvoo and Kirtland to follow the trail of the early church members. Those who had travelled to these places felt that they had a better understanding of the early days of the church and they greatly enjoyed seeing the sites. Nevertheless, the perception remained that it was someone else's history. Some were quite emphatic that they were pioneers themselves, and that their experiences were more relevant for the local members than the traditional LDS pioneer stories. More than one respondent was very happy with the history projects that the church is now doing by appointing local church historians to write down local histories. (In this same context, the lesson manuals were mentioned a number of times. Although there have been some changes in recent years, members still felt that the material was top-heavy with pioneer and agricultural stories that meant little or nothing to urban local members.)

What drew converts to the LDS Church in these decades was the doctrine. Flemish respondents mentioned being attracted to the fact that receiving priesthood was not dependent on education but on worthiness. Work for kindred dead was seen as the ultimate mercy of God. The fact that Christ also visited the Americas and that this event, like those in the Bible, had been written down in the Book of Mormon seemed totally logical, because why would God only speak to one small group of people if He was a loving God? High on the list was also the fact that the church gave answers rather than demanding blind faith and an acceptance of mysteries whenever an answer seemed to be lacking. One respondent who, as a child, was confronted with the consequences of Belgium colonizing the Congo in more than one way, said that she joined the church initially based on the abundance of logic within doctrine in general and the plan of salvation in particular. Soon, however, she discovered that peripherals such as visiting teaching, home teaching, and other activities strengthened her testimony on a daily basis. It felt as if she had come home for the first time in her life. Genealogy and temple work gave her the desire and courage to find her mother and half-siblings. Other respondents mentioned that callings in the church had contributed to better jobs because their callings tapped into unknown talents or helped them acquire new ones.

Most of them also remarked that their extended families, however, reacted in completely the opposite way and that they questioned why their loved ones would want to join an American sect. The fact that there were a fair number of branches with local members was of little importance for their families. The church was an American sect and as such should be feared and avoided. This opposition manifested itself often through little things such as ridiculing the church or suddenly having only coffee, tea, or alcohol in the house when church members visited, or organizing family events during church hours. Some saw their friends buckle under these pressures and leave the church. This feeling was even stronger for those who joined around the time of the Jonestown drama in Guyana, where a sect with American roots committed collective suicide. For one respondent who had by then been a member for about five years, this drama was one more confirmation for his family that American sects were dangerous. One respondent described his father's dramatic reaction to his conversion. The man, upon hearing that his son had joined the church, refused to eat or go to work. At her wit's end, his mother went to her local parish priest to ask counsel. This wise man told her that the Mormons were the best community he knew of and that in any case she would not be able to change her son's mind. His father accepted this, resumed his normal habits, and the church was never again mentioned.

In summary, one could say that the liberating effect of the doctrine far outweighed the origins of Mormonism for the converts themselves. If one were to look at members who joined the church and who remained active, it seems that anything American was placed in a doctrinal context and, therefore, it made perfect sense. Extended family, on the other hand, saw the LDS Church as an American sect; they did not understand why one would want to convert. Some were opposed to the conversion, openly or covertly, and in rare cases they envisioned all sorts of horror scenarios.

1990s

The 1990s saw a shift in Flemish perceptions of the American character and dominance of the church. I see the 1990s as a turning point for the church in Flanders and as the decade when, for want of a better description, the idea was born of *onze kerk en de kerk* (our church and the church). The American roots of Mormonism were being diminished by an increased institutional emphasis on Jesus Christ rather than, for example, the place of the restoration. This included a logo change in 1995 in which the name "Jesus Christ" was emphasized. But another contributing factor was the reorganization in 1994 of the three Dutch stakes and the Flemish mission into four new stakes. Flanders became part of the Antwerp Stake, which incorporated all Flemish congregations and a few Dutch congregations. The fact that the first stake president and one of his counsellors were Flemish and that the name of the stake was the Antwerp Stake was significant.

Quite a few respondents said that the formation of the Antwerp Stake greatly reduced the American influence in the church. A number of

European missionaries, among them also Dutch missionaries, were serving in Flanders, giving the church a more local face in its contacts with investigators. Second-generation members who had themselves served missions were starting to take on leadership positions, frequently as ward or branch mission leaders. This meant that the mainly American mission presidents were no longer involved in the day-to-day running of the church. Local issues could, therefore, be dealt with more easily without cultural faux pas or the need for lengthy explanations. In this context, one respondent who was baptized in the 1970s said that she felt she could now more openly study church history and its sometimes-controversial events.[11]

But the American character of the LDS Church was felt with regard to geopolitical situations such as the Gulf War (1990–1991) in particular. Belgium did not participate in the American-led military coalition, and some respondents felt that the church did not take a clear stand against the war as they would have expected—after all, D&C 98:16, for example, tells members to "renounce war and proclaim peace, and seek diligently to turn the hearts of the children to their fathers, and the hearts of the fathers to the children." One respondent who freely admitted that he and his wife were searching for spirituality, said he would never have joined an "American church." He profoundly disagreed with American foreign policy and felt that America was politically "sticking its nose" into everything and he would not want this kind of intrusion in something as profound as one's religion. (He was not talking about the Gulf War per se because he felt that there was some justification for defending Kuwait and Israel.) They joined the church, however, because of the Dutch missionary who taught them, the local members he met when he came to church meetings, and in no small measure because of the spirit he felt in church meetings and when the missionaries visited them.

When Mormon doctrine was taught by and to Europeans, doctrines about an American Zion, a need to gather the Saints and the lost tribes to Zion in order to prepare for the Second Coming of Christ, and linking this to a sacred place in North America all but seemed to disappear into the background. (For some die-hard doctrine junkies who were baptized in the 1970s this was actually a difficult development to accept.) Also significant is the fact that, with the exception of celebrating the church's sesquicentennial with an elaborate pioneer parade in Charleroi, the stories about pioneers crossing the plains were replaced by stories of local pioneers. Some of these stories centered around a small branch meeting each Sunday in a very long four-hour block, years before the three-hour consolidated program was instituted in the church. The distances the members needed to travel were so great that the branch just added the sacrament meeting that normally took place in the evening to the morning block. Aside from the duration of worship services, this meant that the sacrament was passed twice within the space of about sixty minutes, once during Sunday school and once during sacrament meeting. Children survived this system because there was *de snoepbroeder* (the candy brother) who sat at the back of the chapel and monitored behavior. Good behavior was richly rewarded with sweets.

Another story is about a branch continuing to have Relief Society on a weekday after the three-hour block was instituted because all the sisters were involved in Primary. Visiting sisters from America whose husbands were on business trips to the local Ford factory, would ask where Relief Society was and members took mischievous delight in telling them: "oh, we do not do Relief Society here, you can join priesthood or Primary". The American sisters invariably chose to attend Primary, whereas visiting Flemish sisters usually opted for priesthood.

If we look at the pioneer stories about the early Saints on the American continent, we see that during times of persecution not all things were done "by the book", and new rules and customs came into existence because there was a specific need. Later these rules or customs remained in place because they were deemed beneficial for the church and its members. A similar Flemish "pioneer" action appears to have at least contributed to a church-wide change with regards to access to the temple for unendowed adult sisters. There was a Flemish branch president with a married sister who had a great desire to go to the temple. She had not gone because her husband was not a member and the accepted policy seemed to be that she could not go, even for baptisms. He discussed this with the district president, who noted that there were quite a number of faithful sisters in that position. Together they combed through the *General Handbook of Instructions* to see whether there was an injunction against allowing these sisters to do baptisms for the dead together with the youth. There was not and it appeared it was just something nobody ever thought about, perhaps because it was a problem unique to the mission field. They contacted the temple president and got his permission to organize a temple trip to Switzerland with the youth and with about six of these sisters. The then mission president tried

THE LDS CHURCH IN FLANDERS | 199

to stop it because "it was not allowed," but the district president would not give up and asked him to show where it was written. He could not, but tried to assert his authority anyway on the grounds that it was not done in America. These brothers went ahead anyway in faith and confidence and in spite of the mission president's opposition. This trip became a spiritual highlight for the youth as well as for these sisters and bonded them through fond memories as no other activity could ever have done. Incidentally, all of these sisters remained active and eventually, when the rules changed, had the opportunity to be endowed themselves.

Significantly, as the overarching American influence disappeared, the differences between Dutch and Flemish members became more prominent and frustrations surfaced at times. It was often said that the Dutch were brazen and always thought they knew best and that they tried to take over. It was felt that, while it was true that the Dutch had perhaps more experience in church leadership, they understood little about Flanders and its ways. The Flemish members, in true character, complained about it among themselves but let the Dutch get on with it and quietly did their own thing. This was illustrated by one respondent's story in which all the branch presidents and bishops were called together for a meeting without a public agenda. The Dutch were rather vocal in their opinion about the fact that there was no agenda as they wanted to know what the meeting was going to be about. The Flemish bishops and branch presidents just came quietly. After the meeting the Dutch went home obedient to what they had heard while the Flemish bishops and branch presidents gathered quietly in a corner to discuss how they could adapt the instructions to local circumstances.

2000–PRESENT

Identity-conscious Flemish Mormons today generally have a strong testimony of the gospel, but they are also seekers who abhor the blind obedience they feel general authorities advocate. This group exemplifies the approach of obeying through adaptation. Significantly, those who identify with this group tend to have teaching callings and very few hold leadership positions beyond the local level. Some said with a twinkle in their eyes that the reason for this was the fact that they were not "obedient" enough. Many are well-read, both in books and on the internet. The idea of *onze kerk* (our church) versus *de kerk* (the church) or even *het evangelie* (the gospel) versus *het instituut kerk* (the church as an institution) appeals to this group, although it is not taken to extremes.[12]

Political events such as the American "war on terror" post-2001 continue to introduce secular break lines into the way Flemish Mormons live their faith. American militarism conflicted with widespread European opposition to the Iraq War. Flemish members felt that the Church's silence meant it tacitly supported the war. Another break line was the perception that the LDS Church is aligning itself with the Christian Right, symbolized (according to respondents) by intolerance, disrespect for the environment, and gun culture. The Flemish are very socially conscious and open-minded people: pragmatism and a "live and let live" attitude is a major part of the Flemish psyche. In their eyes, the church's deeply engaged support for California's Proposition 8 in 2008 did a lot of damage to the LDS Church. Flemish Mormons did not necessarily want the LDS Church to change doctrine or to perform same-sex marriages, but they felt that this was simply a non-issue if you truly separated church from state. This was seen as a perfect example of an essentially American domestic issue spilling into the global church.

The younger people in this group had completely different issues and they, too, perceived the church as becoming more and more American. Only with a promise of anonymity did they reveal some of these concerns. Several reasons were given for their thoughts on the Americanization. One was the obsession with the world versus the church. When I asked for more explanation, they said that unlike youngsters in Utah, they had to live in the world, that their friends are in the world, and that the constant insinuations that the world was bad and evil, and LDS members were good and pure, essentially condemned their friends who were also good people.

Another issue was church camps and activities. Although seen as a great opportunity to spend time with friends, there were mixed reactions and the phrase "not so exciting" was used a few times. Some, in talking to their parents who went to church camps some thirty years ago, noted that now there was a lot less fun. In the past, there were many spiritual activities but they were combined with practical lessons such as first aid, hikes, camping skills, and afternoons of sports and adventure. The parents, too, felt that the old four-year church program taught them self-reliance, perseverance, and was character building. Granted that times have changed, most of the youth agreed that now the whole emphasis has shifted to being "peculiar" or unique—the last thing that teenagers want because "belonging to" is very important.

Some youngsters, male as well as female, mentioned the church's modesty discourse. While all of them thought that there was no problem with teaching them about modesty and respect for their bodies, they found the manner in which it was taught irritating. Quite a number of young women and young men were bothered by the insinuations that the female styles of clothing were the cause of young men's inappropriate thoughts. Both young men and women perceived this as demeaning. The majority said they were quite happy to conform in church but that they equally wanted to blend in with society outside a church setting. The internet proved a rich source of answers for them. Some had found church-related articles in which even adults addressed the concerns of the teenagers.[13]

CONCLUSION

Flemish Saints occupy a complicated position as a double minority. Most seem to have adapted to the American institutional and cultural privileging within Mormonism—as long as there is room for adaptation and a bit of complaining to each other rather than to the people who could possibly bring about a change. Institutional efforts to de-emphasize the special theological and historical background of the United States and to emphasize Jesus Christ and a recentering around local rather than American pioneer stories have assisted with this adaptation. The Gulf War and its aftermath have been obstacles. But now resisting cultural and political impositions by The Netherlands seems more important to Flemish Mormons than addressing the persisting colonial dynamics of the American church. I have heard many a Fleming complain about the brazenness of the Dutch Saints and their reputed tendency to think they know it all or that they have to be in charge, no matter what. However, I have thought many a time to myself and sometimes said aloud that the Flemish Saints need to make their displeasure known rather than complain to people who cannot change the situation.

Eleven

SISTER ACTS

Relief Society and Flexible Citizenship in Hong Kong

STACILEE FORD

These are the unspoken legacies we inherit when we belong to a people: not only luminous visions of eternal expanses of loving-kindness, but actual human histories of exclusion and rank prejudice. We inherit not only the glorious histories of our ancestors, but their human failings, too, their kindness, their tenderness, and their satisfaction with easy contradictions: their wisdom as well as their ignorance, arrogance, and presumption, as our own.

We inherit all the ways in which our ancestors and parents and teacher were wrong, as well as the ways they were right: their sparkling differences, and their human failings. There is no unmixing the two.[1]

Joanna Brooks' notion of inheritance is on my mind each Sunday when I attend church in Hong Kong. As a cultural historian, I observe that Mormonism's "unspoken legacies" here are shaped by American, British, Chinese, and pan-Asian histories as well as transnational nineteenth and twentieth century waves of migration and settler capitalism, colonialism and postcolonialism, post–World War II/Cold War national identities and exceptionalisms, and recently, China's rise or return (depending on your viewpoint) to global prominence. Prayers, lessons, and corridor chatter frequently reference pasts, places, and power differentials of various sorts.

What follows is a hybrid of cultural history and a participant observer's analysis based on well over two decades as a member of the LDS Church's Hong Kong China District. I agree with Mary Catherine Bateson's assertion that "participant observation is more than a research methodology. It is a way of being, especially suited to a world of change. A society of many traditions and cultures can be a school of life."[2] I will argue here that

Relief Society, the LDS Church's women's organization, is a school of life and an ideal site for illustrating how multiple pasts shape the present in a more globally connected world. This admittedly abbreviated account zeroes in on some of the legacies that are generally unspoken but ever-present in the district, a predominantly "foreign" (non–Cantonese-speaking) cluster of congregations drawing membership from mostly transplanted residents from across the world living on Hong Kong and outlying islands, the Kowloon Peninsula, and the New Territories.

My participant observation is informed by the perspectives of postcolonial and diaspora/Asian-American studies as well as by concepts from transnational feminist and narrative enquiry. But it is most importantly a collection of stories, and as ethnographer Molly Andrews reminds us, "Stories Matter. They do things."[3] Relief Society stories chronicle micro and macro change and offer glimpses of globalization on the ground. Women's stories are told in church meetings (as talks, lessons, or testimonies) or in interviews, conversations, or emails that connect individual to collective inheritance. They shed light on some of the challenges facing LDS leaders and congregants in Asia today.

This chapter benefits from work on Mormonism in Asia including, in addition to some of the essays in this volume, Grace Kwok Ka Ki's work on gender and Americanization among local Cantonese-speaking women in Hong Kong; Beau Lefler's work on links between LDS communities in Hong Kong and the Philippines; Taunalyn Rutherford's work on Latter-day Saint communities in India; Mei Li Inouye's autoethnography, fiction, and essays engaging memory and transnationality in LDS society; A.A. Bastien's provocative framing of "Mormon as Global" and "Mormon as NOT American"; and most importantly for this chapter, Melissa Inouye's work on women's narratives in the Asian-American and Asian-Canadian Mormon Women's Oral History project.[4]

HONG KONG AS LDS CONTACT ZONE

LDS communities in Hong Kong are, to use postcolonial studies scholar Mary Louise Pratt's terminology, contact zones: places "where cultures meet, clash, and grapple with each other, often in contexts of highly asymmetrical relations of power, such as colonialism, slavery, or their aftermaths as they are lived out in many parts of the world today."[5] Each Sunday there are differences on display between affluent, middling, and indigent members, Chinese and non–Chinese speakers (and speakers of various other languages, including diverse Chinese dialects), short-term and permanent residents, old and young, CEOs and struggling refugee families, and recent converts and life-long members. We profess that we are "all alike unto God" (2 Nephi 26:33), but the differences in how we speak, sit, eat, feel, hurt, exult, and worship indicates that we are not all alike.

And what of Hong Kong itself, the incubator of the Hong Kong China District? This Special Administrative Region (SAR) of the People's Republic of China (hereafter PRC) is largely (95–98 percent) ethnically Chinese, but the district draws from Hong Kong's multicultural minority. Since 1997, all residents of the SAR have been beholden to leaders in Beijing, yet civil society is cosmopolitan and marked by a high degree of freedom of movement and thought. While Hong Kong's daily life is still visibly connected to legacies of colonialism, Confucian and occasionally Communist shibboleths pepper political rhetoric and civil society, and neoliberalism drives business practices and popular culture.

As Adelyn Lim writes, Hong Kong may have "a certain amount of autonomy as an SAR, yet it is neither independent nor sovereign; it is also highly transnational in both its economic and social conditions." As such, "it is a classed, gendered, and racialized space through which ideas, practices, and resources are unequally exchanged, organized, and transformed."[6] Challenging "first world/third world" "north/south" binaries, "through the heritage of its colonial past, its autonomous yet neither independent nor sovereign specificity as a SAR, the opportunities of 'the world's freest economy,' and its salient urbanism, Hong Kong has emerged as a transnational space in terms of politics, commerce, mass media, and movement."[7]

Hong Kong is a symphony of sea, city, mountain, and green space that offers the good life to many "expatriates" as well as to upwardly mobile "local" residents (the terms are a convenient but outdated shorthand thanks to diasporic and migratory flows to and from Asia and the West). Like Singapore and many other places in the region, it relies on a pool of subaltern foreign migrant laborers (approximately 380,000 Filipina and Indonesian citizens) who keep the city running by cooking and cleaning, caring for children and the elderly, and offering a range of services in hospitality and entertainment venues. These female laborers comprise a clear majority of our Relief Society sisterhood here in the Hong Kong China District, and their stories matter in ways that church leaders—and here I speak as someone who served as a district Relief Society president twice over the past two decades—find concurrently heartbreaking and inspiring.

As Nicole Constable asserts, "Hong Kong—which has one of the largest gaps between rich and poor in the world—relies economically on its mainland neighbors, but it also fears an influx of poor and 'other' migrants."[8] The "poor" and the "other" not only fuel much of Hong Kong's success today (they have always done so), they embrace Mormonism at a clip that outpaces the "local" Cantonese-speaking/ethnically Chinese population. They are also, if one looks at conversion rates, the future of the church in Asia. The final section of this chapter will focus specifically on LDS foreign domestic workers and the ways in which they shape and are shaped by LDS culture in Hong Kong, and possibly beyond. However, I would first like to lay a little groundwork to place these sisters' stories in the context of others that also shed light on changes taking place in LDS communities in Hong Kong—and arguably in other Asian cities—today.

GENDER, GENERATION, AND GLOBALIZATION

Melissa Inouye has noted the power of women's narratives as a way of understanding how Mormonism goes global. Her groundbreaking work on Asian-American and Asian-Canadian Mormon women's oral histories highlights key individual insights and hints at broader trends.[9] Inouye has also lived and worked in Hong Kong and she continues her work on Mormonism and transnationality from the University of Auckland in New Zealand. She characterizes Hong Kong as a place "famous for its diversity and discontinuities. Its tiny borders create a crowded space for the confluence of wealth, poverty, tradition, transience, centrality, marginality, urban, rural, East, West, and nearly everything else." For Inouye, "Mormonism comes into focus as a dynamic global religion in which powerful forces of homogeneity and heterogeneity exert themselves side by side."[10]

Inouye's rendering of Mormonism in Asia as manifesting concurrent homogeneity and heterogeneity is particularly apt for those of us, like myself, who grew up in more ethnically homogenous environments in Utah or in heavily Mormon populations elsewhere in North America. We may

recognize many of the trappings of our childhoods in meetinghouse architecture or Relief Society meetings, but it is the increasingly heterogeneous
membership to which we all belong that moves the LDS Church forward,
towards what Inouye calls "instrumental" rather than "ornamental" internationalization. My current home branch (congregation) is an ethnically
diverse cohort containing a sizeable population of what Aihwa Ong has
called "flexible citizens," ethnically Chinese Latter-day Saints who are mid-
wives to the internationalization of Mormonism in Asia. Ong's anthropological research on the Chinese Diaspora in the late twentieth to early
twenty-first century can be appropriated to discuss how individual Latter-
day Saint narratives inform various aspects of globality. She writes,

> Global capitalism in Asia is linked to new cultural representations
> of "Chineseness" (rather than "Japaneseness") in relation to trans-
> national Asian capitalism. As overseas Chinese and mainland Chi-
> nese become linked in circuits of production, trade, and finance,
> narratives produce concepts such as "fraternal network capitalism"
> and "Greater China," a term that refers to the economically inte-
> grated zone comprising China, Taiwan, and Hong Kong, but some-
> times including the ethnic Chinese communities in Southeast
> Asia . . . The changing status of diaspora Chinese is historically
> intertwined with the operations and globalization of capital . . .
> discourses such as "Asian values," "the new Islam," "saying no to
> the West," and "the clash of civilizations" can occur in the context
> of fundamentally playing (and competing) by the rules of neolib-
> eral orthodoxy. Despite the claims of some American scholars and
> policy makers that the emergence of the Pacific Rim powers her-
> alds an irreducible cultural division between East and West, these
> parallel narratives, I argue, disguise common civilizational refer-
> ences in a world where the market is absolutely transcendental.[11]

I find Ong's discussion of the ways in which economic conditions shape individual and cultural identities helpful for understanding how LDS flexible
citizens (men and women) from several Asian countries bring their own
experiences and expertise as a highly mobile and flexibly minded cohort to
bear on my home branch (and other branches in the district). Often these

flexible citizens exhibit attitudes and leadership styles that allow for greater internationalization as well as decolonization of mindsets.[12]

LDS flexible citizen stories matter because they connect economic, national, and increasingly transnational histories to LDS history in North America and to various other nations. As Ong notes, transnational flows of people, capital, ideas, and goods create opportunities for those who are willing to negotiate a high degree of uncertainty. These same flows create conditions where resistance to change is often manifest in anxiety and prejudice on the part of those who are left behind by globalization. In church settings, flexible citizens may have the inside track in terms of understanding certain cultural references from multiple worlds but they may also experience various types of marginalization. For example, some are from families who have lived in the US for decades but they are identified there as perpetually foreign—and are often the victims of microaggressions or worse—because of their skin tone and other physical characteristics. However, in Hong Kong, they may be seen as "less Chinese" and marginalized in different ways.

Some flexible citizens in my branch belong to families who were part of the influx of post-1965 immigrants to the US (many have now returned to Hong Kong or the Greater China region). They are part of what is colloquially referred to as the "brain drain" from Hong Kong and the PRC to various places throughout the world between the 1989 Tiananmen Square protests in Beijing and the 1997 resumption of Chinese sovereignty marking the end of British rule in Hong Kong. They are sensitive to nuances of multiple identities, cultures, and histories. They are also, in my experience, patently committed to forging a more inclusive religious community. They manifest an impressive ability to deal with insensitivity or ignorance although doing so must be wearing at best. Inouye sheds light on the burden of representation placed on Mormon flexible citizens when she writes:

> The category "Asian" is the result of the phenomenon of panethnicity, in which individuals from hitherto distinct national, cultural, and linguistic origins are lumped together by outsiders who see them as homogenous. For example, Korean, Japanese, Chinese, and Vietnamese all become "Asian" to North Americans who view Korean and Japanese scripts as equally unintelligible, who find

Chinese and Vietnamese tonal languages equally sing-song, and who attach Asian-ness to the basic physical appearance of black hair, dark eyes, and darker skin tone. While these general physical similarities have certainly contributed to the racialization of immigrants from Asia in North American societies, appearance alone cannot meaningfully define a cultural group. On the other side of the coin, diverse "Asian" ethnic groups have at times embraced panethnic categorization for their own purposes, creating a powerful coalition for exerting political, social, and economic influence in the pursuit of shared goals.[13]

Inouye herself embodies flexible citizenship (her own multiethnic family includes Chinese and Japanese as well as European heritage). She travels across and interprets difference in affirming but critically contextualized ways as she explores the double-sided nature of panethnicity within Mormonism. She notes that while

> using "Asian" as an ethnic or cultural category can be problematic, the fact that it exists as a category of some significance within the Mormon ecclesiastical organization and in the minds of many Mormon believers means that it certainly bears discussion as such.[14]

An early exemplar of LDS flexible citizenship (Ong asserts that the initial template was Japanese and Japanese American) was the late educator and General Relief Society First Counselor, Chieko Okazaki. She was part of a prescient Relief Society presidency that charted a course of multiculturalism and inclusion despite resistance from those who were anxious about the impact of feminism and other social changes accompanying the shifting demographics of the US and the LDS Church during the "culture wars" of the late twentieth century. Okazaki, a Japanese American woman born in Hawai'i, was the child of immigrant parents who nurtured her intellect and talents. As a young wife, mother, and educator in post–World War II Salt Lake City, she learned to juggle multiple roles and navigate the choppy seas of anti-Japanese sentiment and sexism.[15]

Not only was Okazaki keenly attuned to the needs of rapidly growing immigrant populations in the US, and to the challenges accompanying the internationalization of the LDS Church, she spoke candidly about sensitive subjects such as domestic abuse, addiction, sexism, and racism. She was an advocate for LDS women who chose to pursue careers outside of their homes, and she promoted a model of sisterhood that embraced diversity and eschewed competition and judgment. Okazaki was unstinting in her insistence that LDS congregations and leaders could "draw circles that include" rather then exclude those who were, seemingly, on the margins of Mormon orthodoxy.[16]

Like Okazaki at the end of the twentieth century, LDS women in twenty-first century Hong Kong nudge the institutional church forward with little fuss, deftly negotiating between locations, expectations, and generations. Inouye asserts that while

> many of the Asian Mormon women [in her oral history archive] affirm the patriarchal order of hierarchal priesthood authority in a theological context, they simultaneously circumvent it [when they deem it necessary] through seeking direct personal communion with God in their everyday practice.[17]

For those whose stories follow, other types of authority and hardship are seen as more pernicious than patriarchy (although patriarchy is in the mix, it is not seen as a driving force) including colonial legacies that stratify the city, abusive employers, poverty and subsequent financial bondage, racism, and physical and mental abuse.

MULTIPLE CHINESE MORMONISMS

One recent Relief Society meeting offered a glimpse into Mormonism's global trajectory in East Asia via Sharon (name changed), one of many converts to the church who came of age in Cold War Hong Kong. Born in the mid-1960s and baptized in her teens, Sharon graduated from BYU-Hawai'i, served a mission in Hong Kong, and is now raising bilingual/multiculturally fluent children with her Caucasian American husband. Like many other children growing up during the last decades of the Cold War, Sharon's parents were from the Chinese Mainland. Although her mother was allowed to immigrate to Hong Kong, her father remained in the PRC, and Sharon spent two months there with him each year.

Sharon speaks of growing up in Hong Kong with the symbols of colonialism all around her, including British flags and portraits of the Queen. She attended a Catholic kindergarten and an Anglican primary school. As for the PRC, however, she recalls:

> The China I knew growing up was nothing like the China we know today. I was old enough to appreciate the stark contrast. I saw extreme poverty, heard "The East is Red" Revolution song blaring everywhere in my father's village. I heard it so much that I actually fell in love with it because it sounded almost like a very solemn yet enthusiastic hymn. Seeing young people my age wearing the red scarf and waving the little red book as they marched almost gave me goose bumps. That was exciting to me. Then there was the paranoia amongst my relatives and my parents as I was constantly hushed whenever I said the name Mao Ze Dong.[18]

Connecting her ethnic and cultural heritage to her newfound faith, Sharon spoke of temples and ancestral halls in the PRC "destroyed or filled with propaganda banners." She later realized that she was witnessing the Chinese Communist Cultural Revolution. But she also recalls that she "saw acts of kindness and selflessness in these difficult circumstances." She was deeply touched by the fact that her relatives—who had little to eat—made sure she had food for her trips back to Hong Kong. When Sharon met LDS missionaries in Hong Kong at age fourteen she drew comparisons between the Mormon Church and what she had seen in China:

> I found the Joseph Smith story and Book of Mormon a bit strange but no stranger than what I had seen in China during the Cultural Revolution. Interestingly, there is a parallel between Mormon history and China under Mao for me: The Little Red Book and the Book of Mormon, the revolutionary song "The East is Red" and one of our hymns "Praise to the Man," Communism and the law of consecration, the March of the Red Army and the Mormon Trail, etc., etc. There was also the desire of a young person to belong to a passionate group that stands for something good. Nonetheless the message of love, forgiveness, and eternal life was clearly missing

from the Cultural Revolution. Living in Hong Kong helped me choose where to put my faith. I attribute it to the freedom I enjoyed, the more opportunities to serve and to be served here.[19]

Sharon recalled that it was only in hindsight that she was able to see that not only were there parallels between Mormonism and Maoism, there were other messages that came through her LDS Church experiences as well. She continues:

Quite possibly the fact that both Christ and Joseph Smith appeared white to me, I now suspect represented a "better way" to an impressionable teenager. It is possible that I was influenced by the subliminal messages I received whenever I saw the governor on TV or the Queen's portrait as well. Of course I do not believe any one race is superior to another. Most importantly, the nice people from different cultures and races involved in my conversion to Christianity, in many ways put Christ's teachings into action. I was touched by their kindness. But I now [as an adult] see Christ not just in people in the Mormon Church. I often see Christ outside the Church, too. It has been an adjustment in thinking for me in recent years. I now realize that I saw Christ in my relatives who gave us their precious eggs during the Cultural Revolution in "godless" China.[20]

The ability to "see Christ" in her relatives on both sides of the Hong Kong/China border, as well as her adult realization that her colonial upbringing, in part, underpinned her conversion to Mormonism (she aspired to "whiteness" as a way to access colonial privilege) has altered Sharon's perspective on many of the conversations she hears at church. While she is still an active member of her LDS congregation (as are her children and husband), and someone who displays flexible citizenship in her cooking, child-rearing, church service, and multilingual code-switching, she bristles at China-bashing in lessons and sermons at church and wishes non-Chinese newcomers would be more careful about the careless generalizations they make about Chinese people and cultures. However, she is guarded in her public judgments, self-deprecating about her own flaws, and feels that it's best to try to "live the gospel and be honest with ourselves about how we feel—not how we 'should' feel."[21]

DUELING EXCEPTIONALISMS:
SINO-US NATIONAL IDENTITY AT CHURCH

While Sharon deconstructs her colonial heritage from her vantage point as a member of one of the English-language "expatriate" branches in Hong Kong, sisters in the Mandarin Chinese-speaking branch have a different relationship with notions of national and cultural identity. The Chinophobia or demonization of China that is common in Western media often accompanies newcomers to Hong Kong, but in the Mandarin branch (as it is colloquially called), it is more common to hear expressions of admiration for Chinese culture and history. One woman who was born in the PRC but had lived in the United States for several years was happy to return to Hong Kong because she looked forward to "watching China become a global power" at close range. She speaks for many of the members, including Caucasian Americans who have served Mandarin-speaking missions or married Chinese spouses who have high hopes for China's rise. Sometimes sacrament meetings or Relief Society lessons reflect American and Chinese notions of exceptionalism blurring and blending in surprising ways.

The Mandarin branch is "the space between" for various sub-ethnic groups within the Chinese diaspora, and their Putonghua-fluent family and friends. Members range from recent converts to life-long church members from varied educational and socio-educational backgrounds. Deborah (name changed), who served as a Relief Society leader at both the branch and the district levels, categorizes the Mandarin-speaking congregation into three groups: Mandarin-speaking families with deep roots in the church (and often ties to the US and Brigham Young University); young, single, and upwardly mobile PRC college students or recent graduates who have found employment in Hong Kong (most of whom are women); and Mandarin-speaking single mothers, many of whom married Hong Kong men in hopes of a better life only to be abused or abandoned once they moved across the border.

Each Sunday, and at gatherings such as Christmas or Chinese New Year socials, the Mandarin branch welcomes a range of Chinese "investigators" (individuals interested in learning more about the church) and each week there are opportunities to see how changes in the region shape women's stories and attest to the fluidity of both "Chineseness" as an identity as well as the adaptability of the LDS Church. In speaking about how LDS flexible citizenship looks in her congregation, Deborah sketches a community that struggles for stability in some respects but adapts creatively and in culturally sensitive ways to the needs of its members. She writes:

> We have baptisms almost every month but the branch attendance hasn't grown much. For new members, I believe they are drawn to church as they can seek social, financial support, parenting ideas and wholesome activities for youth, and leadership training experience. A good practice unique in our branch is members enjoying integrating Chinese literature into lessons, and there have been discussions comparing Chinese philosophy with gospel principles which I found interesting, although sometimes deviating from the core meaning of the lesson. But the problem is we have a hard time retaining them [new converts] and the inactivity rate is high. . . . Those who tend to stay long-term have strong testimonies and spiritual experiences but don't rely so much on temporal needs. I personally was touched many times when I witness how investigators convert to church and hear stories about how some members strive to read scriptures even though they have had very limited education.[22]

ALL THE SINGLE MORMON LADIES

Within all of the branch Relief Societies containing a high proportion of LDS flexible citizens—and the Mandarin Branch is a good example of the trend—there is a growing population of upwardly mobile singletons who seek refuge in a church that, while it doesn't render them as *sheng nu* or "leftover women" (the English translation of a Chinese term for women who are not married by the time they turn twenty-seven), still has some pretty clear gendered expectations to navigate.[23] Some unapologetically embrace feminism in various forms—American, British, Chinese, Hong Kong, or a mix of some or all of the above—while others are ambivalent or hostile to it. Most have ambitions to combine motherhood and a career, and they hope to find LDS men (as partners and ecclesiastical leaders) who understand and support the delicate balancing act. As a cohort they seem to me to be more socially progressive than their elders but genuinely committed to being filial daughters and faithful Latter-day Saints.

These cosmopolitan and devout Mormon women are equally passionate in conversations about spiritual or socio-political topics. Many have traveled, studied, or worked in the US, or in other "foreign" countries. Some are returned missionaries. They engage in what I call "reasonable domesticity." (They are appreciative of a culture that values homemade food and goods, provident living, and feminine flourishes, but are not overly invested in the aforementioned.) All are comfortable with social media and most are thoughtful about connections between histories and legacies of colonialism and Americanism as encountered at church or at LDS affiliated educational institutions. Some blog about their experiences. When pressed to do so, many of them admit they endure a range of insensitive or even racist comments at church. They bear their burdens of representation with good humor, but I worry that in a public sphere growing increasingly impatient with discussions of "identity politics" or "political correctness," a long-overdue and sorely needed broadening of mindsets will be deferred indefinitely.

The most recent reminder of distances left to travel on the path to genuine internationalization occurred in a Sunday school lesson/discussion with a group of twenty-something LDS students and professionals of Asian or Asian American heritage, some of whom were returned missionaries, and a few who had returned to Hong Kong for the Christmas holidays. Several shared stories of how they were often singled out or misunderstood in the US (or in other Western countries) because of their "foreign-ness" or "Asian-ness." They are all good-natured about their experiences, but it is disheartening to hear that even among roommates and close friends, mission companions, and priesthood leaders in non-Asian countries, they are regularly referred to as "Orientals," or are mistakenly identified with a particular Asian ethnic group not their own, or subjected to various expressions of Chinaphobia, Orientalist slurs, and racist jokes.

At the same time, these YSA flexible citizens (YSA is the official acronym for Young Single Adult Latter-day Saints) strike me as centered in ways that bode well for the future of the LDS Church should they remain within the fold (and many of their age cohort elsewhere are battling to do so). They profess and model commitment to their church community as well as to the gospel principles on which the organizational scaffolding is based. They are a new generation of increasingly internationalized believers, navigating their own paths through family, religious, and professional challenges with an insight born of their transnational ties. They, like the LDS Church (and other organizations which must function within national boundaries even as their sights are set beyond the nation), will have to reckon with rising nationalisms as well as familial, political, and cultural rifts even as they try to honor but ultimately transcend them.

Additionally, despite the very real changes that have occurred in terms of empowering women in the LDS Church, including attempts to solicit women's views in councils at all levels of the organizational hierarchy, it is not uncommon to hear these young LDS women of Asian heritage complain that they are assumed to be "submissive Asian girls" or cultural oddities if they do not conform to particular stereotypes. (Asian-heritage LDS men have their own gendered battles to fight and that is another chapter to be published elsewhere.) I also see common ground between these flexible citizens and LDS youth on the other side of the Pacific who struggle to help parents and church leaders understand that they are not compromising gospel principles when they seek more inclusive congregations. Whether expressing support for LGBTQ+ members or claiming feminism in various ways, they gingerly choose battles and listening ears, but they are watching their elders, and they appreciate opportunities to engage in challenging conversations across generational divides. Most keep their own counsel at church. As leaders, we see many of them walk or fade away from active participation for many reasons. When they do so, it is our loss.

FOREIGN DOMESTIC WORKERS IN HONG KONG

We came here as domestic workers with different goals for our families and ourselves. Decisions to leave home are not made carelessly. Some domestic workers have come to Hong Kong to escape from abusive husbands or take refuge abroad from a broken marriage. Some are widows who work to sustain their children's needs. Others work to save for business capital or investments, houses and lots, or to save for retirement. I came to work as a domestic helper with the thought that it would be a stepping-stone to land a job in an office or company here. But it's not possible because only residents can work in offices here, so there's no chance at all for me to achieve my dream. . . . [S]ome women do not plan to stay in Hong Kong. They came to work as their gateway to obtain entrance to other countries such as Britain, Russia, Canada, Italy and the United States among others. . . . In Hong Kong then, rather than finding professional success or an abundance of worldly treasures, I, like many of my sisters in the church, have found heavenly treasures that all of the money in the world can't buy. I found the restored gospel of the Savior instead.[24]

In her thoughtful analysis of the Relief Society sisters who attend her branch, Meldrid Lusterio introduces us to the largest group of LDS women in the Hong Kong China District—domestic workers who bear a heavy burden of caretaking and who are required to be flexible without claiming citizenship. Their struggles are, I believe, difficult to comprehend for those of us who live more stereotypically "expat" lives. I appreciate the opportunities church organizational structures afford to learn from these sisters while worshiping and serving with them. Relief Society sisters who are migrant domestic workers (colloquially referred to as "helpers" or as FDWs—foreign domestic workers, or as OFWs for overseas foreign workers) are for the most part from the Philippine Islands. (There is also a small cohort of LDS laborers from Indonesia, Thailand, and Nepal in the district.) As noted previously, LDS domestic workers constitute the bulk of the district membership, making it arguably among the most gender-imbalanced entity of its type in the LDS Church anywhere in the world. Of approximately 1,800 members, about 1,350 are women (including female and children adolescents) and 1,000 or so are employed as domestic workers.

Latter-day Saint migrant domestic workers in Hong Kong live between homes, nations, and cultures, constantly adapting and accommodating. The flexibility required of them is on an entirely different scale than others discussed previously. Legacies of British colonialism as well as PRC government authoritarianism and American neocolonialism in Hong Kong bear down differently on these Relief Society sisters, as many come from countries with their own histories of colonialism. The women who faithfully relinquish their only day off each week to worship, serve, and support each other are buoyant and devout in the face of tribulation. For me, their narratives chronicle particularly poignant challenges accompanying efforts to globalize and decolonize Mormonism.

DOMESTIC WORKERS IN HONG KONG: A BRIEF INTRODUCTION

The LDS Church is, of course, one of many churches in Hong Kong dealing with the highly diverse and often economically imbalanced status of its congregants, particularly its women. A gendered analysis of globalization is imperative in understanding how to support and sustain communities of faith and Adelyn Lim's study of women's activism in Hong Kong illustrates how "economic restructuring has variously shaped women's positions."[25] As Rhacel Parreñas reminds us in her work on the Philippines and families in migration, "care inequities trouble the global economic landscape."[26] In my work as a district Relief Society president I observed that our well-meaning valorization of motherhood and a particular vision of an ideal family can at times, unwittingly, help to underwrite a Hong Kong—and ultimately global—economy of unpaid or undercompensated care that disadvantages women, especially poor women of color and their families, for generations to come. For a church that is deeply committed to a particular model of "the family" (and has built so much of its public image around that model, although it is increasingly sensitive to differences in specific families), domestic workers present a particular challenge. How do we honor caretaking without dooming women to lives of poverty because that is all they are allowed to do?

This is, of course, not just a Hong Kong challenge. Women continue to perform the bulk of caring/nurturing labor in most places across the globe. Although this labor is often attached to positively charged affects (i.e., caregiving is pleasurable or at least rewarding as well as challenging and is a responsibility gladly assumed even if it is undercompensated or done for free), for many women who leave their own children in villages/cities/nations elsewhere to care for others' children in Hong Kong, the work of care comes at a high personal cost. Parreñas reminds us: "Women do not uniformly experience the gender inequities of globalization."[27]

Again, the mixed legacies of history matter. Domestic workers drawn from impoverished Chinese communities were a part of the social landscape from Hong Kong's mid-nineteenth century beginnings as a British colony. In the 1970s, as Hong Kong transitioned from a manufacturing to a service economy, guest workers from the Philippines were welcomed as a source of cheap labor to free Chinese women to work in factories and offices, but were barred from accessing legal rights and achieving meaningful social status. While affluent Chinese and expatriate families were among the earliest employers of migrant domestic workers, before long they were regularly employed in Hong Kong's middle-class families. Today there are approximately 140,000 Filipina domestic workers in Hong Kong and they have been joined by a slightly larger number of women from Indonesia, and by several thousand from Thailand and other Southeast Asian countries.

High unemployment, corruption, poverty, and familial stress in their home countries fuel the continued migration of generally highly educated and multilingual women to Hong Kong and other global cities. While as individuals they find themselves in diverse situations with their respective employers, it is fair to say that by any standard, as a cohort they are an exploited population who work long hours for less than the Hong Kong minimum wage (less than $HK 4,000, roughly $500 USD per month). They perform a range of tasks including child and elder care, cooking and cleaning, shopping, dog walking, and other miscellaneous tasks. They are required to live with their employers and as such, their living conditions vary, but many domestic workers sleep with children, or in closets and bathtubs.

Nicole Constable, who has spent over two decades conducting ethnographic research among the foreign domestic worker population in Hong Kong, writes that while they "sometimes face excruciating violence [and] debilitating mental and physical abuse," their lot is generally "better than asylum seekers and refugees, who have no legal right to work in Hong Kong." Domestic workers are fortunate in that "they are permitted to work, and their work legally entitles them to certain rights and protections." However, Constable reminds us, "their lives overlap and intertwine in important ways with those of refugees and asylum workers. . . . Domestic workers are welcomed to Hong Kong as workers and not as people or citizens."[28] Moreover, the Hong Kong government does very little to guarantee their limited rights. Despite their contribution to society, they are denied full membership in it.

A significant amount of thought and effort is expended trying to figure out how to best support our sisters who do so much caretaking for so little remuneration. In the early 1990s, when the Hong Kong International District (which later became the current Hong Kong China District) was created to serve all non–Cantonese-speaking Saints in Hong Kong, domestic workers, many of whom were already meeting in separate groups in some congregations, were given the choice of attending "family branches" (traditionally expatriate units on both sides of Hong Kong Harbor or in Discovery Bay), or one of four special units (branches) where all meetings and activities are held on Sundays. Services are also held throughout the week to accommodate workers who do not have Sundays off.

Decisions to separate Latter-day Saints from each other on the basis of language, marital status, or other circumstances are made a matter of prayer, fasting, and careful consultation among leaders and members; nonetheless, opinion is divided on these special units (I refer to them as sister branches). In the sister branches, domestic workers are able to claim the space of church buildings as a temporary home one day a week (even more so when LDS families return to their homes after morning services). They speak up more frequently in Sunday school and Relief Society lessons, and assume more responsibility than in family branches. There is less of the lingering colonial deference one sees domestic workers exhibit towards authority figures outside of LDS meetinghouses and more parity between members and leaders.

While I am at times struck by the ways in which gendered American Mormon assumptions piggyback on Confucian and neocolonial utterances and attitudes, I have also observed priesthood leaders exhibit deep and sustained compassion for domestic workers. There are also some genuinely hopeful signs that branch and district leaders, Asia Area authorities, and various church officials in Salt Lake City, Hong Kong, and the Philippines are better coordinating efforts for short-term relief and long-term opportunity for domestic workers.[29] But there are also concerns that the division of the domestic workers into units of their own denies them a chance to feel equal to members in the "expatriate" branches.

Undeniably, though, for most LDS domestic workers, the Sabbath is a lively and rewarding—if lengthy—day of worship, fellowship, and food that extends beyond the three-hour block most other members attend. Sundays in the sister branches include the typical lineup of sacrament meeting, Sunday school, and Relief Society/priesthood auxiliary meetings; but in addition, there is home and visiting teaching, Relief Society activities, and family home evening. While domestic workers are limited in their ability to physically visit each other in their homes, they are constantly looking out for one another in myriad ways, via phone calls, text messages, and various social media sites, particularly Facebook. The pastoral care extends throughout the week in spite of long days and difficult working conditions. Those of us who assist in small ways marvel at the cheerful and meaningful service rendered on multiple levels in the face of significant odds.

At times, however, the tight-knit sisterhood has an underside. As a vulnerable population lacking full citizenship rights, domestic workers are easy prey for business or visa scams. Along with several other members of one of the weekday branches, Reggie (name changed) was the victim of a fraudulent promise of employment. Reflecting on what she had learned as a result of her trauma, she writes:

> My experience was life-changing, bitter, and killed much of my confidence. I learned that it's very easy to give away 100 percent trust to anyone, especially a member of the church. It is my mistake to believe that because a person goes to church that s/he becomes a true saint. I've truly realized that nobody is perfect. . . . [A]nother matter that made me really sad is the attitude of people making judgment and spreading rumors about each other. All of us were victims and we all suffered because of our bad misjudgment and carelessness. We all are responsible for our individual decisions and no one is to blame but the person who swindled us. Instead of hurting each other, blaming each other and talking negatively or spreading false rumors, we should have exercised godliness by being there for each other and helping one another to get back to our feet again—after all, we're all children of God, sisters in Christ, attending church to grow and improve ourselves.[30]

When several Relief Society sisters decide to act together and are swindled collectively, the fallout not only devastates individual bank accounts and dreams of returning home—or to another country with better hopes for work or family reunification—it can wreak havoc with the dynamics of a congregation. Reggie, like so many other women I know in Hong Kong, continues to live with grace and hope in the face of tremendous difficulties, but as an organization we are still working to provide meaningful long-term solutions and opportunities for women who so sorely need and deserve both.

SISTERLY ADAPTATIONS

There are successes and genuinely hopeful signs that organizational structure can accommodate many of the unique and pressing needs of our highly mobile laboring sisterhood. Even the patriarchal scaffolding can, at times, be modified. For example, due to a shortage of men, women are at times called and set apart as administrative assistants (performing some of the duties of an executive secretary—a priesthood calling in other branches), as branch mission coordinators (with responsibilities similar to those of branch mission leaders), as Sunday school superintendents or coordinators (with assistants rather than counselors and responsibilities similar to those of a Sunday school president/presidency), and as assistant membership clerks. As a visiting leader who had the opportunity to attend branch leadership councils, it was refreshing to see so many women sitting around a table generally occupied by a majority of men. Such measures are in line with recent policy decisions made in Salt Lake City to be more inclusive of women. They are gestures of respect our Relief Society branch leaders appreciate and celebrate.

Perhaps the most extraordinary example of church leaders responding to the spiritual needs of LDS migrant domestic workers is the fact that the Hong Kong Temple opens once a quarter for a special Sunday temple day to accommodate the highly controlled schedules of domestic workers. This institutional accommodation (temples are closed on Sundays worldwide) requires substantial support from district leaders, senior (couple) missionaries and other members. More importantly, though, it affirms migrant domestic workers as valued children of God. All who are involved in facilitating temple Sundays see what it means to be flexible in ways that inspire. As one friend living in California who heard about the Sunday temple opening commented, "the global church may be where we learn where there is give [flexibility] and where there is not for Salt Lake."[31]

While institutional and structural decisions that depart from standard practices and procedures are a significant marker of the church adapting to specific circumstances, it is the individual claiming of LDS principles and practices that I admire. Monthly fast and testimony meetings are one of many examples of Melissa Inouye's aforementioned notion of heterogeneity within homogeneity. Testimony meetings also affirm Inouye's assertion that differences in worship styles and manifestations of spirituality from the Global South often invigorate more conventional practices. Sacrament meeting guidelines are handed down from Salt Lake City, but women flex the structure to meet their needs in small but significant ways with their atypically (for Mormondom) charismatic expressions of devotion. They sometimes sing part of their testimonies and share intimate stories of their challenges with homesickness, culture shock, difficult living conditions, and unkind employers.[32]

Occasions for expression of individual and communal creative energy and pathos in these congregations are valued opportunities for women to step outside of their weekday routines and elevate their sense of self-worth as they worship, steeling themselves for the week ahead. Relief Society and Sunday school lessons, choir numbers, skits, and dance performances— when not over-managed by well-meaning leaders or missionaries with overly rigid expectations of what "should" be happening at church—present gospel teachings in creative, inspiring, and often surprising ways. Visiting teaching conventions and Relief Society anniversaries are carefully orchestrated productions that reflect weeks of thoughtful preparation and displays of beauty on a shoestring budget. Decorations, costumes, mementos, and comfort food are important accompaniments that reflect how women express individual beliefs in accordance with their own cultural frameworks and circumstances. I have witnessed a host of performances from lively parody to deeply stirring readers' theatre circles at these events.

Reenactments of nineteenth-century LDS church history are commonplace, including the Mormon pioneer trek along the North American frontier (complete with full-scale representations of handcarts, jagged cardboard rocks, and imitation snow squirting out of bubble guns). But the ingenious efforts to recreate the past in twenty-first century Hong Kong is not celebrating Euro-American Mormon Manifest Destiny via tribute to "the builders of the nation," the "blessed honored pioneer(s)" (of course, the narrative is a stretch, considering that Mormon pioneers were forced to flee beyond the legal and geographic borders of the nation). Domestic workers in Hong Kong reclaim and revise pioneer narratives to sustain hope for a better future in twenty-first century Asia. Although they parallel their nineteenth-century ancestors in their embrace of the notion of chosen-ness, the "promised land" is more figurative and other-worldly. Meanings are mobile and reflective of challenges that come by living between and beyond national borders.

The LDS emphasis on traditional gender roles, including encouraging women to value (if not actually demonstrate) homemaking skills and provident living is embraced with gusto. When I was first called as a district Relief Society president, I implored branch Relief Society leaders to reduce the amount of labor spent in preparation for social events. The energy exerted cutting out stenciled lettering for banners introducing a particular theme, or the seemingly endless rehearsals for a particular dance number seemed superfluous given domestic workers' limited leisure time. My request that they abandon such high-energy preparation was met with respectful compliance (colonial deference), but it became clear in conversations with women who were comfortable being more direct with me that I had overstepped in my admonition to simplify and undervalued what engaging in domesticity meant to women in the sister branches.

Since those early months, I have changed my tune and decolonized my own thought about various types of empowerment for women at church as well as in Hong Kong society. As Caroline Kline, who has written about LDS Relief Societies in Mexico argues,

> When we pay attention to women's unique particularities of location, nationality, class and race, we can see that programs and processes that do not feel particularly liberating for white middle class US women actually can be liberating for women in different parts of the world.[33]

My vision of "reasonable domesticity" that would free women to worship and recharge their spiritual batteries was at odds with their desire to do just that. The difference was that they sought spiritual rejuvenation via domesticity as it allowed for creativity and expressions of homemaking at church.

The intersectional analysis that Kline advocates is unfortunately something that we do not implement as often as we might in Mormonism for a number of reasons, including that we are keen to celebrate a unified sisterhood and church membership. That is a noble ideal, but in so doing, we may be ignoring economic, historical, political, and personal realities that shape us in profoundly different ways and that demand more thoughtful attention and action. Likewise, those of us who are committed intersectional Mormon feminists (and that designation draws fire in a number of ways from all directions) need to learn to be more flexible citizens in terms of understanding what women deem as empowering in various circumstances. Decolonizing our minds as a global community of Latter-day Saints means being cognizant of both where we can find common cause with each other and where we are different and in need of highly individualized ministry that acknowledges and compensates for historical or structural asymmetry.

Strategies for flexing the organizational structure in order to meet economic as well as spiritual needs of domestic workers are the source of lively debate inside and outside of leadership councils and meetings. Branch and district leaders often approve funds for various types of assistance to individual domestic workers and their families on a case-by-case basis according to need and with careful consideration. Additionally, from time to time the church has helped fund selected social welfare organizations or humanitarian projects; however, most of this support is given quietly, so it is difficult to know the type or extent of resources allocated. To date, there has been a reluctance to approve various proposals for assistance to domestic workers as a group. Although each request or proposal has a story of its own, and it is difficult to generalize, it is clear that the church prefers to maintain a sense of political neutrality and to prioritize some needs over others. There is also concern about the sustainability of various programs or projects. As the church grows (and the Asia Area is the largest in the church) and temporal needs multiply, leaders must make difficult decisions about the allocation of resources. Still, there is a concern among some members (myself included) that as an organization we are overly cautious in our reluctance to engage in civil society in ways that other churches in Hong Kong do quite routinely.

Additionally—and this reflects my own experience as someone who has spent significant time researching, teaching, and writing about gender in transnational contexts—I believe that it is important to consider the ways in which culturally bound LDS ideals of motherhood and fatherhood, manhood and womanhood, family, and patriarchy may constrain rather than empower. While church leaders have generally been respectful of individual domestic workers and their agency, particularly when it comes to preaching to those who are providing an economic lifeline to many family members, there is still a clear expectation that men are supposed to be (primarily) bread-winners and women are supposed to be (primarily) caretakers. But as Meldrid Lusterio argues in discussing her own experience, as well as those of her Relief Society sisters in Hong Kong, there is the ideal, and there is the real. How do we reconcile the two? She responds:

> Sometimes things happen over which we have no control. When tragedy, disaster, calamities, accidents and sickness strike in the family of the overseas workers, it often extends their stay as workers in a foreign land. I hear many leaders (men and women) remind us that while we are working here, our children at home grow up without mothers. I understand their concerns, but when I chat with those mothers, I admire their sacrifices for their children and family. They want their children to have an education. They work and hope for a brighter future where their children won't struggle in the same way their parents have when the time comes for them to have their own family. That's why so many mothers sacrifice. They choose to work abroad so that their children may not have to go through the hardships of life. But it is a very difficult choice and it does not help when others judge their choices without truly understanding their individual circumstances. . . . One white sister, the wife of one of our leaders, wonders why, if there are so many big companies in the Philippines, so few men there have work. The reality is that if a person does not have connections to a politician or someone who holds a big position in the company, then there's no chance for work. On top of the corruption and the need for connections, there are many men who do not have the educational backgrounds required for certain jobs or they are unable to perform physical labor. When men do secure employment, the income is usually not enough to send children to college. So there are many (and individual) reasons why a mother may feel like she has no real choice but to go abroad and sacrifice time with her children.[34]

CONCLUSION: FLEXIBLE FAMILIES?

Meldrid's thoughtful analysis of LDS domestic workers in Hong Kong can be placed in a larger context. As Rhacel Parreñas, an expert on transnational migration from the Philippines, has asserted:

Transnational families are increasingly the norm in Philippine society. If people are not part of a transnational family, they are likely to know someone who is—a friend, co-worker, or neighbor. Yet, despite their ubiquity, the public still maintains quite a dismal view of these families, because transnational families, especially those of migrant women, contest the normative nuclear family with a nurturing (that is, physically nearby) mother and a bread-winning father and conflict with dominant cultural notions of the right kind of family. Despite the state's economic dependence on labor migration and its consequent reliance on the formation of transnational migrant households, the constitution of the Philippines still regards the nuclear family as the norm and denies public recognition of transnational migrant families. Moreover, not only state organizations but schools and churches face public pressure to uphold the nuclear family and consequently enshrine this type of family at the cost of ignoring the different needs of other types of families.[35]

There is a real dilemma for a church that has become so closely associated with the post–World War II male-breadwinner/female-caretaker family model in North America. The individual and intersecting challenges of transnational families in globalization are often met, in part, by governments or institutions calling for a return to patriarchal traditions and conventional family structures as a way to soften the rough edges of globalization. But what if that strategy actually places families in more peril?

In Hong Kong, as in much of rising Asia, rapidly changing economic and political circumstances often generate new opportunities for women as well as backlashes that reinforce various types of patriarchy from neoliberal to authoritarian, and secular to fundamentalist (and a mix of all of the aforementioned). Additionally, Latter-day Saints have inherited legacies of colonialism and patriarchy on both sides of the Pacific, and governments in both places rely on gender stereotypes to uphold exploitative notions of "women's work." Often "Asian values" are invoked to protect structures that rationalize the feminization of poverty, perpetuate sexual violence, subject women to unrealistic demands of marriage and mothering (or surrogate mothering for those who raise children of absent migrant laborers), stall upward mobility for future generations trapped in a cycle of poverty and debt, and shame those who do not conform to a particular type of family structure.

Parreñas argues that for better or worse, transnational families are in situations where gender roles expand. Rather than doubling down on tradition, why not think about how economic and domestic labor can be shared and valued by fathers and mothers? She writes:

> In households of both migrant mothers and migrant fathers, the expansion of either mothering or fathering means the achievement of closer intergenerational ties. . . . [M]igrant mothers who not only relegate the emotional care of their children to other relatives but assist them in doing so achieve closer ties with their children than migrant women who reduce mothering to the role of economic provider. Following the same logic of the expansion of parental responsibilities for both men and women in transnational families, not only must mothers who care for the homes of migrant men impose discipline and authority on their children, but fathers left behind by migrant women must in turn nurture their children and care for them. Crossing the boundaries of the gender ideology of separate spheres via the mutual expansion of men's and women's gender responsibilities, accommodates the caring needs created by migration's reorganization of the family better than does a division of labor that maintains gender boundaries. Such a strategic shift in the performance of gender, while requiring more work from all care providers, leads to fewer emotional rifts and greater tolerance of geographical distance. . . . [A]ccepting the gender boundary crossings initiated by women's migration, and accordingly meeting this crossing with the expansion of the gender boundaries of men, could only benefit families. It would not just lessen the emotional upheavals endured by transnational family members in the Philippines, but by example it would also pave the way for women's equality in globalization.[36]

Migration (and other aspects of globalization) changes families and ushers in new ways of both liberating and colonizing bodies, material resources, and labor. It is right and good to take strong stances on the importance of the family as a divine institution. But more needs to be done to welcome and serve families who don't fit a particular model. If families are, indeed, supposed to be "together forever," we can do more here and now to honor familial bonds as they—like family members themselves—migrate and adapt in order to survive. Those of us (women and men) who have been changed by our sisters here in Hong Kong, and by their "Sister Acts" of genuine Christ-like love, know we have work to do. That work will be done in diverse ways depending on how flexible the organization itself can reasonably be. To use the language of a children's pioneer hymn, "Some will push, and some will pull." Some will work within existing LDS organizational frameworks. Others will reach beyond them. Perhaps that is what Mormon flexible citizenship is all about. What is certain is that there is much to learn from the flexible citizens who are an important part of Mormonism's past, present, and future. We are stronger when we listen to and learn from them. After all, as a recent "east meets west" love story reminds us, "It's already tomorrow in Hong Kong."

Twelve

A TALE OF THREE PRIMARIES

The Gravity of Mormonism's Informal Institutions

MELISSA WEI-TSING INOUYE

INTRODUCTION

"The Church may or may not be true," quipped my father-in-law, at the time serving as an LDS Church leader in Seattle, "but it is organized." Like all worldwide religious movements, the Church of Jesus Christ of Latter-day Saints relies on an extensive, multi-tiered organizational network to maintain viability. Headquartered in Salt Lake City, Utah, in a high-rise office building, the correlation and centralization of the church's formal ecclesiastical hierarchy is readily apparent at times such as the church's semiannual worldwide "General Conference." And yet this centralized administration is but one of numerous institutions—formal and informal, vertical and horizontal—that shape Mormonism's variegated global matrix.[1]

What is the relationship between Mormonism's formal and informal institutions, and between its local and central institutional structures? This paper will attempt to make sense of the relationship between Mormonism's formal, vertical institutions and local, horizontal institutions within a global context by comparing how each local Primary (the church's program for children ages three to eleven) implemented the annual "Primary Presentation" in three congregations: two in Hong Kong and one in Auckland, New Zealand. It is primarily an ethnographic exploration of Mormon congregational life outside the United States, the fruits of my years as a participant-observer in wards and branches of Mormonism's global (i.e., non–North American) congregations. My participation and observations are shaped by my particular perspective as a practicing Mormon woman of Japanese and Chinese descent. I was born and raised in the same congregation in Southern California. I have subsequently served a Mormon mission in Taiwan, spent the majority of my adult life outside of North America, wedded one Mormon husband, produced four Mormon children, and pursued a career as a historian of Christianity and other religious movements in China.

Because the descriptions of three different congregations are already quite lengthy, I do not have space in this essay to engage in an extended theoretical discussion. Suffice it to say that my view on the relationship between global Mormonism and the forces of colonialism is shaped by my work on native Chinese religion and global Christian history. In this field in the 1970s and 1980s, theories of "cultural imperialism" and "colonization of consciousness" came to the forefront of interpretations of the Protestant missionary project in the nineteenth and early twentieth centuries.[2] More recently, a new wave of mission historiography has emerged that both corrects hagiographic depictions of missionary work and challenges the "imperialist" interpretation as limited to the extent that it oversimplifies complex cultural exchanges and ignores the agency of native Chinese Christians. As Ryan Dunch pointed out in his 2003 article, "Beyond Cultural Imperialism," a view of the missionaries as representatives of a supposedly distinct, unitary culture engaging in "purposeful aggression" against members of another such culture is problematic because it essentializes "missionary" and "Native" culture, confuses the intent and the effect of the missionary project, and reduces a complex set of interactions to a dichotomy between actor and acted-upon.[3] He suggests that a more fruitful approach, in China and elsewhere, is to understand the missionary encounter as part of the "broader global transformation of the nineteenth and twentieth century," including the spread of certain assumptions and norms such as rationality, a new focus on clock-time and efficiency, and the desirability of literacy.[4]

Other recent scholarship has criticized "imperialist" and "colonialist" interpretations on the basis that such interpretations overlook native Christians' demonstrated agency to embrace, redefine, and reproduce.[5] The work of Lamin Sanneh and Ogbu Kalu has demonstrated how native Christian leaders accepted or rejected missionaries and their teachings according to their own interests. Lamin Sanneh argued that the overemphasis on the "colonialism paradigm" in mission history ignored the agency of native Christians and overlooked how they "translated" the gospel into their own social and spiritual realities for the fulfilment of their own goals.[6]

The significance of native Christians' ownership of Christian ideas, practices, and propagation has become more evident as scholars began to recognize that Christianity has become a largely non-Western religion. In the words of Dana L. Robert in 2008,

> Flaws emerged in a scholarly paradigm that saw the primary significance of the Western missionary movement to be the monolithic imposition of European domination. After all, only an excruciating paternalism would attribute "false consciousness" to the majority of Christians in the twenty-first century.[7]

THIS DEMOGRAPHIC SHIFT TO THE GLOBAL SOUTH IS ALSO OCCURRING WITHIN MORMONISM

In sum, recent mission historiography has recognized that the paradigms of colonialism and imperialism fail to capture the complex, multilateral, and global character of the interaction between Western missionaries and native Christians. Other recent scholarship has demonstrated the phenomenon of "glocalization," meaning the way in which the spread of global organizations, culture, and modes of living is not simply a macro-level, homogenizing process. Rather, processes of globalization also provoke increasing heterogeneity, including distinctive local cultural forms.[8] The "tales of three Primaries" that follow demonstrate the fact that heterogeneity, especially at the local level, is a constant of Mormon globalization and that the cultural gravity of these local particularities rivals the influence of correlated central administration. The view of Mormonism as a homogenized, centralized production is but the tip of the iceberg.

One final thing to note about all three Mormonisms that we will encounter in this essay is that they occur within liminal spaces characterized by overlapping nationalities, ethnicities, languages, and spheres of cultural reference. Multiple degrees of marginality have historically characterized life in Hong Kong and New Zealand, both former British colonies, hubs of trans-Pacific trade, and societies with a complex and turbulent ethnic history.

In Hong Kong, Mormons have occupied a marginal place in the local religious landscape since the church's earliest history there. The three Mormon elders who arrived in Hong Kong in April 1853 lasted only six weeks before returning home. They blamed part of their lack of success on the fact that local newspapers were reporting negatively on the Mormon practice of polygamy.[9] Significant social distance between Mormons and members of the colony's Christian establishment was still the rule even over a century later, when in 1966 the magazine of the Church Missionary Society categorized Latter-day Saints along with oddly named Chinese churches and Pentecostal denominations that good-hearted Anglicans should remember were part of God's "infinite diversity of operation": "Roman Catholic orders work in one street, in the next, perhaps, the True-Jesus Church or, yes, it is so, the "True True-Jesus Church", the Assemblies of God, Latter Days [sic] Saints, Seventh Day Adventists. . . ."[10]

Contemporary Mormonism in Hong Kong is structured along ethnic and linguistic lines and so in many ways reproduces the fractured and transient character of the city's many subcultures.

A similar degree of marginality characterizes Mormonism in New Zealand. In New Zealand, as Marjorie Newton has shown, Mormonism was established by missionaries who came as exiles from the United States and who lacked access to substantial institutional resources. It quickly became a majority-Maori faith that spread along the lines of *whanau* (family) and *iwi* (tribe). Its exclusivist doctrines and lay priesthood practices challenged the authority of the Anglican colonial establishment, and gave expression to certain Maori notions of sacredness, ancestry, and hierarchical kinship that had been suppressed by colonial rule.[11] Mormonism in New Zealand offered an alternative cosmological structure, a self-contained spiritual and social world that could exist in the interstices between the fragmented indigenous order and the colonial status quo by virtue of its inherent marginality.

In her work on Mormons in the Pacific, Laurie Maffly-Kipp has argued that it was in fact the Mormon missionaries' marginality "that attracted the initial interest of indigenous peoples" and that this marginality "had unintended and even positive consequences for their ability to communicate with Native peoples." She points out that Mormon missionaries' youth, poverty, and lack of education separated them from the European and American colonial class, which separation from Europeans and Americans yielded benefits in terms of Mormons' "proximity to Native peoples" and their ability to learn Native languages.[12] Hence Mormonism, while certainly being implicated in and in some instances benefiting from structures of colonial power, was also excluded or alienated from the colonial establishment in significant ways that improved the quality and parity of the exchange between Mormonism and Native culture.

Generally speaking, in the postcolonial era, the fall of the British empire and the rise of heavily North American global capitalism situates Mormonism in a different position, one that aligns more neatly with the longstanding view of the colonizing culture as hegemonic. The "colonizer" could now be seen to be the centralized North American church administration, while the "colonized" could be defined as all local units within global Mormonism (Hong Kong and New Zealand) that are the recipients of centralized church media in which Jesus speaks with an American accent and looks like the Hollywood actor Ashton Kutcher. And yet I would argue that the in-between, alternative character of Mormonism still remains and helps to mitigate this potentially unbalanced relationship. As I hope to show in my study of three Primary Presentations in Hong Kong and New Zealand, the marginal religious position and the lay leadership structure of global Mormon congregations create an environment in which strong local institutions heavily shape Mormons' religious experiences. The structural significance of Mormonism's informal institutions helps us to understand the dynamic between the centrally administered global church and the sprawling network of local religious communities that possess a great deal of de facto autonomy.

It seems important to point out that as far as religious traditions go, rampant institution-building is in Mormonism's DNA. A local Mormon congregation is indefinitely under construction. As Kathleen Flake has pointed out, "one of Mormonism's most fundamental and enduring paradoxes" is that "it attempts to create highly individuated persons with rights to exercise the powers of heaven by attaching them to a tightly bound, earthly community."[13] Practicing Mormons are engaged in a collective, organized spiritual life in which formal and informal institutions play a key role in shaping Mormonism's radically individualistic concepts of agency and divine personhood.[14] Mormonism, as Jim Faulconer has argued, is strongly atheological in character. Therefore, "being Mormon" is not so much a matter of adhering to a set of doctrines as it is functioning within the Mormon community. Hence in understanding Mormonism, it is not enough to simply shoulder the twin buckets of "doctrines" and "practices." We must also examine its organizational structure as manifest in its formal and informal institutions.

I define "institutions" as permanent or semipermanent organizational structures within a local congregation that actively channel and constrain the flow of the congregation's collective life. Another metaphor that might characterize "institutions" are the ruts through which church members' wheelbarrows travel as they trundle to and fro between meetings, classes, activities, social interactions. Like the earth in rain and drought, these ruts are malleable under some conditions, set and rigid under other conditions, and able to guide certain forms of mandated (formal) and spontaneous (informal) group work. Institutions can include official organizational structures, local traditions, and even individuals whose strong personalities exercise significant influence within a congregation. In my childhood congregation in Southern California, for instance, I can name half a dozen individuals whose distinctive influence on the culture of the ward over the course of multiple decades and in a variety of different capacities could qualify them as "institutions." I have chosen to discuss informal institutions instead of "culture," which is too nebulous and also too large a concept. I see informal institutions as an important part of culture, but more elemental, discrete, and contingent.

I would like to point out a distinction—though drawing the bounds of this distinction in every case may not be so easy—between informal institutions and "practices." I believe that it is possible to use this notion of informal institutions to analyze practice at a greater level of detail. For instance, one way in which we might talk about the Mormon sacrament ritual is a practice variously shaped by a centralized liturgy, local conventions, and the size and variety of sacrament meeting attendees on a given day. From an institutional perspective, we see that the text for the sacrament prayer is printed out on a card published by the formal ecclesiastical structure based in Salt Lake City, and that the correct words for this prayer as they are uttered before the congregation are certified as verbatim by the bishop, the designated representative of this formal ecclesiastical structure. But whether or not the bishop decides to be lenient about a slightly misspoken prayer offered by a nervous young man or forces him to repeat it over and over again depends largely on the bishop's individual personality and perspective—that is, on his informal institutional presence. Both "institutions" (the bishop's formal authority and the bishop's informal personal influence) are part of this practice of the sacrament. We can further use this sacrament example to see that informal institutions can be more rigid and "institutional" than formal institutions. For instance, in one of my former LDS congregations in Auckland, the dress code for deacons and teachers who "pass the sacrament" was black coat, tie, white shirt, and either black pants or a black lava lava (skirt). These precise specifications were not even close to what is set forth in the official worldwide *General Handbook of Instructions* (the operating manual for lay priesthood leaders), and yet adherence to this code carried a sense of conspicuous moral force within this particular congregation.

Formal institutions comprise the hierarchical "priesthood chain of authority" whose links include bishops and branch presidents of local units, stake or district presidents, area presidents of the twenty-four global administrative regions, and the top central leadership in Salt Lake City. The vast bureaucratic apparatus that manages the *General Handbook of Instructions*, curriculum, periodicals, welfare, corporate property, public affairs, and so on is also part of Mormonism's formal institutional structure.

Informal institutions exist at or below the stake level and include the particular forms of implementation of official church programs unique to a given local unit (ward, branch) or cluster of units (stake, district) and placed under the stewardship of individuals who are given callings. In this sense the men and women within those units or clusters may also in some circumstances themselves be informal institutions. Examples of informal institutions include, for instance, the usual format for opening exercises of a certain Relief Society (the women's meeting), the way that members of a certain Elders' Quorum (a men's meeting) sing hymns together, the activities for an annual ward party, or the way that speakers for district conference are chosen and listed on the program each year. Informal institutions may or may not have a formally declared structure or be officially sanctioned in their every detail, but they are part of the structure of the local congregation and carry significant weight in shaping choices made by local members, including leaders, that create the collective life of the congregation.

Around the world, Mormonism's formal and informal institutions interlock, overlap, and blur. Every informal institution is directly linked to a formal institution. For instance, a local ward's practice of considering only music from the official "green hymnbook" as appropriate for worship services may arise from the sensibilities of the currently serving bishop, a male member whose usual informal personal influence within the ward has been temporarily harnessed to the formal administrative institution for the length of his term of service ("calling"). And yet even after the green hymnbook-loving male member/bishop ceases to be formally linked to the church administration (i.e., "released from his calling"), his influence on the ward's music culture may be perpetuated by his direct successor or by ward members generally.

Crucially, however, ties between formal and informal institutions do not necessarily create a global culture that is uniform or homogenous, despite the centrally correlated nature of church publications and curricula intended for local use. On the contrary, in local Mormon informal institutions it is often the case that the link to formal institutional authority functions not as a conduit for global sameness, but as the justification or impetus for highly particularistic informal institutions. At times the most original local innovations are produced out of a straightforward desire to adhere with absolute fidelity to formal central directives. Hence, Mormonism's centralized structure does not merely control and constrain but also legitimates and enables local agency and innovation.

At the local level, most callings last for a few years at most (with bishops and their counselors sometimes serving several years). Because of relatively rapid turnover in formal institutions, these informal institutions can be even more subject to fluctuation; on the other hand, precisely because of the structurally high turnover in formal institutions, informal institutions can in many cases be much more long-standing and robust than the formal institutions in terms of determining congregational norms and shaping congregants' experience of Mormonism.

Informal institutions are relatively under-studied. This is partly because researchers have tended to view Mormonism in terms of its central-administrative institutions linked vertically to Salt Lake City and not in terms of its local manifestations blooming horizontally around the globe. This is also partly because currently the most well-established field of Mormon Studies is history, which relies on the kinds of primary sources that tend to reflect formal priorities and realities, such as individuals' narratives written with devotional intent, didactic literature, and official church histories.

The "Primary Presentation," also known as the "Sacrament Meeting Presentation" or the "Primary Program," is both a formal and informal Mormon institution. On the one hand, the official prescription for the content of the Primary Presentation is set out in annual "Outline for Sharing Time" distributed before January of each year. Five correlated outlines are cycled through a yearly rotation: "I Know My Savior Lives," "I Know the Scriptures Are True," "Choose the Right," I Am A Child of God," and "Families are Forever." The differences implied between each of these yearly themes are actually minimized as each month works through a list of stock subtopics such as the life of Christ, prophets, commandments, the "Restoration" through Joseph Smith, and so on, each slightly inflected by the theme. Each outline specifies a topical verse of scripture that fits the sub-theme for each month of the year and provides a lesson plan for the twenty-minute "Sharing Time" complete with attention activities, key points for discussion, and suggestions for adaptation to individual Primary children's ages and circumstances. The Outline also specifies specific visual aids, object lessons, or games, along with suggestions for accompanying songs. The climax of the year is the annual "Primary Presentation," usually—but not always, as we shall see—held in November. The Primary Presentation is intended to showcase that year's doctrinal and musical learning for the entire congregation and to give the children an opportunity to perform, prepare talks, and speak before a large sacrament meeting audience. The Primary Presentation is semi-scripted. Young children often contribute to writing their own lines and older children usually prepare their own talks (usually with parents' help).

On the day of the Primary Presentation, the Primary is in charge of the entire content of the meeting after the sacrament rite. The Presentation generally begins with an opening song, an introduction of the yearly theme, progresses through songs and the spoken word that correspond to the Outline's monthly sub-themes (often in the order of the youngest children to the oldest children), and concludes with a song. Adults such as the Primary president and often the bishop/branch president often participate in short interjections near the beginning or end.

The Outline is translated at church headquarters into thirty-seven languages and distributed worldwide. Were a child to attend church in a different country each month, it would be theoretically possible for her to learn all of the songs for the Primary Presentation (though in several different languages). Although the text for an individual Primary Presentation is written by local leaders, because they are basing the text on the set of sub-topics set forth in the Outline and writing in relatively simple language so that children can memorize or read their lines, the topical range of what is said and sung is circumscribed. From this point of view, therefore, the Primary Presentation is a highly centralized, vertically correlated, content-controlled performance that directly transmits the perspectives of Mormon administrators in Salt Lake City.

On the other hand, the Primary Presentation can be a highly idiosyncratic and extremely local informal institution. It involves singing, public speaking, young children, and individual Primary leaders who feel personally responsible for the success of the Presentation in the doctrinal, pastoral, and performative sense. It varies not only from country to country but also from unit to unit. It is an integral part of the yearly calendar of the local congregation and a fundamental part of how that congregation imagines and identifies itself as a whole.

To get a sense of the diversity and robustness of the informal institution that is the local Mormon Primary Presentation, I will describe the Primary Presentation in three different Mormon congregations that took place within roughly a year's time, from the fall of 2013 to the fall of 2014. In the course of this year I happened to be a member of the congregations, an attendee of the Primary Presentation, and an active participant in the Primary culture of the following three units:

- The Victoria First Branch (an English-speaking branch in Hong Kong, hereafter "International Primary"), where my children attended Primary from October 2011–June 2014;
- The Victoria Third Branch (a Mandarin-speaking branch in Hong Kong, hereafter "Mandarin Primary"), where I was first the Primary chorister/counselor and then the Primary president from October 2011–June 2014);
- The Auckland Ward (an English-speaking branch in Auckland, New Zealand, hereafter "Auckland Primary"), where I was Primary pianist from June 2014–April 2016.

In addition to attending Sunday Primary meetings in these three branches, I have also attended numerous congregational and Primary activities and have interacted socially with Primary leaders and families. I am therefore familiar with the distinctive culture of each of these units as a participant-observer.

Aside from the Primary Presentation, each of these units is characterized by distinctive informal institutions that are a combination of local context and individual personalities that happen to be inserted into the formal institution at a given point in time. For instance, in the Hong Kong International District Primary one of the chorister's many ingenious singing games involves passing out festive "red envelopes" (traditionally containing folded banknotes, given to children around Chinese New Year) that contain instructions for singing a given song. In the Hong Kong Mandarin Branch, children are so adept at reading and memorizing from their local school education, which emphasizes rote memorization and recitation, that even very young children can memorize passages of scripture, Articles of Faith, the canonized text of Joseph Smith's First Vision, and so on. In the Auckland Primary, before every prayer in the junior Primary (the group of children under eight years old), the entire Primary recites the following verses, composed by a member of the Primary presidency in recent years:

> Before we say a little prayer
> Let each one of us[15] prepare
> Our arms we fold, our heads we bow
> We close our eyes, and: Ready NOW!

After the "now," there is instant silence, with all of the children in the prescribed posture, and the designated child launches into the prayer.

All three of these examples of informal institutions in Primary contrast with each other and with the other versions of Primary that I've encountered in other parts of the world. Primary is not simply a place where Mormon children go during Sunday church meetings, but a powerful expression of how members of local congregations constitute themselves and create Mormonism in distinctive and innovative ways, even when linked to a centralized, hierarchical formal structure.

In the bulk of the essay that follows, I will first provide a detailed description of each of the three Primaries in terms of demographics, leadership, and relationship to the congregation.[16] Then I will briefly survey the three Primary Presentations that I observed in 2013–2014 and point out one distinctive element that helps us to understand informal institutions within global Mormonism. (Of course any Primary organization anywhere in the world is distinctive simply by virtue of its demographic makeup and human individuality.)

I am not trying to pinpoint the "unique essence" of a given Presentation or Primary, but instead to use examples from actual Primary Presentations to support general propositions about Mormonism as a global church tradition. The Hong Kong International Branch Primary shows the real institutional gravity that a Primary can have within a congregation, amplifying the influence of informal institutions. The Mandarin Branch Primary demonstrates the improvisational, flexible nature of global church units in accessing resources for the benefit of the local congregation. The Auckland Primary is an example of how the discourse of centralized hierarchical authority can be enabling as well as constraining for local leaders.

PART I: INTRODUCING THE HONG KONG INTERNATIONAL, HONG KONG MANDARIN, AND AUCKLAND PRIMARIES

Busy and Cosmopolitan: The Hong Kong International Branch Primary

Demographics

In November 2013, the International Primary met on the sixth floor of the Wanchai building on Gloucester Road and was composed of around 150 children of English-speaking expatriates in Hong Kong, most of them employed by multinational corporations or by the governments of wealthy nations. Parents came from countries such as the United States, the United Kingdom, Australia, Japan, South Korea, New Zealand, and the People's Republic of China. The majority of the children were Americans of European descent; a significant minority were Asian, of Asian descent, or mixed; one or two were African. Many of the Primary children had fathers who earn high salaries in finance, business, or law, and mothers who did not work full-time. Many of them lived in homes with a live-in domestic maid who cooked, cleaned, and did some childcare. Nearly all of them attended private international schools in Hong Kong that charged annual fees ranging from $6,000 to $25,000 USD. When not in school, the children were busy with a full schedule of extracurricular activities, including music lessons, sports, language tutoring, dance, and so on. On Sunday, girls wore dresses and skirts, usually major Western brands. Boys wore a range of collared shirts and pants, with some but not all boys dressing in white shirts and black pants. There was a large contingent of nursery children under three years old who were divided into older and younger groups and had their own large classrooms with toys and snacks.

President

In the fall of 2013, the Primary leadership was composed of a group of four women who fit the general profile described above. The Primary president— let's call her "President I," for "International Primary"—was a woman in her mid-thirties with a masters degree in public administration from the University of Southern California, a couple of children, and a corporate lawyer husband who was also a member of the bishopric. She had a warm, effusive personality that made her a natural leader (she had served as Relief Society president in a previous ward) and a clear vision for her executive priorities and the significance of Primary's influence within the branch. "I'm in charge of 150 people!" she once exclaimed to me in a discussion about how Mormon women should be better represented in administrative structures such as the morning bishopric meeting. "I should be in that meeting!"

Format and discipline

President I's manner in running Primary functions was engaging and firm, a style shared by her counselors and the Primary chorister. During opening exercises, the Primary presidency sat in a row of chairs facing the assembled children in the same way that the branch presidency faced the congregation during sacrament meeting. When the children got noisy, Primary leaders restored order by pausing, adopting an expectant expression, and waiting for silence. Primary teachers were generally parents of Primary children as well as young couples without children. These teachers generally had several years of experience as Primary teachers or as former Primary children. Because of the size of the Primary, the younger children had Sharing Time and Singing Time together for the second hour of the three-hour Sunday meeting block and then broke up into smaller age-group classes on the second and sixth floors for the third hour. The older children had a reverse schedule.

Relationship to the rest of the congregation

Primary activities comprised a major facet of general branch culture. For instance, the "Fall Festival" was technically a branch activity but was run by the Primary. Because of the large number of families that comprised the branch membership, a Primary event was effectively a branch event, attended by mothers and fathers who held callings as Sunday school teachers, branch presidents, and so on. Because of the heavy American majority within the branch congregation, many of the Primary activities existed to stand in for typical American childhood community experiences not readily available in Hong Kong, such as Halloween trick-or-treating, Easter egg hunts, and talent shows. Active adult participation in Primary events was linked to the fact that branch activities not only provided a cultural refuge within Hong Kong but also afforded opportunities for socializing and networking with other expatriates. Relationships with other Primary parents formed an important network for sharing information, hand-me-down clothes, and so on, and many Primary children met regularly for playdates. The Primary Presentation was a time when parents and other members of the congregation celebrated their children's religious learning and the unity of their close-knit expatriate community. The Primary Presentation was also valued for its simple, authentic, child-proclaimed religious messages. Children's testimonies were viewed as refreshing and powerful when delivered to an audience of sophisticated, well-educated expatriates in Asia's world city.

Free-Form and Fluctuating: The Victoria Third Branch (Mandarin) Primary

Demographics

In January 2014, the Victoria Second Branch Primary (hereafter "Mandarin Primary") met on the seventh floor of the Wanchai building on Gloucester Road, crossing paths with the International Primary when the latter came up the elevators and stairs to use the sixth-floor chapel as their Primary room. On a given day the Mandarin Primary had between two and twenty children in attendance, some of whom were multilingual (Mandarin, Cantonese, English, and/or other local mainland dialects) and some of whom spoke only Mandarin or only Cantonese. They were all ethnically Han Chinese. A slight majority were the children of citizens of the People's Republic of China (PRC) who had grown up in Hong Kong, but a significant proportion had arrived in Hong Kong more recently from the PRC, Taiwan, or Canada. About half attended local Hong Kong public schools and half attended private international schools (the same as those attended by International Branch children). Their parents' occupations fell into a wide range, from public welfare recipients to bankers, with divisions of labor from single working mothers to two working parents to a father-breadwinner and stay-at-home mother. When not in school, in keeping with the general Hong Kong culture, Mandarin Primary children were involved in extracurricular activities such as soccer, music lessons, Boy Scouts, dance, and so on. On Sunday, girls' dress varied from neat dresses and tights to very casual shirts and pants. Boys' dress varied from the white shirts and black pants to very casual shirts and pants. There was no Mandarin nursery; Mandarin Branch toddlers were either tended by their parents or sent to the International Primary's Nurseries on the second floor.

President

For most of 2013 and early 2014, the Primary leadership consisted of the Primary president/pianist and a counselor/chorister, both of whom had children in the International Primary but who served in the Mandarin Primary. The Primary president ("President M," for "Mandarin") was raised in Japan with an undergraduate degree from Brigham Young University. She was the mother of several children, the wife of a district leader, and the founder of a charitable organization dedicated to helping Japanese tsunami orphans. She was a singularly energetic person—generous, perceptive, and very involved in providing support for other women in the Mandarin and International Branches by helping them move, caring for their children, and so on.

For years, President M was a one-woman show in the Mandarin Primary in the sense that she ran both Sharing Time and Singing Time in the second hour and then also taught a lesson to an age-group class in the third hour. This was due to a chronic shortage of members available to serve. All of the Mandarin Branch members had converted as adults. No one had grown up attending Sharing Time, singing Primary songs, or otherwise experiencing any sort of institutional Primary contours and culture. In addition to this, the Mandarin Branch children had the well-deserved reputation of being wild. Intimidated by Primary institutions and the Primary children themselves, until recently most people whom the branch president asked to

244 | *Melissa Wei-Tsing Inouye*

serve in Primary simply turned down the calling (with a couple of notable exceptions of people who served as teachers for a period of time).

President M had lasted in her calling so long because of her executive/musical/pedagogical skill set and also because she had a genuine love for the children and a heartfelt desire to see them identify themselves with the church and with Christ. "I just want every child to like coming to church," she said once after a rowdy meeting in which seemingly little formal doctrinal instruction had been accomplished.

Format and discipline

President M's style of running Primary was cheerful and upbeat. During opening exercises, if not standing in front of the children to lead the music or play the piano, the leaders sat with the children in their rows of chairs or around a table (the latter designed to minimize the children's tendency to play with the chairs). In times of unruliness, President M's response was to fold her arms, smile, and look expectantly at the children. When this didn't work, she called their names. When this didn't work, she or I (or some other leader, such as a member of the bishopric who had been called in as a policeman) might have to physically guide a child to a seat, or drag a child off another child, and so on. There were three chief causes for unruliness during lessons and transitions: first, the shortage of experienced adult supervision; second, because the children saw Sunday as their day of rest from Hong Kong's disciplinarian educational culture; and third, because the small and frequently fluctuating numbers of children in attendance obstructed efforts to build an institutional culture. Sharing Time and Singing Time would come first, followed by a ten-to-fifteen minute break (often supplemented by snacks that had been bribes during the lesson in the preceding hour), followed by a Small Class and a Big Class that I and President M taught.

Because of the considerable energy and planning required to pull off Sharing Time and Singing Time in the second hour, by the third hour President M and I often ended up teaching the lesson extemporaneously, without prior preparation. If I did rely on an official church lesson manual, it was a lesson selected at random. The result was that these lessons were seldom systematic in their themes, but rather irregular and spontaneous, shaped by the children who happened to be in attendance that day and by the ways the adults compelled the children to pay attention.

Relationship to the congregation

Within the Mandarin Branch, the Primary was a small institution compared to the large Relief Society, comprised mostly of single university students and middle-aged PRC women who had divorced their Hong Kong husbands. The Relief Society dominated the branch by virtue of numbers, activity, and strong personalities. Within the branch, two-parent families with children were a minority form of household. A majority of Primary children lived with a single parent. President M, with her characteristic sensitivity, saw that the project of Primary was as much about helping the children's parents as about helping the children themselves, an aid to parents who struggled to adapt traditionally authoritarian Chinese habits of parenting to Mormon teachings of Christlike tolerance and the individual worth of each soul. Despite its small demographic gravity, the Primary was very significant in terms of branch members' views of the validity of Mormonism. Chinese culture's framing of moral behavior in the context of family relations, particular the deference of the young to their elders, meant that within the Mandarin Branch members felt entitled and indeed obliged to comment on children's behavior. Criticizing an unruly child's behavior could also be a form of questioning the moral rectitude of his parents. The project of shaping children's behavior was seen as an important test for the validity of Mormon teachings and lifestyle standards. On multiple occasions I heard members' testimonies from the Mandarin Branch pulpit about how "the gospel was clearly true because President M's children are so well-behaved." Hence for a branch of Mormon converts, the Primary Presentation represented a crucial validation of gospel efficacy and the hope of a future in which Mormonism was experienced not in isolation, but en masse. Through the Primary Presentation, usually rather notorious children were transformed through singing and talks into models of moral earnestness and testaments to the good fruits of the congregation's commitment.

Committed and Inspired: The Auckland Primary

Demographics

The Auckland Primary met in a [regular LDS chapel in a] suburb of Auckland and had around forty regularly attending children, though attendance at meetings could fluctuate widely. Most of the children were Samoan,

Tongan, or Maori, and a number of them were more fluent in Samoan than they were in English. There were a number of children from mixed ethnic backgrounds. The children's parents are generally working class, with both parents holding jobs. The children attend local public schools and tend to have a lot of free time compared to those in the International and Mandarin branches, due to New Zealand's generally relaxed educational culture. On Sunday, Primary girls of all ages wore dresses and skirts. Primary boys wear a range of clothing but many of the older boys wear either black coats and ties, or white shirts and black pants, or white shirts and lava lavas (skirts). Both teachers and children are sometimes barefoot while teaching or attending Primary. The nursery is medium-sized and well-staffed, with nearly as many teachers as children.

President

The Primary presidency was composed of four women who represented the diversity of the Primary demographic. The Primary president—"President A," for "Auckland Primary"—ran a tight ship, with frequent presidency meetings and a set plan for each week of the year. She spoke Samoan and had a child in Primary. President A was genial; she was gracious; she ruled Primary with an iron hand. Her counselors were a Samoan woman who frequently taught Sharing Time barefoot and a young American woman who had married a New Zealander. The secretary was a young single adult woman who at the time did not teach Sharing Time.

Roles within the Auckland Primary were well delineated and these delineations were publicly reinforced. The verbal ritual of "turning the time over" to another leader was never omitted and denoted a real transfer of leaders' attentions, presence within the group, and sense of being summoned into the spotlight. At the end of every large group meeting of Primary, President A thanked the counselors, the music leader, and pianist in turn with the same formality of the bishop's manner in thanking speakers and musicians at the end of the ward sacrament meeting. In another example of formal structure of Primary leadership, President A delegated one of her counselors to meet with the music leader and the pianist (myself) to discuss songs to learn in the upcoming year. (In the more casual International or Mandarin branches, President I or President M would have likely communicated directly with the music leader.) This meeting began with the counselor explaining that she was the counselor with the duty of overseeing music. It ended with a prayer in which the counselor gave thanks for "Sister A and the keys that she holds."

Format and discipline

During opening and closing exercises, Sharing and Singing Time, the Primary leaders and teachers, mostly middle-aged adults with one young single adult man and a young single adult woman, sit in a row at the back of the Primary room while the Primary children sit together in rows in front of them. When Primary children in the Auckland Primary become unruly, President A pauses, folds her arms, and stares at the children. If chatter persists, she will call on individual children or threaten to not release the children until they are quiet. "Do you want to go home?" she may say at 12:00 p.m., when the three-hour block is supposed to conclude. "No one's going home until everyone is quiet." Like the International Branch, junior Sharing/Singing Time meets first, followed by individual classes, while the older children follow this schedule in reverse.

Relationship to the congregation

Within a socially conservative ward influenced by Samoan and Tongan cultural norms, including general acceptance of the principles of patriarchy, hierarchy, and obedience, the Primary functions as an institution that helps children understand the gospel context for these norms. Primary is seen as an institution where the children develop testimonies and learn appropriate behavior. The Primary Presentation is widely viewed as the most important event of the year for the Primary. For the leadership, it represents a way for the children to contribute to the spiritual life of the congregation by performing in such a way that the sacrament meeting audience "feels the Spirit" and a way to demonstrate the children's religious and musical learning that year. For the members of the congregation, who bring their children to church with the expectation that they will sit quietly and who rarely provide young children with the sorts of elaborate diversions that International Branch families bring out during sacrament meeting, the Primary Presentation is not only a yearly affirmation of their children's learning but also a demonstration of their children's ability to sit obediently and follow directions. While many International Branch and Mandarin Branch children might have expressed reluctance to sing solos or in small ensemble numbers in front of the entire congregation, several Auckland Primary children were called upon to sing at short notice and stepped up to practice without a fuss.

The Auckland Primary has a strongly established institutional culture to the extent that its well-organized activities rarely "piggyback" on activities for the entire congregation, as International Branch and Mandarin Branch activities often do. For example, some of these activities include the Primary disco, the Primary quiz night (trivia night), a Saturday morning Primary breakfast cooked and served by the bishopric, and the annual trip in a chartered bus to Hamilton (two hours away) to picnic near the lake and see the Hamilton temple's Christmas lights.

The bishopric's active involvement with Primary activities was notable. For instance, the bishop and the first counselor and their families accompanied the Primary children and teachers on the long bus trip to the Hamilton temple. The other side of this close relationship between the Primary and the bishopric is that—in keeping with the strong cultural norms of deference to patriarchal authority that I have mentioned above—directives from the bishopric to the Primary were not generally seen as being open to negotiation. For example, one week before Mother's Day, the second counselor in the bishopric asked the Primary president to arrange a musical number involving four Primary children singing a Mother's Day song during the Mother's Day sacrament meeting. I protested that this was not only logistically difficult because it would require the four chosen children to convene for emergency rehearsals in the middle of the week, it was also less than ideal because on Mother's Day all of the mothers in the audience wanted to hear from their own children, not just four "representative children." Moreover, the song that the bishopric had prescribed was an unfamiliar song with uninspiring lyrics. The Primary president generally agreed, but was not willing to raise the issue with the bishopric herself. I therefore took the matter to the second counselor in the bishopric, who took the matter to the bishop and then came back with approval for the new plan (all the primary children singing a familiar song) with the condition that no extra elements such as accompaniment with musical instruments be added. Hence cultural norms of deference to patriarchal authority even on seemingly insignificant matters such as the format of a musical number in sacrament meeting were very strong in the Auckland Primary.

PART II: COMPARING THE PRIMARY PRESENTATIONS AS
EXPRESSIONS OF MORMON INFORMAL INSTITUTIONS

Having introduced the three Primaries' demographics, leadership, structure, and relationship to the conversation, let me now turn to examining
how these local differences dramatically shaped the production of the Primary Presentation despite the fact that in theory (i.e., on paper) they are
all following the same Outline for Sharing Time prescribed by the Church's
centralized formal institutions in Salt Lake City.

International Branch Primary Presentation: Nexus of Collective Investment

As I have explained above, although the theme for the Primary Presentation changes each year, in effect the fundamental format and content of
the Primary Presentation is very similar from year to year because of the
comprehensive nature of each Outline and the young children's rudimen-
tary rhetorical capacity. First, I will describe the Primary Presentation of
the International Branch in the fall of 2013, in which my children participated and which I attended. Next, I will describe the Primary Presentation
of the Mandarin Branch in January of 2014, which I helped to organize
and rehearse, and in which my children also participated. Finally, I will
describe the Primary Presentation of the Auckland Ward in November
2014, in which my children participated and which I also helped to rehearse
as pianist.

The theme for the International Branch Presentation in November
2013 was "I Am A Child of God." The designated theme song for the year
was titled "If the Savior Stood Beside Me," a generally lyrical and easy-to-
memorize three-verse song that was a series of questions and then answers.
For example, the first verse lyrics begin "If the Savior stood beside me,
would I do the things I do? Would I follow His commandments and try
harder to be true?" All of the songs for the Presentation had been taught
to the children over the course of the preceding months by a veteran music
leader with decades of Primary experience and that enviable quality of
invisible authority. When she raised her arms, they rose together, and when
she lowered her arms, they sat. Altogether, the children sang all six of the
Outline-specified songs, along with four additional songs that the music
leader chose:

2013 Outline:
    "I Am A Child of God"
    "My Heavenly Father Loves Me"
    "If the Savior Stood Beside Me"
    "When I Am Baptized"
    "Families Can Be Together Forever"
    "A Child's Prayer"
Music leader's choices:
    "On A Golden Springtime"
    "Keep the Commandments"
    "I Love to Pray"
    "I Pray In Faith"

The Primary Presentation began after the sacrament rite was concluded. Thereupon the members of the bishopric left their seats on the stand from which they usually "presided" in accordance with church regulations and sat in the congregation. Accompanied by the sound of piano prelude, the children filed out of the pews, up onto the stand, and into the rows of choir seats. The children were so numerous that they filled all of the choir seats. Adult teachers sat with their classes at strategic intervals. Songs were interspersed with speaking. Children's scripted lines had been composed with some degree of child participation. For instance, in the class assigned to talk about gratitude for the earth, a child might have been given the prompt "On the earth, I am grateful for _____". One of these answers, "dinosaurs," drew a laugh. The Primary president sat next to the pulpit and prompted the youngest children on their scripted lines. Toward the latter half of the Presentation, older children delivered talks that they had written themselves with help from their parents. One of these older children was a Hong Kong city public speaking champion. "Good morning, brothers and sisters," she began, looking straight into the audience with almost unnerving self-assurance. Despite the quality of the older children's talks, from a certain point of view the participation of the very young children was the highlight of the Presentation because of their charming shyness and unfamiliarity with speaking into microphones. Even when a short line such as "I can follow Jesus Christ" was blared out in a childish monotone, it drew an appreciative laugh from the congregation.

Such widespread responses to obvious bloopers was not merely because of the entertaining spectacle of an innocent, attractive child in front of an audience for the first time, but because of the extensive network of intracongregational connections routed through the Primary institution. Because of the sheer size of the International Primary, including not only the children of large families inserted at intervals throughout the age groups but also the many leaders and teachers required to serve full-time as Primary workers, it would be hard for even members of the ward with no children to have more than "one degree of separation" away from Primary. In other words, even people with no official Primary calling, including members of the bishopric, were married to, friends with, or parents of someone with a direct Primary connection.

The institutional gravity of the International Primary exerted a powerful influence on the branch. Primary, with its formal institutions including its leadership and teaching network, and with its informal institutions including its close-knit, participatory culture, was perhaps the most compelling nexus of congregational identity and purpose. The children's formidable presence on the stage, their well-rehearsed singing and transitions from singing to silence, their intelligent and articulate speaking, and their childish attractiveness all combined to impress the audience with a sense that this performance was the result of sustained and monumental effort by many people who were connected through overlapping church, professional, school, and social circles in Hong Kong's dense cultural environment. The Primary Presentation was not merely a presentation in the sense of delivering religious messages, but was actually really about the presentation of the children themselves to the congregation. This public presentation of the children, so obviously the work of many hands, reinforced local members' feelings of investment in the children and thereby in each other.

Mandarin Branch Primary Presentation:
Pragmatic Adaptation of Resources

Up until January 2014, the Mandarin Branch Primary Presentation had been held not during the Outline-prescribed months of October or November, but during the month of January. This was partly because Primary leaders had generally had a hard time getting the children ready by November, and partly because the natural climax of the year was not Christmas in December, but Chinese New Year in late January or February. At Chinese New Year, Hong Kong schools and businesses shut down for an extended period of time and many children returned home to their parents' native cities in mainland China. The Primary Presentation in January was hence the closing event for the year. This significant deviation of the informal institution (i.e., the Mandarin Branch's implementation of the Primary Presentation) from the formal institution (the schedule clearly set forth in the Outline for Sharing Time) once again demonstrates the variability of informal institutions despite formal institutions' apparent rigidity. This January 2014 Primary Presentation was considered successful by the Mandarin Branch congregation and miraculous by those with firsthand knowledge. The Mandarin Branch children who attended regularly spoke with great decorum, poise, and earnestness and sat quietly on the stand under the eyes of the congregation.

President M had delegated the job of writing the script for the Primary Presentation to me. In the same manner as the International Branch, the younger children's scripted lines had been written with their input, such as "When I [insert a wrong choice here], I can repent. I can [insert a way to make amends for the wrong choice here]." Older children wrote their own talks, unfolding them carefully from pockets when they approached the pulpit. Songs were interspersed between talks. These songs had not been learned by heart and the children had to rely on prompt cards.

Because the theme of the Presentation was "I Am a Child of God," we began with the song of that same name. This song was chosen not only because it matched the theme and was prescribed in the Outline, but because it was a song that the children could sing well. The same criterion—the children's ability to sing a song—was a top priority in choosing the other songs. The Outline-mandated, multi-verse song "My Heavenly Father Loves Me" is lovely in English but clunky in Mandarin. As the chorister, frazzled by the long blocks of time in which I had to "perform" in front of the children, I had long ago lost my Outline and was not aware that I was supposed to teach this song. Even so, had I consulted the Outline every week, I still would have had reservations. Instead, we opted for a short, simple song: "I am like a star, shining brightly/Shining for the whole world to see/I can do and say/Happy things each day/For I know Heavenly Father loves me." In a similar vein, we chose "Book of Mormon Stories" and "Choose the

Right" for the Presentation because the children were familiar with these songs and sang them enthusiastically. We did sing the Outline-mandated theme song, "If the Savior Stood Beside Me," which was nicely translated and lyrical in Mandarin. Below is the list of the eight songs performed in the Presentation, only two of which were specified by the 2013 Outline:

"I Am A Child of God" (Outline-specified)
"I Am Like A Star"
"Book of Mormon Stories"
"I'm Trying to Be Like Jesus" (English)
"Choose the Right"
"I Hope They Call Me On A Mission"
"If the Savior Stood Beside Me" (Outline-specified)
"I'm Trying to Be Like Jesus" (Mandarin)

Another informal institution that is probably not unique to the Mandarin Branch Primary is the presence of native English-speakers and English songs within the Primary Presentation. The Hong Kong city speech champion whom I mentioned in the International Branch Presentation was a competitor in both English and Mandarin divisions (the daughter of an American lawyer and a mainland Chinese housewife, she attends a Mandarin immersion school). This family's children, along with President M's children, my children, and two other children who usually attend the International Primary, were all mustered into service to swell the ranks of children on the stand during the Mandarin Primary Presentation. In keeping with the freewheeling, improvisational character of the Mandarin Primary, the Hong Kong speech champion had forgotten, in fact, to prepare her talk for this Presentation (she always attended the International Primary and so had not been part of our rehearsals). Being a speech champion, however, and as fluent in Mandarin as she was in English, she winged it admirably with the help of her father, a counselor in the branch presidency, who scribbled some scriptures down on a piece of paper before the start of the Presentation.

The pianist on the day of the Presentation was the former branch president and then-counselor in the district presidency, President M's husband. He had been pressed into service on the spot because both President M and I were sitting on the stand with the children to help keep them quiet. When not playing, he, too, sat on the stand with the children, whom he knew well.

254 | *Melissa Wei-Tsing Inouye*

Because we had never rehearsed together with him, we coordinated piano playing using the printout of the script and silent gesticulations. The music leader for the Presentation was Sister Li, one of the mothers of the children. On the day of the Presentation, Sister M and I asked her to hold up the signs or prompt cards with the lyrics for the songs so that we could sing with the children, boosting their confidence and directing the sound out into the audience. There were no other adults in the congregation who knew these songs. Because Sister Li did not know the songs herself, at a certain point she mixed up the prompts for the verses and we sang them out of order (though no one in the audience could tell because they didn't know the songs in the first place).

Importing pinch-hitting, extemporaneously speaking Primary children, musicians, and music leaders at the last minute on the day of the Presentation would be considered highly irregular and potentially a sign of disaster in a well-established Mormon unit, but in the Mandarin Primary it was one of the many "normal" modes of functioning by which local leaders blurred formal protocols to help the show go on. The critical mass of children and Primary leaders on the stand was important to the success of the Presentation because it encouraged the children to sing more loudly, it was more impressive for the audience, and it helped the children feel an esprit de corps.

In each of the three Primary Presentations that I have observed in the Mandarin Branch, one of the songs has been in English. In January 2014, it was "I'm Trying to Be Like Jesus." In January 2013, it was "Keep the Commandments." In January 2012, it was "I Pray in Faith." This last song, "I Pray in Faith," was particularly impressive in its English iteration since the children had to sing two different sets of lyrics and melodies in harmony. Since this is a volume on "decolonizing Mormonism," the reader's knee-jerk reaction may be to exclaim at the hegemonic presence of the Church's main administrative language within a Presentation that was supposed to authentically reflect the experiences and prerogatives of the members of the Mandarin Branch. Of course it would be easy to attribute this colonial influence within the Primary Presentation to the chauvinistic sensibilities of Americanized or American expatriates (i.e., President M and myself) who imposed their will on the local Primary.

And yet while it is true that the legacy of British colonialism in Hong Kong and hegemonic American cultural influence throughout the world has led to what may be an unfair privileging of English over the world's many languages, it would be a mistake to depict the role of English within the Mandarin Branch Primary Presentation as a one-way project of linguistic subjugation. As a matter of fact, parents of the children in the Mandarin Branch Primary see English language training as one of the major perks that their children stand to gain from being Mormon and attending Primary. In Hong Kong, millions of parents spend thousands of dollars each year on English language tutoring and after-school classes. Good command of English is a key qualification for nearly any job, from an ordinary secretary to a convenience store cashier to a lawyer or doctor. This is certainly due to the legacy of colonialism, imperialism, and global capitalism, but the practical fact of the matter is that English education has high economic value. Some Mandarin Branch parents have even tried to send their children to the English primary on the second and sixth floors of the Wanchai building in order to improve their English. They ultimately return to the Mandarin Branch primary because their children's English levels were not sufficient for meaningful classroom interactions. On the other side of this coin, I initially tried to send my children to the Mandarin Branch Primary in order to improve their Mandarin, but ultimately had to switch them to the International Branch primary because their Mandarin levels were not sufficient for meaningful classroom interactions.

The thrust of this discussion of English and Mandarin in Primary and the flexible strategies that Primary parents pursued to take advantage of these church language environments is that the global character of the Church of Jesus Christ of Latter-day Saints can reflect unfortunate global imbalances, such as the way that local behavior is shaped by a global, modern, capitalist system in which English is a hegemonic language that people on the periphery must master in order to become upwardly mobile. Disentangling church structures from this larger capitalist system is nigh impossible. Still, within these global realities, local members act autonomously. Quietly downplaying Americanized church institutions that do not resonate locally, they actively and strategically appropriate aspects of the Church's multinational structure and culture. For certain ethnic or socioeconomic groups in many countries and certainly in Hong Kong and New Zealand, active church participation may offer significantly increased opportunities for upward mobility in terms of a high cultural emphasis on education, role models and mentors, access to inexpensive tuition at a church educational institution, jobs and career tracks as local church administrators, and so on.

Auckland Ward Primary Presentation: Called to Serve

The Auckland Ward's Primary Presentation in November 2014, "Families Are Forever," was the most seamless Primary Presentation that I have ever witnessed.[17] On the day of the Primary Presentation, girls were dressed in blue, red, or yellow (the official "Primary colors"). Boys were dressed in dark slacks and white shirts. Each of the fifty or so children wore either a hairpin or a bowtie that had been carefully knitted from colorful blue, red, and yellow rubber bands by a member of the ward. Transitions were smooth. Nearly all speaking parts (with the exception of the very young children) were delivered by heart, without notes, including the longer talks. Special arrangements of songs, including obbligatos played by children on the organ and small singing groups, unfolded according to plan.

The polish of this Primary Presentation was largely due to the fact that the children had five full-length rehearsals before the Presentation—three Tuesday evenings and two Saturday mornings. Such a repeated commitment on valuable scheduling real estate would have been unheard of and simply impossible in the International Branch and Mandarin Branch in Hong Kong, in which children have a packed schedule of extracurricular activities after school and on weekends. The Auckland Ward children are simply less busy and the Auckland Ward Primary institution is simply more demanding in terms of asking the children's families to prioritize Primary.

In the weeks leading up to the Primary Presentation, President A ran the children and teachers like a general preparing troops for war. During the last Saturday morning practice, after the children had already run through the entire forty-minute Presentation one time and when even the adults were eagerly expecting to be dismissed, President A said to the fidgeting children: "Do you want to go home? If you want to go home, sit down, be quiet, and pay attention. We're going to run through the whole thing one more time." It was almost unbelievable that she would require this of everybody in that moment. Yet she did, and both adults and children complied, through her sheer force of will. She repeatedly reminded children of her expectation that their parts in the Presentation would be learned by heart, and her expectation was fulfilled.

These high expectations that Primary children would prioritize Primary activities were combined with an institutional culture of comprehensive adherence to central Church programs and directives. The official song designated for the 2014 Presentation was titled "The Family Is of God." The lyrics in its four verses rather tediously prioritize ideological precision over poetic resonance, making the verses difficult for children to learn. For example, the second verse reads like a long list of randomly interchangeable verbs: "A father's role is to provide, preside/To love and teach the gospel to his children/A father leads in family prayer, to share/His love for Father in Heaven." The chorus, however, is extremely catchy, and the children always perked up to sing it: "God gave us family/To help us become all He wants us to be/This is how He shares His love/For the family is of God."[18]

Throughout June, July, August, and September, the children had learned only the first verse plus the chorus of this song, which I thought was quite sufficient. However, one month before the Primary Presentation, the music leader and I were informed that "because it's the song for this year's theme, the children have to learn all the verses." I protested that it was simply impossible to teach the additional three verses with their difficult lyrics and to polish them for performance in the time remaining. I was ignored and over the course of the remaining Sundays and the five additional practices—most impressively—the children learned the remaining verses.

Months later, when the music leader and I met with President A's counselor to discuss the music for the coming year, including the Primary Presentation, I noted that this year's Outline for Sharing Time included three songs that were duplicated from last year's Presentation. Instead of wasting a whole month on songs that the children had already mastered, I proposed, could we substitute other songs covering the same topic? This suggestion was met with the firm assertion that "there's a reason why these songs are in [the Outline]," that we would stick with the official Outline, and that this decision was backed by the music leader's revelatory authority. My initial reaction was one of disbelief: how could Primary leaders could be so rigid in implementing central Presentations when clearly—in my mind—a degree of local flexibility in implementing the Outline was assumed by the authors of the Outline themselves? And yet as I reflected on this incident, I realized that this response of affirming conformity through revelatory authority was itself a highly localized expression of the Auckland Primary's informal institutions.[19]

As Marie Griffith has noted in her studies of Pentecostal and evangelical women, in American church cultures with a conservative view of gender, women gain power through asserting their submissiveness to God's power and the patriarchal ecclesiastical structures through which it is formally mediated.[20] The informal institutions of the Auckland Primary similarly supply a discourse of straightforward deference to both central Church and local patriarchal authority. One of the major influences on this Primary informal institutional culture is Pacific Islander culture, which is similarly patriarchal and hierarchical. And yet this discourse of deference enables local Primary leaders to position themselves firmly within a formal structure of authority and revelation. By acting strictly within what they see as the bounds of authority, they view themselves as entitled to the full exercise of their authority. The formal gravity with which they approach their assignments in Primary goes quite beyond the "someone's got to run this outfit, and I guess right now it's me" attitude of leaders in the International Branch and Mandarin Branch. In a sense it is a weighty and empowering privilege, from their perspective, to be reliable instruments in implementing a divinely appointed plan that transcends national and cultural divides.

Hence, although Mormon Primary institutions clearly lack formal ecclesiastical or sacerdotal power in terms of overseeing the entire membership or performing religious ordinances, it would be a mistake to dismiss Primary and the members who serve in Primary as inconsequential. On a global level, Mormonism is administered centrally but experienced locally. The locally coordinated effort and individuated personal talent—that is, the informal institutions—within individual congregations repeatedly transform formal curricular prescriptions such as the Outline for Sharing Time into a powerful vehicle for affirming collective Mormon identity rooted in highly personal intracongregational relationships.

Indeed, it seems relevant to point out here that while Primary assignments are often seen as "low status" or "low influence" positions within a Mormon congregation, in fact, because young children are involved, it is within the Primary institution that the levers of hierarchical power can be operated most authoritatively in terms of demanding obedience and instructing directly. The informal institutions of the Auckland Ward Primary draw on the authority of central formal institutions in a way that sharpens individual sensibilities and local cultural prerogatives. In other words, the non-negotiable authority of the central formal institutions is a resource for local informal institutions. Because formal and informal institutions are constituted in completely different mediums, with formal institutions on television, on the internet, in print, and over the pulpit, and informal institutions in the room, in the next seat, and in person, they each hold sway over the other in different ways. In this sense the relationship between formal and informal influence and between "glocal" (global, local) Mormonism and centralized Mormonism is dynamic and strategic.

CONCLUSIONS: MANY MORMONISMS

The three examples of distinctive Primary informal institutions upon which I have drawn in this essay come from Hong Kong and New Zealand, but they could very well have come from any three adjacent congregations any-place where Mormonism has a presence. Any two Mormon congregations can have wildly divergent informal institutions and hence, I argue, Mormon experience worldwide is much more heavily shaped by local context than by central directives. For Mormons who live in Utah (the physical seat of the central administration, with a local economy in which many Mormons are actually employed within the church bureaucracy), their sense of the significance or the cultural weight of Mormonism's formal institutional structures vis-à-vis local informal institutional structures may be amplified, but this is an local exception to the worldwide norm, which follows the spirit of this Chinese saying: "The mountains are high, and the Emperor is far away." In such a structural situation, global Mormon experience is char-acterized by extremes of diversity.

One of the reasons that the International Branch and Mandarin Branch cultures were so different even though they met in the same building at the same time and overlapped in their membership was the character of Hong Kong itself as a major global way-station for commerce and culture. And yet this sort of transnational, multiethnic, multilingual diversity increas-ingly can be found all over Mormondom, not only in Tokyo and London but also in places such as Alpharetta, Georgia, and Trieste, Italy. Given the diversity of lived Mormon experience found in just a thumbnail sketch as this essay, it seems clear that scholars have their work cut out for them in understanding how global Mormonism really works. The formal institu-tions are well known because their skeletal nature is simple and straightfor-ward in comparison to the complex, striated, vascular network of informal institutions they support.

Examining how some of these informal institutions vary at the local level helps us to appreciate how they function in relation to Mormonism's central authority. In the case of the International Primary, the sheer gravity of the Primary's formal and informal manifestations makes Primary and its individual leaders active shapers of the life of the congregation and of the way in which Mormonism is experienced at the local level.

In the case of the Mandarin Primary, the international and multilingual connections afforded through the branch's situation within Mormonism's unified global network provide opportunities for Primary children and their parents that have not only spiritual but also economic and social value. The case of the peculiar English-language song tradition within the Mandarin Primary Presentation shows how local Hong Kong Mandarin Branch members engage flexibly and strategically with the cultural resources available within the global Church.

In the case of the Auckland Primary, conformity to central authority constitutes not an abdication of individual agency but rather a choice to align with a particular discourse of hierarchical authority and revelatory entitlement. This culture of authority permeates the Primary's informal institutions within a larger cultural context of Pacific Islander hierarchical culture and produces a strong, cohesive Primary culture.

Taken together, these three examples also illustrate two larger points. First, the leadership of the Primary institution is, according to current church policy, overwhelmingly female. The gendered nature of Primary assignments is for many evidence of Mormon women's lack of power because they have authority over only children (in Primary) and women (in Relief Society) at the lowest (i.e., local) level, while men exercise formal ecclesiastical and sacerdotal power over both men and women throughout Mormonism's tiered global administrative hierarchy. I certainly agree that Mormon women's formal institutional power is circumscribed. However, Mormon women's lack of formal institutional authority does not mean that we should dismiss their informal institutional power in creating the world in which Mormons live, both through the socialization of Mormon children and through the role of the Primary in the life of the local congregation.

From a certain point of view, Mormonism is only ever experienced at the local level. The pronouncements of the far-off prophet and general authorities and the disciplinary and organizational preferences that are the prerogative of mid-level priesthood authorities are tied to a global corporate-style rhetorical and administrative apparatus. But the gravity of informal institutions within a local congregation, many of them shaped or

constituted by women, should not be overlooked. Intracongregational relationships are a critical factor in regulating the exercise of formal and informal power within a local congregation, and female Primary leaders' control
of the institution that often constitutes the focal point of a congregation's
collective life should not be dismissed lightly.

Second, Mormonism is always experienced collectively, in relationship
to others. One Mormon Primary culture that I have experienced would
have added a great contrast to this paper: the Primary of a ward in Likasi,
the Democratic Republic of the Congo. I have not included it as one of the
three Primaries for analysis in this paper because of my fleeting contact and
because I did not see the Primary Presentation. On the Sunday that I visited
the Likasi Primary, I saw that no female leaders or teachers were present
at the start of Primary and the lesson was taught by a man who was not
called to Primary but who just came in because a teacher was needed. During Sharing Time, a Primary lesson manual was occasionally consulted but
not the Outline, even though the Outline has been translated into French.
The fifty or so children sat in rows of plastic chairs, trickling in throughout
the course of Sharing Time and Singing Time. There were no small classes;
the Sharing Time lesson started late and lasted for a long time. Eventually
a female leader arrived and gave a similar lesson for about half of the time
of the preceding lesson. The chorister was a boy of perhaps ten or eleven.
Two of the Singing Time songs, including "I Am A Child of God," were
from the Primary songbook, but the others were from the green congregational hymnal. No teachers sat with the children throughout the entire two
hours of Primary. Older girls with infant siblings strapped to their backs sat
toward the back of the classroom, occasionally transferring the babies to
their laps and jiggling them intermittently. Most of the children who raised
their hands to answer questions were older boys.

The Likasi Primary appeared to be like all three of the aforementioned
Primaries, but in different ways. Like the International Primary, it was large
in terms of numbers. The children sang loudly. In sacrament meeting, they
filled many seats in the chapel. Like the Mandarin Primary, the balance
tended to skew toward informal institutions. The "standard program" prescribed by central administration was not present. Like the Auckland Primary, the children sat in their seats with a patience and quietness that would
be unusual for a congregation of white North American children. In some
ways it was most like the Mandarin Primary because of its improvisational

quality. But in other ways it was least like the Mandarin Branch Primary because the large numbers of children gave it its own shared, distinctive cultural mass. The collective energy and sense of group identity among the children in the Likasi Primary was palpable.

To be a Latter-day Saint is to believe in collectivity, in gathering, in organization. In many cases Mormons choose institution-building over the cultivation of charisma, for feasibility over worthiness. In many instances this proves to be a dull and conservative choice. But I would argue that the tradition of institution-building, especially informal institutions created by local Mormons for local Mormons, is among the most valuable and distinctive things that Mormonism has to offer as a religious tradition. With Mormonism's liberal attitude about who will be saved and its generous estimation of each individual human being's divine potential, the question of heaven, or an eternal kingdom of glory, is not really a question of attendance, but of organization. Mormons' instinctive penchant for organization is developed early through their participation in Primary, including Primary Presentations, which show them both the hazards and the rewards of the work of collective religious endeavor.

AFTERWORD

P. JANE HAFEN

[Aunt Susie] was of a generation,
the last generation here at Laguna,
that passed down an entire culture by word of mouth
an entire history
an entire vision of the world
which depended on memory
and retelling by subsequent generations.
—Leslie Marmon Silko

Although this is an afterword, let me start at beginnings. If any question is universal it would be: where do we come from? Origins clearly represent cultures, illustrate levels of colonization, and raise problems of reconciling conflicting belief systems. As scholar James E. Faulconer observes, when origins are fixed or determinate, by text or by practice, they may lead to racism and nationalism. These origins designate inside/outside definitions, who belongs to the community and who cannot. If an origin is indeterminate, or perhaps simply figurative, a door is opened to multiple interpretations and understandings. These various understandings decolonize the dominating culture.[1] Mormon origins of the human experience, as determined by canonical texts and temple rituals, collide with oral and indeterminate indigenous origins of not only humanity, but all living beings. This collision sets the stage for colonial processes. Those processes of dominion and determination in practice can be decolonized to find a communal space for all to become alike before God.

For most people of Western culture, and for Mormons in particular, as ritually reiterated in the temple endowment ceremony, the world was created by a patriarchal God (Elohim) as outlined in Genesis. Human beings were part of that creation; heteronormativity reigned. God commanded moral behaviors, first by forbidding the taking of the fruit from the tree of knowledge, and then by delineating good and evil as binary opposites, establishing knowledge as a basis of behavior or agency. Adam and Eve were given dominion over all things. The familiarity of this story does not require a close reading here. However, this beginning also fits a framework of sacred literature by establishing moral boundaries, by being divinely revealed, and by addressing the complications of life—particularly the universality of death ("for in that day you shall surely die"). Another characteristic of sacred literature is that it is absolutely true to the culture wherein it was created.[2]

If the creation story from Genesis has absolute veracity, it is also determinate. Therefore, indigenous creation stories are, by comparison, often categorized in terms of "myth" or fables, rather than true. A personal belief in determinate sacred text (Genesis) creates an intellectual distance from the self's text to the "other" origin text and allows such dismissal. The point of view of subject and internal belief system permits the objectification of an "other" belief. Consider, then, the 566 American Indian tribes in the United States representing a multitude of cultures and languages and origin stories. Each of these tribes addresses questions of where they come from, why they are here, how moral behavior is defined, and what happens after death. Rather than simple good and evil, many stories demonstrate complexities of choices and behaviors. Deities are often female, relationships are not always male/female. However, if the hundreds of origin stories from tribal nations are valid, they are indeterminate. Some of these stories may be told only at certain times of the year or in particular sacred spaces. Indigenous origin stories are often relative to their geographic area. In the Southwest, many stories are emergence stories in which human beings come from lower worlds. In many Plains tribes, human beings fall through a hole in the sky. In some woodland tribes, a turtle or some other diver goes to the bottom of the ocean and brings back a patch of earth.

Additionally, many native stories incorporate all living characters, including those from the animal world who speak (not unlike a talking serpent in the Genesis story). Coyote may steal fire; Iktomi, the L/N/Dakota spider, may demonstrate morals by his excessive behaviors; raven may show gluttony by eating too many blueberries and shitting out human beings.

(Yes, the language of some of these stories is crude in order to show the spectrum of human experience.)

As scholar Michael Dorris notes, the talking animals are stylistic conventions rather than literal. Humans do not have dominion over the natural worlds, but interact with all living things. To understand these stories, several contexts of time, place and oral storytelling should be in place, thus rendering the tales as indeterminate.[3] By contrast, Mormon scriptural texts can be read anywhere and in almost any language. Temple participation is becoming more accessible to all people around the world and the liturgy remains constant. Native origin practices are reserved for specific communities in designated times and places.

The uniqueness of Mormonism not only provides a contrasting origin story from indigenous origin stories, but the Book of Mormon also offers another origin story for the inhabitants of the western hemisphere. Rather than recognizing indigenous inhabitants and their own understandings of origins, the Western world struggled to fit Native people into its own cosmology. The idea that indigenous people descended from the Twelve Tribes of Israel was not new to Mormonism, but creating an entire book of scripture with that explanation, and a tale of an epic journey by Lehi, is singularly colonizing.

Religionists and scientists have long asked questions about origins of peoples of the Western hemisphere. The best-known scientific answer is the Bering Strait theory that postulates that large populations migrated from Asia. Dakota scholar Vine Deloria Jr. presents a book-length rebuttal of the simplicity and flaws of that theory in *Red Earth, White Lies: Native Americans and the Myth of Scientific Fact*. The 1491s, a comedy group, satirizes those problems of origins and colonization:

> [We] would like to see a conversation between white people who think Natives came across the Bering Strait and white people who think Natives came from aliens. If they can figure that out, then they can tell us where we came from since we are just Indians and have no idea.[4]

Colonization of Native origins, defining origins for Indigenous peoples rather than letting them state clearly their own origins, has both religious and political implications. The challenge for Western European governments and religions was to fit (all) peoples of North and South America into the Genesis narrative. Whether or not these people had souls was a major cause of contention among Catholics and led to a long debate, with one possible alternative being that Natives belonged to Aristotle's theory of natural slavery;[5] that Natives were part of the Lost Tribes of Israel idea also seemed a workable idea.

The missing component of all this theorizing is what Natives say about themselves. Listening to Natives tell their own stories about their origins is a decolonizing act. Two sets of Mormon creation stories colonize Native peoples: the creation of the earth and human beings from Genesis (and the Pearl of Great Price) that is ritually enacted in LDS temples, and a more specific story of origins in the Western Hemisphere in the Book of Mormon, in which Lehi and his family leave Jerusalem to find the Promised Land.

The Book of Mormon rhetoric of universal heritage for indigenous peoples has changed in the past twenty years. Amateur and professional archaeologists have tried to pinpoint geographic locations described in the Book of Mormon narrative from South America up to New York state where Joseph Smith obtained the golden plates for translation. However, with the challenges of DNA evidence showing no connection between Hebraic peoples and Western Hemispheric indigenous peoples, the comprehensive historicity has changed to a limited geography model. Additionally, the introduction to the Book of Mormon was edited in 2007 from claiming that the book identified "the principal ancestors of the American Indian" to a more limiting identification of the people who were "among the ancestors of the American Indians."[6]

Usurping origin stories, stories that establish moral boundaries and address life questions, is a disruptive and colonizing act.[7] The looming issue is how an indigenous person can decolonize such an act after converting to the Church of Jesus Christ of Latter-day Saints. Louise Erdrich, Ojibwe writer, observes in *The Last Report on the Miracles at Little No Horse* that "conversion . . . [is] a most ticklish concept and a most loving form of destruction."[8] Undoubtedly some might say that conversion would require a sacrifice of traditional beliefs. However, if culture is a set of behaviors based on foundational beliefs, then those moral behaviors may supersede differences in culture. In other words, if truth-telling is a basic value ("I took the fruit and I did eat"; "the truth shall set you free"), its origin story supports that value. As part of foundational Mormon morality, the church's thirteenth Article of Faith states,

We believe being honest, true, chaste, benevolent and virtuous, and in doing good to all men; indeed, we may say that we follow the admonition of Paul—We believe all things, we hope all things, we have endured many things, and hope to be able to endure all things. If there is anything virtuous, lovely, or of good report or praiseworthy, we seek after these things.

These values are not culturally specific and reflect many values among American Indian peoples.

With a multiplicity of American Indian tribes in the United States, many different nations live in close proximity to one another. Linguistic and cultural differences are common. Conflicts did not occur over ideology as much as over competition for resources. Living with this pluralism opened the door for many tribal peoples to live with complex and mixed belief systems, especially after Euro-American contact. Consider this condensed history of the Pueblo peoples: after Spanish conquest, Catholic conversion, and violent early settler colonialism, the Pueblos revolted. On August 9, 1680, they drove out the Spanish and slew twenty-one Catholic priests. When the Spanish returned in 1692 with a terrible vengeance, a compact was reached that allowed the Pueblo peoples to continue their traditional practices while also becoming nominal Catholics. When I last attended Mass at the Taos Pueblo Church, the entrance processional was a traditional Pueblo song, performed by tribal members. Before acknowledging the authority of the Catholic priest to conduct the Mass, the tribal authority thanked the Great Spirit, Our Lord and Savior, Jesus Christ.[9]

Another example of melding spiritual beliefs is Black Elk, Oglala seer, and source for the seminal spiritual book, *Black Elk Speaks*, wherein he has a Great Vision of the Universe. While the book is a classic in American Indian literatures, what is less known is that Black Elk became a Catholic catechist. John Neihardt's role as amanuensis colonizes Black Elk's story to complete a vanishing American trope, yet Black Elk's vision and spiritual practice extends beyond the text itself.

Laura Tohe (Diné) addresses the lack of religious exclusivity in her poetry collection *No Parole Today*. In the section of the book about the Albuquerque Indian School, a boarding school for American Indian students,[10] Tohe describes "Christianity Hopping"—how the students choose a denomination based on benefits. The Presbyterians offer coffee and Oreos;

the Christian Reformed were farthest away from the school and allowed escape; the Catholics were scary. Of the LDS Church she says: "Mormons don't drink coffee so we reserved Wednesday afternoons to be *Gáamalii*, Mormon. They let us slap dough into fry bread in the little kitchenette in the back as long as we cleaned up afterwards."[11] This little prose piece is effective because it decolonizes the various Christian religions and shows how the Indians students used each to their own advantage. However, if any of the listed denominations was looking for exclusivity, the Indians students generally were not compliant because their basic beliefs were found in Navajo/ Diné cosmology.

Nevertheless, the poem that immediately follows "Christianity Hopping" is steeped in Mormonism with an ironic contrast. Called "The Sacrament," the speaker, probably Tohe herself, goes behind the Mormon church with her friend, Mary Ann, and together they "scoop a handful of dirt /into our mouths." She describes the sense of "marbles/rolling and scattering/ crunching between our teeth." Generally, children eat dirt to compensate for some lack in the diet. Here, Tohe, the boarding school student deprived of language, culture, place and family, seeks nourishment in the earth itself. She concludes the poem:

> Later we sat in a neat row
> of metal folding chairs
> while the acne-faced Mormons
> broke up slices of white bread
> as we sang,
> ". . . as we eat the broken bread
> thine approval on us shed,
> as we drink the water clear. . . ."
> Occasionally a grain or two of sand
> still crunched in our mouths.[12]

Though participating in a ritual of renewing baptismal covenants and cleansing, the earth itself still remains in her mouth and fills her spiritual desires.

Another contemporary Native poet captures problems of Mormon colonialism. Turtle Mountain Ojibwe Heid Erdrich's poem "Upon Hearing of the Mormon DNA Collection" begins with this epigraph of origin from

William Blake: "Little Lamb who made thee?/Dost thou know who made thee?" Bits of DNA from "curious genome-seekers" are stored "Deep [. . .] underground," probably referring to the LDS Church's Granite Mountain Records Vault storage of genealogical records. The poem conflates family histories and God-created humans with the science of DNA:

> whoever made you
> never imagined consignment
> to secure storage—
> your bitsy cells forever property,
> awaiting the Angel Moroni.

By imagining one's DNA as property, Erdrich underscores the colonial ownership of individual story and genetic identity. She plays with the inside joke/trope of persons claiming "(really) you are Cherokee" ancestry as proved by both family and DNA.

The poem then shifts to some particularities of Mormon doctrine: "your name has been recorded/for Baptism of the Dead./We'll all go Mormon for the end." While the idea of universal redemption of the dead may be one of the primary missions of the Church, it is also presumptive that all humanity will become Mormon. Of course, the caveat of agency is implied; nevertheless, that assumption is part of a pattern that includes postmortem colonialism.[13] Erdrich concludes the poem with reference to the Book of Mormon idea that dark-skinned people will become lighter as they become more righteous:

> . . . our samples
> glimmer in the dim vaults,
> grow lighter by a shade,
> whiten like unto Little Lambs
> ready to enter heaven.[14]

The implication is that heaven will be populated with homogenous white people. Of course, the poem is full of irony. If identity is determined by DNA or "bitsy cells," then the historicity of the Book of Mormon must be addressed, as it is in an expansive essay, "Book of Mormon and DNA Studies" on the LDS Church's official website.[15] If a person must become white to enter heaven, then God is a racist. If one must deny racial identity in addition to discarding culture, then a religious institution, Mormon or non-Mormon, is colonizing ethnicity.

These colonizing perceptions that Erdrich unmasks are not uncommon among Native non-Mormons. However, even though the church has acknowledged that its attitudes and practices toward African Americans were steeped in nineteenth-century racism (see "Race and the Priesthood"[16]) there has yet to be such a discussion about racism toward Indigenous peoples, especially in regard to origins and the Book of Mormon. A section of the online essay, "Peace and Violence among 19th-Century Latter-day Saints" recounts some of the conflicts between Indians and Mormons in the West and describes, without using the term "settler colonialism."[17] Certainly part of this official effort along with scholars and historians reconfiguring historical perceptions is a decolonizing methodology.

An LDS writer who accommodates both her traditional Hopi beliefs and Mormonism is Helen Sekaquaptewa in *Me and Mine*, a life story "as told to Louise Udall," her visiting teaching companion. Sekaquaptewa does not dwell on her conversion and discusses it only near the end of the volume. She begins the chapter "My Church" with a recounting of the Hopi emergence origin story, "Once the people lived in the underworld." After summarizing the story and making some Biblical comparisons, Sekaquaptewa observes that "[w]hile the ritual part of the Hopi religion had no appeal to me—it was crude—the things my parents taught me about the way to live were good." Her father admonishes her to "choose the right church [. . .] There will come a time when all the people of the earth will belong to the one true church, and we will all speak the same language and will be as one people."[18]

Sekaquaptewa says she had heard these teachings prior to ever knowing about the Book of Mormon. She then transitions into a brief history of the church, Jacob Hamblin (a Mormon missionary to southwest indigenous peoples), and Mormon relations with the Hopi. She tells of various encounters with missionaries over the years and in 1953, at the age of fifty five, she, along with her children Edward and Marlene, were baptized by her son Wayne, who had already converted. She says "I have no doubt I did right. I have never been sorry. It has made a better woman of me, and I have sure been happy in my church."[19] Her narrative is a decolonizing gesture in that her Hopi life is not subsumed by her Mormon life. Her discussion of her conversion is important but secondary to the whole of her life experiences as a twentieth-century Hopi woman.[20]

Nevertheless, the problems of origins remain and lead to a fundamental question of how an indigenous person can be a faithful member of the church and still hold traditional beliefs. In colonizing acts, some former mission presidents and local church authorities have insisted that traditional beliefs be abandoned. Perhaps the height of this attitude of total assimilation and high rhetoric about Lamanites came with the presidency of Spencer W. Kimball. Kimball, from Arizona, was well-known for his affinity for Native Peoples and earned the accolade Apostle to the Lamanites. He was sympathetic to American Indian practices but also believed in literal prophecies about Lamanites as chosen people and in actual transformations regarding skin color. I believe it is more common for Indigenous church members to hold both traditions as the literal historical rhetoric retreats, especially with younger generations who do not see themselves as Lamanites. This plurality is consistent with the scope of history and survival among Native peoples. Consider Sekaquaptewa's life narrative where Mormonism is a complement to her Hopi life. Consider also Tohe's writing. Tohe is a Diné woman who, while exposed to various denominations of Christianity, remains a Diné woman. She has written poetry about boarding school, the iconic Tseyi Canyon in Dinétah, the Navajo Reservation, and the libretto for a Navajo-themed oratorio, *Enemy Slayer*. Most of her works are written in English; she has a doctorate from the University of Nebraska and has engaged critical discourse with an essay, "There is No Word for Feminism in My Language."[21] Clearly she cannot be parsed into separate pieces.

Additionally, I see a parallel in coping with conflicting ideologies as both a Native person and a citizen of the United States. As early as the founding of the nation, the Declaration of Independence refers to Natives as "merciless Indian savages." The country was driven by Manifest Destiny and Indians stood as a roadblock to movement west. The institutional project to assimilate or to exterminate Natives is a shameful part of United States history. Almost every tribal nation has a confrontational moment when their universe changes beyond repair: the Trail of Tears for the Five Civilized Tribes, the Bear River Massacre, the Sand Creek Massacre, the Long Walk, the Baker Massacre at the Marias River, the Wounded Knee Massacre, virgin soil diseases, and so on. Although most Indians were not allowed to become United States citizens until 1924, over twelve thousand

Indians served in the military in World War I. They continue to serve in the armed forces at a higher rate (5 percent) than their representation in the general population (1.5 percent). Many Indians ritually demonstrate patriotism at powwows with flag and honor songs. In discussing Independence Day, Dennis Zotigh (Kiowa/San Juan Pueblo/Santee Sioux) of the National Museum of the American Indian talks about military support and the origin of the Taos Pueblo: "The idea of protection goes deeper than for most Americans because this land is where our people emerged and that any threat to it is met from a place of deep, deep meaning."[22]

On several occasions I have heard Spokane/Coeur d'Alene author Sherman Alexie quote F. Scott Fitzgerald: "the test of a first-rate intelligence is the ability to hold two opposed ideas in the mind at the same time, and still retain the ability to function."[23] Perhaps that is one dilemma of colonialism. Recognizing that more than one origin story can co-exist with another does not require the dismissal of either. Life's experiences are not a singular narrative, but full of complexities. Origin stories may echo those complexities.

Linda Tuhiwai Smith lists twenty-five projects of decolonizing indigenous peoples. Of "storytelling," she says,

> Oral traditions [...] are still a reality in day-to-day indigenous lives. Importantly, storytelling is also about humour and gossip and creativity. Stories tell of love and sexual encounters, of war and revenge. Their themes tell us about our cultures.[24]

Origin stories fall into this description. They reveal moral foundations of cultures. Their oral nature renders them indeterminate. They are complex.

Another aspect of decolonizing is testimony. In the essays in this volume, many of the authors give testimony of their experiences with Mormonism and its conflicts with their own culture or race. By bearing witness, these writers show how community can exist even when these differences are painful. Gina Colvin tells of her family history and the consequences of colonial practices, both good and bad, in conversion; she sees individual reconciliation through faith but acknowledges the hurtful marginalization of Indigenous peoples. Rolf Straubhaar boldly acknowledges white privilege in structural practices and the need for "critical consciousness" in addressing practical inequalities. Thomas Murphy, Angelo Baca (Navajo) and Elise

Boxer (Dakota) show the dissonance of Indigeneity and the literal textual readings of the Book of Mormon. Alicia Harris (Assiniboine) also feels that conflict but situates it within her own multiracial identity. Mica McGriggs addresses Mormon cultural racism in her own biracial experience. Melissa Wei-tsing Inouye, Ingrid Sherlock, and Stacilee Ford contextualize their international observations and experiences in contrast to the unspoken, yet determinate culture of the central Mormon practices of Utah. Ignacio Garcia outlines how restructuring can decolonize according to the needs of his congregation. Joanna Brooks reframes the historical narrative of race relations in a new historical pattern that reveals the complexities of Mormon history with minority populations.

Each of the writers in this collection shows in some way how determinate or formal practices and texts colonize marginalized LDS peoples. They each, in their own way, decolonize those practices and texts through informal adjustments, by telling their own stories, and by illustrating the complexities of Mormon life.

Also complex is the balancing of determinate and indeterminate understandings of origins. As Faulconer also observes, determinate and indeterminate origins render possibilities that would bring us together in the community of saints: Past and future make us. Concrete past and future—together a determinate origin that is incapable of final determination, so always giving rise to new meanings and possibilities—are transcendent and our relation to them is transcendence. Our origin constantly draws us beyond ourselves and constitutes us in doing so. However, second, this historical origin is not the only kind of transcendence, for in it we find interruption, the interruption that makes the determinate origin also indeterminate. Our origin is broken, incapable of final determination, so it always draws us beyond not only ourselves but also beyond our historical context and constitution.[25]

For Mormons to see Indigenous peoples as "alike unto God" (2 Nephi 26:33), the relationship must decolonize. We need to see, as Black Elk saw, that we are all children of one mother and one father. In dedicatory prayers at three temples with proximity to Indian reservations, Vernal, Utah; Monticello, Utah; and Snowflake, Arizona, Gordon B. Hinckley expressed a common sentiment: "May old animosities be dispelled, and may there come a renewed spirit of brotherhood and love and respect."[26] That is a beginning.

NOTES

INTRODUCTION

1. Hugh Nibley, *Approaching Zion*, ed. Don Norton (Salt Lake City: Deseret Book Company, 1989) 28–30.
2. "American Samoa—LDS Statistics and Church Facts" Mormon Newsroom, accessed October 23, 2017, http://www.mormonnewsroom.org/facts-and-statistics/country /american-samoa/.
3. For contemporary introductions to theories and practices of decolonization, see Linda Tuhiwai Smith, *Decolonizing Methodologies: Research and Indigenous Peoples*, 2nd ed. (London: Zed Books, 2012); Waziyatawin Angela Wilson and Michael Yellow Bird, *For Indigenous Eyes Only: A Decolonization Handbook* (Santa Fe: School of American Research, 2005); and Waziyatawin and Michael Yellow Bird, *For Indigenous Minds Only: A Decolonization Handbook* (Santa Fe: School of American Research, 2012). These authors provide a helpful and practical point of entry into the much larger body of decolonizing thought and writing produced by thinkers such as Aime Cesaire, Frantz Fanon, Albert Memmi, and Vine Deloria.
4. Samuel Brown, *In Heaven as It Is on Earth: Joseph Smith and the Early Mormon Conquest of Death* (New York: Oxford University Press, 2012).
5. Richard Jackson, *Places of Worship: 150 Years of Latter-Day Saint Architecture* (Provo, UT: Brigham Young University Press, 2003).
6. Walter Benjamin, *Illuminations* (New York: Schocken, 1968), 257–258.
7. Ibid., 255.
8. James Cone, *Risks of Faith: The Emergence of a Black Theology of Liberation, 1968–1998* (Boston: Beacon, 1999), 11.
9. "Our Glory or Our Condemnation," in Nibley, *Approaching Zion*, 20–21.
10. "We Will Sing of Zion," hymn no. 47, *Hymns of The Church of Jesus Christ of Latter-day Saints* (Salt Lake City: Corporation of the President, 1985).

CHAPTER 1

1. A *marae* is a traditional meeting place which often includes a meeting house, kitchen, dining room, and ablutions. Marae are often given the name of ancestors associated with that area and are thus a place of belonging and ancestral/tribal identity.

Hinerupe was the wife of Hukarere, brother of Tuwhakairiora, both descendants of Porourangi for whom many of the people of the East Coast district are named—Ngāti Porou—"Ngāti" being the suffix used to express one's descent. Thus, those of the tribe Ngati Porou are descendants of Porourangi. Hinerupe marae remembers this ancestress of Te Araroa who along with her two sisters were known as Nga Kopara o Rongomaitapui. Mead (2004) interprets this proverb as meaning: "'Rongomaitapui's bellbirds are chirping.'" The saying was originally aimed at the three daughters of Rongomaitapui and Uetaha, but may be applied to any group of talkative women (p. 163).

2. *Tangi* means literally 'to cry', but is also used to refer to funereal ceremonies, particularly those held at a marae.

3. *Koroua*—male elder.

4. *Tikanga*—protocols, rituals, and procedures. The "right" things to do.

5. *Kuia*—old women.

6. *Whare Whakairo*—carved house.

7. *Advances to Settlers Act* (1894): low-interest loans made available to white settlers to buy land from the government.

CHAPTER 2

1. *History of Montgomery and Fulton Counties, N.Y.* (New York: F.W. Beers & Co., 1878), 108. See also Thomas W. Murphy, Jessyca B. Murphy, and Kerrie S. Murphy, "An Indian Princess and a Mormon Sacagawea: Decolonizing Memories of Our Grandmothers," in *Race, Gender, and Power on the Mormon Borderlands*, ed. Andrea Radke-Moss, Dee Garceau, and Sujey Vega, forthcoming.

2. Karen Boren, "Indians to Settlers: 'We Must Help One Another,'" *Church News*, July 5, 1997.

3. Murphy, Murphy, and Murphy, "Indian Princess."

4. Thomas W. Murphy, "Laban's Ghost: On Writing and Transgression," *Dialogue: A Journal of Mormon Thought* 30 (Summer 1997); Thomas W. Murphy, "Sin, Skin, and Seed: Mistakes of Men in the Book of Mormon," *Journal of the John Whitmer Historical Association* 25 (2004): 36–51.

5. *History of the Church of Jesus Christ of Latter-day Saints* (Salt Lake City: Deseret Book, 1949), 2:362.

6. *Journal History of the Church*, November 20, 1850.

7. Lori Elaine Taylor, "Telling Stories About Mormons and Indians" (PhD diss., State University of New York at Buffalo, 2000). W. Paul Reeve, *Religion of a Different Color: Race and the Mormon Struggle for Whiteness* (New York: Oxford University Press, 2015).

8. David Martin, *Tongues of Fire: The Explosion of Protestantism in Latin America* (New Jersey: Wiley, 1993); Mark P. Leone, *Roots of Modern Mormonism* (Cambridge: Harvard University Press, 1979); F. LaMond Tullis, *Mormons in Mexico: The Dynamics of Faith and Culture* (Logan: Utah State University Press, 1987).

9. Thomas W. Murphy, "Reinventing Mormonism: Guatemala as a Harbinger of the Future?" *Dialogue: A Journal of Mormon Thought* 29 (Spring 1996): 177–192.

10. Thomas W. Murphy, "Fifty Years of United Order in Mexico," *Sunstone* 20, (October 1997): 69; Murphy, "'Stronger Than Ever': Remnants of the Third Convention," *Journal of Latter Day Saint History* 10 (1998): 1, 8–11.

11. Thomas W. Murphy, *Imagining Lamanites: Native Americans and the Book of Mormon* (Seattle: University of Washington, 2003); Thomas W. Murphy and Simon G. Southerton, "Genetic Research a 'Galileo Event' for Mormons," *Anthropology News* 44, no. 2 (2003): 20.

12. Murphy, *Imagining Lamanites*, 142–43; Murphy and Southerton, "Genetic Research a 'Galileo Event,'" 20.

13. Linda Tuihiwai Smith, *Decolonizing Methodologies: Research and Indigenous Peoples*, 2nd ed. (New York: Zed Books, 2012); Susan A. Miller and James Riding In, *Native Historians Write Back: Decolonizing American Indian History* (Lubbock: Texas Tech University Press, 2011).

14. Thomas W. Murphy, "Lamanite Genesis, Genealogy, and Genetics," in *American Apocrypha: Essays on the Book of Mormon*, ed. Dan Vogel and Brent Lee Metcalfe (Salt Lake City: Signature Books, 2002), 47–77.

15. Ibid., 68.

16. Suzan Mazur, "Mormons in the Olympic Spotlight: Polygamy and Scripture Threaten to Steal Some of the Thunder from Winter Games in Utah," *Financial Times*, February 9, 2002; William Lobdell, "Bedrock of a Faith Is Jolted," *Los Angeles Times*, February 16, 2006.

17. William Lobdell and Larry B Stammer, "Mormon Scientist, Church Clash over DNA Test," *Los Angeles Times*, December 8, 2002.

18. Smith, *Decolonizing Methodologies*; Margaret E. Kovach, *Indigenous Methodologies: Characteristics, Conversations, and Contexts* (University of Toronto Press, Scholarly Publishing Division, 2010).

19. Dozens of short videos produced from a decolonization perspective are available on YouTube and other online media. See https://www.youtube.com/user/takinitbakk/videos for a good selection.

20. Joel Kramer and Jeremy Reyes, *DNA Vs. The Book of Mormon* (Brigham City, Utah: Living Hope Ministries, 2003); Scott Johnson and Joel Kramer, *The Bible vs. The Book of Mormon* (Brigham City, Utah: Living Hope Ministries, 2005).

21. Angelo Baca, *In Laman's Terms: Looking at Lamanite Identity* (Seattle, WA: Native Voices, 2008).

22. Catherine Bell and Robert Paterson, *Protection of First Nations Cultural Heritage: Laws, Policy, and Reform* (Vancouver: University of British Columbia Press, 2009).

23. Thomas W. Murphy and Angelo Baca, "Rejecting Racism in Any Form: Latter-Day Saint Rhetoric, Religion, and Repatriation," *Open Theology*, no. 2 (2016): 700–725; Samuel Morris Brown, *In Heaven as It Is on Earth: Joseph Smith and the Early Mormon Conquest of Death* (New York: Oxford University Press, 2012).

24. Vine Deloria, Jr., *God Is Red: A Native View of Religion, the Classic Work Updated* (Golden, CO: Fulcrum Publishing, 1994), 99–100.

25. Vine Deloria Jr. "Vision and Community," in *For This Land: Writings on Religion in America*, ed. James Treat (New York: Routledge, 1999), 116–17.

26. Douglas Campbell, "'White' or 'Pure': Five Vignettes," *Dialogue: A Journal of Mormon Thought* 29 (Winter 1996): 119–135.

27. Tom Porter, *And Grandma Said . . . Iroquois Teachings as Passed Down through the Oral Tradition* (Bloomington, IN: Xlibris Corporation, 2008); Barbara Alice Mann, *Native Americans, Archaeologists, & the Mounds* (New York: Peter Lang, 2003); Mann, *Iroquoian Women: The Gantowisas* (New York: Peter Lang, 2011).

28. Thomas W. Murphy, "Simply Implausible: DNA and a Mesoamerican Setting for the Book of Mormon," *Dialogue: A Journal of Mormon Thought* 36, no. 4 (2003): 109–131. Murphy, "Inventing Galileo," *Sunstone*, no. 131 (2004): 58–61.

29. See Sandy Grande, *Red Pedagogy: Native American Social and Political Thought* (Lanham, MD: Rowman & Littlefield Publishers, 2004); Paulo Freire, *Pedagogy of the Oppressed: 30th Anniversary Edition* (London: Bloomsbury Publishing, 2014); bell hooks, *Teaching Community: A Pedagogy of Hope* (United Kingdom: Taylor & Francis, 2013); Devon A. Mihesuah and Angela C. Wilson, *Indigenizing the Academy: Transforming Scholarship and Empowering Communities* (Omaha: University of Nebraska Press, 2004).

30. Eugene Hunn, *A Zapotec Natural History: Trees, Herbs, and Flowers, Birds, Beasts, and Bugs in the Life of San Juan Gbëë* (Tucson: University of Arizona Press, 2008).

31. See Melissa Nelson, *Original Instructions: Indigenous Teachings for a Sustainable Future* (Rochester: Bear and Company, 2008); Daniel Wildcat, *Red Alert! Saving the Planet with Indigenous Knowledge* (Golden, CO: Fulcrum Publishing, 2009); Gregory Cajete, *Native Science: Natural Laws of Interdependence* (Santa Fe: Clear Light Publishers, 2000).

32. See Daniel S. Blumenthal, et al., *Community-Based Participatory Health Research: Issues, Methods, and Translation to Practice* (New York: Springer Publishing, 2013); Nina B. Wallerstein and Bonnie Duran, "Using Community-Based Participatory Research to Address Health Disparities," *Health Promotion Practice* 7, no. 3 (2006): 312–323.

33. Jessyca B. Murphy, "The White Indin': Native American Appropriations in Hipster Fashion," in *Unsettling Whiteness*, ed. Lucy Michael and Samantha Schulz (Oxford: Inter-Disciplinary Press, 2014), 127–138.

34. Thomas W. Murphy, review of *The Book of Mormon: A Biography*, by Paul Gutjahr, *Nova Religio* 17, no. 3 (2014): 128–129.

35. Thomas W. Murphy, review of *By the Hand of Mormon: The American Scripture That Launched a New World Religion*, by Terryl L. Givens, *Journal of Mormon History* 28, no. 2 (2002): 192–198.

36. American Friends Service Committee, *Tribal Journeys Handbook and Study Guide* (Seattle: Cedar Media, 2011).

37. Mark Celletti, *Canoe Way* (Tacoma, WA: Cedar Media, 2009).

38. Hokulani K. Aikau, *A Chosen People, a Promised Land: Mormonism and Race in Hawai'i* (Minneapolis: University of Minnesota Press, 2012); Angela Waziyatawin Wilson and Michael Yellow Bird, *For Indigenous Eyes Only: A Decolonization Handbook* (School of American Research, 2005); Michael Yellow Bird and Angela Waziyatawin Wilson, *For Indigenous Minds Only: A Decolonization Handbook* (Santa Fe: School of American Research Press, 2012); Mark G. Brett, *Decolonizing God: The Bible in the Tides of Empire* (Sheffield, England: Sheffield Phoenix Press, 2009); David Joy and Joseph F. Duggan, *Decolonizing the Body of Christ: Theology and Theory after Empire?* (New York: Palgrave Macmillan, 2012); Richard Twiss, *Rescuing the Gospel from the Cowboys: A Native American Expression of the Jesus Way* (Downers

Grove, IL: IVP Books, 2015); Amos Yong and Barbara B. Zikmund, *Remembering Jamestown: Hard Questions about Christian Mission* (Eugene, OR: Pickwick Publications, 2010); James Treat, *Around the Sacred Fire: Native Religious Activism in the Red Power Era* (New York: Palgrave Macmillan, 2003).

CHAPTER 3

1. George P. Lee, *Silent Courage: An Indian Story, the Autobiography of George P. Lee, a Navajo,* (Salt Lake City: Deseret Book, 1987), 40.
2. Baca, *In Laman's Terms.*
3. Terry Macy and Daniel W. Hart, *White Shamans, Plastic Medicine Men: A Documentary,* (Native Voices Public Television, 1996).
4. Taiaiake Alfred, *Wasase: Indigenous Pathways of Action and Freedom.* (Toronto: University of Toronto Press, 2005), 157.

CHAPTER 4

1. Adria L. Imada, "'Aloha 'Oe': Settler-Colonial Nostalgia and the Genealogy of a Love Song," *American Indian Culture and Research Journal* 37, no. 2 (2013): 36.
2. Jared Farmer, *On Zion's Mount: Mormons, Indians, and the American Landscape* (Cambridge: Harvard University Press, 2008).
3. Patrick Wolfe, "The Settler Complex: An Introduction," *American Indian Culture and Research Journal* 37, no. 2 (2013): 1.
4. Ibid.
5. Patrick Wolfe, "Settler Colonialism and the Elimination of the Native," *Journal of Genocide Research* 8, no. 4 (2006): 388.
6. Ibid.
7. Myla Vicenti Carpio, "(Un)disturbing Exhibitions: Indigenous historical Memory at the NMAI," *American Indian Quarterly* 30, no. 3 & 4 (Summer/Fall 2006): 620.
8. Ibid.
9. Newspaper clippings, 1831–1993, in "Editorial Correspondence" section of *Evangelical Magazine and Gospel Advocate* (Utica: New York, June 1831): 2. MS 8648 in the archives of the Church of Jesus Christ of Latter-day Saints (hereafter "LDS Archives"), Salt Lake City, Utah.
10. Newspaper clippings, 1831–1993, "The Golden Bible," *Painesville Telegraph,* November 16, 1830. MS 8648, LDS Archives.
11. Ibid.
12. In addition to fears raised by Mormon expansion and intolerance towards Mormons' use of the Book of Mormon, other LDS religious beliefs and practices also disturbed non-Mormons, including polygamy, which was announced as a formal policy and practice in 1852. Despite claims that the majority of the membership did not practice polygamy, the practice remained controversial and did little to abate increasing pressures by non-Mormons. The initial policy on polygamy began with Joseph Smith (see D&C 132). Both Smith and his successor, Brigham Young, endorsed and practiced polygamy. Mormon religious ideologies and beliefs stirred intolerance

because they did not align with those of other Christian sects and defied widely accepted norms of morality; further, Mormons followed their religious leaders' teachings and believed that their actions were sanctioned by a higher authority than that of the US government.

13. The Church of Jesus Christ of Latter-day Saints, *Teachings of Presidents of the Church: Joseph Smith*, 11. "New Jerusalem" is simply a new term for "Zion." Faithful members are told that "ye shall assemble yourselves together to rejoice upon the land of Missouri, which is the land of your inheritance, which is now the land of your enemies." See also D&C 52:42.

14. The Church of Jesus Christ of Latter-day Saints, *Church History in the Fulness of Times* (Salt Lake City: Corporation of the President, 2003), 201.

15. Ibid., 278.

16. *The Mormons,* PBS documentary, 2007.

17. Minnesota Historical Society, "Alexander Ramsey," accessed February 6, 2017, http://sites.mnhs.org/historic-sites/alexander-ramsey-house/history

18. Angela Cavender Wilson, "Decolonizing the 1862 Death Marches," *American Indian Quarterly* 28, no. 1 & 2 (Winter/Spring 2004): 191.

19. Ronald K. Esplin, "A 'Place Prepared' in the Rockies," *Ensign* (July 1988): 7.

20. Clifton G. M. Kerr, "God Made the Choice . . ." *Millennial Star* 120, no. 7 (July 1958): 189.

21. Esplin, "A 'Place Prepared,'" 12; Harold H. Jenson, "Utah's First 24th Celebration," *The Improvement Era* 45, no. 7 (July 1942): 435; Kerr, "God Made the Choice," 189.

22. Wolfe, "Settler Colonialism and the Elimination of the Native," 388.

23. Henry A. Smith, "Achievements of Mormon Pioneers Now Recorded in Enduring Granite and Bronze," *Deseret News,* July 19, 1947.

24. Thomas P. Brown, "'This is the Place' Monument," *The Headlight,* November 1945, 5.

25. Wolfe, "Settler Colonialism and the Elimination of the Native," 388.

26. Ned Blackhawk, *Violence over the Land: Indians and Empires in the American West* (Cambridge: Harvard University Press, 2008). Brigham D. Madsen, *The Shoshoni Frontier and the Bear River Massacre* (Salt Lake City: University of Utah Press, 1985).

27. Carpio, "(Un)disturbing Exhibitions," 621.

28. Statistics for Toppenish, WA, accessed November 23, 2014, www.quickfacts.census.gov/qfd/states/53/5371960.html

29. Elise Boxer, "'The Lamanites Shall Blossom as a Rose': The Indian Student Placement Program, Mormon Whiteness and Indigenous Identity," *Journal of Mormon History* 41, no. 4 (October 2015): 132–176.

30. Ibid. See also 2 Nephi 5:20–23 (author's emphasis).

31. For examples, see: *Our Heritage: A Brief History of The Church of Jesus Christ of Latter-day Saints* (Salt Lake City: Corporation of the President, 1996); The Church of Jesus Christ of Latter-day Saints, *Truth Restored: A Short History of The Church of Jesus Christ of Latter-day Saints* (Salt Lake City: Corporation of the President, 2001); Leonard J. Arrington and Davis Bitton, *The Mormon Experience: A History of the Latter-day Saints,* 2nd ed. (Urbana: University of Illinois Press, 1992); Richard E. Bennett, *Mormons at the Missouri, 1846–1852: "And Should We Die . . . ,"* 1st ed. (Norman: University of Oklahoma Press, 1987); Richard L. Bushman, *Joseph Smith: Rough Stone Rolling: A Cultural Biography of Mormonism's Founder* (New York: Alfred A. Knopf, 2005).

32. Haunani-Kay Trask, *From a Native Daughter: Colonialism and Sovereignty in Hawai'I*, rev. ed. (Honolulu: University of Hawaii Press, 1999), 252.
33. Attributed to Capt. Richard H. Pratt, 1892.

CHAPTER 5

1. Paulo Freire, *The Pedagogy of the Oppressed*, (New York: Continuum, 1970), 58.
2. Ibid., 51.
3. Ibid., 59.
4. Judy M. Cornett, "A Dialogue Commemorating the Fiftieth Anniversary of *To Kill a Mockingbird*'s Publication: Atticus Finch, Christian or Civic Hero? A Response to Professor McMillian," *Tennessee Law Review* 77, no. 4 (2010): 701–802. See also Brett C. McInelly, "Expanding Empires, Expanding Selves: Colonialism, the Novel, and Robinson Crusoe," *Studies in the Novel* 35, no. 1(2003): 1–21.
5. Julio Cammarota, "Blindsided by the *Avatar*: White Saviors and Allies Out of Hollywood and in Education." *Review of Education, Pedagogy, and Cultural Studies* 33, no. 3 (2011): 242–259. See also Matthew W. Hughey, "The White Savior Film and Reviewers' Reception." *Symbolic Interaction* 33, no. 3 (2010): 475–496; Paul R. Ketchum, David G. Embrick, and B. Mitch Peck. 2011. "Progressive in Theory, Regressive in Practice: A Critical Race Review of Avatar." *Humanity & Society* 35 (2011): 198–201.
6. Joseph M. Larkin and Christine E. Sleeter, eds., *Developing Multicultural Teacher Education Curriculum* (Albany: State University of New York Press, 1995); Peggy McIntosh, "White Privilege: Unpacking the Invisible Knapsack," *Independent School* 49, no. 2 (1990): 31–36; Christine E. Sleeter, "How White Teachers Construct Race," in *Race, Identity and Representation in Education*, edited by Cameron McCarthy and Warren Crichlow, (New York: Routledge, 1993), 157–171; Christine E. Sleeter and Peter McClaren, eds. *Multicultural Education, Critical Pedagogy and the Politics of Difference*, (Albany: State University of New York Press, 1995).
7. See Freire, *Pedagogy of the Oppressed*. See also Paulo Freire, *Cultural Action for Freedom*, (Cambridge: Center for the Study of Development and Social Change, 1970); Paulo Freire, *Education for Critical Consciousness*, (New York: Continuum, 1973).
8. Paulo Freire, *Pedagogy in Process: The Letters to Guinea Bissau*. (New York: Continuum, 1978), 15.
9. Ibid., 16.
10. Paulo Freire, *The Politics of Education: Culture, Power and Liberation*, (South Hadley, MA: Bergin & Garvey, 1985), 105.
11. Freire, *Cultural Action for Freedom*, 27.
12. Freire, *Pedagogy of the Oppressed*, 60–61
13. Paulo Freire and Antonio Faundez, *Learning to Question: A Pedagogy of Liberation*, (New York: Continuum, 1989), 37.
14. Paulo Freire, *Política e Educação: Questões de Nossa Época*, (São Paulo: Cortez Editora, 2001), 11.
15. Paulo Freire, *Pedagogy of Freedom: Ethics, Democracy, and Civic Courage*, (Lanham, MD: Rowman and Littlefield, 2000), 33.
16. bell hooks, *Teaching to Trangress: Education as the Practice of Freedom* (New York: Routledge, 1994), 56.

17. Freire, *Pedagogy of the Oppressed*, 32.
18. Ibid., 56–57.
19. Ibid., 85.

CHAPTER 6

1. For a comprehensive view of the history of racial passing, see Elaine K. Ginsburg, ed., *Passing and the Fictions of Identity* (Durham, NC: Duke University Press, 1996).
2. Allyson V. Hobbs deeply explores the losses (rather than the social gains) of passing in *A Chosen Exile: A History of Racial Passing in American Life* (Cambridge, MA: Harvard University Press, 2014).
3. Marianne Hirsch, *Family Frames: Photography Narrative and Postmemory* (Cambridge, MA: Harvard University Press, 1997), 22.
4. Nancy Rose Hunt, *A Colonial Lexicon of Birth Ritual, Medicalization, and Mobility in the Congo* (Durham, NC: Duke University Press, 1999), 8.
5. See "A History, of the Persecution, of the Church of Jesus Christ, of Latter Day Saints in Missouri," in vol. 1 of *Times and Seasons*, ed. Ebenezer Robinson and Don Carlos Smith. The serial article appeared in this monthly broadsheet from December 1839 through October 1840, and is part of a bound volume held at the LDS Church History Library.
6. See Parley P. Pratt, *History of the Late Persecution,* 1839; also Bernard DeVoto, *The Year of Decision 1846* (New York: St. Martin's Griffin, 2000), 84–86.
7. "What Is Religious Freedom?" Mormon Newsroom, the Church of Jesus Christ of Latter-day Saints, accessed February 22, 2015, http://www.mormonnewsroom.org/official-statement/religious-freedom.
8. A 2012 study by the Pew Forum on Religion and Public life is titled, "Mormons in America: Certain in Their Beliefs, Uncertain of Their Place in Society." Reflecting upon the so-called "Mormon Moment" of 2012, the authors write, "Many Mormons feel they are misunderstood, discriminated against and not accepted by other Americans as part of mainstream society. Yet at the same time, a majority of Mormons think that acceptance of Mormonism is rising." The study also found that 46% of Mormons felt that they are actively discriminated against in society today, which is a higher percentage than for African-Americans. See "Mormons In America," Pew Research Center, accessed April 15, 2015, http://www.pewforum.org/2012/01/12/mormons-in-america-executive-summary/.
9. Lubna Kahn, "Tongans Work to Maintain Identity, Many Keep Traditions, But LDS Members are More Westernized," Associated Press Writer, *The Deseret News*, October 9, 1999.
10. A photo of a group of imprisoned Mormon polygamous men is widely published in LDS church literature and shown in seminary and institute classes. The men are in prison at the Utah Territorial Penitentiary in Salt Lake City, all but one person wearing black and white striped prison uniforms. All the men were imprisoned for "unlawful cohabitation" with multiple wives. My ancestor, Jacob Furhiman (in the far left of the photograph), had three plural wives throughout his lifetime, the last of which was my great-great-grandmother, Carolina "Carrie" Bollschweiler Fuhriman.

11. An 1877 Supreme Court decision, *Beecher v. Weatherby* (95 U.S. 517, 525) classified the United States as a "superior and civilized" nation, providing legal justification for the Dawes Act, which passed in 1887. As a result, the United States assumed the legal obligation to act as a trustee over Native American property and affairs, referencing (in the case) the United States as "a Christian people in their treatment of an ignorant and dependent race." This "benevolent" racist institutional classification set a precedent which would perpetuate a legacy of the subjugation of Indian peoples throughout the United States.

12. The current version of the Book of Mormon employs the phrase "pure and delightsome" in 2 Nephi 30:6, reflecting the change to the verse that scholars assume Joseph Smith made in 1840; however, the majority of English-language editions up until 1981 used the phrase "white and delightsome" that appeared in the original version published in 1830.

13. My decision to keep this part of my family story private is one that I have made carefully. I love and respect my grandmother, my adopted grandfather, and all of my aunts, uncles, and cousins. I fear that a deep dissection of this piece of our history would be a disservice and an unwanted exposure. I hope to come to a place of greater understanding about how individuals in my family feel about this story because it has been immensely impactful on me personally, but I don't believe that this is the proper format in which to create that kind of discussion. This said, I intend to be non-divisive, and wish to respect all members of my family. It feels like the most respectful thing to do at this point, to leave it closed here. Please trust that I have not left out anything elemental to the narrative.

14. See, for example, Jodi A. Byrd, *The Transit of Empire* (Minneapolis: University of Minnesota Press, 2011).

15. Vine Deloria Jr., *God is Red: A Native View of Religion* (Golden, CO: Fulcrum Publishing, 1973).

CHAPTER 7

1. Jean S. Phinney, "Ethnic Identity in Adolescents and Adults: A Review of the Research," *Psychological Bulletin* 108 (1990): 499–514.

2. Ibid.

3. Linda M. Chatters, Robert Taylor, and Rukmalie Jayakody. "Fictive kinship relationships in black extended families." *Journal of Comparative Family Studies* 25, no. 3 (1994): 297–312.

4. Robert Keegan, *The Evolving Self: Problem and Process in Human Development*, (Cambridge: Harvard University Press, 1982).

5. Adia H. Wingfield and John H. Wingfield. "When visibility hurts and helps: How intersections of race and gender shape Black professional men's experiences with tokenization." *Cultural Diversity and Ethnic Minority Psychology* 20 (2014), 483–490

6. George B. Ray, *Language and Interracial Communication in the United States: Speaking in Black and White*, (New York: Peter Lang Publishing, Inc., 2009).

7. Ibid.

8. Derald Wing Sue, *Microaggressions in Everyday Life: Race, Gender, and Sexual Orientation*, (New Jersey: John Wiley & Sons, 2010).

CHAPTER 8

1. Most Latino Saints—particularly those who come from countries with an Indigenous history—tend to see themselves as descendants of the Book of Mormon's Lamanite people, and thus heirs of the promises made to them of a future "blossoming like a rose" (D&C 49:24). For the promise about becoming "pure and delightsome," see 2 Nephi 30:6.

2. I realize that some will not see early LDS racial theology as "soft." I call it soft only because much of the LDS explanation for differences in God's children was that race (or color) was based on decisions that individuals made either in the pre-existence or, in the case of Indigenous people, in times past. And from the beginning LDS ideology offered a way out from the curse of color and race through obedience to God's commandments. This is no way prevented a harsh reality for many Saints of color, but it did mitigate to some extent the treatment of them within the church because of the expectation of redemption. Still, I accept that others might have a different way of describing this racialism, and I have no problem with that since we would all agree that this was totally unacceptable.

3. This talk of the promises to the Lamanite, however, seems to have ended for the most part with the death of President Spencer W. Kimball in 1985. Sadly, Latino general authorities who sometimes still allude to it seem to command little attention among the world-wide Saints or the brethren. In recent years illegal immigration has raised concerns among church leaders but there seems to be no consensus on how to deal with this issue beyond tacitly supporting immigration reform and discouraging any serious public discussion about the role of the church in this matter.

4. More ample discussions on the "secondary status" of Saints of color can be found in Armand Mauss's *All Abraham's Children: Changing Mormon Conceptions of Race and Lineage* (Urbana: University of Illinois Press, 2003); Russell W. Stevenson, *For the Cause of Righteousness: A Global History of Blacks and Mormonism, 1830–2013* (Salt Lake City: Greg Kofford Books, Inc., 2014); and Marjorie Newton, *Mormon and Maori* (Salt Lake City: Greg Kofford Books, Inc., 2014). Among the few works dealing with Latinos, see Emily Ann Gurnon, "The Dark Face of a White Church," (Master's thesis, University of California, Berkeley, 1993), and Jessie L. Embry, *In His Own Language* (Provo, UT: Charles Redd Center for Western Studies, Brigham Young University, 1997). My own Mormon History Association plenary address on growing up Mormon also sheds some light on the Latino secondary status experience in the church; see "Finding a Mormon Identity Through Religion and Activism: A Personal Note on Constructing a Latino Time and Place in the Mormon Narrative," *Journal of Mormon History*, vol. 41, no. 2 (April 2015).

5. I grew up at a time when most Latino wards met in their own buildings and the only contact with the stake was an occasional visit from a high councilman or when we attended stake conference. We rarely felt the influence or authority of our stake leaders nor of church headquarters.

6. I attended Texas A&I University in Kingsville, Texas, where I became involved in the Chicano movement, read the works of many activists and revolutionaries, and also found my faith challenge by other Latter-day Saints. I tell that story in my memoir, *Chicano while Mormon: Activism, War and Keeping the Faith* (Madison, NJ: Fairleigh Dickinson University Press, 2015), 161–168.

7. Self-deprecation is often a characteristic of people of color because it helps us deal with our challenges in a funny way. It can be both disparaging to ourselves because of our inability to be like our white brothers and sisters or it can be a way to mock those who might see themselves as superior to us.

8. See Octavio Ignacio Romano, "Intellectual Mercenaries of our Age, the Social Scientists," an editorial in *El Grito* 1 (Fall 1967): 4–5. Social scientists and social workers were particularly disliked in the Mexican barrios of the Southwest. The former were disliked because they tended to see all problems of the Mexican-American people through a "presentist" viewpoint that made them victims of their own bad choices. The latter were abhorred because they entered people's homes, told them how to live, criticized their food and clothing, and sometimes took their children away without ever providing any real help with the problems the people faced.

9. See Romano, "Minorities, History and the Cultural Mystique," *El Grito* 1 (Fall 1967): 9. Romano was particularly scathing about those minorities who once having "solved" their own poverty turned against those left behind. He saw this as a constant in American history, where those who assimilated and found success saw it imperative to teach a "submissive" philosophy to their own so as to keep themselves on top of their people's pecking order.

10. There are many who do engage in this type of discipleship, but many more of us who live a "checklist" religious life that rarely interrupts or complicates our secularism. This checklist approach strengthens the meritocracy view of the Kingdom of God and marginalizes those whose difficult social, economic, or familial circumstances prevent them from living their spiritual lives in such structured ways.

11. That white members can be "cold and distant" is a Latino Mormon complaint that I grew up hearing from the first day I stepped into church. I've come to accept that often white members are as unsure of how to deal with us as we are with how to interact with them.

12. My dissertation became my second book, *Chicanismo: The Forging of a Militant Ethos among Mexican Americans* (Tucson: University of Arizona Press, 1989), and remains one of the most read books on the Chicano movement.

13. Scholars and activists did not use the term "decolonizing" much back then.

14. See my memoir, *Chicano while Mormon*, 164–168, for a discussion of an ill-fated and naïve attempt to mix politics with religion in a ward setting.

15. In the Chicano movement I learned that the support of "natural" leaders was always crucial to getting people to follow.

16. We got one of the members of the ward who was getting a PhD in anthropology to teach the course. She was at first unsure of how to do it but ended up doing a fine job. Just having her in front of the class sent multiple messages to the youth about gender, education, and our history, and made the future "blossoming" a lived reality for one of the sisters at the conference.

17. I reserved the right as a bishop to call them to repentance, but found that private conversations and small-group admonitions worked better than public shaming.

18. This brother moved out because he felt he was no longer needed after being seen as indispensable in the past. We wanted the few white members to stay and help but to do so simply as another member of the ward. Some did—and in fact, for a time one of my counselors was a white fellow with few Spanish language skills who loved the

ward members and was loved just as much by them. Unfortunately, he also moved out because his Latino wife wanted a house in the foothills and loved mingling with the better-educated white sisters.

19. See my memoir, *Chicano while Mormon*.

20. Ironically, the failure to make him the stake president—which all the members in the stake seemed to believe would happen—came to trouble some of these members and caused a crack in their absolute belief that all things were fair in the church. The new stake president liked me and thought I was doing a good job, so I had no problem with him, but like most of the stake members, I, too, believed that our former bishop would have made a good stake president.

21. I want to point out here that we did not solve all the problems and we found that some were caused by personal sin, lack of commitment, and poor choices. We also had a number of middle-class members fully committed to our vision.

22. It is widely perceived that most Latino wards have a sizeable population that is not legal or who are predominantly undocumented, and that concern can at times— quite logically—subsume other important issues in the ward.

23. I recognize that there are some inherent problems, particularly in the view of younger white Mormons, with how Mormons have constructed their local congregations, but to build a sense of community the local ward has advantages over even the Utah-styled Mormon neighborhood in bringing people together and providing them the space and resources to create an extended family. While that is becoming harder and harder to accomplish with the imposition of more and more restrictive rules on the use of the ward buildings, along with a growing individualism among white Mormons, it is still the best place for the larger Mormon family.

24. See Eugene England, "Why The Church Is As True As The Gospel," *Sunstone* 22, no. 3 & 4 (June 1999): 61–69, for a discussion of how the LDS ward setting can serve as a place to develop discipleship.

25. George A. Sánchez, one of the great intellectuals of what is known as the Mexican-American Generation, made this statement. See my book, *Viva Kennedy, Mexican-Americans in Search of Camelot* (College Station: Texas A&M University Press, 2000), 74–84.

26. Many white members will say that equality in the kingdom is now a reality and to continue to focus on past inequalities is to create divisions among the Saints. But as long as history remains a foundation for our faith, the unchallenged racialist theology of the past will continue to hamper some from coming unto Christ. More tragically, new forms of racialism will emerge as long as social and economic inequalities in our world remain. The church may not be able to do much about such inequalities, but it can create—or better said, reclaim—a theology of spiritual equality that pushes back on those socially constructed racial hierarchies.

27. This occurred when the revelation on the priesthood ban was announced without commentary and without official clarification or an apology for what has now been accepted as a pseudo-revelation that harmed many individuals, Black and others, for over a century. Despite the new essay on the priesthood ban on the LDS.org website (https://www.lds.org/topics/race-and-the-priesthood?lang=eng&old=true) there is no formal commentary or denunciation on record from any significant church authority. Our fear of being perceived as inconsistent with our past leaders causes greater conflict among our members than would an apology and a strong statement about

the equality of all of God's children from even before the creation. This would force all church members to confront their own deeply rooted views of race in the church.

CHAPTER 9

1. Brigham Young to King Kamehameha, box 1, folder 2.2, Brigham Young Papers, Utah State Historical Society.
2. Thomas Murphy, "Simply Implausible: DNA and a Mesoamerican Setting for the Book of Mormon," *Dialogue: A Journal of Mormon Thought* 36, no. 4 (2004): 110–131; Blake T. Ostler, "DNA Strands in the Book of Mormon," *Sunstone* (May 2005): 63–71. On racial formation in the LDS Church, see Armand Mauss, *All Abraham's Children: Changing Mormon Conceptions of Race and Lineage* (Urbana: University of Illinois Press, 2003).
3. Thomas W. Murphy, "From Racist Stereotype to Ethnic Identity: Instrumental Uses of Mormon Racial Doctrine," *Ethnohistory* (1999): 457–459.
4. Hokulani Aikau, "Indigeneity in the Diaspora: The Case of Native Hawaiians at Iosepa, Utah," *American Quarterly* 62, no. 3 (September 2010): 483.
5. Leonard J. Arrington, *Great Basin Kingdom: An Economic History of the Latter-day Saints, 1830–1900* (Urbana: University of Illinois Press, 2005); Ned Blackhawk, *Violence over the Land: Indians and Empires in the Early American West* (Cambridge: Harvard University Press, 2006); Jared Farmer, *On Zion's Mount: Mormons, Indians, and the American Landscape* (Cambridge, MA: Harvard University Press, 2009); Milton R. Hunter, "The Mormons and the Colorado River," *The American Historical Review* 44, no. 3 (1939): 549–555; Dale L. Morgan, "The Administration of Indian Affairs in Utah, 1851–1858," *Pacific Historical Review* 17, no. 4 (1948): 383–409; Beverly P. Smaby, "The Mormons and the Indians: Conflicting Ecological Systems in the Great Basin," *American Studies* 16, no. 1 (1975): 35–48.
6. Bruce Burgett, "On the Mormon Question: Race, Sex, and Polygamy in the 1850s and the 1990s," *American Quarterly* 57, no. 1 (2005): 75–102; Nathan B. Oman, "Natural Law and the Rhetoric of Empire: Reynolds v. United States, Polygamy, and Imperialism," *Wash. UL Rev.* 88 (2010): 661. On the politics of sexuality and empire, including the enforcement of "civilized" norms of family life and intimacy as colonization, see also Amy Kaplan, "Manifest Domesticity," *American Literature* 70, no. 3 (September 1998): 581–606, and Laura Stoler, *Haunted By Empire: Geographies of Intimacy in North American History* (Durham, NC: Duke University Press, 2006).
7. On the colonization and assimilation of the Mormon people in late nineteenth and early twentieth centuries, see Richard Bushman, "The Colonization of the Mormon Mind," Annual of the Association for Mormon Letters 2000, ed. Lavina Fielding Anderson (Salt Lake City: Association for Mormon Letters, 2000), 14–23; Kathleen Flake, *The Politics of American Religious Identity: The Seating of Senator Reed Smoot, Mormon Apostle* (Chapel Hill: University of North Carolina Press, 2004); Ethan Yorgason, *Transformation of the Mormon Culture Region* (Urbana: University of Illinois Press, 2003).
8. Norman Douglas, "The Sons of Lehi and the Seed of Cain: Racial Myths in Mormon Scripture and Their Relevance to the Pacific Islands," *Journal of Religious History* 8, no. 1 (1974): 90–104; R. Lanier Britsch, *Moramona: The Mormons in Hawaii* (Laie, Hawaii: Institute for Polynesian Studies, 1989).

9. Brigham Young to King Kamehameha.
10. Hokulani Aikau, "Resisting Exile in the Homeland: He Moʻoleno No Liʻe," *American Indian Quarterly* 32, no. 1 (Winter 2008): 70–95; Lanier Britsch, "Maori Traditions and the Mormon Church," *The New Era*, June 1981, accessed October 16, 2017, https://www.lds.org/new-era/1981/06/maori-traditions-and-the-mormon-church ?lang=eng; Tamar Gordon, "Inventing the Mormon Tongan Family," in *Christianity in Oceania: Ethnographic Perspectives,* ed. John Barker (Lanham, MD: University Press of America, 1990), 197–219; Carl R. Harris, ed., *The Building of the Kingdom in Samoa* (Heber City, Utah: Peczuh Printing, 2006); Adria Imada, "Hawaiians on Tour: Hula Circuits Through the American Empire," *American Quarterly* 56, no. 1 (March 2004): 111–149; Peter Lineham, "The Mormon Message in the Context of Maori Culture," *Journal of Mormon History* 17 (1991): 62–93; Marjorie Newton, *Tiki and Temple: The Mormon Mission in New Zealand, 1854–1958* (Salt Lake City: Greg Kofford Books, 2012); Alec Thornton, Maria T. Kerslake, and Tony Binns, "Alienation and Obligation: Religion and Social Change in Samoa," *Asia Pacific Viewpoint* 51, no. 1 (2010): 1–16; Grant Underwood, "Mormonism, the Maori and Cultural Authenticity," *Journal of Pacific History* 35, no. 2 (2000): 133–146.
11. Tona J. Hangen, *I Remember Placement: Participating in the Indian Student Placement program of the Church of Jesus Christ of Latter-Day Saints* (PhD diss., Massachusetts Institute of Technology, 1992), 6.
12. James B. Allen, "The Rise and Decline of the LDS Indian Student Placement Program, 1947–1996," in *Mormons, Scripture, and the Ancient World: Studies in Honor of John L. Sorenson,* ed. Davis Bitton (Provo, UT: Foundation for Ancient Research and Mormon Studies, 1998), 85–119; Genevieve De Hoyos, "Indian Student Placement Program," *Encyclopedia of Mormonism* (1992), accessed October 16, 2017, http://eom .byu.edu/index.php/Indian_Student_Placement_Services; Matthew Garrett, "Mormons, Indians and Lamanites: The Indian Student Placement Program, 1947–2000" (PhD diss., Arizona State University, 2010); Hangen, *I Remember Placement*; Tona J. Hangen, "A Place to Call Home: Studying the Indian Placement Program," *Dialogue* 30, no. 1 (1997): 53–69; Matt Martinich, "The Impact of Church Schools and Universities on LDS Growth," accessed October 16, 2017, http://www.cumorah. com/index .php?target=view_other_articles&story_id=481&cat_id=30; Steve Pavilk, "Of Saints and Lamanites: An Analysis of Navajo Mormonism," *Wicazo Sa Review* 8, no. 1 (1992): 21–30; Martin D. Topper, "'Mormon Placement': The Effects of Missionary Foster Families on Navajo Adolescents," *Ethos* 7, no. 2 (1979): 142–160; "Worlds of Difference: Latter-day Saints and Indians," NPR, January 23, 2005, accessed October 16, 2017, http://www.npr.org/templates/story/ story.php?storyId=4463101.
13. David Knowlton, "Go Ye to All the World: The LDS Church and the Organization of International Society," in *Revisiting the Mormons: Persistent Themes and Contemporary Perspectives,* eds. Tim Heaton, Cardell Jacobsen, and John Hofman (Salt Lake City: University of Utah Press, 2008), 395.
14. James B. Allen, "Would-Be Saints: West Africa Before the 1978 Priesthood Revelation," *Journal of Mormon History* 17 (1991): 216–217.
15. David Knowlton, "Mormonism and Guerillas in Bolivia," *Journal of Mormon History* 32, no. 3 (1989): 184n9, 185–86.

16. Allen, "Would-Be Saints," 207–247.
17. Ibid., 242.
18. Ibid., 216, 230.
19. Knowlton, "Mormons and Guerillas," 187.
20. Ibid., 198.
21. Lawrence A. Young, "Confronting Turbulent Environments: Issues in the Organizational Growth and Globalization of Mormonism," in *Contemporary Mormonism: Social Science Perspectives*, eds. Marie Cornwall, Tim B. Heaton, and Lawrence Young (Urbana: University of Illinois Press, 1994), 51.
22. Hokulani Aikau, *A Chosen People, A Promised Land: Mormonism and Race in Hawai'i* (Minneapolis: University of Minnesota Press, 2012), 1.
23. Thomas W. Murphy, "Other Mormon Histories: Lamanite Subjectivity in Mexico," *Journal of Mormon History* 26, no. 2 (Fall 2000): 187.
24. Aikau, "Resisting Exile," 79–80.
25. Aikau 2012, 71.
26. See also Hokulani Aikau, "Indigeneity in the Diaspora: The Case of Native Hawaiians at Iosepa, Utah," *American Quarterly* 62, no. 3 (September 2010): 477–500.
27. Jason Brown and Christopher Nielsen, "Plotino Constantino Rhodakanaty: Introduction to a Mormon Anarchist," *The Mormon Worker*, accessed January 31, 2014, http://themormonworker.net/past-issues/mw-issue-8/plotino-constantino-rhodakanaty-introduction-to-a-mormon-anarchist/
28. Murphy, "Other Mormon Histories," 203.
29. Jason Dormady, "'Not just a Better Mexico': Intentional Religious Community and the Mexican State, 1940–1964" (PhD diss., UC Santa Barbara, 2007); Jorge Iber, *Hispanics in the Mormon Zion, 1912–1999* (College Station: Texas A&M Press, 2000); Thomas Murphy, "From Racist Stereotype to Ethnic Identity: Instrumental Uses of Mormon Racial Doctrine," *Ethnohistory* (Summer 1999), 451–480; Thomas Murphy, "'Stronger than Ever': Remnants of the Third Convention," *Journal of Latter-day Saint History* 10 (1998): 1, 8–11; Stuart Parker, "Mexico's Millennial Kingdom of the Lamanites: Margarito Bautista's Mormon Raza Cósmica" (paper delivered at the Rocky Mountain Conference on Latin American Studies, 2009); F. LaMond Tullis, *The Mormons in Mexico: The Dynamics of Faith and Culture* (Logan, UT: Utah State University Press, 1987); Fernando Gómez, *From Darkness into Light* (Mexico City: MHMM, 2005); Margarito Bautista, *La Evolución de México, Sus Verdaderos Progenitores y su Origen: El Destino de América y Europa* (1935).
30. See especially Hangen, (1992) and "Worlds of Difference" (2005).
31. Aikau, *Chosen People*, 123–56.
32. Jessie L. Embry, "LDS Ethnic Wards and Branches in the United States: The Advantages and Disadvantages of Language Congregations," *Deseret Language and Linguistic Society Symposium* 26, no. 1 (2000); Jessie L. Embry, *In His Own Language: Mormon Spanish-Speaking Congregations in the United States* (Provo, UT: Charles Redd Center for Western Studies, Brigham Young University, 1997); Jessie L. Embry, "Separate but Equal: Black Branches, Genesis Groups, or Integrated Wards?," *Dialogue* 23, no. 1 (1990): 11–37; Jessie L. Embry, "Speaking for Themselves: LDS Ethnic Groups Oral History Project," *Dialogue* 25, no. 4 (1992): 99–110.

33. Fernanda Santos, "Some Find Path to Navajo Roots Through Mormon Church," *New York Times*, October 30, 2013, http://www.nytimes.com/2013/10/31/us/for-some-the-path-to-navajo-values-weaves-through-the-mormon-church.html

34. Niko Besnier, "Modernity, Cosmopolitanism, and the Emergence of Middle Classes in Tonga," *The Contemporary Pacific* 21, no. 2 (Fall 2009): 215–262; Knowlton, "Go Ye to All the World," 394; Ronald Lawson and Ryan T. Cragun, "Comparing the Geographic Distributions and Growth of Mormons, Adventists, and Witnesses," *Journal for the Scientific Study of Religion* 51, no. 2 (2012): 220–240; Cathy Small, *Voyages: From Tongan Villages to American Suburbs* (Ithaca, NY: Cornell University Press, 2011).

35. Young, "Confronting Turbulent Environments," 60.

36. Knowlton, "Go Ye to All the World," 389–412.

37. Moana Uluave, "I Can Hear Myself Speak It" (unpublished manuscript, 2014).

38. See for example Gina Colvin, "'Church Instructs Leaders on Same-Sex Marriage'—or did it just make a bad situation worse?," *Kiwi Mormon*, January 12, 2014, http://www.patheos.com/blogs/kiwimormon/2014/01/church-instructs-leaders-on-same-sex-marriage-or-did-it-just-make-a-bad-situation-worse.

39. Françoise Lionnet and Shu-Mei Shih, eds., *Minor Transnationalism* (Durham: Duke University Press, 2005), 7, 21.

40. Knowlton, "Go Ye to All the World," 407. See also Marcus Martins, "The Oak Tree Revisited: Brazilian Leaders' Insights on the Growth of the Church in Brazil" (PhD diss., Brigham Young University, 1996).

41. Aikau, *Chosen People*.

42. Moroni Benally, email to the author.

43. The LDS Church reported 846,931 members in Mexico in 2000; Mexico's census for the same year, which required respondents to self-identify, recorded 205,229 Mormons, about one quarter of the members of record. The LDS Church reported 520,202 members in Chile in 2001—about 4 percent of the country's population; Chile's 2002 census identified 103,735 adult members—again, about one quarter of the members of record. See David Knowlton, "How Many Members are there Really? Two Censuses and the Meaning of LDS Membership in Chile and Mexico," *Dialogue: A Journal of Mormon Thought* 38, no. 2 (2005), 54.

See "Letting Go: Understanding Mormon Growth in Africa," *Journal of Mormon History* 35, no. 2 (2009): 19–23, in which Philip Jenkins addresses retention issues among converts in Africa. He writes, "My impression from anecdotal accounts in many parts of Africa is that the Church has a high dropout rate, far larger than that of other denominations and that a great many reported members remain in the Church for just two or three years before passing on to other groups." Jenkins claims that Mormon failure to acculturate to Africa and accept African indigenizations of the faith—perhaps because there is no Book of Mormon narrative to vest Indigenous African cultures with scriptural sanctity—may contribute to retention failure in Africa. He writes, "In the broad context of religious development in Africa, the LDS Church is extraordinarily unusual, and probably unique: I can't think of a competitor. It is one of the very last churches of Western origin that still enforces Euro-American norms so strictly and that refuses to make any accommodation to local customs. Missionaries have resolutely refused to draw on the historical lessons offered by any other church."

44. Aikau, *Chosen People*, 56.

CHAPTER 10

1. Kim B. Östman, "'The Other' in the Limelight: One Perspective on the Publicity Surrounding the New LDS Temple in Finland," *Dialogue: A Journal of Mormon Thought* 40, no. 4 (2007), 98.

2. Wilfried Decoo, "Mormonism in a European Catholic Region: A contribution to the Social Psychology of LDS Converts," *BYU Studies* 24, no. 1 (Winter 1984), 61–77; Wilfried Decoo, "Feeding the Fleeing Flock: Reflections on the Struggle to Retain Church members in Europe," *Dialogue: A Journal of Mormon Thought* 29, no. 1 (Spring 1996), 97–118; and Wilfried Decoo, "In Search of Mormon Identity: Mormon Culture, Gospel Culture, and an American Worldwide Church," *International Journal of Mormon Studies* 6 (2013), 1–50.

3. Walter E.A. van Beek, "The Temple and the Sacred: Dutch Temple Experiences," *Dialogue: A Journal of Mormon Thought* 45, no. 4 (Winter 2012), 39.

4. Other insights can be found in the works of Armand Mauss, Christian Euvrard, Ronan J. Head, Massimo Introvigne, David M. Morris, Kim Östman, and Bernadette Rigal-Cellard, all of which have been presented at conferences and published in such journals as *Dialogue: A Journal of Mormon Thought* or *The International Journal of Mormon Studies*, the latter linked to the European Mormon Studies Association.

5. Marinel Gerritsen, "Vlaanderen en Nederland: één taal, twee culturen?," *Neerlandia/Nederlands van Nu* 1-2014, www.anv.nl/wp-content/uploads/2014/03/N2014 -1_Marinel_Gerritsen_Vlaanderen_en_Nederland-een_taal_twee_culturen.pdf (Dutch). See also Evert van Wijk, *Waarom Belgen niet kunnen voetballen en Nederlanders nooit wereldkampioen worden: Over de moeizame samenwerking tussen Belgen en Nederlanders*, Tielt: Lannoo, 2010. Other articles that deal with this subject include Evert van Wijk, "Nederlanders zijn voor Vlamingen wat Duitsers zijn voor Nederlanders," *Express.be*,, December 21, 2010 (Dutch), http://www.express .be/joker/nl/nederbelg/nederlanders-zijn-voor-vlamingen-wat-duitsers-zijn-voor -nederlanders/137679.htm and "Nederland en Vlaanderen, twee twistende zusters" (Dutch), http://vosnet.org/nederland-en-vlaanderen-twee-twistende-zusters.

6. George Tuffin, *Mormonen in Vlaanderen—Volume 1: 1840–1959*, Wijk Antwerpen van de Kerk van Jezus Christus van de Heiligen der Laatste Dagen: Antwerpen 2012 (Dutch; self-published via Lulu.com).

7. Ibid., 108.

8. For example, missionaries were allowed to attend the Heilige Bloedprocessie (Holy Blood procession) in Bruges and the world-famous passion play in Oberammergau, Germany. See Tuffin, *Mormonen in Vlaanderen*, 126.

9. See, for example, Wilfried Decoo, "Understanding Anger against Mormon Missionaries," *Times and Seasons*, May 6, 2014, http://timesandseasons.org/index.php/2014 /05/

10. D. Michael Quinn, "I-Thou vs. I-It Conversions: The Mormon 'Baseball Baptism' Era," *Sunstone* 93 (December 1993): 30–44.

11. This respondent recalled an event in the late 1970s when her branch president had asked someone to give a fireside about plural marriage. The mission president, a member of that branch, attended, too, and found the topic wholly inappropriate for a fireside. The members felt that he was projecting his Utah mistrust of

polygamist groups, whereas they were simply interested in the historical events and doctrinal implications.

12. Eugene England, "Why the Church is as True as the Gospel," (1985), http://www .eugeneengland.org/why-the-church-is-as-true-as-the-gospel, accessed February 15, 2015.

13. Sarah Bringhurst Familia, "The Way We Teach Our Children Modesty," *Times & Seasons*, July 26, 2012, http://timesandseasons.org/index.php/2012/07/the-way-we -teach-our-children-modesty/ and Julie M. Smith, "Men, Women, and Modesty," *Times & Seasons*, February 17, 2014, http://timesandseasons.org/index.php/2014/02 /men-women-and-modesty/.

CHAPTER 11

1. Joanna Brooks, *The Book of Mormon Girl: A Memoir of American Faith* (New York: Free Press, 2012), 28.

2. Mary Catherine Bateson, *Peripheral Visions: Learning Along the Way* (New York: Harper Perennial, 1994), 7–8.

3. Molly Andrews, *Narrative Imagination and Everyday Life* (New York: Oxford University Press, 2014).

4. See Joanna Brooks, Gina Colvin, and Melissa Wei-Tsing Inouye's essays in this volume. Additionally, see Inouye, "The Oak and the Banyan: The 'Glocalization' of Mormon Studies" in *Mormon Studies Review* 1 (2014): 70–79; "How Conference Comes to Hong Kong," *Patheos* (March 2013), accessed 13 March 2013, http:// www.patheos.com/blogs/peculiarpeople/2013/03/how-conference-comes-to-hong -kong/; "Culture and Agency in Mormon Women's Lives," in *Women and Mormonism: Historical and Contemporary Perspectives*, eds. Kate Holbrook and Matthew Bowman (Salt Lake City: University of Utah Press, 2016), 230–246. Kate Holbrook, Brittany Chapman Nash, and Elizabeth Heath link LDS communities in Asia to larger trends within global Mormonism in their work. On LDS women in Cantonese-speaking stakes, see Kwok Ka Ki ("Grace"), "Mormon Women's Identity: The Experiences of Hong Kong Chinese Mormon Women" (MA diss., Hong Kong University, 2012); on LDS communities in India, see Taunalyn Rutherford's PhD dissertation "Conceptualizing Global Religions: An Investigation of Mormonism in India (PhD diss., Claremont Graduate University, 2017). For related work that applies various themes discussed here to autoethnographic and fictional texts see that of Karin Mei Li Inouye, particularly her film novella, *Walk Without Notice* (Palmyra, Virginia: Palmyra Press, 2005).

5. Mary Louise Pratt, "Arts of the Contact Zone," *Profession* (1991): 33–40.

6. Adelyn Lim, *Transnational Feminism and Women's Movements in Post-1997 Hong Kong: Solidarity Beyond the State* (Hong Kong: Hong Kong University Press, 2015), 13.

7. Ibid., 127.

8. Nicole Constable, *Born Out of Place: Migrant Mothers and the Politics of International Labor* (Hong Kong: Hong Kong University Press, 2014), 4.

9. Inouye's work is an excellent starting point for this—and any discussion—of the LDS Church and Asia, as well as for the stories of Latter-day Saint flexible citizens

who are part of the Asian Diaspora throughout the world. She draws on the theoretical/literary perspectives of Arjun Appadurai, Roland Robertson, John Tomlinson and others (see particularly Roland Robertson, "Glocalization: Time-Space and Homogeneity-Heterogeneity," in *Global Modernities*, eds. Mike Featherstone, Scot Lash and Roland Robertson [London: Sage, 1995]). Not only has she written/spoken about her own family's "transnational passages," she outlines the challenges facing those who wish to make meaningful assertions about a LDS communities in diaspora/globality. She notes that labels such as "American" and "Canadian" already contain a "multitude of meanings" that vary according to generation, citizenship status, and other factors when considering discussions of people of Asian descent within North America. She writes,

> "Asia," for its part, is a huge geographical area that defies sweeping historical, cultural, or ethnic characterizations. Granted, it is possible to point to certain environmental, historical, or cultural features that unite certain Asian subgroups, such as an economic structure historically based on rice cultivation, entanglements with colonialism, imperialism, and Cold War geopolitics, Confucian family traditions (e.g. filial piety, extended multigenerational family influence, and a patrilineal prizing of male offspring) and social conservatism, and Buddhist cultural influences such as vegetarianism, prohibitions against alcohol, and strict codes for individual moral behavior. Still, no single one of these features appears universally across Asia. ("Culture and Agency," 232–33)

Inouye acknowledges the convenience of the term "Asian" for certain "geographic and ethnic descriptions," but models more care in "attributing cultural traditions to their fundamental origin, such as 'Confucian.'"

10. Melissa Inouye, "How Conference Comes to Hong Kong," Patheos, http://www .patheos.com/blogs/peculiarpeople/2013/03/how-conference-comes-to-hong-kong.
11. See Aihwa Ong, *Flexible Citizenship: The Cultural Logics of Transnationality* (Durham, NC: Duke University Press, 1999), 7.
12. I have written about this elsewhere. See Stacilee Ford, "Crossing the Planes: Gathering, Grafting, and Second Sight in the Hong Kong China International District," in *Dialogue: A Journal of Mormon Thought*, 47, no. 3 (Fall 2014): 23–52. During my service as a District Relief Society president I was appreciative of the ways in which "flexible citizen" priesthood leaders (men with ties to Chinese or Asian diasporic communities) understood the importance of inclusive rhetoric and action.
13. Inouye, "Agency in Mormon Women's Lives."
14. Ibid.
15. See Chieko Okazaki, *Lighten Up! Finding Real Joy in Life* (Salt Lake City: Deseret Book Company, 1993) and *Cat's Cradle* (Salt Lake City: Bookcraft, 1993). Okazaki subtly and diplomatically discussed her views on dealing with various types of bias—including racism—in her books, church talks, and magazine articles in church publications. See particularly *Being Enough* (Salt Lake City: Bookcraft, 2002). The challenges Okazaki and the Relief Society General Presidency experienced with various church leaders have been discussed in several places, but there is

a pithy and insightful discussion of this period—along with relevant primary docu-ments—in Joanna Brooks et al., *Mormon Feminism: Essential Writings* (New York: Oxford University Press, 2015). I believe Okazaki herself was careful not to make too much publicly of the struggles she faced. In this she is like many of the flexible citizens (women and men) I know in Hong Kong and in LDS diaspora communi-ties in North America and across Asia. Generally, they tend to focus on what they appreciate about the church even as they model more inclusive mindsets than those who (often unintentionally) offend. However, one can piece together a pretty sober-ing picture of the difficulties Okazaki faced, particularly if one speaks to those who knew and worked with her. See Ford, "Crossing the Planes," 51.

16. Okazaki, *Cat's Cradle*, 52.
17. Inouye, "Agency in Mormon Women's Lives."
18. "Sharon," Relief Society meeting, Victoria First Branch, October 2016 (cited hereaf-ter as Sharon, RS, October 2016).
19. Sharon, RS, October 2016.
20. Ibid.
21. Ibid., and subsequent conversations and email correspondence, November 2016.
22. "Deborah," email correspondence, October 2016.
23. See Leta Hong Fincher, *Leftover Women: The Resurgence of Gender Inequality in China* (London: Zed Books, 2014).
24. Meldrid Lusterio, *Pioneers and Converts in Hong Kong,* May 2015. Since she wrote the original draft, Lusterio has left Hong Kong and returned to her home in the Philippines.
25. Lim, *Transnational Feminism*, 32.
26. Rhacel Salazar Parreñas, *Children of Global Migration: Transnational Families and Gendered Woes* (Palo Alto, CA: Stanford University Press, 2005), 13.
27. Ibid., 29.
28. Constable, *Born Out of Place*, 13.
29. During the last few years there has been an increase in the coordination between various representatives of the LDS Church at the branch, district, area, and global level. Self-reliance training has been updated and tailored for the region. Church funding is available for families who can identify educational or professional oppor-tunities. Branch Presidents and senior missionaries often have expertise based on previous work in humanitarian service, and those who do are able to hit the ground running. There are also heartening signs that some women have been beneficiaries of church self-reliance initiatives as well as courses run by non-government orga-nizations in Hong Kong. Some are returning home to their families with pragmatic skills, greater confidence, and an increased optimism about what lies ahead. How-ever, it is not uncommon for women to find themselves back in Hong Kong due to a new family or economic crisis of some sort.
30. "Reggie," Facebook Messenger exchange, November 2016.
31. Virginia Hopper Webber to Stacilee Ford, email exchange, 17 August 2015. Ms. Hop-per Webber is a writer who is no longer a practicing member of the LDS Church but who maintains a keen and fair-minded interest in it. She is a thoughtful commenta-tor on many subjects related to this chapter and her feedback has helped me think about the transpacific resonance of many of the lessons I have learned as a Latter-day Saint and a scholar living in Hong Kong. I thank her as well as my husband,

Matthew Hosford, for being particularly thoughtful interlocutors during my time as a Relief Society president.

32. Inouye, "How Conference Comes to Hong Kong."

33. See Caroline Kline, "Navigating Gender, Negotiating Agency: Mexican Mormon Women's Experiences and Self-Constructions in Oral Narratives," in *Race, Gender, and Power in the Mormon Borderlands*, eds. Andrea Radke-Moss and Dee Garceau (Lubbock: Texas Tech University Press, forthcoming). Kline's work is an important intervention in the conversation about gender and Mormonism in globality and her work connecting transnational and intersectional feminist perspectives to LDS realities helps me think about gender, domesticity, and religion in globality.

34. Meldrid Lusterio, "He Can Mend and Fix Broken Things," chapter one in *Pioneers and Converts in Hong Kong*, May 2015.

35. Parreñas, *Children of Global Migration*, 30.

36. Ibid., 165–168.

CHAPTER 12

1. In this article I will use the terms "LDS," "LDS Church," "Mormon," and "Mormonism" to refer to the Church of Jesus Christ of Latter-day Saints, its members, and its culture. I recognize that "Mormonism" and "Mormonisms" are also terms that can be used very broadly to indicate numerous non-LDS strains of Mormonism, but for the sake of using the same language employed by practitioners themselves and also for the sake of variety, I will use variants of the term "Mormon" within this discussion.

2. William R. Hutchinson, "A Moral Equivalent for Imperialism: Americans and the Promotion of 'Christian Civilization,' 1880–1920," in Hutchinson and Torben Christensen, eds., *Missionary Ideologies in the Imperialist Era: 1880–1920* (Aarhus, Denmark: Christensens Bogotrykkeri, 1982), 174; Arthur Schlesinger, Jr., "The Missionary Enterprise and Theories of Imperialism," in *The Missionary Enterprise in China and America*, ed. John K. Fairbank (Cambridge: Harvard University Press, 1974), 363.

3. Ryan Dunch, "Beyond Cultural Imperialism: Cultural Theory, Christian Missions, and Global Modernity," *History and Theory* 41 (October 2002), 301–325.

4. Dunch, "Beyond Cultural Imperialism," 312. This critique of associating modern notions of order and rationality solely with European culture instead of with the spreading condition of global modernity also applies to Linda Tuhiwai Smith's characterization of precolonial and postcolonial realities in *Decolonizing Methodologies: Research and Indigenous Peoples*, second edition (London: Zed Books, 2012), 29.

5. Dana L. Robert, "Introduction," in *Converting Colonialism: Visions and Realities in Mission History, 1706–1914*, ed. Dana L. Robert, (Grand Rapids, MI: William B. Eerdmans Publishing Company, 2008), 1–20.

6. Dana L. Robert, "Introduction," 4, citing Sanneh, "World Christianity and the New Historiography: History and Global Interconnections," in *Enlarging the Story: Perspectives on Writing World Christian History*, ed. Wilbert Shenk (Maryknoll, NY: Orbis Books, 2002).

7. Robert, "Introduction" (World Christianity), 2.

8. Roland Robertson, "Glocalization: Time-Space and Homogeneity-Heterogeneity," in *Global Modernities*, eds. Mike Featherstone, Scott Lash, and Roland Robertson (London: SAGE Publications Ltd, 1995).

9. R. Lanier Britsch, *From the East: The History of the Latter-day Saints in Asia, 1851–1996* (Salt Lake City: Deseret Book Company, 1998), 36.

10. R.O. Hall, "Who is my neighbor in Hong Kong?", *Church Missionary Society Outlook* (London: Church Missionary Society, December 1966), 17–21.

11. See Marjorie Newton, *Mormon and Maori* (Salt Lake City: Greg Kofford Books, 2015).

12. Laurie Maffly-Kipp, "Looking West: Mormonism and the Pacific World," *Journal of Mormon History*, 26, no. 1 (2000), 45–49.

13. Kathleen Flake, "The Emotional and Priestly Logic of Plural Marriage," *Arrington Annual Lecture* (Logan: Utah State University Press, 2009), lecture 15, accessed at http://digitalcommons.usu.edu/arrington_lecture/15.

14. James Faulconer, "Why A Mormon Won't Drink Coffee But Might Have A Coke: The Atheological Character of the Church of Jesus Christ of Latter-day Saints," in *Element*, 2 no. 2 (Fall 2006). Faulconer has also argued elsewhere that Mormon identity is communal, not individualistic. See Faulconer, "Negotiating the Tension between Modernism and Mormonism," Patheos, accessed at http://www.patheos.com//Mormon/Negotiating-Tension-James-Faulconer-07-10-2014.html

15. Until recently the phrase "let each one himself prepare" was used until a member of the Primary leadership pointed out that the Primary included girls as well as boys. For about two months the tendency to lapse back into the old version was strong, depending on which leader was conducting, but the new inclusive version has now taken hold.

16. Because informal institutions are subject to rapid change, I use the past tense to describe all three Primaries at the time of the Primary Presentation.

17. "2014 Outline for Sharing Time: Families Are Forever" (Salt Lake City: The Church of Jesus Christ of Latter-day Saints, 2013). I estimate that in my lifetime I have witnessed at least thirty-two Primary Presentations.

18. "The Family Is of God," words and music by Matthew Neeley, in the "2014 Outline for Sharing Time."

19. As the year unfolded, each month we did in fact sing and teach the children many additional songs beyond those listed in the Outline, a consequence of the children's and leaders' natural desire for variety.

20. Marie Griffith, *God's Daughters: Evangelical Women and the Power of Submission* (Berkeley and Los Angeles: University of California Press, 2000).

AFTERWORD

1. James E. Faulconer, "Philosophy and Transcendence: Religion and the Possibility of Justice," in *Transcendence in Philosophy and Religion*, ed. James E. Faulconer (New York: HarperCollins, 2003), 76.

2. Mircea Eliade, *The Sacred and the Profane: The Nature of Religion*, trans. Willard R. Trask (New York: Harcourt, Brace & World, 1959).

3. Michael Dorris, "Native American Literature in an Ethnohistorical Context," *College English* 41, no. 2 (October 1979): 147–62. Reprinted in *Paper Trails: Essays* (New York: HarperCollins, 1994), 239–40.

4. 1491s, "I would like to see a conversation between white people who think Natives came across Beringia and white people who think Natives came from aliens," Facebook, August 13, 2015, accessed April 10, 2017, https://www.facebook.com/1491s /posts/606211996106448.

5. Lewis Hanke, *Aristotle and the American Indians: A Study in Race Prejudice in the Modern World* (Bloomfield: University of Indiana Press, 1970).

6. I have written about this more extensively in "My Book of Mormon Story," in *Women and Mormonism: Historical and Contemporary Perspectives*, eds. Kate Holbrook and Matthew Bowman (Salt Lake City: University of Utah Press): 274–87.

7. Though not in the scope of this essay, the colonial privilege of definition spills into artistic creation as well. My MA thesis, admittedly dated, "A Pale Reflection: American Indian Images in Mormon Arts" (Brigham Young University, 1984) discusses stereotyped representations. A contemporary example of appropriation might be the *Twilight* series. If Mormons are raised with colonial images of Indigenous peoples, including origins, an entitlement to create stories for them is not surprising.

8. Louise Erdrich, *The Last Report on the Miracles at Little No Horse* (New York: HarperCollins, 2001), 55.

9. I resist calling these practices "hybrid." The post-colonial term implies parity and does not acknowledge imbalance of political power or individual agency.

10. Boarding schools are widely acknowledged as colonial tools of assimilation and their literatures are complex. The motto (attributed to Capt. Richard H. Pratt, 1892) for nineteenth-century boarding schools was "kill the Indian, save the man."

11. Laura Tohe, *No Parole Today* (Albuquerque, New Mexico: West End Press, 1999), 11.

12. Ibid., 13.

13. My thanks to colleague Enyd Green for this apt term.

14. Heid Erdrich, "Upon Hearing of the Mormon DNA Collection," in *Cell Traffic: New and Selected Poems* (Tucson: University of Arizona Press, 2012), 47.

15. The Church of Jesus Christ of Latter-day Saints, "Book of Mormon and DNA Studies," accessed April 10, 2017, https://www.lds.org/topics/book-of-mormon-and-dna -studies

16. The Church of Jesus Christ of Latter-day Saints, "Race and the Priesthood," accessed April 10, 2017, https://www.lds.org/topics/race-and-the-priesthood

17. The Church of Jesus Christ of Latter-day Saints, "Peace and Violence among 19th-Century Latter-day Saints," accessed April 10, 2017, https://www.lds.org/topics/ peace-and-violence-among-19th-century-latter-day-saints

18. Helen Sekaquaptewa, *Me and Mine: The Life Story of Helen Sekaquaptewa as told to Louise Udall* (Tucson: University of Arizona Press, 1969), 224, 234-245.

19. Ibid., 242.

20. I have written previously about Helen Sekaquaptewa in "'A Trail in the Sand': Helen Sekaquaptewa's *Spiritual Frontiers*," *Literature and Belief* 21, no. 1 & 2 (2002): 149–62.

21. Laura Tohe, "There Is No Word for Feminism in My Language," *Wacazo Sa Review* 15, no. 2 (2000), 103.

22. Dennis Zotigh, "Do Americans Celebrate the 4th of July," Blog, National Museum of the American Indian, July 3, 2014, accessed April 10, 2017, http://blog.nmai.si.edu/main/2014/07/july_4_2014.html

23. F. Scott Fitzgerald, "The Crack-up" (1936), *Esquire*, June 9, 2014, accessed April 10, 2017. http://www.esquire.com/features/the-crack-up

24. Linda Tuhiwai Smith, *Decolonizing Methodologies: Research and Indigenous Peoples* (London: Zed Books, 1999), 145.

25. Faulconer, "Philosophy and Transcendence," 73.

26. Gordon B. Hinckley, "Dedicatory Prayer," Vernal Utah Temple, July 13, 2014, accessed April 10, 2017, http://www.ldschurchtemples.com/vernal/prayer/

BIBLIOGRAPHY

Aikau, Hokulani K. *A Chosen People, a Promised Land: Mormonism and Race in Hawai'i.* Minneapolis: University of Minnesota Press, 2012.

———. "Indigeneity in the Diaspora: The Case of Native Hawaiians at Iosepa, Utah," *American Quarterly* 62, no. 3 (September 2010): 477–500.

———. "Resisting Exile in the Homeland: He Mo'oleno No Li'e," *American Indian Quarterly* 32, no. 1 (Winter 2008): 70–95.

Alfred, Taiaiake. *Wasase: Indigenous Pathways of Action and Freedom.* Toronto: University of Toronto Press, 2005.

Allen, James B. "The Rise and Decline of the LDS Indian Student Placement Program, 1947–1996," in *Mormons, Scripture, and the Ancient World: Studies in Honor of John L. Sorenson,* edited by Davis Bitton. Provo: Foundation for Ancient Research and Mormon Studies, 1998.

———. "Would-Be Saints: West Africa Before the 1978 Priesthood Revelation," *Journal of Mormon History* 17 (1991): 216–217.

American Friends Service Committee. *Tribal Journeys Handbook and Study Guide.* Seattle: Cedar Media, 2011.

Andrews, Molly. *Narrative Imagination and Everyday Life.* New York: Oxford University Press, 2014.

Arrington, Leonard. *Great Basin Kingdom: An Economic History of the Latter-day Saints, 1830–1900.* Urbana: University of Illinois Press, 2005.

Arrington, Leonard J., and Davis Bitton. *The Mormon Experience: A History of the Latter-day Saints,* 2nd ed. Urbana: University of Illinois Press, 1992.

Baca, Angelo. *In Laman's Terms: Looking at Lamanite Identity.* Produced by Daniel Hart. Seattle: University of Washington, Native Voices Program, 2008.

Bateson, Mary Catherine. *Peripheral Visions: Learning Along the Way.* New York: Harper Perennial, 1994.

Bautista, Margarito. *La Evolución de México, Sus Verdaderos Progenitores y su Origen: El Destino de América y Europa.* Mexico City: Talleres Gráficos, 1935.

Bell, Catherine, and Robert Paterson. *Protection of First Nations Cultural Heritage: Laws, Policy, and Reform.* Vancouver: University of British Columbia Press, 2009.

Benjamin, Walter. *Illuminations.* New York: Schocken, 1968.

Bennett, Richard. *Mormons at the Missouri, 1846–1852: "And Should We Die. . . ."* 1st ed. Norman: University of Oklahoma Press, 1987.

Besnier, Niko. "Modernity, Cosmopolitanism, and the Emergence of Middle Classes in Tonga," *The Contemporary Pacific* 21, no. 2 (Fall 2009): 215–262.

Boxer, Elise. "'The Lamanites Shall Blossom as a Rose': The Indian Student Placement Program, Mormon Whiteness and Indigenous Identity," *Journal of Mormon History* 41, no. 4 (October 2015): 132–176.

Britsch, R. Lanier. "Maori Traditions and the Mormon Church," *The New Era*, June 1981. https://www.lds.org/new-era/1981/06/maori-traditions-and-the-mormon-church?lang=eng.

Britsch, R. Lanier. *Moramona: The Mormons in Hawaii.* Laie, Hawaii: Institute for Polynesian Studies, 1989.

Brooks, Joanna. *The Book of Mormon Girl: A Memoir of American Faith.* New York: Free Press, 2012.

Brooks, Joanna, et al., *Mormon Feminism: Essential Writings.* New York: Oxford University Press, 2015.

Brown, Jason, and Christopher Nielsen, "Plotino Constantino Rhodakanaty: Introduction to a Mormon Anarchist," *The Mormon Worker* (n.d.): http://themormonworker.net/past-issues/mw-issue-8/plotino-constantino-rhodakanaty-introduction-to-a-mormon-anarchist/

Brown, Thomas P. "'This is the Place' Monument," *The Headlight* (November 1945): 5–6.

Burgett, Bruce. "On the Mormon Question: Race, Sex, and Polygamy in the 1850s and the 1990s," *American Quarterly* 57, no. 1 (2005): 75–102.

Bushman, Richard. "The Colonization of the Mormon Mind," in *Annual of the Association for Mormon Letters 2000.* Edited by Lavina Fielding Anderson. Salt Lake City: Association for Mormon Letters, 2000.

Bushman, Richard L. *Joseph Smith: Rough Stone Rolling: A Cultural Biography of Mormonism's Founder.* New York: Alfred A. Knopf, 2005.

Blackhawk, Ned. *Violence over the Land: Indians and Empires in the American West.* Cambridge, MA: Harvard University Press, 2008.

Blumenthal, Daniel S., et al. *Community-Based Participatory Health Research: Issues, Methods, and Translation to Practice.* New York: Springer Publishing, 2013.

Boren, Karen. "Indians to Settlers: 'We Must Help One Another.'" *Church News*, July 5, 1997.

Brett, Mark G. *Decolonizing God: The Bible in the Tides of Empire.* Sheffield, England: Sheffield Phoenix Press, 2009.

Brown, Samuel M. *In Heaven as It Is on Earth: Joseph Smith and the Early Mormon Conquest of Death.* New York: Oxford University Press, 2012.

Byrd, Jodi A. *The Transit of Empire.* Minneapolis: University of Minnesota Press, 2011.

Cajete, Gregory. *Native Science: Natural Laws of Interdependence.* Santa Fe: Clear Light Publishers, 2000.

Cammarota, Julio. "Blindsided by the Avatar: White Saviors and Allies Out of Hollywood and in Education." *Review of Education, Pedagogy, and Cultural Studies* 33, no. 3 (2010): 242–259.

Campbell, Douglas. "'White' or 'Pure': Five Vignettes." *Dialogue: A Journal of Mormon Thought* 29, Winter (1996): 119–35.

Carpio, Myla Vicenti. "(Un) disturbing Exhibitions: Indigenous Historical Memory at the NMAI." *The American Indian Quarterly* 30, no. 3 (2006): 619–631.

Celletti, Mark. *Canoe Way.* Tacoma, WA: Cedar Media, 2009.

Chatters, Linda M., Robert Taylor, and Rukmalie Jayakody. "Fictive kinship relationships in black extended families," *Journal of Comparative Family Studies* 25, no. 3 (1994): 297–312.

The Church of Jesus Christ of Latter-day Saints. *Church History in the Fulness of Times.* Salt Lake City: Corporation of the President, 2003.

———. *Our Heritage: A Brief History of The Church of Jesus Christ of Latter-day Saints.* Salt Lake City: Corporation of the President, 1996.

———. *Teachings of Presidents of the Church: Joseph Smith.* Salt Lake City: Corporation of the President, 2016.

———. *Truth Restored: A Short History of The Church of Jesus Christ of Latter-day Saints.* Salt Lake City: Corporation of the President, 2001.

Colvin, Gina. "'Church Instructs Leaders on Same-Sex Marriage'—or did it just make a bad situation worse?," *Kiwi Mormon*, January 12, 2014. http://www.patheos.com /blogs/kiwimormon/2014/01/church-instructs-leaders-on-same-sex-marriage-or -did-it-just-make-a-bad-situation-worse.

Cone, James. *Risks of Faith: The Emergence of a Black Theology of Liberation, 1968–1998.* Boston: Beacon, 1999.

Constable, Nicole. *Born Out of Place: Migrant Mothers and the Politics of International Labor.* Hong Kong: Hong Kong University Press, 2014.

Cornett, Judy M. "A Dialogue Commemorating the Fiftieth Anniversary of *To Kill a Mockingbird*'s Publication: Atticus Finch, Christian or Civic Hero? A Response to Professor McMillian." *Tennessee Law Review* 77, no. 4 (2010): 701–802.

Decoo, Wilfried. "Feeding the Fleeing Flock: Reflections on the Struggle to Retain Church Members in Europe," *Dialogue: A Journal of Mormon Thought* 29, no. 1 (Spring 1996), 97–118.

———. "In Search of Mormon Identity: Mormon Culture, Gospel Culture, and an American Worldwide Church," *International Journal of Mormon Studies* 6 (2013), 1–50.

———. "Mormonism in a European Catholic Region: A Contribution to the Social Psychology of LDS Converts," *BYU Studies* 24, no. 1 (Winter 1984), 61–77.

———. "Understanding Anger against Mormon Missionaries," *Times and Seasons*, May 6, 2014. http://timesandseasons.org/index.php/2014/05/

De Hoyos, Genevieve. "Indian Student Placement Program," *Encyclopedia of Mormonism* (1992), accessed online at http://eom.byu.edu/index.php/ Indian_Student_ Placement_ Services.

Deloria Jr., Vine. *God is Red: A Native View of Religion.* Golden, CO: Fulcrum Publishing, 1973.

———. *God Is Red: A Native View of Religion, the Classic Work Updated.* Golden, CO: Fulcrum Publishing, 1994.

———. "Vision and Community." In *For This Land: Writings on Religion in America*, edited by James Treat. New York: Routledge, 1999.

DeVoto, Bernard. *The Year of Decision 1846.* New York: St. Martin's Griffin, 2000.

Dormady, Jason. "'Not just a Better Mexico': Intentional Religious Community and the Mexican State, 1940–1964" PhD diss., UC Santa Barbara, 2007.

Dorris, Michael. "Native American Literature in an Ethnohistorical Context." *College English* 41, no. 2 (October 1979): 147–62. Reprinted in *Paper Trails: Essays.* New York: HarperCollins, 1994.

Douglas, Norman. "The Sons of Lehi and the Seed of Cain: Racial Myths in Mormon Scripture and Their Relevance to the Pacific Islands," *Journal of Religious History* 8, no. 1 (1974): 90–104.

Embry, Jessie L. *In His Own Language: Mormon Spanish-Speaking Congregations in the United States.* Charles Redd Center for Western Studies, Brigham Young University, 1997.

———. "LDS Ethnic Wards and Branches in the United States: The Advantages and Disadvantages of Language Congregations," *Deseret Language and Linguistic Society Symposium* 26, no. 1 (2000).

———, "Separate but Equal: Black Branches, Genesis Groups, or Integrated Wards?," *Dialogue* 23, no. 1 (1990): 11–37.

———, "Speaking for Themselves: LDS Ethnic Groups Oral History Project," *Dialogue* 25, no. 4 (1992): 99–110.

England, Eugene. "Why The Church Is As True As The Gospel," *Sunstone* 22, no. 3 & 4 (June 1999): 61–69.

Erdrich, Heid. "Upon Hearing of the Mormon DNA Collection." In *Cell Traffic: New and Selected Poems*. Sun Tracks: An American Indian Literary Series, Vol. 70. Tucson: University of Arizona Press, 2012.

Erdrich, Louise. *The Last Report on the Miracles at Little No Horse*. New York: Harper-Collins, 2001.

Esplin, Ronald K. "A 'Place Prepared' in the Rockies," *Ensign* (July 1988): 7.

Familia, Sarah Bringhurst. "The Way We Teach Our Children Modesty," *Times & Seasons*, July 26, 2012. http://timesandseasons.org/index.php/2012/07/the-way-we-teach-our-children-modesty/

Farmer, Jared. *On Zion's Mount: Mormons, Indians, and the American Landscape*. Cambridge, MA: Harvard University Press, 2008.

Faulconer, James E. "Philosophy and Transcendence: Religion and the Possibility of Justice." In *Transcendence in Philosophy and Religion*. Ed. James E. Faulconer. Bloomington: Indiana University Press, 2003. 70–83.

Fincher, Leta Hong. *Leftover Women: The Resurgence of Gender Inequality in China*. London: Zed Books, 2014.

Fitzgerald, F. Scott. "The Crack-up" (1936). *Esquire*, June 9, 2014. http://www.esquire.com/features/the-crack-up

Flake, Kathleen. *The Politics of American Religious Identity: The Seating of Senator Reed Smoot, Mormon Apostle*. Chapel Hill: University of North Carolina Press, 2004.

Ford, Stacilee. "Crossing the Planes: Gathering, Grafting, and Second Sight in the Hong Kong China International District." *Dialogue: A Journal of Mormon Thought*, 47, no. 3 (Fall 2014): 23–52

Freire, Paulo. *Cultural Action for Freedom*. Cambridge, MA: Center for the Study of Development and Social Change, 1970.

———. *Education for Critical Consciousness*. New York: Continuum,1973.

———. *Pedagogy in Process: The Letters to Guinea Bissau*. New York: Continuum, 1978.

———. *Pedagogy of Freedom: Ethics, Democracy, and Civic Courage*. Lanham, MD: Rowman and Littlefield, 2000.

———. *The Pedagogy of the Oppressed*. New York: Continuum, 1970.

———. *Pedagogy of the Oppressed: 30th Anniversary Edition*. New York: Bloomsbury Publishing, 2014.

———. *Política e Educação: Questões de Nossa Época*. São Paulo: Cortez Editora, 2001.

———. *The Politics of Education: Culture, Power and Liberation*. South Hadley, MA: Bergin & Garvey, 1985.

———, and Antonio Faundez. 1989. *Learning to Question: A Pedagogy of Liberation*. New York: Continuum.

García, Ignacio M. *Chicanismo: The Forging of a Militant Ethos among Mexican Americans*. Tucson: University of Arizona Press, 1989.

———. *Chicano while Mormon: Activism, War and Keeping the Faith*. New Jersey: Fairleigh Dickinson University Press, 2015.

———. "Finding a Mormon Identity through Religion and Activism: A Personal Note on Constructing a Latino Time and Place in the Mormon Narrative." *Journal of Mormon History* 41, no. 2 (2015): 69–90.

———. *Viva Kennedy, Mexican-Americans in Search of Camelot*. College Station: University of Texas A&M Press, 2000.

Garrett, Matthew. "Mormons, Indians and Lamanites: The Indian Student Placement Program, 1947–2000." PhD Diss., Arizona State University, 2010.

Gerritsen, Marinel. "Vlaanderen en Nederland: één taal, twee culturen?," *Neerlandia/Nederlands van Nu* 1–2014, www.anv.nl/wp-content/uploads/2014/03/N2014-1_Marinel_Gerritsen_Vlaanderen_en_Nederland-een_taal_twee_culturen.pdf

Ginsburg, Elaine K., ed., *Passing and the Fictions of Identity*. Durham, NC: Duke University Press, 1996.

Givens, Terryl L. *By the Hand of Mormon: The American Scripture That Launched a New World Religion*. Oxford and New York: Oxford University Press, 2002.

Gómez, Fernando. *From Darkness into Light*. Mexico City: MHMM, 2005.

Gordon, Tamar. "Inventing the Mormon Tongan Family." In *Christianity in Oceania: Ethnographic Perspectives*. Ed. John Barker. Lanham, MD: University Press of America, 1990. 197–219.

Grande, Sandy. *Red Pedagogy: Native American Social and Political Thought*. Lanham, MD: Rowman & Littlefield Publishers, 2004.

Gurnon, Emily Ann. "The Dark Face of a White Church." MA thesis, University of California, Berkeley, 1993.

Gutjahr, Paul C. *The Book of Mormon: A Biography*. New Jersey: Princeton University Press, 2012.

Hangen, Tona Jean. "I Remember Placement: Participating in the Indian Student Placement Program of the Church of Jesus Christ of Latter-day Saints." PhD diss., Massachusetts Institute of Technology, 1992.

———. "A Place to Call Home: Studying the Indian Placement Program," *Dialogue: A Journal of Mormon Thought* 30 (1997): 53–69.

Harris, Carl R., ed. *The Building of the Kingdom in Samoa*. Heber City, Utah: Peczuh Printing, 2006.

Heller, Monica. *Codeswitching: Anthropological and Sociolinguistic Perspectives*. Vol. 48. *Contributions to the Sociology of Language*. Berlin: Walter de Gruyter, 1988.

Hinckley, Gordon B. "Dedicatory Prayer." Vernal Utah Temple, July 13, 2014, accessed April 10, 2017. http://www.ldschurchtemples.com/vernal/prayer/

History of Montgomery and Fulton Counties, N.Y. New York: F.W. Beers & Co., 1878.

History of the Church of Jesus Christ of Latter-day Saints, Vol. 2. Salt Lake City: Deseret Book, 1948.

Hirsch, Marianne. *Family Frames: Photography Narrative and Postmemory*. Cambridge, MA: Harvard University Press, 1997.

Hobbs, Allyson. *A Chosen Exile: A History of Racial Passing in American Life*. Cambridge, MA: Harvard University Press, 2014.

hooks, bell. *Teaching Community: A Pedagogy of Hope*. New York: Taylor & Francis, 2013.

———. *Teaching to Transgress: Education as the Practice of Freedom*. New York: Routledge, 1994.

Hughey, Matthew W. "The White Savior Film and Reviewers' Reception." *Symbolic Interaction* 33, no. 3 (2010): 475–496.

Hunn, Eugene. *A Zapotec Natural History: Trees, Herbs, and Flowers, Birds, Beasts, and Bugs in the Life of San Juan Gbëë*. Tucson: University of Arizona Press, 2008.

Hunt, Nancy Rose. *A Colonial Lexicon of Birth Ritual, Medicalization, and Mobility in the Congo*. Durham, NC: Duke University Press, 1999.

Hunter, Milton R. "The Mormons and the Colorado River," *The American Historical Review* 44.3 (1939): 549–555.

Iber, Jorge. *Hispanics in the Mormon Zion, 1912–1999*. College Station: Texas A&M Press, 2000.

Imada, Adria. "'Aloha 'Oe': Settler-Colonial Nostalgia and the Genealogy of a Love Song," *American Indian Culture and Research Journal* 37, no. 2 (2013): 35–52.

———. "Hawaiians on Tour: Hula Circuits Through the American Empire," *American Quarterly* 56, no. 1 (March 2004): 111–149.

Inouye, Mei Li. *Walk Without Notice*. Palmyra Press, 2005.

Inouye, Melissa. "Culture and Agency in Mormon Women's Lives." In *Women and Mormonism: Historical and Contemporary Perspectives*. Edited by Kate Holbrook and Matthew Bowman. Salt Lake City: University of Utah Press, 2016. 230–246.

———. "How Conference Comes to Hong Kong," *Patheos*, March 2013. http://www.patheos.com/blogs/peculiarpeople/2013/03/how-conference-comes-to-hong-kong/;"Culture.

———. "The Oak and the Banyan: The 'Glocalization' of Mormon Studies." *Mormon Studies Review* 1 (2014): 70–79.

Jackson, Richard. *Places of Worship: 150 Years of Latter-Day Saint Architecture*. Provo: Brigham Young University Press, 2003.

Jenkins, Philip. " Letting Go: Understanding Mormon Growth in Africa." *Journal of Mormon History* 35, no. 2 (2009): 1–25.

Johnson, Scott, and Joel Kramer. "The Bible vs. The Book of Mormon." Brigham City, Utah: Living Hope Ministries, 2005.

Journal History of the Church. Church History Library, The Church of Jesus Christ of Latter-day Saints, Salt Lake City, Utah.

Joy, David, and Joseph F. Duggan. *Decolonizing the Body of Christ: Theology and Theory after Empire?* New York: Palgrave Macmillan, 2012.

Kahn, Lubna. "Tongans Work to Maintain Identity, Many Keep Traditions, But LDS Members are More Westernized," *Deseret News*, October 9, 1999.

Kaplan, Amy. "Manifest Domesticity," *American Literature* 70, no. 3 (September 1998): 581–606.

Keegan, Robert. *The Evolving Self: Problem and Process in Human Development*. Cambridge, MA: Harvard University Press, 1982.

Ketchum, Paul R., David G. Embrick, and B. Mitch Peck. "Progressive in Theory, Regressive in Practice: A Critical Race Review of Avatar." *Humanity & Society* 35 (2011): 198–201.

Ki, Kwok Ka ("Grace"). "Mormon Women's Identity: The Experiences of Hong Kong Chinese Mormon Women." MA thesis, Hong Kong University, 2012.

Kline, Caroline. "Navigating Gender, Negotiating Agency: Mexican Mormon Women's Experiences and Self-Constructions in Oral Narratives." In *Race, Gender, and Power in the Mormon Borderlands.* Edited by Andrea Radke-Moss and Dee Garceau. Lubbock: Texas Tech University Press, forthcoming.

Knowlton, David. "Go Ye to All the World: The LDS Church and the Organization of International Society." In *Revisiting the Mormons: Persistent Themes and Contemporary Perspectives.* Edited by Tim Heaton, Cardell Jacobsen, and John Hofman. Salt Lake City: University of Utah Press, 2008.

———. "How Many Members are there Really? Two Censuses and the Meaning of LDS Membership in Chile and Mexico," *Dialogue: A Journal of Mormon Thought* 38, no. 2 (2005), 53.

———. "Mormonism and Guerillas in Bolivia," *Journal of Mormon History* (1989), 389–412.

Kovach, Margaret E. *Indigenous Methodologies: Characteristics, Conversations, and Contexts.* Toronto: University of Toronto Press, Scholarly Publishing Division, 2010.

Kramer, Joel, and Jeremy Reyes. *DNA vs. The Book of Mormon.* Brigham City, Utah: Living Hope Ministries, 2003.

Larkin, Joseph M. and Christine E. Sleeter, eds. *Developing Multicultural Teacher Education Curriculum.* Albany: State University of New York Press, 1995.

Lawson, Ronald, and Ryan T. Cragun. "Comparing the Geographic Distributions and Growth of Mormons, Adventists, and Witnesses." *Journal for the Scientific Study of Religion* 51, no. 2 (2012): 220–240.

Lee, George P. *Silent Courage: An Indian Story, the Autobiography of George P. Lee, a Navajo.* Salt Lake City: Deseret Book, 1987.

Leone, Mark P. *Roots of Modern Mormonism.* Cambridge, MA: Harvard University Press, 1979.

Lim, Adelyn. *Transnational Feminism and Women's Movements in Post-1997 Hong Kong: Solidarity Beyond the State.* Hong Kong: Hong Kong University Press, 2015.

Lineham, Peter. "The Mormon Message in the Context of Maori Culture," *Journal of Mormon History* 17 (1991): 62–93.

Lionnet, Françoise, and Shu-Mei Shih, eds. *Minor Transnationalism.* Durham: Duke University Press, 2005.

Lobdell, William. "Bedrock of a Faith Is Jolted." *Los Angeles Times,* February 16, 2006.

———, and Larry B. Stammer. "Mormon Scientist, Church Clash over DNA Test." *Los Angeles Times,* December 8, 2002.

Macy, Terry, and Daniel W. Hart. *White Shamans, Plastic Medicine Men: A Documentary.* Native Voices Public Television, 1995.

Madsen, Brigham D. *The Shoshoni Frontier and the Bear River Massacre.* Salt Lake City: University of Utah Press, 1985.

Mann, Barbara Alice. *Iroquoian Women: The Gantowisas.* New York: Peter Lang, 2011.

———. *Native Americans, Archaeologists, & the Mounds.* New York: Peter Lang, 2003.

Martin, D. *Tongues of Fire: The Explosion of Protestantism in Latin America.* New Jersey: Wiley, 1993.

Martinich, Matt. "The Impact of Church Schools and Universities on LDS Growth," http://www.cumorah. com/index.php?target=view_other_articles&story_id=481& cat_id=30.

Martins, Marcus. "The Oak Tree Revisited: Brazilian Leaders' Insights on the Growth of the Church in Brazil". PhD diss., Brigham Young University, 1996.

Mauss, Armand. *All Abraham's Children: Changing Mormon Conceptions of Race and Lineage.* Urbana: University of Illinois Press, 2003.

Mazur, Suzan. "Mormons in the Olympic Spotlight: Polygamy and Scripture Threaten to Steal Some of the Thunder from Winter Games in Utah." *Financial Times,* 2002.

McInelly, Brett C. "Expanding Empires, Expanding Selves: Colonialism, the Novel, and Robinson Crusoe." *Studies in the Novel* 35, no. 1 (2003): 1–21.

McIntosh, Peggy. "White Privilege: Unpacking the Invisible Knapsack." *Independent School* 49, no. 2 (1990): 31–36.

Mihesuah, D.A., and A.C. Wilson. *Indigenizing the Academy: Transforming Scholarship and Empowering Communities.* Omaha: University of Nebraska Press, 2004.

Miller, Susan A., and James Riding In. *Native Historians Write Back: Decolonizing American Indian History.* Lubbock, TX: Texas Tech University Press, 2011.

Morgan, Dale L. "The Administration of Indian Affairs in Utah, 1851–1858," *Pacific Historical Review* 17, no. 4 (1948): 383–409.

The Mormons. Directed and produced by Helen Whitney. Frontline and American Experience with Helen Whitney Productions, 2007.

Murphy, Jessyca B. "The White Indin': Native American Appropriations in Hipster Fashion." In *Unsettling Whiteness.* Eds. Lucy Michael and Samantha Schulz. Oxford: Inter-Disciplinary Press, 2014. 127n–138.

Murphy, Thomas W. "Fifty Years of United Order in Mexico." *Sunstone* 20 (Oct. 1997): 69.

———. "From Racist Stereotype to Ethnic Identity: Instrumental Uses of Mormon Racial Doctrine," *Ethnohistory* (1999): 457n459.

———. *Imagining Lamanites: Native Americans and the Book of Mormon.* Seattle: University of Washington, 2003.

———. "Inventing Galileo." *Sunstone,* no. 131 (2004): 58–61.

———. "Laban's Ghost: On Writing and Transgression." *Dialogue: A Journal of Mormon Thought* 30 (Summer 1997): 105–26.

———. "Lamanite Genesis, Genealogy, and Genetics." In *American Apocrypha: Essays on the Book of Mormon,* edited by Dan Vogel and Brent Lee Metcalfe. Salt Lake City: Signature Books, 2002.

———. "Other Mormon Histories: Lamanite Subjectivity in Mexico." *Journal of Mormon History* 26, no. 2 (2000): 179–214.

———. "Reinventing Mormonism: Guatemala as a Harbinger of the Future?" *Dialogue: A Journal of Mormon Thought* 29 (Spring 1996): 177–92.

———. Review of *The Book of Mormon: A Biography* by Paul Gutjahr. *Nova Religio* 17, no. 3 (2014): 128–29.

———. Review of *By the Hand of Mormon: The American Scripture That Launched a New World Religion* by Terryl L. Givens. *Journal of Mormon History* 28, no. 2 (2002): 192–98.

———. "Simply Implausible: DNA and a Mesoamerican Setting for the Book of Mormon." *Dialogue: A Journal of Mormon Thought* (2003): 109–31.

———. "Sin, Skin, and Seed: Mistakes of Men in the Book of Mormon." *Journal of the John Whitmer Historical Association* 25 (2004): 36–51.

———. "'Stronger than Ever': Remnants of the Third Convention," *Journal of Latter-day Saint History* 10 (1998): 1, 8–11.

Murphy, Thomas W, and Angelo Baca. "Rejecting Racism in Any Form: Latter-Day Saint Rhetoric, Religion, and Repatriation." *Open Theology,* no. 2 (2016): 700–725.

Murphy, Thomas W, Jessyca B. Murphy, and Kerrie S. Murphy. "An Indian Princess and a Mormon Sacagawea: Decolonizing Memories of Our Grandmothers." In *Race, Gender, and Power on the Mormon Borderlands*, edited by Andrea Radke-Moss, Dee Garceau, and Sujey Vega, in review.

Murphy, Thomas W., and Simon G. Southerton. "Genetic Research a 'Galileo Event' for Mormons." *Anthropology News* 44, no. 2 (February 2003): 20.

Neihardt, John G. *Black Elk Speaks*. With a new introduction by Philip J. Deloria and annotations by Raymond J. DeMallie. Lincoln: University of Nebraska Press, 2014; William and Morrow Co., 1932.

Nelson, Melissa. *Original Instructions: Indigenous Teachings for a Sustainable Future*. Rochester, New York: Bear and Company, 2008.

Newton, Marjorie. *Mormon and Maori*. Salt Lake City: Greg Kofford Books, Inc., 2014.

———. *Tiki and Temple: The Mormon Mission in New Zealand, 1854–1958*. Salt Lake City: Greg Kofford Books, Inc., 2012.

Nibley, Hugh. *Approaching Zion*. Ed. Don Norton. Salt Lake City: Deseret Book Co., 1989.

Okazaki, Chieko. *Being Enough*. Salt Lake City: Bookcraft Publications, 2002.

———. *Lighten Up! Finding Real Joy in Life*. Salt Lake City: Deseret Book Company, 1993.

Oman, Nathan B. "Natural Law and the Rhetoric of Empire: Reynolds v. United States, Polygamy, and Imperialism," *Wash. UL Rev.* 88 (2010): 661.

Ong, Aihwa. *Flexible Citizenship: The Cultural Logics of Transnationality*. Durham: Duke University Press, 1999.

Ostler, Blake. "DNA Strands in the Book of Mormon," *Sunstone* (May 2005): 63n71.

Östman, Kim B. "'The Other' in the Limelight: One Perspective on the Publicity Surrounding the New LDS Temple in Finland," *Dialogue: A Journal of Mormon Thought* 40, no. 4 (2007), 71.

Parker, Stuart. "Mexico's Millennial Kingdom of the Lamanites: Margarito Bautista's Mormon Raza Cósmica." Paper delivered at the Rocky Mountain Conference on Latin American Studies, 2009.

Pavilk, Steve. "Of Saints and Lamanites: An Analysis of Navajo Mormonism," *Wicazo Sa Review* 8.1 (1992): 21–30.

Phinney, Jean S. "Ethnic Identity in Adolescents and Adults: A Review of the Research," *Psychological Bulletin* 108 (1990): 499–514.

———. "Ethnic Identity in Adolescents and Adults: A Review of the Research," *Psychological Bulletin* 108 (1990): 499–514.

Porter, Tom. *And Grandma Said..: Iroquois Teachings as Passed Down through the Oral Tradition*. Bloomington, IN: Xlibris Corporation, 2008.

Pratt, Mary Louise. "Arts of the Contact Zone," *Profession* (1991): 33–40.

Quinn, D. Michael. "I-Thou vs. I-It Conversions: The Mormon 'Baseball Baptism' Era," *Sunstone* 93 (December 1993): 30–44.

Ray, George B. *Language and Interracial Communication in the United States: Speaking in Black and White.* New York: Peter Lang Publishing, Inc., 2009.

Reeve, W. Paul. *Religion of a Different Color: Race and the Mormon Struggle for Whiteness.* New York: Oxford University Press, 2015.

Romano, Octavio. "Intellectual Mercenaries of our Age, the Social Scientists," *El Grito*, vol. 1 (Fall 1967): 4–5.

Romano, Octavio. "Minorities, History and the Cultural Mystique," *El Grito* vol. 1 (Fall 1967): 9.

Salazar Parreñas, Rhacel. *Children of Global Migration: Transnational Families and Gendered Woes.* California: Stanford University Press, 2005.

Santos, Fernanda. "Some Find Path to Navajo Roots Through Mormon Church," *New York Times*, October 30, 2013. http://www.nytimes.com/2013/10/31/us/for-some-the-path-to-navajo-values-weaves-through-the-mormon-church.html

Sekaquaptewa, Helen. *Me and Mine: The Life Story of Helen Sekaquaptewa as told to Louise Udall.* Tucson: University of Arizona Press, 1969.

Silko, Leslie Marmon. *Storyteller.* New York: Arcade Publishing, 1981.

Sleeter, Christine E. "How White Teachers Construct Race." In *Race, Identity and Representation in Education*, edited by Cameron McCarthy and Warren Crichlow. New York: Routledge, 1993. 157–173.

Sleeter, Christine E., and Peter McClaren, eds. *Multicultural Education, Critical Pedagogy and the Politics of Difference.* Albany: State University of New York Press, 1995.

Smaby, Beverly P. "The Mormons and the Indians: Conflicting Ecological Systems in the Great Basin," *American Studies* 16, no. 1 (1975): 35–48.

Small, Cathy. *Voyages: From Tongan Villages to American Suburbs.* Ithaca: Cornell University Press, 2011.

Smith, Julie M. "Men, Women, and Modesty," *Times & Seasons*, February 17, 2014. http://timesandseasons.org/index.php/2014/02/men-women-and-modesty/.

Smith, Linda Tuhiwai. *Decolonizing Methodologies: Research and Indigenous Peoples.* London: Zed Books, 1999.

———. *Decolonizing Methodologies: Research and Indigenous Peoples.* 2nd ed. London: Zed Books, 2012.

Stevenson, Russell. *For the Cause of Righteousness: A Global History of Blacks and Mormonism, 1830–2013.* Salt Lake City: Greg Kofford Books, Inc., 2014.

Stoler, Laura. *Haunted By Empire: Geographies of Intimacy in North American History.* Durham, NC: Duke University Press, 2006.

Taylor, Lori Elaine. "Telling Stories About Mormons and Indians." PhD diss., State University of New York at Buffalo, 2000.

Thornton, Alec, Maria T. Kerslake, and Tony Binns. "Alienation and Obligation: Religion and Social Change in Samoa," *Asia Pacific Viewpoint* 51, no. 1 (2010): 1–16.

Tohe, Laura. *No Parole Today.* Albuquerque, New Mexico: West End Press, 1999.

Topper, Martin D. "'Mormon Placement': The Effects of Missionary Foster Families on Navajo Adolescents," *Ethos* 7, no. 2 (1979): 142–160.

Trask, Haunani-Kay. *From a Native Daughter: Colonialism and Sovereignty in Hawai'I*, revised ed. Honolulu: University of Hawaii Press, 1999.

Treat, James. *Around the Sacred Fire: Native Religious Activism in the Red Power Era.* New York: Palgrave Macmillan, 2003.

Tuffin, George. *Mormonen in Vlaanderen—Volume 1: 1840–1959, Wijk Antwerpen van de Kerk van Jezus Christus van de Heiligen der Laatste Dagen.* Antwerpen: n.p., 2012.

Tullis, F. LaMond. *The Mormons in Mexico: The Dynamics of Faith and Culture.* Logan, Utah: Utah State University Press, 1987.

Twiss, Richard. *Rescuing the Gospel from the Cowboys: A Native American Expression of the Jesus Way.* Downers Grove, IL: IVP Books, 2015.

Uluave, Moana. "I Can Hear Myself Speak It." Unpublished manuscript, 2014.

Underwood, Grant. "Mormonism, the Maori and Cultural Authenticity," *Journal of Pacific History* 35, no. 2 (2000): 133–146.

van Beek, Walter E.A. "The Temple and the Sacred: Dutch Temple Experiences," *Dialogue: A Journal of Mormon Thought* 45, no. 4 (Winter 2012), 39.

van Wijk, Evert. "Neederlanders zijn voor Vlamingen wat Duitsers zijn voor Nederlanders," *Express.be*, December 21, 2010. http://www.express.be/joker/nl/nederbelg/nederlanders-zijn-voor-vlamingen-wat-duitsers-zijn-voor-nederlanders/137679.htm

———. *Waarom Belgen niet kunnen voetballen en Nederlanders nooit wereldkampioen worden: Over de moeizame samenwerking tussen Belgen en Nederlanders.* Tielt: Lannoo, 2010.

Wallerstein, Nina B. and Bonnie Duran, "Using Community-Based Participatory Research to Address Health Disparities," *Health Promotion Practice* 7, no. 3 (2006): 312–323.

Wildcat, Daniel. *Red Alert! Saving the Planet with Indigenous Knowledge.* Golden, CO: Fulcrum Publishing, 2009.

Wilson, Angela Cavender. "Decolonizing the 1862 Death Marches." *The American Indian Quarterly* 28, no. 1 (2004): 185–215.

Wilson, Angela Waziyatawin, and Michael Yellow Bird. *For Indigenous Eyes Only: A Decolonization Handbook.* Santa Fe: School of American Research, 2005.

———, and Michael Yellow Bird. *For Indigenous Minds Only: A Decolonization Handbook.* Santa Fe: School of American Research Press, 2012.

Wolfe, Patrick. "The settler complex: an introduction." *American Indian Culture and Research Journal* 37, no. 2 (2013): 1–22.

———. "Settler Colonialism and the Elimination of the Native." *Journal of Genocide Research* 8, no. 4 (2006): 387–409.

"Worlds of Difference: Latter-day Saints and Indians," NPR, January 23, 2005. http://www.npr.org/templates/story/story.php?storyId=4463101.

Yong, Amos and Barbara B. Zikmund. *Remembering Jamestown: Hard Questions about Christian Mission.* Eugene, OR: Pickwick Publications, 2010.

Young, Lawrence A. "Confronting Turbulent Environments: Issues in the Organizational Growth and Globalization of Mormonism." In *Contemporary Mormonism: Social Science Perspectives.* Eds. Marie Cornwall, Tim B. Heaton, and Lawrence Young. Urbana: University of Illinois Press, 1994. 43–63.

Yorgason, Ethan. *Transformation of the Mormon Culture Region*. Urbana: University of Illinois Press, 2003.

Zotigh, Dennis. "Do American Indians Celebrate the 4th of July." Blog, National Museum of the American Indian, July 3, 2014, accessed April 10, 2017. http://blog .nmai.si.edu/main/2014/07/july_4_2014.html

CONTRIBUTORS

Angelo Baca (Navajo and Hopi) is a Native American filmmaker who works on educational films, fiction and non-fiction. A graduate of the Native Voices Documentary Master's Program at the University of Washington in the Department of Communications and American Indian Studies, he has done numerous documentaries and collaborative works with other filmmakers, both Indigenous and non-Indigenous. His 2008 documentary film, *In Laman's Terms: Looking at Lamanite Identity*, is one of the only films that speaks back to the LDS Church from a critical Indigenous perspective. He has taught at Northwest Indian College, Edmonds Community College, and Shoreline Community College in Washington State. Recently, he taught at Brown University both Native American Literature and Native American Media/Film courses as a Visiting Lecturer and now attends New York University's PhD program in Anthropology focusing on Documentary Film, Indigenous Food Sovereignty, and International Repatriation of ancestral remains and culturally significant items.

Elise Boxer is an enrolled citizen of the Fort Peck Assiniboine and Sioux Tribes. She is Dakota from the Sisseton and Wahpeton bands. Boxer received her PhD in history from Arizona State University. She is an Assistant Professor of History at the University of South Dakota. Dr. Boxer is currently working on her manuscript, *To Become White and Delightsome: The Church of Jesus Christ of Latter-day Saints and Construction of a "Lamanite" Identity*. Her manuscript explores the construction of race in the LDS Church and the manner in which race and identity has been defined, constructed and maintained. Her primary focus is on Indigenous peoples in the United States and the creation of a religious identity (or using Mormon terminology, a "Lamanite" identity). She has published her research in the *Western Historical Quarterly* and the *Journal of Mormon History*.

Joanna Brooks is Associate Vice President of Faculty Advancement at San Diego State University and a Professor of English. She has written or edited nine books about religion, race, colonialism, gender, and culture including the anthology *Mormon Feminism: Essential Writings* (Oxford University Press, 2015).

Gina Colvin is a New Zealander of Māori (Ngāti Porou, Ngapuhi) and Pakeha (European) descent. She the author of the blog *KiwiMormon* and host of the podcast *A Thoughtful Faith*. She holds a PhD in Journalism from the University of Canterbury.

Stacilee Ford is a cultural historian who has lived in Hong Kong since 1993 and is an Honorary Associate Professor in the Department of History and the American Studies Program at The University of Hong Kong. She is also a board member of the HKU Women's Studies Research Centre. Her scholarship focuses on the intersection of gender, generation, ethnicity, national identity, and culture. Published works include *Troubling American Women: Gender and National Identity in Hong Kong* and *Mabel Cheung Yuen-Ting's An Autumn's Tale*. She earned a Bachelor's degree from Brigham Young University, a masters degree from Harvard University (EdM), and doctorates from Columbia University (EdD) and Hong Kong University (PhD). She has served two terms as a District Relief Society President in Hong Kong and is currently a Young Single Adult Sunday School Teacher. She is working on a book on Sinophone/Asian American men and leadership.

Ignacio M. García is the Lemuel Hardison Redd, Jr. Professor of Western & Latino History at Brigham Young University, and the author of seven books on Mexican American/Chicano civil rights and politics as well as a study of sports in the Latino community. His most recent book, a memoir, is *Chicano while Mormon: Activism, War and Keeping the Faith*, which chronicles his life as a young Mormon Chicano rights activist. He has twice served as a bishop in the Church of Jesus Christ of Latter-day Saints.

P. Jane Hafen (Taos Pueblo) is a Professor of English at the University of Nevada, Las Vegas. She serves as an advisory editor of *Great Plains Quarterly*; on the editorial board of Michigan State University Press, American

Indian Series; on the board of the Charles Redd Center for Western Studies; and is an Associate Fellow at the Center for Great Plains Studies. Dr. Hafen is a Frances C. Allen Fellow at the D'Arcy McNickle Center for the History of the American Indian, The Newberry Library. She received the William H. Morris Teaching Award for the College of Liberal Arts, UNLV, and the UNLV Foundation Distinguished Teaching Award. She edited *Critical Insights: Louise Erdrich, Dreams and Thunder: Stories, Poems and The Sun Dance Opera* by Zitkala-Ša, and co-edited *The Great Plains Reader*. She is author of *Reading Louise Erdrich's Love Medicine*, and articles and book chapters about American Indian literatures.

Alicia Harris is the embodiment of the American West. Cowboys and Indians and the frontier of American expansion are her ancestors. Born in Ogden, Utah, and raised in San Diego, California, her work deals with the myth and memory of America. She is an art historian, and has interest in understanding the ways that indigenous peoples aesthetically express their relationship to place. Alicia holds a BA in Art History and Curatorial Studies from BYU, a masters degree in Art History from the University of Nebraska-Lincoln, and and is currently a PhD candidate in Native American Art History from the University of Oklahoma. Alicia is Assiniboine (Fort Peck), and very American.

Melissa Wei-Tsing Inouye is a lecturer in Asian Studies at the University of Auckland. She holds a PhD in East Asian Languages and Civilizations from Harvard University and is interested in the history of Christianity in China, Chinese religions, and global Mormonism. She served a mission for The Church of Jesus Christ of Latter-day Saints in Kaohsiung, Taiwan, and has been a member within LDS congregations overseas for many years. Melissa, her husband, and their four children currently live in Henderson Valley, Auckland.

Mica McGriggs is a postdoctoral fellow in psychology at Columbia University. Her academic research is primarily in the area of multicultural sensitivity in psychology. Her social justice interests are broadly defined, but can expressed through the term intersectional feminism. She contributes to several online outlets, including the Huffington Post.

Thomas W. Murphy has a PhD (2003) in anthropology from the University of Washington. His critical theory-inspired article, "Laban's Ghost: On Writing and Transgression," won a Scripture and Theology Writing Award from the Dialogue Foundation in 1998. He is Chair of the Department of Anthropology at Edmonds Community College in Lynnwood, Washington. In 2006, he founded the Learn and Serve Environmental Anthropology Field (LEAF) School, a multi-campus decolonization partnership with Coast Salish Tribes to apply traditional knowledge to local sustainability projects. Students at Edmonds CC selected Dr. Murphy for the Lifetime Honorary Triton Outstanding Faculty Award in 2005. The Board of Trustees followed with an Excellence in Education Award in 2008. The Snohomish Tribe of Indians recognized the LEAF School and Dr. Murphy as its Partner Team of the Year in 2011. The Washington Association of Conservation Districts named him the 2011 Washington State Conservation Educator of the Year and the Puget Sound Regional Council gave Edmonds CC a VISION 2040 Award in 2012 for the LEAF School's role in the Japanese Gulch Fish Passage Improvement Project. In 2014, KSER Public Radio recognized Dr. Murphy with a Voice of the Community Award for Community Impact by an Individual.

Ingrid Sherlock-Taselaar was born in The Netherlands but grew up in the Flemish-speaking part of Belgium. After secondary school she attended the Hebrew University of Jerusalem in Israel, where she received a BA in ancient Semitic languages, a BA in Assyriology, a MA (cum laude) in ancient Semitic languages, and a PhD at the School of Oriental and African Studies (SOAS), University of London, under the supervision of Professor Tudor V. Parfitt. She was the co-ordinator of The Centre for Jewish Studies at the School of SOAS, taught in the Religious Studies department at Middlesex University, and taught Hebrew and Dutch language and literature in the International Baccalaureate programme at Southbank International School in London. Currently, she is a teacher at the International Language and Literature Teachers' Cooperative and the associate editor of the *International Journal for Mormon Studies*.

Rolf Straubhaar is an anthropologist of education whose research focuses on the global spread of US-centric educational policies and the educational experiences of Latino immigrant students in the United States, particularly in the "New South." He is an Assistant Research Scientist and the Director of Research at the University of Georgia's Center for Latino Achievement and Success in Education. He received his PhD from the University of California, Los Angeles, where his dissertation on the adaptation of US-derived educational policies in Rio de Janeiro (funded by a Fulbright-Hays Doctoral Dissertation Research Abroad fellowship) received the 2014 Frederick Erickson Outstanding Dissertation Award from the Council on Anthropology and Education (a division of the American Anthropological Association).

INDEX

Mormonism/Mormon faith: as American, 187, 190, 196, 201; ancestral legacy in, 125; angels' role in, 11; in Asia, 202–28; Chinese, 209–11; communities at margins of, 15; conclusion about, 263–73; and cultural hubris, 45; decolonization of, 49, 51–55, 62–64, 182–84; demographic studies of, 177, 231–40; fear within, 120–21; and flexible citizens, 206–8, 213–15, 225–28; gender role issues, 224–27; as a global religion, 161, 171–73, 183–84, 205–6, 230, 233, 259; great trial of, 14; as an identity component, 124–25; informal and formal institutions, 233–36; internationalization of, 206, 207, 208, 214; leadership issue, 172, 232; many types, 259–62; and Maoism, 211; and Māori people, 33; and middle-class ideal, 9–10; migrant workers embracing, 205; as minor transnationalism, 181; origins story, 263–66, 273; personal narratives, 184, 185; and racism, 60, 93–94, 97–99, 180–81; religious colonization, 17, 95, 168; and temple experiences, 68–69; and tikanga, 39; "unspoken legacies," 202; value of belonging in, 116, 117
Mormon movements, 11, 17, 164, 168, 185
Mormon privilege, 103–13
Mormons: about, 2, 19; and being born in the covenant, 107–9; "cold and distant," 285n11; colonial projects by, 166; education enterprises by, 170–71; Flemish, 188, 189, 191, 199–201; and institution-building, 262; marginalization of, 231–33; migration of, 80–82, 165–66; and Mormon privilege, 103–13; pragmatic choices made by, 168; as a special class, 167–68; and tribe termination, 51
Mormon settlers: about, 19, 68, 74; annual and sesquicentennial celebrations, 94–97, 125; and mob violence, 165; monument related to, 83–88; perspective on land, 94, 95; as "pioneers," 77, 78, 79, 82, 94–97; in Utah, 78. See also colonialism
Mormons of color. See Indigenous peoples; people of color
Mormon testimony, 27–46, 124, 272–73
Mormon theology, 1, 13, 15, 179, 180
multiculturalism, 132, 204, 208, 209
Murphy, Dr. Tom, 73, 272

Native American Village, 86–87
native Christians, 230, 231
Native heritage, 115, 120, 125

Native peoples. See Indigenous peoples
Native Voices Program, 71
Navajo Reservation, 67, 177, 271
Neo-colonization and neocolonialism, 6, 172, 174, 177, 216
neoliberalism and neoliberal networks, 173, 174, 182, 204
New Jerusalem, 80, 192, 280n13
New Zealand: biculturalism in, 42; Māori resistance in, 37, 40, 67; marginality issues in, 232; missionaries to, 168, 232–33
Ngāti Porou people, 27–30, 275–76n1
Nibley, Hugh, 2, 4, 14
non-Mormons, 80, 82, 85, 270, 279n12
North Island, 27

Okazaki, Chieko, 208, 209, 293–94n15
Ong, Aihwa, 206, 207
On Zion's Mount: Mormons, Indians, and the American Landscape (Framer), 78
oppression: Freire's views on, 104, 112; and Indigenous peoples, 44, 45, 52; of Mexican-Americans, 144–45; and pioneer ancestors, 122; tangible, 68. See also racism/racialism
oral traditions, 56, 71, 272
origins story, 263–66, 273
overseas foreign workers, 215–20

Paddle to Bella Bella, 62, 65
paradox and biracial person, 133–34
parental rights, 51–52
Parreñas, Rhacel, 217, 225, 227
participant observation, 202–3, 230
passing process, 115, 116
pecking order, 140, 157, 285n9
Pedagogy of the Oppressed (Freire), 104
people of color, 136, 137, 149, 174, 285n7
pioneer ancestry, 104, 108, 113, 115, 122
"pioneers," Mormon settlers as, 77, 78, 79, 82, 94–97
pioneer stories, 198–99
plural marriage, 51, 291–92n11
polygamy: about, 32, 48, 120, 122; imprisonment for, 282n10; policy on, 279–280n12; Reynolds case about, 168
Polynesian Cultural Center (PCC), 62, 73, 184
poor people, 13, 141, 143, 147, 149
postmemory idea, 118, 119
power imbalances, 52, 53, 57
Pratt, Mary Louise, 203
President A, 246–48, 256, 257